Fredric Jameson and
Film Theory

Fredric Jameson and Film Theory

Marxism, Allegory, and Geopolitics in World Cinema

EDITED BY KEITH B. WAGNER, JEREMI SZANIAWSKI, AND MICHAEL CRAMER
Afterword by Fredric Jameson

Rutgers University Press
New Brunswick, Camden, and Newark, New Jersey, and London

Library of Congress Cataloging-in-Publication Data
Names: Szaniawski, Jeremi, editor. | Wagner, Keith B., 1978– editor. | Cramer, Michael,
    1981- editor.
Title: Fredric Jameson and film theory : Marxism, allegory, and geopolitics in world
    cinema / edited by Keith B. Wagner, Jeremi Szaniawski, and Michael Cramer.
Description: First edition. | New Brunswick : Rutgers University Press, [2022] |
    Includes bibliographical references and index.
Identifiers: LCCN 2021016519 | ISBN 9781978808867 (paperback) |
    ISBN 9781978808874 (hardback) | ISBN 9781978808881 (epub) |
    ISBN 9781978808898 (mobi) | ISBN 9781978808904 (pdf)
Subjects: LCSH: Jameson, Fredric—Criticism and interpretation. | Motion pictures—
    Philosophy. | Marxist criticism. | Geopolitics in motion pictures. | Philosophers—
    United States—Biography.
Classification: LCC PN75.J36 F745 2022 | DDC 801/.95092—dc23
LC record available at https://lccn.loc.gov/2021016519

A British Cataloging-in-Publication record for this book is available from the British Library.

www.rutgersuniversitypress.org

Manufactured in the United States of America

To our communities—knowable, unknowable, and yet to be discovered.

Contents

**Fredric Jameson and
Film Theory**

Introduction: Always Historicize the Moving Image!

Fredric Jameson's Place in Film Studies

MICHAEL CRAMER,

JEREMI SZANIAWSKI, AND

KEITH B. WAGNER

Fredric Jameson has never sought to position himself as a film theorist, nor does he wish to be labeled one now. Yet Jameson's work on film (and indeed all of his work) has had an immense impact on the field of film studies, and on the study of culture as a whole. He is, of course, not alone in this position: we might think of the work of Slavoj Žižek, Jacques Rancière, and most of all Gilles Deleuze as occupying a similar position in respect to the discipline. Like these three thinkers, Jameson examines film rather differently than most scholars within film studies proper, and this difference, in his case, resides in his resolute and consistent *Marxist* approach, one that is not merely "leftist" but that seeks to synthesize over a century of Marxist perspectives on culture, perspectives that are largely absent from film studies today (and indeed have largely always been, despite the discipline's frequent pretentions to radicalism). While Marxist thinkers like Louis Althusser were instrumental in influencing the film theory of the 1960s and 1970s (however problematically, and often in a way that detaches their insights from a properly materialist framework), which could be broadly described as leftist, there are very few film scholars who approach film in a broad enough way so as to see its history as inextricable from the development of capitalism itself. Jameson's unflagging attention to capitalism and the concrete social and economic relations it creates allows for a large-scale, *longue durée* historical perspective that yields tremendous insights about cultural production that a more local or philosophically idealist approach prevents. We cannot talk about culture, Jameson reminds us, without talking about capitalism, not as an idea or an ideology (as it is predominantly treated now, both by mainstream liberals and by those who proclaim themselves Marxists), but as a historical and material process; indeed, what we might now call "capitalism studies" was, in some ways, brought into the humanities by Jameson himself. While he was certainly not without predecessors in his insistence on the utility of Marxism for the study of culture—we might mention, limiting ourselves to scholars writing in English, Raymond Williams and E. P. Thompson[1]—Jameson has masterfully examined the full breadth of different class cultures on a broader and more global scale than either and has observed the rapid change of culture as a whole (the only way, he insists, that it can be treated) within the era of late capitalism. What begins to emerge as we consider his contribution is the glaring lack of attention, with some major exceptions, to both class and capitalism in the field of film studies,[2] with most considerations of these issues staying on a superficial level that considers how they are literally represented in film.

Perhaps paradoxically, Jameson has nonetheless been deeply influential upon a field that sees him as an outsider and that has largely ignored the concerns and methodologies of Marxism, as his key concepts and methods—whether used in a Marxist context or "cherry picked" in such a way that detaches them from the greater whole that gives them meaning—have gained widespread familiarity and employment in the discipline. Despite his seemingly marginal position with respect to film studies, a Jamesonian approach has been central to the work of a number of prominent film scholars, and seems to be increasingly so. The essays in this book provide ample evidence for this influence, and we might also note several other works that rely heavily on his thought, for example, Eric Cazdyn's *The Flash of Capital: Film and Geopolitics in Japan* (2002),[3] which elegantly blends nuanced analysis of Japanese cinema with a Jamesonian Marxian dialectic, highlighting the country's historical changes through its history of moving images, and Clint Burnham's 2016 book *Fredric Jameson and* The Wolf of Wall Street, which considers the relevance of Jameson's Marxist cultural theory for analyzing the relatively new genre of what Burnham and others have called "finance films."[4] In the same year, film scholars Damon R. Young, Nico Baumbach, and Genevieve Yue edited a special issue in *Social Text* that found a range of distinguished scholars reengaging with Jameson's cultural logic of capitalism (or neoliberalism's triumphalism), deploying materialist perspectives (both old and new) to examine topics ranging from new media (Alexander Galloway) to affect in

Hollywood cinema (Sulgi Lie), from an NGO aesthetic in Nairobi by producers of audiovisual media (Jennifer Bajorek) to global television and Adorno (Amy Villarejo); these articles share a Marxist or neo-Marxist commitment to Jameson's political critique of culture. The list could go on (and would of course include work by the editors of this volume), but instead of providing an extensive literature review, in the remainder of this introduction we highlight the crucial interventions made by Jameson and our assessments of their value as well as their appropriation, redeployment, and refinement by other scholars. Before moving on to more abstract and conceptual terrain, however, it is worth briefly taking account of Jameson's impact upon the field in a way that, however crudely, proves that he indeed has been and continues to be read by film studies scholars, even if his work has not (yet) generated the subfield or "school" that has formed around more visible "outsiders" such as Deleuze.

We can begin to measure Jameson's impact on the field of film studies from what is perhaps an unexpected direction, namely by looking at quantitative evidence in the form of the citation rate of his edited books and monographs since the 1990s.[5] Although many may shudder to think of measuring scholarly importance in this manner and would see such "tallying up" as un-Jamesonian, the quantitative does, albeit in a coldly rational and reifying way, allow us to trace the "value" of an oeuvre within the context of platform capitalism. If we look at Jameson's citation rate, we find that he stands in a more or less virtual tie with fellow Marxist thinker Žižek (who is of course younger, but who has been far more proactive about promoting himself through the media).[6] While Žižek might enjoy a slightly higher number of citations overall than Jameson (127,948 vs. 120,468),[7] the latter's two most successful books (*Postmodernism; or, The Cultural Logic of Late Capitalism* [27,941 citations as of July 2020] and *The Political Unconscious: Narrative as a Socially Symbolic Act* [12,317]) have garnered many more citations than Žižek's (*The Sublime Object of Ideology* [10,173 citations]). Undoubtedly, while Žižek and Deleuze are better known in the broader cultural sphere (having become pop culture icons), Jameson's work on postmodernism is some of the best known and respected in the humanities, and such quantitative data only confirm this impression.

As far as the two cinema books by Jameson—*Signatures of the Visible* and *The Geopolitical Aesthetic*—are concerned, they come respectively in seventeenth and eighteenth positions of his personal ranking on Google Scholar, virtually tied at 1,367 and 1,359 citations respectively—closely followed by the famous "Reification and Utopia in Mass Culture" chapter, reprinted in *Signatures of the Visible* (1,347 mentions). From a film studies perspective, this is a towering achievement: suffice it to look at two eminent and widely cited film scholars: Edward Branigan has around 1,300 citations for his single most cited volume (*Narrative Comprehension and Film*), while Thomas Elsaesser's two most frequently cited texts, *European Cinema* and *Tales of Sound and Fury*, have roughly 730 citations each. When one acknowledges the prominence and influence of

Branigan or Elsaesser on film studies, it is easy to gain a sense of the tremendous citation rate accomplished by Jameson—not only in numbers (which of course can always be used in such a way as to mean everything and its exact opposite), but also in terms of the wide range of scholars in the field who have channeled, engaged with, challenged, or at least mentioned his work. Indeed, a closer look at the range of film and media scholars to have cited Jameson's work allows one to surmise that Jameson may be the most widely cited living English-speaking scholar by the field of film studies—his impressive "penetration rate" into the discipline also a function, to be sure, of his prodigious productivity.

Given the fact that there is hardly a Jamesonian school or subfield of film studies, how might we explain Jameson's simultaneous presence and absence in/from the discipline? In part, this may be due to the difficulty of digesting his work as a whole, which is in many respects essential for its most productive usages (much like that of Freud or Lacan), or to its enormously broad scope; indeed, the deployment of his analytic approaches within "local" contexts risks missing what is most important about his contributions—his dialectical, synthetic, and totalizing method. We might also attribute his arm's-length distance from the field to the fact that his method has largely been one of applying "literary categories to film rather than studying film as film," to borrow a turn of phrase from film and affect / material textures scholar Pansy Duncan.[8] Yet while literature and literary theory provide the foundations of Jameson's work, this does not mean in any sense that his ideas are applicable to or exclusively about only literature; rather he insists on an approach in which all cultural production needs to be studied as part of a greater ensemble, rather than a set of discrete fields or languages, since all of these are symptomatic and expressive of the same concrete, material processes. Jameson and his work are thus hardly in the mainstream of film studies, yet this is at least one reason why they are so productive: Jameson as a thinker largely eschews any disciplinary boundaries (as any totalizing thinking must), but also reminds us that any discourse or "code," any specific approach, reveals its full hermeneutic potential only when juxtaposed with others.

Jameson's background in comparative literature allowed him to reveal the various discursive frameworks for the study of film (many indebted to structuralism and poststructuralism) that had developed in the preceding years as both highly productive and highly limited in manifold ways (a question to which we will return), whether in terms of their scope (historical and theoretical analysis that was wedded to the limited context of single nation-states or an exclusive or myopic focus on the "language" of film itself) or in terms of their ideology (a predilection for undialectical and idealist thinking). While we will return in more detail to how Jameson's approach responds to these limitations, we should here note, first and foremost, the importance of the totalizing character of Jameson's approach, which insists that the broadest possible interpretive framework be used, and has proven especially productive (albeit often criticized) for thinking about how film can be studied in a quite literally global context (both in the geographical sense of breadth and as part of a larger, more abstract totality), one in which the "smallest variations of meaning" are seen to come from various "levels of textual and cultural differentiation."[9] Jameson's equal attention to textual nuance and form and to large-scale thinking allows us to see how world-scale processes manifest in specific cultural forms: from his own definition of "magic realism" (and its iterations in Soviet cinema as well as in films from communist Poland and Latin America) to the cultural appropriation of L'art naïf and its conflation with tropical modernization (villages in the jungle set next to images of rapid urban expansion in Manila) seen as unique to Filipino cinema, the rise of global Asia and the resulting technocratic auteurism in Taiwanese cinema, national allegory and multinational capitalism in Senegalese cinema, and theories of conspiracy in 1970s and 1980s American and Canadian cinema. This is perhaps where Jameson's relative absence or failure to form an identifiable subfield in film studies becomes the most surprising, given the local-global connections examined by his research and the growing interest in approaching film in these terms. Before turning to the specific interventions in this volume that, we hope, will begin to change this situation, we now take stock of Jameson's impact first through a consideration of how he enacted something like a paradigm shift that both synthesized and sublated earlier theoretical work on film (particularly that of the 1960s and 1970s) and then through an examination of his essential contributions to the discipline in his works dedicated specifically to film.

Jameson, Marxism, and Film Theory

Jameson's synthetic and totalizing approach, not to mention his commitment to Marxism, meets, predictably enough, with resistance from multiple tendencies within film studies, particularly those that have attempted, in the wake of David Bordwell and Noel Carroll's *Post-Theory* (1996), to eradicate the interdisciplinary and politically critical character of many of the major currents of film theory that had developed up to that point (particularly those that relied heavily on psychoanalysis and Marxism). To take a present-day example, we might look to scholars such as Andrew Klevan, who takes quite seriously the view that the disciplinary roots of film studies as a specialist field are sacrosanct and that a focus on film aesthetics is the most valuable way to study the moving image. Many scholars still treat the moving image as a precious and unique device, a visceral signifier that should be considered apart from macro-level thinking or attempts to account for the crucial material foundations that underlie all cultural production. To scholars taking this approach, there is nothing beyond the image that would warrant or merit attention within the scope of a film studies approach. Jameson, to the contrary, welcomes the broader inclusion of ideas related to geopolitical or global thinking (whether about literature, film, or broader political, social, and economic concerns) and rejects what "purists" see as the vulgarity, or even irrelevance, of economic or social conditions, which they jettison in favor of exclusively aesthetic concerns, often considered within the framework of aesthetic philosophy and analytic philosophy in particular. For Jameson, the aesthetic is not some separate realm but rather the expression of the "raw material" that exists outside of it, processed by the subject and disclosing a "political unconscious." At the same time, Jameson distinguishes himself from many (or even most) scholars who take a more politically or socially minded approach due to the attention his work devotes to form, taken not as an object of aesthetic contemplation but as the means through which what lies beyond the surface of the texts, the concrete "content" that serves as their raw material, discloses itself indirectly (which is, indeed, the only way it can be disclosed); as Jameson writes, "all visible matter is form, and all meaning or expression concrete embodiment."[10] This is obviously an important corrective to any approach that ignores form and focuses instead on what is now commonly called "representation," as though that representation itself were simply a direct reflection of material reality, or something that "makes a statement" about reality in a transparent, direct sense, not to mention one that would reject an attention to form as a sign of the kind of fetishistic aestheticism or apoliticality that we find in theorists such as Bordwell, Carrol, and Klevan. We might also mention here, in passing, the way in which such an approach also serves as a riposte to similarly limited methodologies rooted in cognitive or experimental psychology, and even neuroscience, which often treat film as a kind of ahistorical machine that works upon a subject conceived of as uniform and outside of any particular historical context.

Jameson's comparativist outlook and interdisciplinary strengths have for decades (and even now) shown the validity of large-scale thinking for film theory regardless of whether or not we can count him as one of us. Indeed, film theory has always borrowed and even developed key methodologies by drawing on thinkers who are hardly film scholars, and in some cases hardly speak about film at all: Freud, Benjamin, Barthes, Althusser, Bourdieu, Agamben . . . (the list goes on). It would not be farfetched to say that scholars who do not write exclusively or primarily about film have contributed just as much or more to the discipline than those who do (in some cases, like that of Jameson, precisely because they illustrate how one cannot study film in any kind of isolation). That these thinkers and critics are more influential than many film theorists and critics working today is not disconcerting to us because they are not part of film studies as a discipline; instead, the problem is that the discipline itself is largely populated by specialists focusing on a narrow and/or local domain of expertise, with many concerned only with territorialized cultures or single moments in history (both of which amount, of course, to a denial of history itself, at least in any Hegelian or Marxist sense). This is of course encouraged by the structure of academia itself and reminds us how much the demands placed upon today's scholars (find something no one else has written about, do it quickly, "publish or perish," etc.)

block anything *other* than local inquiry. The "local" or the limitation in question here operates on several levels: first delimiting or blocking off world-scale analysis, second isolating the study of film from the broader study of culture, and finally making it impossible to situate film in anything like a more holistic or *longue durée* account of history, in which political economy and the class struggle are given the central position they deserve.

Jameson's contributions to film studies began long before he started writing about film. Most importantly, he played a key role in bringing thinkers from the Frankfurt School, as well as Lukácsian and Althusserian thought, into American academia beginning in the 1970s, although given his slow incorporation into film studies, today scholars of film are far more familiar with *Marxism and Form: Twentieth-Century Dialectical Theories of Literature*, published in 1971, than they would have been decades earlier. Here, Jameson announces the tasks of dialectical criticism and explains, "For a genuinely dialectical criticism, indeed, there can be no pre-established categories of analysis: to the degree that each work is the end result of a kind of inner logic or development in its own content, it evolves its own categories and dictates the specific terms of its own interpretation. Thus dialectical criticism is at the other extreme from all single-shot or univalent aesthetic theories which seek the same structure in all works of art and prescribe for them a single type of interpretive technique or a single mode of explanation."[11] Dialectical criticism, therefore, cannot seek recourse to a closed model or static structure as a way to disclose the meaning of any given text or object. The "univalent aesthetic theories" Jameson mentions here encompass a wide variety of approaches but are most obviously those of aesthetic formalisms or aesthetic philosophy; at the same time, his criticism can apply to any methodology that closes the text off from a truly historical and dialectical ground, reifying it in the process. We might begin to evaluate the impact of Jameson's employment of a Western Marxism-derived dialectical criticism upon film studies by considering how many of his core ideas pose challenges to those very methodologies (primarily structuralist and poststructuralist in character) that had been developed by the discipline by the early 1970s. What is essential to note here, though, is that Jameson's interventions never seek the absolute negation or rejection of what they react to and critique: he does not seek to show what is wrong with any given theory so much as to show what might be useful about it, and this is usually revealed through its juxtaposition with some other theoretical paradigm or methodology, or through the repurposing of its fragments that one can then reposition (as Marx did with Smith and Ricardo's work) "in perspective as parts or functions of some larger totality."[12]

A wide number of French thinkers (working both specifically in the realm of film, as in the case of the critics of *Cahiers du cinéma* or *Cinéthique*, or in a broader cultural and more scholarly realm, as in the case of *Tel Quel*), as well as their British counterparts at *Screen*, had of course by the 1970s formulated an array of dazzling theories heavily informed by psychoanalysis (Freud, but perhaps even more importantly Lacan), structuralism (especially Althusser, but also various theorists working more specifically with semiotics, such as Metz), and later poststructuralism (the later Barthes, Kristeva). Despite these thinkers' frequent attention to Brecht, German sources were far less predominant than francophone ones: indeed, the primacy of place that Jameson devotes to the German-language Marxist tradition (including not only more friendly faces like that of Benjamin but also the dreaded Lukács, who by that time had been reified and was largely seen as nothing more than a shill for socialist realism) allowed him to carry out a dialectical negation and sublation of these methodologies, which would continue slouching toward their death into the 1980s.

Jameson himself gives us a suggestion as to how we might conceive of this intervention in "The Existence of Italy" (1992). Here he positions *Screen* theory's approach as a "postmodern critique of representation" that encompasses both realism (in the form of "Classical Hollywood Realism") and modernism (in the form of auteurist cinema). For the *Screen* theorists, Jameson notes, the process of criticism is purely negative: they do not operate dialectically or try "to escape from the image by means of the image," but instead enact "an iconoclastic and negative or sheerly deconstructive project, which undermines all forms of representation and yet thereby in some form requires representation to do its work."[13] This provides a good explanation of why so much theory of this time insists that the only truth content that film can reveal is the falseness of its own claims to knowledge and the essential falseness of any image or code that claims to give us access to the real. Jameson thus hits on the deeply undialectical thinking at the core of so much of structuralist/poststructuralist film theory: it continues to think in terms of binaries that oppose and negate each other, thus locking itself into a structure in which the initial terms can never be transcended but are simply remapped onto various texts and codes.

In Jameson's view, the endeavor to negate all existing forms of representation (which can of course extend beyond art, once we realize that everything else is a "text" as well), denouncing them as equally false, furthermore locks theory into making the same critique over and over again. (If all codes are simply ideological and propagate illusion, what is left to say?) We end up, he argues, with an idealistic, even ethical binary of bad and good objects, in which the former are said to perpetuate deception while the latter reveal it, but refuse to put anything in its place. The implications of this position on radical film practice are of course enormous as well: if one can never truly get outside of the image, the only thing to do if one wishes to be "political" is to destroy it. And herein lies the larger problem, and the importance of Jameson's interventions: for the leftist theorists and filmmakers of the 1960s and 1970s (particularly those associated with Third Cinema), the political character of film (and culture in general) is located in what it *does* in an instrumental sense. The value of culture for the left (unsurprisingly, given the Chinese Cultural Revolution and the increasing influence of Gramsci) is seen to lie in its ability to cause change in an immediate and concrete sense, whether this means accomplishing some specific political goal or simply "deprogramming" the mind of the spectator. For Jameson, meanwhile, the political value of film is part of a far more complex and mediated process, in which ideology is conceived of not as a "bad" thing that must be eradicated completely but as a necessity whose function cannot be filled *without* representation (and correspondingly, without form). We, then, grasp history or gain knowledge and understanding of the real not by negating representation but rather by understanding that "history is not a text, not a narrative, master or otherwise, but that, as an absent cause, it is inaccessible to us except in textual form, and that our approach to it and to the Real itself necessarily passes through its prior textualization, its narrativization in the political unconscious."[14] Given the necessity of this process of representation, and its status *as* representation, any study of film must thus take account first and foremost of the *form* that representation takes (form here being something that must be thought of at once in terms of the work's particular construction—which can be historicized and used as a means for comparison with other works) and as something that stands at a remove from that invisible, ultimately ungraspable thing we call "content," insofar as it constitutes the manifestation of a whole concrete situation in a kind of disguised or distorted form. Form is "the final articulation of the deeper logic of the content itself,"[15] which calls upon us to draw out that absent, ungraspable content of the concrete that it mediates.

For Jameson, the ideological work of cinema is not simply negative, one of deception or containment (even if, in its final moment, a film usually affirms the status quo), but also positive in the way it gives voice to fantasy and wish fulfillment (both of which often imply some kind of desire to grasp a totality, however repressed), which reveals a political unconscious that registers the concrete that lies beneath it and says more through its omissions and failures and through the ideology of form ("the determinate contradiction of the specific messages emitted by the varied sign systems which coexist in a given artist process as well as in its general social formation")[16] than through its manifest content. This account of film's ideological function avoids the abstract and systematizing strictures of *Screen* theory and its ilk precisely by reopening the text onto history, implying a larger totality of which not only the text but also the audience and the film's "author" (whether thought of as an individual in a specific historical situation or as a kind of consciousness that supersedes any individual and comes into being only through the act of creating the text itself) are a part, and which is ultimately a historically specific concrete situation. Thus to critiques of *Screen* theory like that of Stuart Hall (and many others in his wake), which cast it as an essentializing, closed paradigm that posits a universal subject,[17] we can add, via Jameson, that a liberation from this paradigm not only allows for a more nuanced picture of the present but enables a whole array of diachronic comparisons.

This intervention, as may already be obvious, also radically changes the way in which psychoanalysis is incorporated into film theory: the subject (whether author or spectator) must be precisely historicized, and becomes not a deceiver or a dupe (the closed binary so often inscribed in 1960s and 1970s theory), but must instead be positioned as part of a broader totality that is in itself deeply contradictory; to put it in perhaps overly clichéd terms, Jameson moves us outside of Plato's (and Baudry's) cave, revealing film theory itself to have been confined to the very same prison to which it consigned the naïve spectator, believing itself to be superior due to its supposed realization of the illusory quality of all images. For scholars like Jameson, the operations of the psyche are no longer mechanisms that allow ideology to exercise its supposedly diabolical function but rather creative, generative ones, which allow the subject to express lived experience in a given concrete situation through the work of art, and which in turn allow us to draw out both the political unconscious of the text and the concrete that lies beneath it. On the other hand, there is a kind of trade-off here, which may account for the reluctance of activist-minded academics to embrace Jameson's approach: this means that the function of the Marxist scholar is not to critique the flaws of existing practices and then prescribe better ones in a highly normative way (a practice present in the Zhdanovite Soviet Union and certainly still with us now in no small way) but rather to excavate the concrete of history, and hence also the lived experience that was part of it; to draw out that which could not be said, or could not even be conceived of. The study of film becomes useful for us as a means to uncover a history that can never be apprehended as whole, and then to understand the ways in which our political unconscious grapples with the concrete historical situation and points to ways out of it, and indeed reveals that the utopian impulse, the drive toward true collectivity, toward something better, still remains, not crushed or completely enclosed by some dehumanizing and totalizing system. A dialectical account of any given cultural text thus allows us to understand our own situation, the limits that fetter our thought, so that we can conceive of the present in terms that are commensurate to it rather than letting it outrun us as we stick to old oppositions and paradigms that prevent us from grasping the unrepresentable real.

One can hardly separate Jameson's work on film from his approach to culture more broadly, but it is nonetheless true that film provides a privileged site for thinking about how culture functions in a mass-mediatized, spectacularized postmodern culture in which ideology is almost always conveyed in visible form, just as the totality that lies beneath it becomes increasingly abstract, invisible, and unthinkable. This certainly goes some way in explaining why it is the films of the 1970s and onward that have occupied most of Jameson's attention, insofar as they exist in a situation that takes us beyond that of the modern, one in which the visual plays an unprecedented role. We should thus take stock of what Jameson has to say about film specifically, or perhaps what film in particular allows him to say.

Visual Pleasure, Intellectual Joy: Visible Utopias and Invisible Communities in *Signatures of the Visible*

"Films . . . ask us to stare at the world as though it were a naked body," writes Jameson in the introduction to *Signatures of the Visible*—his first collection of essays dedicated strictly to film.[18] Pornographic in essence, Jameson argues, the visual must be probed beyond the raptness it induces in the viewer. And the only way to apprehend and go beyond film's sensuous and overwhelming "all-pervasive visuality as such" (which distinguishes it from the novel, although they are both rooted in the senses through perception and memory) is to look at its emergence in historical terms. It is this process that gives the volume its polysemous title: the "signatures" are at once the imprints or traces films leave on our senses, but they are also the act of writing, which the necessary reflection on film elicits. Jameson has compared the experience of film viewing to a form of drug taking or the euphoria of being intoxicated, and the process of responding to the film by way of analysis and criticism as the remedy that at once cures one and redoubles one's pleasure. Such a strong metaphor allows us to get a glimpse of Jameson's deeply affective relationship to cinema and gives us occasion to point to an important element in his biography. Born in 1934, Jameson grew up in South Jersey, outside of Philadelphia—a stone's throw from a movie theater, which meant that from an early age he would go see movies on a regular and frequent basis.[19] Jameson recalls that he saw "everything made in Hollywood" between 1944 and 1950 (when he left to attend college), an era brimming with studio classics and masterpieces as well as inventive B movies. He started discovering foreign films when he was old enough to take a quick bus ride to Philadelphia: Italian neorealism, first and foremost, but also films from France (his very first was Julien Duvivier's *Panique*) and Sweden (Bergman—*Sawdust and Tinsel* particularly) and those of Luis Buñuel's Mexican period. But, unsurprisingly, it was Hitchcock who evoked the great cinephilic emotion of Jameson's early life ("One of the great moments of my life was seeing the world premiere of *Notorious* on Steel pier in Atlantic City—we used to take vacations in Atlantic City in the summer. . . . Generally Hitchcock would come out around the time of my birthday in April"). Later, while in France (1954) and Germany (1958), Jameson expanded on this body of knowledge, watching, for example, Eisenstein's films at the Paris cinémathèque. Through these biographical reminiscences we can better understand the affective dimension with which Jameson's writing on film is infused—also because these film-going experiences predated his exposure, in college, to theory, and thus played an important formative role in his life as a pre-Marxist thinker; he was then able to revisit and understand these experiences all the more perceptively once he became equipped with the necessary scholarly background, but without relinquishing a sense for the medium that may be characterized as intuitive or instinctual for lack of a better term (hence Jameson's emphasis on the sensory dimension when engaging with film). This is an experience shared by many film scholars, one that makes Jameson's writing on film all the more relatable.

We thus find in Jameson both a need to move beyond the immediate experience of visual pleasure and a great value placed upon that pleasure. This can be detected in the rich, indeed lush and colorful descriptions found in *Signatures of the Visible*. While history and its actors—social classes—are of course the great protagonists of the book, and while each of the discrete chapters is rife with discussions that broach a vast gamut of ideas—as per Jameson's habit (Lukács, Marx, Althusser, Bloch, Freud, Sartre, Adorno, Macherey, Deleuze and Guattari, Coleridge, Márquez, Steinbeck, Dreiser, and Doctorow, among many others, are summoned here, as are a select few film theorists and critics—Bazin, Cavell, Metz)—the case can be made that the central or connecting methodological feature resides in Jameson's allegorical readings. Thus he reminds us of the indispensable need to always periodize and place the films in their historical context, but also to see their historical meaning as something that needs to be excavated or drawn out, moving beyond or behind their manifest content. This, he suggests, is the only way to totalize and, however momentarily, "escape the image by means of the image."[20] To read allegorically and to historicize allows the viewer to escape the anesthetizing or overwhelming effect of the visual/aesthetic per se and to engage in a productive reading of the text in its interplay with history.

History and the visual, the visual and history are the two key terms of *Signatures of the Visible*. But, like Goldmannian "hidden Gods" of sorts, there are also two less discussed elements that seem to animate the volume, namely community and authenticity, both of which are in a way correlated with a utopian drive or yearning.[21] Community is conceived, of course, as the lost (and longed for) element conducive to authenticity, which is still being pursued and renegotiated in the symbolic solutions and answers to social and historical problems proposed by films themselves. So that, throughout the book, Jameson not only seeks to make the reader aware of the importance of unmasking filmic texts for what they are (an apparatus, allegorical, and "mind control" critique), but also stresses their importance in potentially reawakening the drive toward collectivity that cinema at once replays and neuters.

Slicing through Hitchcock, 1970s American genre films (*Jaws*, *The Godfather*, *Dog Day Afternoon*, *The Shining*) but also European and Latin American auteur cinema, with each individual chapter Jameson performs a variety of illuminating interventions. On a local level, he examines how these films deal with questions of class and community. But on a broader one, he challenges the common assumption that there is a hard and fast distinction between "high" and "popular" art, one that obfuscates the true nature of the problem of symbolic production and its alienating quality within capitalism. Indeed, as Jameson makes clear, the desires and problems that animate "popular" (or mass) culture exist within the same framework, and carry out the same operations as those in high art, also because "popular"' or "folk" art can no longer exist as something of its moment in a fully reified twentieth-century Western culture.

On another note, perhaps Jameson's most important contribution to the humanities is his reflection on postmodernism, and in the book he addresses both the aesthetic aspects of this phase in American and Western European films of the 1970s and 1980s and the entanglement between late capitalism and these postmodern films. While the latter express in their form and content modes of a cultural logic that is now mired in a perpetual present and reifies the past in the form of glossy images, Jameson also points to coexisting alternative modes, such as that of late auteur or modernist cinema, which were still able to promote a form of transcendental effect, albeit one that was out of joint with its own era and socioeconomic environment. These late modernist auteur films also display a stimulating rapport with the past, a yearning for a society where social class was still a recognizable entity, to the point where it can haunt both film and viewer (this is precisely Jameson's thesis in his chapter dedicated to "historicizing" Stanley Kubrick's *The Shining*).

While Jameson does not jettison postmodern cinema as uninteresting or a "bad object" wholesale, he clearly sees it as a reflection of a negative development in capitalist society. He remains clear, all the while, that this should never lead one to idealize earlier periods. Yet not all forms of postmodernism are the same, even if they emerge when modernization is completed, alongside the correspond-ing stage of capitalist development. In his provocative revisiting of the "magic realist" category Jameson opposes American postmodern cinema to films from Latin America and communist Poland, which correspond in chronological terms with postmodern pastiche: these magic realist texts differ from their Western counterparts in terms of their engagement with a "perforated" history (as opposed to the nostalgia mode found in Hollywood cinema: while the former takes a cer-tain sense and knowledge of history on the part of the viewer for granted, the latter discards it and reduces the past to glossy, presentified images; again, the sense of community and the latter's relationship to history are a strong unspoken sub-text here), their colorful rather than glossy images, and their drive not so much toward spectacle and commodification of the narrative as toward pure image, denarrativized fragments centering around the body, with sex and violence as their purest expression. Jameson sees these texts as in dialogue with capitalism's history, the spread of which is still resisted in socialist or communist countries, even as they convey a sense of the imminent spread of postmodern impulses to the whole world, as per the logic of a multinational-neoliberal idiom.

"The Existence of Italy" reiterates Jameson's periodizing schema (realism, modernism, and postmodernism), debunking commonplaces about each moment: realism is shown by definition to be impossible as a symbolic or artistic idiom (the moment it is realized, it disappears), and appears to be nothing if not the most artificial of the three modes, in its demiurgic creation of worlds which parade as "natural"; modernism's cult of the auteur and the autonomy attached to it are likewise strongly challenged and debunked, although also celebrated and redeemed through its transcendental aspirations, which possess metaphysical, existential, and often self-referential resonances impossible in realism and undesirable in postmodernism. In the last part of the chapter, Jameson shows how, following a phase of "cultural asphyxiation," the autonomy of culture willed by modernism dissolves in postmodernism, "which can accommodate the molecular fancy of isolated difference with genuine and visceral sympathy and delight,"[22] not by disappearing, but by becoming universal.[23] This is a process through which the ability to see is lost, and one that can be resisted only by reinstating, against capitalism's inscrutable one(s), history as the true transcendental horizon of interpretation.

In a key passage that aptly reveals such a historicizing, totalizing, and synthetic method,[24] Jameson shows how the proto-modernist *politique des auteurs* of the *Cahiers* Young Turks—and their appreciation for Hitchcock but also for less prestigious directors such as Nicholas Ray and Samuel Fuller—is not formulated sui generis but happens just as, in Hollywood itself, the system, following the consequences of the 1948 enforcement of the Paramount Decrees and end to the studios' monopoly, evolves from the mode of massive production of B and genre films to one that casts the director in a new role, much closer to the auteur model of Truffaut, Godard, and company. This exemplar of historicizing film analysis shows the interconnectedness of phenomena, refusing to view them as isolated and without a connection to the industrial, social, political, and—at the base of it all—economic developments of capitalism.

In the end, Jameson's demonstration might appear in equal degree sophisticated and maddeningly nihilistic, were it not for the nearly subliminal but frequent returning to the idea of community (including the references to the end of "traditional" society).[25] While the volume seems to rely mostly on strictly dialectical thinking (hence the many pairings resurging throughout: the modernist tension between the principle of totality and the content of episodes themselves; autonomy and repetition; the molecular and the molar; Coleridge's imagination and fancy; etc.), it is a trinity (the three stages of capitalism and their corresponding cultural "modes" or "codes," but also the subject, community, and history) that effectively guides its triangulated and dynamic reasoning, moving from the intellectual and individual subject to the interplay of subjects and system to a quasi-mythical precapitalist, not yet alienated community connected with authenticity, and which the reified images of cinema nonetheless allow us, paradoxically enough, to envision. In the end, then, two things haunt *Signatures of the Visible* in equal parts: the ghost of human community and the pleasure of an unadulterated (or rediscovered) text.

What also appears evident, in retrospect, is that while he does not yet call it such (although he does mention the concept in closing his "Class and Allegory in Contemporary Mass Culture" chapter), *Signatures* announces the important methodological feature of its more celebrated sequel, *The Geopolitical Aesthetic*, namely its famous application of cognitive mapping. Here, Jameson's method throughout is already one of cognitive mapping in the making, and one to which cinema lends itself as well as—if not better than—its next of kin, the novel.

Global Jameson: *The Geopolitical Aesthetic*, Scale, and World Cinema Studies

Jameson's extensive travel for academic purposes allowed him to develop a global consciousness, with conferencing, keynote lectures, plenary sessions, and visiting professorships accumulating over the past five decades. What made this international travel and his various academic fellowships so important (at Peking University and elsewhere) is that they allowed a cultural and physical distance from the United States to influence his thinking. This expansion of his Marxist-inspired, European-trained perspective, gained through his geographical movement and the encounters he had with distant geographies and unfamiliar cultures, would profoundly transform his scholarship.

Jameson has thus personally experienced globalization in two ways. First, the forces that propel globalization propelled him as a thinker: the scholarly research by thinkers all over the globe that he was consuming, the flight paths he took to get out into the world (outside of the neo-Gothic confines of Yale and Duke), and the computer screens that enabled learning, movement, and interaction through their technological ubiquity. All of these material drivers, utilized by Jameson and those around him, form part of "the real material of globalization, the things that count, the things that guide or impose outcomes."[26] Those outcomes in this context are knowledge and reflexivity about globalization and a conceptualization of a globalized world through his "intellectual effort to recover the object, . . . and the total historical situation underneath and around it."[27]

Second, Jameson's foray into theorizing "cultural globalization"—an allusive, almost amorphous condition and process that creates different "inter-cultural contacts, global migration and changing subjectivities that unfold unevenly across many different fields and dimensions"[28]—was largely excogitated through these very material experiences. The premises of Jameson's theses on cultural globalization were first developed in *The Cultures of Globalization* (1998) and placed a renewed emphasis on its "push-pull" effect, beyond its economic and political vectors, attending to what he saw as three possible consequences of increased worldwide interconnectedness: (1) "the enlargement of communicational nets," (2) "postmodern difference," and (3) new "national situations."[29] Globalization's effects on modes thus could take the form of geocultural assimilation (for example, filmic melodramas and their global ubiquity), hybridity (via coproductions in the film industry), and insistence on cultural uniqueness (films with an emphasis on national figures through heritage cinema and biopics and local suspicion of import-only culture): communication and technological entwinement and expansion thus elicited three different reactions to the conditions and processes of planetary scale.

In effect, these three vectors of global culture let Jameson bypass older, more binary views that held the grand concept of globalization to be a social and economic phenomenon only; instead, Jameson takes a cautious tone and distills from Néstor García Canclini's impassioned notion of cultural globalization a tripartite set of possibilities, ones that give "ammunition to the most vital Utopian visions of our time, of an immense global urban intercultural festival without a center . . ."[30] By making globalization a new "object of study," he is thus able to expand his theoretical toolkit to include ideas not native to the United States or Europe and to attempt to quantify something that seemed almost unquantifiable at the time and still does today. Indeed, much of Jameson's global consciousness about the cinemas he theorizes connects to how he positions these national cinemas as part of a supranational system, one that globalization creates. Yet few have given his treatment of cultural globalization—a phenomenon once viewed as too multidimensional in scope, a flimsy and wooly concept, not worthy of sustained elucidation—much of a second thought in terms of what it might offer to film theory.

Looking back over Jameson's expression of his worldview in interviews and publications formulated during the 1980s and 1990s, it is refreshing to see his development of a countervailing approach to area studies and a refutation of the nation-state framing that had largely compartmentalized the study of film. Despite some early efforts to formulate a global approach to film studies (we find important precursors in Ella Shohat and Robert Stam, and Roy Armes),[31] national case studies continued to dominate into the 1990s. Jameson's intervention into this made clear the necessity of looking at local examples as revealing a particular culture's partial globality, rather than its absolute difference or uniqueness and the reification of culture itself that this would imply. He put films in conversation with globalization by drawing on world-systems theory, which structured his core argument in *The Geopolitical Aesthetic: Cinema and Space in the World System* (1992). Here, his tracing of capital's impact on cinematized societies from the North Atlantic, Europe, Southeast Asia, and East Asia allows him to analyze their film cultures as "units inside the world."[32] By putting world-systems theory to good use, Jameson discerns texts not just as resonating with political and economic concerns but also as a means to analyze culture as affected by, transformed by, or antagonistic to different para-sovereign realities. World-systems theory was, of course, a mode of analysis developed by sociologist Immanuel Wallerstein that serves as a conceptual and theoretical mechanism to see a macro-scale picture of capitalism through an overlap of its systematic reach at a number of different levels as in a Venn diagram. The scalar arrangements proposed by Wallerstein are tripartite and take the form of a constellation of political and economic units: "core" (Western Europe, the United States, England, and Japan), "semi-periphery" (South Korea, Taiwan, Argentina, Israel, and parts of

Eastern Europe), and "periphery" (China, India, most of Africa, the Middle East, Latin America, the Caribbean, and Southeast Asia). All of these political and economic units then animate nation-state rivalries, competing with one another for interstate power, production capabilities, or solely for profit and financial hegemony.

Jameson's systematization of not only geopolitics but more importantly geo-cultural difference and overlaps offers a transnational system of analysis that res-onates just as much today, largely because of the continuing predominance of what he calls "a host of partial subjects, fragmentary or schizoid constellations, [things that] can often now stand in allegorically for trends and forces in the world system."[33] The wide-ranging analyses of *The Geopolitical Aesthetic* demon-strate how films from around the globe can be read as manifestations of world-wide historical processes while still maintaining local specificity, as in his discussions of "magic realism" as a global tendency that manifests differently in different contexts (exemplified by his chapter on Alexander Sokurov's *Days of the Eclipse* [1988]), and Taiwan's transformation as it became a vassal state for global capitalism, as manifested in *The Terrorizers* (Edward Yang, 1986).

Jameson's "geopolitical aesthetic" showed that globalization's center never emanated from one place but was shaping human activity, cultural production, visualities, and ideas in film—all simultaneously and unevenly—at a rapid pace around the world. More recently, Jameson has taken his perspective on global culture one step further in a chapter titled "Globalization and Hybridization," published in Nataša Ďurovičová and Kathleen Newman's edited collection *World Cinemas, Transnational Perspectives* (2010). Keenly aware of the cultur-ally hybrid nature of film and its transnational promotion of a creolizing world, Jameson provides a coda to his work related to cultural globalization with a short piece devoted to Wong Kar-wai's *Happy Together*. A globe-trotting story shut-tling between the Southern Cone and Pacific Rim, the queer escapade of two young men, on a short sojourn from Hong Kong to Buenos Aires, left stranded without money to pay for a return flight home, forces one to find employment at a rundown bar and the other to pursue sex work, with both squandering money and not too concerned with their waywardness.

Focusing on the film's refutation of a "superstate centrality" (i.e., that of the United States)[34] in favor of attention to more far-flung outposts of globalization, Jameson observes that Wong's characters seem unfazed by having to live within the context of the Global South. Here Jameson's own sentiments can be seen, like the film (and his long-awaited official departure from using the Third World descriptor), to ascribe to the Global South (a term he never uses) the function of "a crucible for sustaining popular agency, one that allows for old and new forms of cultural freedom to express themselves through a myriad of mediums against structures of power, national and international alike."[35] Like other global art cinema from the period, *Happy Together* may be referred to retrospectively as "a theater for other liberatory dramas which draw attention to the ordinary and peripheral,"[36] where the polyvalent imprint of these regions of the world—truer melting pots of culture and languages than the United States with its segregated or multicultural approach to difference—is enough for these transient characters to stay entertained and in places that one normally imagines as more distant from the reach of globalization: milieus full of tango, street football, and asado in Argentina, which complement and are fused with Hong Kong's cramped livings spaces, karaoke bars, and packed tram cars and night market. Yet all these spaces are connected at the end of the film where an airport and a flickering television screen reveal the world in miniature. Ultimately Jameson's reading of *Happy Together* is consistent with the Global South's cultural self-determination, and he sees Wong's film as being ahead of its time in its depiction of the global present that has made migrant mobility a necessary part of one's worldliness.

This section, and indeed our introduction, should not end without mentioning the frequent accusations of Eurocentrism that have been leveled at Jameson. Catherine Liu's rebuttal of Jameson's instinctual application of Cold War politics to Edward Yang's *The Terrorizers*, for example, is not without merit. Liu notes how Jameson treats East Asia—save Japan—as the backwater of global modernity. This positioning of the region finds its meaning specifically in its relationship to the West, insofar as Asia's delayed modernization/postmodernity comes to function as a critical tool to carry out a critique of the West (or if we summon Shu-mei Shih's argument, built upon Michel Foucault's work, a technology of recognition of the West). Like Liu, Deborah Dixon and Leo Zonn criticize Jameson's Western-centric viewpoint, in this case in their response to his discussion of *The Perfumed Nightmare* (Kidlat Tahimik, 1977), in which these two postcolonial scholars incorporate a concept original to film studies and overlooked by Jameson, namely Third Cinema.[37] The emancipatory fervor related to the core logic of Third Cinema is used by Dixon and Zonn to discard Jameson's Francophilic anticapitalist critique in favor of seeing the Filipino jeepney driver from this canonical Southeast Asian film as subjugated by American militarism in the Philippines but ultimately liberated from his fanciful revery for France though newfound agency and historical awareness. This brings us back to our opening statement: while Jameson has given much to film studies, and his separateness from the discipline indeed has its virtues, he has also refused to make use of some of the discipline's most innovative and polemical concepts, a shame perhaps, given that this Southern Cone–related term holds deep relevance to his Marxist beliefs.[38]

Critiques of Jameson, however, can also, perhaps more productively, place him in the position that he places others, using his insights and tools while in other ways transcending them or placing them into a broader framework of which they initially took no account. A Jamesonian approach need not be ruled out or discounted due to the sometimes Western-centric approach of his work, but can instead show, as Naoki Yamamoto does in his contribution here, how Jameson's own thought reveals deeper meanings and potential uses when confronted with cultural and theoretical discourses that largely exclude or contest it (here, in the Japanese context), and indeed should never be taken as sufficient in itself, in the lack of more local-level discourses generated *from* the region in question. Alvin Wong's chapter in this volume, meanwhile, considers what we might make of Jameson's "lack of acknowledgment of his own positionality vis-à-vis the Chinese and Taiwanese young intellectuals to whom he exported Marxist theory of postmodernism," but also argues that experiences from which Jameson himself remains irremediably distant on a personal level—in this case, those of young gay men in Sinophone Asia—can nonetheless be productively examined through his critical framework (as indeed Jameson himself would agree, having written about *Happy Together* in the vein discussed above). What is perhaps most productive here is not debating who has a "right" or is locally informed enough to write about a particular topic, but rather how, in both of these cases, Jameson's work should not be rejected due to an authorial subject position that like any subject position, is inevitably biased and limited, but rather as something that can be used productively and built off of, and in need of supplementation. These supplements, however, are not merely local knowledges or expertise that flesh out Jameson's thought, or even ideological corrections to a perceived Western-centrism, but rather dialectical complements to that thought, which reveal its assumptions and lacunae while at the same time incorporating it into a new, expanded map of sorts. This applies not only to cases in which Jameson's Western-centrism blocks the consideration of certain geographical specificities, but to fields such as queer studies (also addressed by Wong) and affect studies (whose productive encounter with Jameson is staged in this volume by Pansy Duncan), which Jameson has largely excluded from his toolbox.

On a somewhat more obvious note, whatever objections one might have to Jameson's approach to the global, it nonetheless remains the case that theories laid out in *The Geopolitical Aesthetic*, *The Cultures of Globalization*, and, more recently, the "Globalization and Hybridization" essay remain highly relevant today largely because they insist upon the importance of examining social forces and cultural forms spread across the globe as inseparable from their positioning as part of a global, late capitalist context. This approach has provided a foundation for an emerging generation of critically engaged and interdisciplinary film scholars, and it is our view that Jameson is partly responsible—along with Wallerstein, Roland Robertson, Arjun Appadurai, Jan Nederveen Pieterse, Kōichi Iwabuchi, and others—for the "global turn" in film studies, a turn that can certainly do much to remedy the kinds of Western-centric perspectives that still inhere in Jameson himself.

Sprawling, Dialectical, Cinematic: Jameson's Prose Style

We should briefly note here other aspects of Jameson's work that have been—sometimes rightly—held against him. These range from the more general (Jameson as a haughty, at times overly authoritative voice—Liu's criticisms a case in point here) to the more topical (his claims about the death of affect [1991], which came under much fire from affect studies scholars and have been engaged with productively by others)[39] and his alleged overly masculine approach and limited interest in queer theory (his otherwise masterful reading of Alexander Sokurov's work is entirely oblivious to the Russian director's homosocial imagery).[40] Many of these issues can be attributed to Jameson's seemingly anachronistic standpoint as a modernist and the quasi-dogmatic role that (Lukácsian) Marxist doxa plays therein. While one can in no way attempt to gloss over the divide that may appear to exist today between a new generation of scholars and Jameson's ongoing body of work, one can see the very same tendencies in his work that may seem outmoded as a demonstration of his intellectual consistency, and the steadfast attachment he has had to a specific method, one that, whatever its omissions, is unrivaled in its synthetic and catholic character.

In addition to the objections catalogued above, Jameson's dense prose style has often been held against him. Its difficulty, however, is a sign not of negligence or willful obscurity but of the expression of a precise poetics that allows for the theorist's refined crafting of narratives that lead the reader through a labyrinth that feels almost spatial in its construction and at the same time necessitates a decisively temporalized and irreversible unfolding, both of which suggest that his writing operates much like cinema itself. While many scholars, particularly those who consider him a dilettante in film studies, might reproach Jameson's lack of interest in precise terminology and relatively cursory familiarity with canonical texts of the field, one could argue that his approach to writing is the most cinematic that one could possibly imagine and therefore a more appropriate means to approach its object than any sterile or pared-down analytical style. It may be thus productive to further consider the relationship between Jameson's dialectical method and cinema specifically, particularly insofar as both offer a particular form of *experience* to the subject who confronts them (again, this is one of the key premises of *Signatures of the Visible*).

Jameson is quite clear about the rationale behind his prose style: indeed, we could see *Marxism and Form* as laying out what a dialectical criticism should be and his subsequent works as then demonstrating it, hence their increasing "difficulty." In the very first pages of the book, he notes how, beginning with Hegel, "dialectical thought turns out to be nothing more or less than the elaboration of dialectical sentences"; the "clarity and simplicity" that are demanded by the Anglo-American tradition are thus hopelessly impotent and mystifying, insofar as "they were intended to speed the reader across a sentence in such a way that he can salute a readymade idea effortlessly in passing, without suspecting that real thought demands a descent into the materiality of language and a consent to time itself in the form of a sentence."[41] Jameson insists that we see thought as "a form in time, as process, as a lived experience of a peculiar and determinate structure."[42]

These two terms—materiality (or form) and time—are of course eminently related to cinema, which engages with them in a way that no medium had before. While there is plenty more to be said about Jameson's writing style more broadly (as Terry Eagleton has done in two separate essays),[43] we can quickly note two fundamental ways in which we might think of it in "cinematic" terms. First, Jameson's insistence on the materiality of thought, as Eagleton notes, allows him to endow "ideas with a sensuous body, translating conceptual matters into visual, dramatic, or corporeal terms; Jameson's own translation of concepts into material images is yet another way of reuniting the sensible and the intelligible."[44] As in cinema, thought here becomes palpable, visible, experienced in a way that goes beyond any conceptual abstraction and instead offers a visceral experience, full of sensuality and pleasure. Second, that experience is in both Jameson's writing and cinema in some sense uncontrollable or elusive: one cannot pause to pin down any givens or absolutes, since to pause (to still the image, we might say) would be to reify the object, to deny all experience and all concrete phenomena their historical dimension. As soon as the projector stalls, the image melts away rather than manifesting itself with some greater form of visibility.

Although the two thinkers engage with cinema in very different ways, and indeed from antagonistic philosophical positions, the parallels between cinema and thought we find in Jameson are curiously echoed in the work of Gilles Deleuze—not least in the emphasis they have placed on periodizing and on epistemic "breaks." In both cases, it would probably not be going too far to say that this cinematic prose attests to the fact that cinema itself constitutes a kind of language or code that is particularly suitable for expressing our experience of reality in the modern period, not because it reproduces it in some perfectly mimetic or accurate way, but precisely because it inscribes within itself the very spatio-temporal terms in which that reality is experienced, while at the same time giving specific form to the modern alienation of the subject from the world (that visible from which the spectator is in fact always estranged, whether it is mistaken for an illusory plenitude or acknowledged as Debordian spectacle).

This all raises the question, of course, of what sort of writing would be suitable for grasping not the modern but instead the postmodern; indeed, one of the paradoxes of Jameson's work is that his own approach still hews so closely to modernism itself, even as it speaks of that which has come to fulfill or sublate it (in however undesirable a fashion). But to be in this sense anachronistic is also to insist that the promises that modernism offered, as noted above in relation to *Signatures of the Visible*, are something that the postmodern does not, and that to hold out any hope, to retain any kind of utopian dimension, necessitates a kind of deferral, an insistence that the kind of future modernism could still imagine can still be glimpsed on the horizon if one can find it between the cracks of the total spectacle of the postmodern. Style itself, perhaps inescapably modernist in Jameson, thus becomes a kind of never-fulfilled figure of utopian desire, as it "both compensates for and adumbrates pleasures historically postponed," as

Eagleton puts it.[45] One might say the same of cinema (especially that of Godard), insofar as it holds out (or at least did in the past) the promises of a reconciliation between subject and world, and a moment at which the visible and the sensible will be commensurate with meaning itself.

All of this brings us, of course, to the question of Jameson's relevance in an age in which his thought itself seems to have been outstripped by new paradigms that make a more decisive break with the modern. What might Jameson have to offer us in thinking about a moment that no longer seems to be "his"? One answer, to be sure, is that he provides a set of "raw materials" that can in turn dialectically confront or be sublated into new forms of thought, something that we can see in some of the chapters in this collection, to which we now turn.

Chapter Synopses

Several of the essays included here deal with films and filmmakers to which Jameson has already devoted considerable attention, but build upon and recontextualize his insights. Dudley Andrew's contribution, for example, returns to Jameson's famous reading of Beineix's *Diva* (1981), considering in greater depth how the film articulates "the force of a conjuncture" specific to France, already remarked upon by Jameson as a historical situation that gives it a different kind of significance than American postmodern films that were released at around the same time. In addition to considering the concept of conjuncture itself and its importance for the analysis of the postmodern culture industry, Andrew situates *Diva* within a succession of phases specific to the history of French cinema, showing how Jameson's use of periodization can be articulated at a more local and nationally specific level, all the while connecting such a local case to the global development of capitalism. Positioning it in relation to a dizzying array of French films and novels, Andrew considers how Beineix's film both parallels and breaks with earlier films that marked similar ruptures within French cinema, and how Jameson's identification of it as heralding a new film style has been borne out by subsequent developments in France.

Likewise delving into Jameson's writings on a single filmmaker, but also considering his methodology and style more broadly, Paul Coates juxtaposes the critic's works with the films of Theo Angelopoulos. Dazzlingly eloquent and erudite in his comparison of both men's methods ("long ground-swells of thought in Jameson, like the long takes of Angelopoulos") in terms of their relationship to Lukácsian totality and Adornian negative dialectics and a melancholy resistance to exchange, Coates interrogates the act of redeeming "the image by the image" that Jameson explicated in *Signatures of the Visible*—or perhaps it is the opposite. Coates perceptively identifies a sympathy or homeostatic affinity between the American critic and the Greek filmmaker, "kindred spirits" and both, of course, late moderns in a sea of postmodernity. In both men he sees a "process of advance and continuous suspension" consubstantial with their method. In the lyrical yet rigorous prose that characterizes his output, Coates focuses here on a variety of motifs in Angelopoulos's later work (mists, bodies of water to cross, borders, trees) and finds in them a meaning that reaches beyond the poetic or lyrical, while still accounting for the "mystery" Jameson acknowledges in cinema at large (and is skeptical of, in turn, in Angelopoulos's later films). Coates redeems this mystery, seeing in it a representation of the impossibility of totalizing the world system, a kind of utopian absence.

Michael Cramer's contribution, meanwhile, focuses on Jameson's reading of 1970s conspiracy films, and on *All the President's Men* (1976) in particular. Cramer places the conspiracy film within the context of the broader movement/cycle of what is now commonly referred to as New Hollywood, demonstrating how it offers not only a solution to the "form-problem" of how to bridge the gap between individual experience and an ungraspable totality (i.e., a practice of cognitive mapping), but also Hollywood's own solution to largely negational films that launched New Hollywood. Rather than casting serious doubt on both the form and ideology of Classical Hollywood cinema (as did films like *Easy Rider, Two-Lane Blacktop*, and those of Robert Altman), *All the President's Men* seems to mark a moment of restoration of faith both in American ideology and institutions and in the goal-based, "happy ending" narrative characteristic of Classical Hollywood. Cramer argues, however, that the film is not a restoration at all but rather carries out a kind of sublation of the qualities that were cast as negative in earlier New Hollywood films (minimization of individual agency, open endings, lack of clear values or beliefs) and uses them to produce something like an instruction manual of how the subject might navigate a new information-based form of late capitalism, one already strongly characterized in the film in a way that aligns closely with what would later be called neoliberal ideology. At the same time, the film retains a kind of ambivalence about this kind of "adaptation" of the subject to the neoliberal context and hints at the darkness and violence that lie behind its championing of "transparency" and affirmation of the function of the press.

Focusing, like Cramer, on conspiracy, Mike Wayne moves beyond Jameson's case studies of Nixonian thrillers made during the 1970s to instead consider a whole new array of "conspiracy films," all the while building off of and revising Jameson's ideas. One of the most fascinating analyses of conspiracy film comes via Wayne's look at *The International* (2009), a film that shows an admiration for the 1970s conspiracy films but faces the problem of responding to the way that social content of advanced capitalism threatens to overwhelm the limits of the classical narrative form. Wayne proposes that the entity of the multinational bank and the CEO-villain who runs it (the polyglot and cosmopolitan executive from Scandinavia), "as the Interpol detective hero Salinger is also supported by a team of detectives internationally in all the different locations of the action (Jameson's point about spatializing narratives)," allow the film to link one industry to another through its transborder crimes (assassinations and loan addiction by

Global South nations). Ultimately, the bank in *The International* reveals by the end sequence its supranational dominance: what this means is that "business as usual" will prevail, and the film exemplifies a neoliberal thought increasingly willing to accept illicit transactions to keep industries solvent. It is this kind of cultural logic, in Wayne's reconsideration, that perhaps allows the conspiracy film to retain a form of goal-oriented storytelling.

The three chapters dealing with East Asia move beyond any of Jameson's readings of specific films and instead pursue analyses in a Jamesonian vein and explore how certain terms central to his work (namely cognitive mapping, allegory, and postmodernism) can be deepened and revised by being placed in contact with more local and particular situations. Alvin Wong's chapter updates Jameson's cognitive mapping concept, showing how the films of Tsai Ming-liang offer an account of what Wong calls "queer cognitive mapping," that is, the way in which queer subjects in particular understand and experience urban dystopia, spatial compression, and claustrophobia in places like Taipei. With a particular focus on Tsai's use of doubled or overlapping spaces, Wong shows how his films articulate "the existing logics of queer claustrophobia while self-reflexively providing alternatives through queer cognitive mapping." Wong's keen attention to the interplay between space, sexuality, and relationships (particularly familial ones) in Tsai's *Rebels of the Neon God* (1992) and *The River* (1997) allows him to show the inextricability of these categories from each other in queer Sinophone cinema and to illustrate how these films were ahead of most Asian art cinema produced in the early 1990s in their representation of how libidinal and familial spaces are subject to negotiation and contestation and how they give visual form to queer urban experience in spatial terms.

Zooming in on the Oscar-winning film *Parasite* (2019) by Korean filmmaker Bong Joon-ho, Keith B. Wagner emphasizes the juxtaposition of the sociological and global in conjunction with Jameson, extracting theories from his *Geopolitical Aesthetic* and *Postmodernism* to think about real estate speculation in post-IMF South Korea. Jameson's views about postmodern architecture and neonoir film deepen Wagner's theorization of the worship of property and the implications of the location of the properties the film's diegetic world depicts in real-life Seoul. Wagner also revises Jameson's notion of allegory, showing that it can be conceived of not only as the expression of a fixed social totality, but also as a way to gesture toward something that has not yet occurred but seems imminent, in this case the burst of the real estate speculation bubble.

Naoki Yamamoto's contribution, meanwhile, focuses less on any particular media text than on what he calls a "virtual dialogue" between Jameson and Japanese theorists of the postmodern. Yamamoto begins by considering Jameson's interactions with the theorists Karatani Kōjin and Asada Akira, and his objection to their tendency to consider Japanese postmodernity as unique in such a way as to undermine his position that there is indeed only one postmodernity, given its global scale. The remainder of his account, however, seeks to explain the relative disappearance of Jameson's name from Japanese discourse around postmodernism while at the same time showing the relationship between Jameson's work and that of two more recent Japanese theorists who do not engage with him directly, namely Ōsawa Masachi and Azuma Hiroki. Focusing in particular on how the latter have developed theories in which new media play a central role, Yamamoto shows at once how much analyses of new media and Japanese popular culture can contribute to our understanding of the postmodern and the shortcomings of approaches to such phenomena that would fail to see Marx's value as "a shrewd commentator on the oxymoronic nature of capitalism and its ever-shifting strategies for survival." Just as importantly, Yamamoto insists upon the necessity for Western scholars to pay more attention "to previously neglected non-Western theorizations of the present and its dominant cultural forms" given capitalism's now global totalizing logic and reminds us that we should not see them "as a credible empirical account of the cultural specificity of given national contexts," but instead "use them creatively, highlighting their epistemological potentials to enhance and complicate our imperfect understanding of late capitalism and its inherently global nature."

Two chapters here examine through a Jamesonian lens the specter that haunts twentieth-century communism, namely Stalin. In his contribution, John MacKay addresses this fraught legacy by way of Dziga Vertov's *Three Songs of Lenin* (1934). Unlike certain Soviet films (Eisenstein's late oeuvre a case in point) where the dictator does not literally appear but looms as an omnipresent but invisible quasi-divinity, "present only in metonymic indicators" (Bulgakowa), MacKay persuasively demonstrates that Stalin is indeed *not* absent from *Three Songs*, even in its de-Stalinized version, from which his image has been all but excised. What effect, then, MacKay asks, "should this knowledge have on our *reading* of the film, in contrast to our necessary efforts to establish a correct original text? That is, what precise difference does the presence or absence of Stalin make to our considerations of Vertov's artistic evolution and of the structure and ideology of *Three Songs*"? However, even as Vertov deliberately incorporated the dictator into his uncensored film, MacKay suggests that Stalin (or rather "Stalin") was not particularly essential to the overall structure and rhetoric of *Three Songs of Lenin*. MacKay argues this not on the basis of Vertov's political allegiances but on the basis of his peerless knowledge of Vertov's films and their mechanisms. This MacKay does using Jameson's categories based on the four medieval exegetical levels (borrowed in turn from Northrop Frye) to show that Stalin is more or less absent from the highest, or anagogical, layer of interpretation of the film's political unconscious. All the while Stalinist repression and censorship are still present in the film, and thus Vertov, the avant-gardist, must remain true to his favored modes and motifs, not through an appeal to progress or science, but by reaching out for "the folk" and "subjectivities," making "the story of Vertov's own creative passage from the Old of the 1920s to the New of the 1930s a peculiarly Soviet one."

Turning to the legacy of twentieth-century communism as it manifests itself in the present, Jeremi Szaniawski offers his take on the films of Paweł Pawlikowski and neoliberal politics in Poland, using a Jamesonian foundation as a springboard for his own specific pursuits. In 2015, Szaniawski predicted, through his analysis of *Ida* (2013),[46] the dialectics at play and the turn in politics that would a few months later see the populist right seize power in the country, over the more overtly pro-European neoliberal party (a "battle" replayed again in favor of the former, but in a much more closely contested election, in July 2020). Here, Szaniawski again turns to *Ida*, but then moves on to *Cold War* (2018), Pawlikowski's sophomore effort in his Polish phase. This allows us to see clearly the influence of changes of regime on film form, through comparison of the apparently more subtle (and minority-friendly) narrative of *Ida* with the higher contrasts and egotistically sweeping tale of *Cold War*. These tonal and thematic modulations, however, are mostly cosmetic, Szaniawski argues: beneath the lush black-and-white cinematography of the films, we witness a reflection of the continuous development of neoliberalism in the former communist satellite country (dating back to the late 1980s), of which the "global auteur" is a function or byproduct. Beyond this, we witness another variation on late capitalism's cinematic idiom and its grip on this new aesthetic category or product—the festival or middlebrow art house film, hailed as the toast of the town of an all but fully reified world cinema. Borrowing from by now canonical Jamesonian categories and a Lukácsian skepticism of aesthetic ideology, Szaniawski expands his intervention by probing the politics of melancholy, which constitutes another veneer obscuring truth content yet also betrays the sobering and pedestrian political unconscious of Pawlikowski's films: a covert or unconscious fascination for the Big Other (here, again, Stalin). The latter is perceived as more vibrant and paradoxically empowering when set against the tedium of a late capitalism that does not seem intent on either authentically questioning itself or thinking historically, and of which totalitarian Stalinism represents, against the odds, the negative but increasingly realized or inescapable "utopia"—in the form of an unbridled hyperneoliberal society of technological oligarchy and discipline, control, and constraint.

Likewise exploring the status of utopias in the present-day, Dan Hassler-Forest builds upon Jameson's crucial work on science fiction engaging with "An American Utopia: Dual Power and the Universal Army," in which Jameson seeks to reignite our utopian imagination by way of a "collectivity one does not choose" and provocatively interrogates the suggestion that mandatory and universal military conscription could offer a solution to global capitalism's escalating crisis of socioeconomic inequality. Hassler-Forest finds many examples of precisely this kind of imaginary in science fiction, including the genre's most notorious franchises: *Star Trek*, whose futuristic utopia is firmly rooted in military hierarchies, and *Star Wars*, the archetypal Jamesonian nostalgia film that associates the military with political oppression and imperial power. He likewise casts his attention on *Starship Troopers*, illustrating its transformation from a politically reactionary novel to a much more ambivalent film adaptation that fully embraces some of the key contradictions of fantastic military utopias and "Hollywood's fascist unconscious," which Paul Verhoeven's unsung masterpiece is one of the rare films to uncover from within the system. Then turning to the literary realm, Hassler-Forest shows how Kameron Hurley's *The Light Brigade* manages to bring together two contradictory aspects of Jameson's utopian vision: on the one hand, the book powerfully dramatizes the transformative solidarity among military conscripts and the social benefits contained in service. On the other, it shows the military's top-down hierarchies' congeniality with fascist ideology. Finally, Hassler-Forest looks at the recent development in Chinese blockbusters, with the film *The Wandering Earth*, an adaptation of Liu Cixin's successful novel *The Three-Body Problem*. These texts push our cultural and political imaginations from individualism to collectivism, but at the same time their geopolitical context—the nominally communist, single-party, authoritarian PRC—lies much closer to authoritarian capitalism than Jameson's utopian horizon of dual power. From this perspective, the heavily militarized collective future articulated by *The Wandering Earth* is also close to a fascist imaginary, "where a remarkably homogeneous humankind forms a natural and organic collective that has fully internalized the state's authority alongside the hierarchical military organization of its social system." Ultimately, the chapter shows how difficult it is to even imagine the kind of revolutionary transformation that Jameson proposes and shows that the American utopia predicated on the dual power of the universal army still seems a far cry away indeed.

Attending to another one of Jameson's key concepts for analysis, namely class, Mercedes Vázquez's contribution illustrates the utility of a Jamesonian approach for the study of the contemporary Latin American *cine clasemediero* (middle-class cinema) that has emerged in the wake of the increasing fortunes of the middle classes in Mexico and Brazil brought about through neoliberalism. Vázquez considers how recent films by middle-class directors, namely Carlos Reygadas's *Post Tenebras Lux* (Mexico) and Anna Muylaert's *Que horas ela volta?* (Brazil), both exhibit a consciousness of the director's middle-class status and its relationship to working class characters and deploy "strategies of containment" that dramatically limit their political perspective. Drawing on Jameson's theorization of such strategies, Vázquez shows them at work through the articulation of space in both films, grounding her analysis in Jameson's observations about the relationship between space and class. Both films, Vázquez argues, depict space in such a way that it becomes the marker of both a kind of atomization or isolation that both keeps members of the working class and the reality of class itself at a distance (Reygadas) and functions a site of contestation (Muylaert). The relationship between characters and space is further articulated through formal techniques that, as Vázquez shows through close analysis, express a resolutely middle-class perspective. Both films, despite their foregrounding of class difference, ultimately shy away from the realities underlying class conflict and largely isolate themselves to the spaces and perspectives with which the middle-class directors feel most comfortable, carrying out an operation of containment that is at once ideological and spatial.

Pansy Duncan's chapter, finally, considers Jameson's work in conjunction with questions of affect that have so recently dominated the study of culture. Duncan focuses on the illustrations included in *The Geopolitical Aesthetic*'s "Conspiracy as Totality" chapter and, noting that most are medium shots, those "unremarkable, undistinguished staple[s] of popular Anglo-American narrative cinema," inquires as to their political and hermeneutic value. Such shots, she argues, may serve to address a critical impasse in Jameson's own project of cognitive mapping: because cognitive mapping is, by Jameson's own admission, fundamentally impossible, it calls for a supplementary aesthetic strategy that would provide a set of affective tools for responding to and navigating its impossibility. Contending that the formal logic of the encounter lies at the very heart of the medium shots, Duncan also argues that they represent a case of what Jonathan Flatley calls "affective mapping," an "aesthetic technology" that "provide[s] a nugget of affective experience for the audience, one with direct historical resonance and relevance, and . . . tell[s] the reader something about that experience within the narrative itself."[47] Duncan demonstrates how the "encounters" between the individual and the cognitive mapping-resistant world around them that are articulated in these medium shots serve as allegorical articulations not of social totality as such, but of the moment of spectatorial confrontation with the allegorical articulation of social totality, in which we confront the sense of defeated curiosity or confounded aspiration that arises from our inevitably feeble attempts to grasp it. From this perspective, the medium shot emerges as an allegorical mise en abyme in which the simultaneously unrealizable and insatiable spectatorial desire for the representation of what it is properly impossible to represent and its affective component achieve graphic cinematic inscription.

The chapters included here, of course, hardly begin to scratch the surface of let alone exhaust the possible applications, broadenings, and revisions of Jameson's work that will surely emerge in years to come, in part, we hope, under the impetus of this volume. While wide-ranging, the geographical scope on display here could easily be expanded, in particular to address parts of the world (Africa, India) that have received comparatively little attention from Jameson and Jamesonians. There is likewise far more to be done to place Jameson in dialogue with theoretical paradigms largely outside of his purview, both ones that are considered here (queer studies, affect studies) and those that are not (feminist theory, Indigenous studies). It is our hope that whatever limitations or elisions characterize this volume (and they are many!) might be seen as so many empty or unexplored locations on a map whose filling in would represent the full achievement and apotheosis of a Jamesonian study of contemporary global culture.

In closing (but also in opening!), what emerges from this volume, completed in some of the most troubling times we have witnessed in our lifetimes (and also at a time when cinema itself is going through a profound crisis of its own—look no further than the rise of platformization and the hegemony of companies such as Amazon and Netflix in the United States and Tencent and iQIYI in China), against those voices that would cast theory as impotent "ivory tower" chatter, is that we *need* theory, and particularly a theoretical method such as the one Jameson's work exemplifies, more than ever today. The vast majority of scholars represented in this collection illustrate how interdependent our world has become and suggest that it is perhaps in cinema that images come, in the words of Bruce Robbins, to "make global feeling possible."[48] This "global feeling," however, can be traced only to the material conditions that create it through the work of theory: the generic and textual conventions that give it concrete form require a global comparativist analysis and a contextualization within world capitalist systems and the forms of subjective experience that they engender. Jameson has taught us to historicize and more recently to globalize these universal processes and conditions, not only insisting on the unity of the world of late capitalism but also revealing the interconnected and hybridized nature of the Global North and South. As we enter into a historical period in which global neoliberalism attempts to reassert its afflicted powers through the imposition of a fully mediatized authoritarian and surveillance-based system of control that would seem to bring everything into the realm of the visible, we must take from Jameson the lesson that these global-scale processes are, first, almost always occulted, absent from the surface-level conflicts that present themselves as foundational, and, second, never in fact hidden at all but embedded into every single cultural object that surrounds us. To theorize is to dismantle this spectacle, not by denouncing it as false, but by unearthing its formal mechanisms and material foundations, insisting on both the specificity of any text in question and the historical conditions that give it possibility. At the same time, it is important to keep in mind the extent to which the possibility of finding hope or solace through critical and totalizing thinking can itself be dangerous, perversely enough, and risks ultimately reifying and aestheticizing the reified and aestheticized itself. We must always be on guard against truisms and formulas, against a category or concept itself taking the place of the concrete; one must theorize, but theory must never become the response to its own questions. This is a conundrum with which we find ourselves confronted, reminding us of the limits of any thinking, even the most ambitious and comprehensive kind, and of our need to never take it as fixed or final but, instead, to use the legacy of great thinkers to refine our own methods, however modestly, in an age of global discontent, in which we find ourselves standing at a threshold that seems to open onto a dystopian future, but nonetheless should not deter us from seeking its utopian potential.

Notes

1 See Dana Polan's excellent "Raymond Williams and Film Studies," *Cinema Journal* 52, no. 3 (Spring 2013): 1–18.

2 For scholarship that provides an appraisal and interrogation of class and capitalism, see Jyotsna Kapur and Keith B. Wagner, eds., *Neoliberalism and Global Cinema: Capital, Culture and Marxist Critique* (London: Routledge, 2011); Derek Nystrom, *Hard Hats, Rednecks and Macho Men: Class in 1970s American Cinema* (Oxford: Oxford University Press, 2009); David E. James and Rick Berg, eds., *The Hidden Foundation: Cinema and the Question of Class* (Minneapolis: University of Minnesota Press, 1996).

3 Eric Cazdyn, *The Flash of Capital: Film and Geopolitics in Japan* (Durham, NC: Duke University Press, 2002).

4 Clint Burnham, *Fredric Jameson and* The Wolf of Wall Street (London: Bloomsbury, 2016). On the "finance film," see Keith Wagner, "Giving Form to Finance Culture: Neoliberal Denizens in *Wall Street* (1987), *Boiler Room* (2000), and *Margin Call* (2011)," *Journal of Film and Video* 68, no. 2 (2016): 46–60, and Constantin Parvulescu, ed., *Global Finance and Screen: From Wall Street to Side Street* (New York: Routledge, 2018).

5 We would like to thank Dylan Davidson, a graduate student in film and media studies at Yale University, for his extensive and remarkable work tracking down the scholars in the field having quoted texts by Jameson and the rate of citation.

6 Gilles Deleuze stands far ahead of the rest, with an unassailable lead (332,000 citations), which his presence in both Anglo-American and Francophone academia (and many others), as well as the importance of texts such as *A Thousand Plateaus* (over 41,000 citations) in spheres others than the humanities, explains in part.

7 All references to Google Scholar figures listed here date back to a search conducted in July 2020.

8 Pansy Duncan, "Once More, with Fredric Jameson," *Cultural Critique* 97 (Fall 2017): 1–23.

9 Colin MacCabe, preface to Fredric Jameson, *The Geopolitical Aesthetic: Cinema and Space in the World System* (Bloomington: Indiana University Press, 1992), x–xi.

10 Jameson, *Marxism and Form: Twentieth-Century Dialectical Theories of Literature* (Princeton: Princeton University Press, 1971), 39.

11 Jameson, *Marxism and Form*, 333.

12 Jameson, *Marxism and Form*, 183.

13 Fredric Jameson, *Signatures of the Visible* (New York: Routledge, 1992), 160–162.

14 Jameson, *The Political Unconscious* (Ithaca, NY: Cornell University Press, 1981), 35.

15 Jameson, *Marxism and Form*, 329.

16 Jameson, *Political Unconscious*, 98–99.

17 Stuart Hall, "Recent Developments in Theories of Language and Ideology: A Critical Note," in *Culture, Media, Language: Working Papers in Culture Studies, 1972–79*, ed. Stuart Hall, Dorothy Hobson, Andrew Lowe, and Paul Willis (London: Routledge, 1980), 150.

18 Jameson, *Signatures of the Visible*, 1.

19 Jameson remembers that his very first solo outing to that local theater was to see *House of Frankenstein* (Earle C. Keaton, 1944). "The first film I was able, allowed to see on my own, because it meant walking down two blocks and crossing the street

with the light . . . was the *House of Frankenstein*. I still remember the moment in the wall when you get to see the monster's fingers begin to stir" (unpublished interview with Jeremi Szaniawski, August 2016).

20 Jameson, *Signatures of the Visible*, 162.

21 One would be remiss to not point out the fact that the book is dedicated to Peter Fitting, a scholar who has written extensively on the topic of utopia, including with the forthcoming *Utopian Effects, Dystopian Pleasures*.

22 Jameson, *Signatures of the Visible*, 208.

23 Jameson, *Signatures of the Visible*, 202.

24 Jameson, *Signatures of the Visible*, 199–200.

25 Jameson, *Signatures of the Visible*, 227.

26 Nigel Thrift and Steve Woolgar, *Globalization in Practice* (Oxford: Oxford University Press, 2014), 1.

27 Benjamin Kunkel, *Utopia or Bust: A Guide to the Present Crisis* (London: Verso, 2014), 55.

28 Jan Nederveen Pieterse, *Globalization and Culture: Global Melange* (Lanham: Rowman & Littlefield Publishers, 2009), 26.

29 Fredric Jameson and Masao Miyoshi, eds., *The Cultures of Globalization* (Durham, NC: Duke University Press, 1998), 56–61.

30 Fredric Jameson, "Notes on Globalization as a Philosophical Issue," in Jameson and Miyoshi, *Cultures of Globalization*, 66.

31 Ella Shohat and Robert Stam, *Unthinking Eurocentrism: Multiculturalism and the Media* (New York: Routledge, 1994); Roy Armes, *Third World Film Making and the West* (Berkeley: University of California Press, 1987).

32 Immanuel Wallerstein, *World-Systems Analysis: An Introduction* (Durham, NC: Duke University Press, 2004), 23.

33 Jameson, *Geopolitical Aesthetic*, 5.

34 Fredric Jameson, "Globalization and Hybridization," in *World Cinemas, Transnational Perspectives*, ed. Nataša Ďurovičová and Kathleen Newman (New York: Routledge, 2010), 318.

35 Pamila Gupta, Christopher J. Lee, Marissa J. Moorman, and Sandhya Shukla, "Editors' Introduction: The Global South: Histories, Politics, Maps," *Radical History Review* 131 (May 2018): 3–4.

36 Gupta et al., "Editors' Introduction," 5.

37 Deborah Dixon and Leo Zonn, "Confronting the Geopolitical Aesthetic: Fredric Jameson, *The Perfumed Nightmare* and the Perilous Place of Third Cinema," *Geopolitics* 10, no. 2 (2005): 290–315.

38 For a synthesis of Jameson's ideas and Third Cinema, see Mike Wayne's *Political Film: The Dialectics of Third Cinema* (London: Pluto Press, 2001).

39 See, for instance, Eugenie Brinkema, *The Forms of the Affect* (Durham, NC: Duke University Press, 2014).

40 See Jeremi Szaniawski, *The Cinema of Alexander Sokurov: Figures of Paradox* (New York: Wallflower Press, 2014).

41 Jameson, *Marxism and Form*, xii–xiii.

42 Jameson, *Marxism and Form*, 307.

43 Terry Eagleton, "Fredric Jameson: The Politics of Style," *Diacritics* 12, no. 3 (Autumn 1982): 14–22; Terry Eagleton, "Jameson and Form," *New Left Review*, no. 59 (September/October 2009): 123–137.

44 Eagleton, "Jameson and Form," 126–128.

45 Eagleton, "Fredric Jameson," 17.

46 Jeremi Szaniawski, "Benefits of the Doubt: Pawlikowski's *Ida* and the Taste(s) of Ambiguity," *Academia*, February 21, 2015, https://www.academia.edu/11032531 /Benefits_of_the_Doubt_Pawlikowski_s_Ida_and_the_taste_s_of_ambiguity.

47 Jonathan Flatley, *Affective Mapping: Melancholia and the Politics of Modernism* (Cambridge, MA: Harvard University Press, 2008), 4, 7.

48 Bruce Robbins, *Global Feelings: Internationalism in Distress* (New York: New York University Press, 1999), 95.

1

Feeling Film as
the Pulse of the
Postmodern Condition

On Jameson's "On *Diva*"

DUDLEY ANDREW

Periods and Conjunctures in General

At the outset of the 1980s *Diva* (1981) preened as the most talked about French film around. Yet it failed to become a classic and is better known today for having occasioned a short, seemingly offhand essay by the leading Marxist cultural critic of the past half century, Fredric Jameson. Jameson opens his review with two sentences, full of terms whose significance it will be my task to tease out.

> The first French postmodernist film enjoys an advantage denied its American equivalents (those of Brian De Palma): the privilege of a historical *conjuncture*. May 10, 1981, the date of the first left government in France for thirty-five years, draws a line beneath the disappointing, neo-romantic and post-Godard French production of the 1970s and allows *Diva* to emerge (rightly or wrongly) with all the prestige of a new thing, a break, a turn.[1]

Let me begin with the term Jameson troubled to italicize, *conjuncture*. Indeed, let me reinvest in it with compound interest, for extraordinary timing linked something momentous in three spheres: a new phase in French cinema, in French politics, and—here's the added interest—in Jameson's writing and influence. What is the force of a conjuncture, as opposed to a mere coincidence?

Jameson asked this question a year and a half later in a major article with the pertinent title, "Periodizing the 60s." It was in the 1960s (by coincidence?) that Louis Althusser articulated the coordination or balance of forces that produce a "current moment" as a conjuncture. In his essay, Jameson follows in this direction,[2] for after he warns against idealist notions of the "organic unity" of history, he itemizes four levels of social existence that course through any given time span: philosophy, political theory and practice, cultural production, and economic cycles. We may presume these levels to be autonomous (or at least semiautonomous), but sometimes they can be taken together when there arises "a hypothesis about the rhythm and dynamics of the fundamental situation in which those very different levels develop according to their own internal laws."[3] The lines representing the activity of those levels that meander as they move along the horizontal x-axis on a graph of historical time come into phase and seem to run parallel for a time, producing an echo effect, not quite an analogy, that almost demands a label like those we use to discuss "The Postwar" or "The 60s." A conjuncture occurs at certain rare points on the graph where "significant homologies between the breaks in those forms and their development" stand out, signaling the change that has been ongoing.

Jameson marked a clear conjuncture in France in spring 1981 when a major event in political praxis (the election of François Mitterrand) intersected one in cultural production (the brash appearance of *Diva*). Beneath changes in both these levels but running parallel to them, Jameson sees a "new structural moment in capital in our own time [as] has been theorized by Ernest Mandel . . . involving a technological revolution under the radically different industrial dynamic of the computer, of nuclear energy and of the media."[4] Mandel, a Belgian Trotskyite and fellow contributor to the *New Left Review*, had just published *Long Waves of Capitalist Development* in 1978, which Jameson welcomed as serious support for his historical views. If a new wave of "Late Capitalism" followed the exhaustion of the 1940 to 1973 wave, as Mandel demonstrated, then postmodern culture, first visible in the 1960s, was right on time when it had its growth spurt everywhere as the 1970s wore on, blossoming in France with the florid *Diva*.

Theory, Marxist or otherwise, doesn't observe and analyze culture and politics from a timeless perch; it constitutes another level itself, and it too wanders along the historical axis on which literature, political praxis, fashion, and other levels can be tracked as lines moving in semi-independence. Jameson signals the connection between these fields by situating his reading of *Diva* in relation to the work of intellectual stars of the 1970s like the flashy Bernard-Henri Lévy, and the cloudy thinkers of the Nouvelle Philosophie, which he dismisses before fixing momentarily on Michel Foucault's *History of Sexuality* (vol. 1, 1976). The figures that bear directly on issues that *Diva* brings into his viewfinder are Christopher Lasch, famous for his 1979 *The Culture of Narcissism*, and Daniel Bell, whose *The Cultural Contradictions of Capitalism* was a mainstay republished three times in the 1970s. More surprising and specific is Jameson's mention of Reyner Banham, the architectural historian of contemporary urban life, whose *Megastructure: Urban Future of a Recent Past* came out in 1976 when Jameson was teaching in Southern California, where he became alert to architecture at the moment of its postmodern turn.

So it is symptomatic that "Periodizing the 60s" came out in *Social Text*, the journal Jameson cofounded in 1979, and where three of his first four essays on film appeared, including "On *Diva*." This journal announced a turn, a new emphasis that would include film and postmodernism (between 1979 and 1991 eighteen of Jameson's articles have "Postmodern" in their titles, culminating in the massive *Postmodernism; or, The Cultural Logic of Late Capitalism*). Hence the aptness of the first clause of "On *Diva*" where "the first French postmodernist film" ran into Jameson at the outset of his own new phase. They arrived, by very different routes, at a certain conjuncture where François Mitterrand came to meet them, too.

Jameson has taught us to look for punctuating moments like this when culture, or at least its cutting edge, can be seen to have mutated due to underlying social and economic developments. While the act of what he calls "periodizing" inevitably courts distortions, comparative cultural analysis depends on such temporal as well as geographical demarcations, even if time periods are usually shown to be smudged, crossed, distended, obliterated. I have long followed Jameson's decision to boldly periodize, most obviously in my effort to organize the cumbersome field of "world cinema" under his standard terms: classic,[5] modern, postmodern.

Jameson, largely following Mandel, intimates that these stages of culture follow socioeconomic developments. However, it wasn't only Marxists who identified 1940 as a gaping fault line separating phases (or cycles, in Mandel's economic parlance). André Bazin explicitly recognized that a "modern" conception of cinema was replacing a "classic" one, right as this was happening at the time of World War II; later, Gilles Deleuze followed suit, even breaking his grand *Cinéma* project into two volumes, using the war as cleaver.[6] According to Mandel the next break, the next economic wave or cycle, came on schedule; Jameson had sensed it coming in the late sixties, in both the political and the cultural levels. The defeats of the left in Latin America (1966–1967) and throughout the First World in 1968 became definitive with the overthrow of socialism in Chile in 1973.[7] Nearly the entire world was now ready to be networked into a global market for multinational capitalism led by an America that had just ignominiously pulled out of Vietnam and in compensation planned to dominate the world commercially. The media, and movies most of all, became the most visible product and vehicle of this invigorated, utterly dominant culture industry at the outset of the postmodern cultural phase. Already an accomplished reader of "the political unconscious" as figured in modern fiction (and science fiction), Jameson had now "turned" to the cinema through particular films that seemed to choose him.

In his inaugural essay in *Social Text* no. 1, "Reification and Utopia in Mass Culture," Jameson elaborated the dialectical interplay of high and mass culture operating in the postmodern era of consumerism, and he did so by turning to vivid film examples to seal his argument. He chose blockbusters from the New Hollywood, *Jaws* (1975) and *The Godfather* (1972–1974), the first because it is "an excellent example" of the system tapping into and expressing incendiary issues of "genuine social content," that it then manages to contain. As for *The Godfather*, both parts, but especially the second, "offer a virtual textbook illustration of my propositions . . . and dramatize the thesis that all contemporary works of art—whether those of high culture and modernism or of mass culture and commercial culture—have as their underlying impulse our deepest fantasies about the nature of social life, both as we live it now, and as we feel in our bones it ought rather to be lived."[8] Jameson's next film essay, also for *Social Text*, returned to these inklings of the lost community in American life, this time figured in Kubrick's *The Shining*. But now the film, rather than serving as an illustration of Jameson's "propositions," takes the lead in opening the terms and avenues of the essay's meditation on "Historicism."[9] And then came *Diva*, propelling Jameson's ideas by the sheer force of its new images and characters. *Diva* was an event whose significance Jameson intuited, but could not immediately explain. Insubstantial in itself, perhaps it took on weight by conjoining with what was occurring simultaneously around it: the political moment of socialism and the cultural moment of postmodernism. Only a close examination of the film could measure this conjuncture.

We can backtrack from this 1981 conjuncture to look for earlier such moments in the history of French cinema, early places where its phases can be recognized. For if Jameson has taught us anything, it is that general shifts need to be tracked within particular situations. Even the most universal forces (nationalism in politics or sound in cinema, for example) take particular shape and have their effect in localities that are literally ruled by language, traditions, and politics.

France has cultivated its overweening cinema sector as if it were self-sufficient. Conspicuously fashion conscious, and taking the screen as a mirror before which films strut, French critics, even more than their counterparts elsewhere, like to announce dramatic new cinematic styles each "season." However, changes at a scale as large as something called classic, modern, and postmodern take time to develop before a shift finds itself noticed as instantiated. The real drama of French cinema style, one that has gone on for over a century, seems best broken not into years but into acts, with the curtain falling, then rising, between acts just about every twenty years. This corresponds closely to the general phases just outlined.

As if on schedule, right around 1940, 1960, 1980, and 2000, something noticeably changed in the way French cinema looked at itself in the mirror of the silver screen. Given this rhythm, we should be on the lookout right now in 2021
for the next act. What will it hold in store?

The films announcing these observable changes are easy to name; that's the
point. When they came out, everybody immediately remarked on the style of
Port of Shadows (*Le Quai des brumes*, 1938), *Breathless* (*A bout de souffle*, 1960),
Diva (1981), *Amélie* (*Le fabuleux destin d'Amélie Poulain*, 2001). The first three
were in sync with major political changeovers: the end of the Third Republic,
the birth of the Fifth Republic, and the election of a socialist government. As
for *Amélie*, it was still in the theaters when Jean-Marie Le Pen of the Front
National defeated the socialist Lionel Jospin, to reach the 2002 runoff election.

These four films do have certain things in common; Jean-Paul Belmondo's
character in *Breathless* was immediately taken to be the wayward son of Jean
Gabin's deserter in *Port of Shadows*. Both wind up shot down on the street. Like
them, *Diva*'s protagonist finds himself on the run from both the police and a
criminal gang, but neither his face nor his demeanor bear the weight of a worldview the way Gabin's and Belmondo's do. Neither the actor nor his character carries the authority of personal style, the way those two did. As for the female
leads, all of them except the one playing the diva were unassuming ingénues who
were made instantly famous. Although their characters avoid the limelight, the
actresses themselves—Michèle Morgan in a trench coat, Jean Seberg in a T-shirt,
and Audrey Tautou in a rainbow of colors—were themselves exposed in newspapers and on billboards. Coiffeuses worldwide learned to imitate the distinctive hairdo of each. As for Wilhelmania Fernandez, *Diva*'s title alone solicits the
male gaze and female envy; however she was, and remained, a genuine opera
singer, wishing to become neither actress nor model, indeed never again playing
in a motion picture.[10] Still, her image (silver gown draped on dark skin) promoted
the look of a film that inaugurated precisely "Le Cinéma du Look."

Diva's Postmodern Turn and Political Conjuncture

When Jameson opened his article by pointing to *Diva* as "a new thing, a break,
a turn," he was acknowledging that it (and perhaps he) had sped past an exhausted
modernity. He later put it this way: "Modernity, in the sense of modernization
and progress, or *telos*, was now definitively over; and what I tried to do, along
with many others, working with different terminologies no doubt, was to explore
the shape of the new historical period we had begun to enter around 1980."[11] This
language is close to that which François Mitterrand used in his inaugural address
and interview: "There was only one victor on May 10—hope," the hope specifically to overcome the "mechanized system in which thinking has become ste-
reotyped, and in which people have not fully assimilated in their minds and in
their hearts the new power of the information media, and because most leaders

tend to take a 'technocratc' approach."[12] After the stagnant Giscard years, which in the cinema sector resulted in "the disappointing . . . French production of the 1970s," a new attitude of openness, even of optimism, conjoined *Diva* to Mitterrand's political rhetoric, because it produced new images, an entirely new kind of character, and a satisfying negotiation with technology.[13]

Hovering nearby right from the start, however, is the inevitable and mercurial Jean-Luc Godard, whose name Jameson invokes twice in the first paragraph. *Diva* might be "the first [commercially successful] French postmodernist film," but Jameson had the previous year nominated Godard's video work as "resolutely postmodernist,"[14] and in his article on *Passion* says outright, that "Godard [was] surely as postmodern *avant la lettre* as one might have wished in the heyday of auteurist high modernism."[15] For in the late 1960s Godard already sensed modernity and modernist art to be passé, and so he declared fiction films (including his own) to be disposable consumer products. Renouncing authorship, he joined the Dziga Vertov collective and turned to video with Anne-Marie Miéville through the mid-seventies. He was proud to trade in cinema's highly produced packaging (made for consumption) and adopt the ease and direct address of the small, workaday format, the "numéro deux" of audiovisual media. But then, sensing a new insidious cultural and political atmosphere phasing in with the eighties, he returned to thirty-five-millimeter feature production and "has today in full postmodernism become the ultimate survivor of the modern as such."[16]

Jameson was completing the essay on *Diva* as *Passion* (1982) was coming out. That film appeared so pertinent to the issues of postmodernism and socialism that he needed to mention it, if only on the fly. *Diva* and *Passion* both connect exquisite classic humanist art (opera and painting) with the outdated factories of modernity through new technologies of reproduction. But "the comparison stops there." In his later full-blown essay on late Godard, Jameson insists that *Passion*'s refusal of a satisfying narrative, its longing for meaning that never arrives, should be seen as a modernist, and preferable, way of conceiving film art, "requiring active analysis, whereas the postmodern option would seem to involve little more than sitting back to watch it all hang out."[17] What hangs out in postmodern art might be the incongruities that can indeed fill up Godard's works the way they fill up our lives, or the "far older and pre-capitalist vocation of decoration and ornament [that] has been reborn."[18] *Diva* is a postmodern film of this latter sort. Its narrative is so neatly wrapped up that it exists merely as another additional ornament. *Diva* certainly does not exhibit, as *Passion* does, that "longing for monadic closure about which the postmodern text could care less."[19]

Godard confuses all categories. In *Passion*, the postmodernist cineaste of the 1960s now questions postmodernist art and derides "the demarxified postmodern France of the Parti Socialiste." He thus mocks both terms in Jameson's title, "*Diva* and French Socialism." His persistence makes us question Jameson's way of characterizing French production of the seventies, as "neo-romantic and post-Godard," simply because he outlasted those years. For in the eighties Godard is himself post-Godard; moreover, from *Passion* to *King Lear,* "who else today [other than Godard] would reaffirm—by way of that unexpected permutation of his otherwise grotesque self-mockery—the conception of the Romantic genius and creator in the strongest and most unseasonable expressions it has found in our own time?"[20]

"Unseasonable," indeed. Romanticism, as a period term, dates to the French Revolution and is generally thought to have petered out by 1850. It doesn't figure except tangentially in Jameson's periodization, standing as a particular reaction to industrialism at the beginning of the modern period. But this movement, rebellious and self-assertive, also harked back to an earlier, preindustrial era. Hence the term is commonly applied to twentieth-century figures and works that blithely aim to return to an imagined purity whether or not in the style of the romantic poets, painters, and composers. In denigrating the state of French cinema as "neo-romantic," was Jameson thinking of the rural and melancholy sensibility of the mid-twentieth-century painters for whom the term was coined?[21] This conceivably could apply to Truffaut's *Adèle H* (1975) and *The Green Room* (*La Chambre verte,* 1978) or André Techiné's *Wuthering Heights* (*Les hauts de Hurlevent,* 1977) and Bertrand Tavernier's *A Week's Vacation* (*Une Semaine de vacances,* 1980), but that makes for a small selection. Likely using "neo-romantic" more loosely, he targeted a general return across the spectrum of French production to the absolute primacy of the individual, which he saw as a doleful retreat after the socially radical output of the late 1960s. But is *Diva* so very different? After all, it flirts with neoromantic themes like purity and authenticity. As for "the conception of the Romantic genius and creator," Beineix could at times adopt this mantle too: "My characters are carried by a passion that brings them beyond the limits. This is exactly the way I picture being a director. That's why I've never matched with the system because I'm so intense when I do a picture, I'm so dedicated, that slowly the people surrounding me become enemies—I see that they don't believe, they have no faith. They try to reduce everything to some kind of a standard. They try to understand everything. But you do not explain what faith is. Either you believe or you don't. I'm a believer."[22] Truffaut and Godard definitely used such florid language in speaking for, and to, the ultramodern existentialist youth culture of the fifties, which Beineix, born in 1946, aspired to join. They proclaimed allegiance to Balzac and Stendhal when lambasting the professional *savoir-faire* of the insipid *cinéma de papa.* Their early films often exude neoromanticism (*Jules et Jim,* 1961; *Pierrot le fou,* 1965). Beineix undoubtedly felt an affinity between his situation in 1980 and Godard's in 1960, as the entry on *Diva* in Magill's *Survey of Foreign Language Cinema* makes clear: "Not since the initial wellspring of New Wave directorial debuts in the late 1950s . . . has a French filmmaker emerged with as confidently polished and stylistically assured a first feature as Jean-Jacques Beineix's *Diva.* Yet while Godard, Truffaut . . . were preoccupied with the passion of politics and social ecology, cast into a constantly evolving framework of experimentation with the formal attributes of the Hollywood classical narrative style, Beineix exhibits a cool and often bemused postmodern sensibility, less concerned with an ideological perspective than with a dazzling presentation of contemporary culture."[23] The parallel "conjunctures" are indeed striking. *The 400 Blows* (a favorite of Beineix) and *Breathless* breathed the new air that had just blown in with the Fifth Republic and its leader Charles de Gaulle. When he appointed the dashing André Malraux to a brand-new Ministry of Culture that was tasked, among other things, with nurturing cinema, Godard, who venerated him at the time, was ecstatic, for he seemed a benevolent uncle of the rambunctious new wave. When Malraux chose *The 400 Blows* for Cannes, Godard exulted, "The face of the French cinema has changed. Malraux made no mistake. The author of *La Monnaie de l'absolu* could hardly help recognizing that tiny inner flame, that reflection of intransigence shining in the eyes of Truffaut's Antoine as he sports a man's hat to steal a typewriter in a sleeping Paris; for it is the same as that which glittered twenty years ago on Tchen's dagger on the first page of *La Condition humaine*."[24] Twenty-two years later, does that romantic "reflection of intransigence" reappear in the eyes of Jules as he surreptitiously tapes the aria and then grabs the diva's gown, dashing home into the Paris night, to make a shrine to her as Antoine had done for Balzac? Like the New Wave moment, the shock Beineix delivered to a stale production system punctuated the arrival of a new government, with its own flamboyant minister of culture, Jack Lang, whose mandate was as broad as the one Malraux had enjoyed under de Gaulle, and whose belief in cinema was, if anything, greater.[25] Both new governments (one right, the other left) challenged France to become a leader in the modern world, believing it could rival the United States, thanks to the nation's unfathomably deep and noble traditions.[26] Both governments put stock in the cinema as inheritor of the literary and artistic values of the past and as forger of France's international cultural presence for the future. In popular parlance, these noble aspirations were quite romantic.

Perhaps Jameson felt *Diva* to be a retort to neoromanticism because that particular sensibility needs to be unalloyed; otherwise, like the experience of the sublime with which it is related, it dissipates. And *Diva* is unquestionably impure, for its romanticism colors just a single panel of Beineix's jarringly variegated mural. Jules's devotion to the purity of lyric song and the diva appears romantic but is just as stereotypical as the fixed demeanor of the methodical Taiwanese, or the cartoonish cruelty of the villain's two thugs (a fifties greaser, a seventies skinhead). Mixing characters like these and the genres they come from, while spinning them in the agitator of a double plot, "Beineix exhibits a cool and often bemused postmodern sensibility," as the Magill entry put it.

Diva did not impress Jameson with its plot, which he rightly identified as a fairly standard *policier* of the sort the French have mastered. He is a connoisseur of Raymond Chandler, after all. And if each of its characters had been a stereotype like those just mentioned, there would have been nothing to catch his interest—and no conjuncture to point to. *Diva* stands out because of "that rare thing, the emergence of a new kind of *character*," Gorodish. Looking at the constellations of social actors that inhabit French cinema's night sky, this one is completely unfamiliar and therefore disorienting. Gorodish is also luminous, indeed bright enough to let Jameson imagine him drifting into the political sphere. He is the new element that Beineix introduced into something like a difficult problem in organic chemistry, helping solve that problem (or "contradiction") at the level of the filmic imagination. Citing Lévi-Strauss, Jameson implies that viewers come away satisfied aesthetically, while also sensing that they have overcome, or can live with, an analogous contradiction in social life.[27] In *Diva*, class, race, and gender are all obviously involved.

Gorodish seems to float above all contradictions. Jameson calls him a late product of the sixties, not of its radical politics, but of the alternative lifestyle that went along with it, where dropouts from the system enjoyed drugs, sex, and zen. The dull seventies provided enough leisure for the "idle rich" among these to acquire idiosyncratic expertise (memorably, Gorodish demonstrates how properly, exquisitely, to butter bread), and random skills like completing an oceanic jigsaw puzzle. Able to look down on such a puzzle and intuit where the pieces fit, this character of "angelic stature" will watch over and solve two interlaced criminal intrigues, so as to guard the life and innocence of the young hero, Jules. Like Oberon in *Midsummer Night's Dream*,[28] he has his own slightly troubled life high up in the loft that he shares with Alba, the Vietnamese pixie he sends on missions to do his bidding and reorganize the strings of the plot, by crossing them. "The sixties have come to this, the unexpected emergence not of . . . students, blacks, marginals, women, but of a hip new countercultural businessman who wishes us well, who *loves* us."[29]

But what kind of businessman is Gorodish and what kind of business is he in? With a well-placed parenthesis, "(see Daniel Bell)," Jameson gives us an answer. Bell's 1970s books *The Coming of Post-industrial Society* and *The Cultural Contradictions of Capitalism* identified the emergence of a new technical elite that was reshaping traditional social strata. Whether in his loft in some old building in La Villette, or in a lighthouse, or from an I-beam high above the cavernous shell of a disused industrial hangar, Gorodish surveys the confusing and corrupt world on and beneath the streets of Paris, engineering outcomes that restore order and bring him sums of money. Like a film director, he establishes the mise-en-scène of every dramatic confrontation, never raising his voice (calmed by years of zen). He gives orders to Saporta, the corrupt *commissaire* of police, first via the Citroën's tape player, then live over a walkie-talkie in what is the huge hulk of the old car factory. From his perch, he dangles the tell-all tape just out of Saporta's reach. Gorodish here takes on the tone of a CEO in the information age who lords it over a clumsy power broker of the industrial era whom he has cleverly disarmed. This reverses the tilt of the producer-consumer relation that has characterized capitalism till now. Gorodish produces nothing. The old institutions of police, of organized crime, of copyright, are at the mercy of this unpredictable new character who deliberately chooses what he likes and is master of everything he uses: home décor, kitchen implements, music (lyric, New Age, Tibetan) transportation (roller skates, classic Citroën cars), electronics.

Jules is another such consumer; a low-wage earner, a postman, he too has set himself up just as he pleases in what we might call a "studio," though not in the usual sense of a small prefab apartment. Jules's unique space, contiguous with a body shop and reached by an industrial elevator, resembles a movie studio filled with props—bric-a-brac from earlier decades—and behind it looms an enormous mural depicting vintage cars in a scene out of some 1950s film. At once minimal and cluttered, his room expresses his taste: without standard amenities, it nevertheless features professional-grade stereo equipment for playback, reproduction, and transfer. Jules is a fetishist of sound, of opera, of a particular soprano's voice. The plot, at least half of it, and such as it is, turns on that fetish. By the third sequence, thanks to his secret recording of her live performance, Jules's studio will be filled with Cynthia Hawkins's incomparable (and unreproducible) voice, not to mention her silver gown. Jules curls up with gown and music in an adolescent erotic fantasy that might have led to a puerile comedy had he not been inadvertently drawn into another plot, also tied to a secret tape of the voice of a woman. Because of this second plot, he will require help from Gorodish, obtained through Alba who skates between them as the free spirit of taste and instant judgment ("c'est chic," she declares definitively, or "pas mal"). Alba may be capricious, but she brings Jules into the orbit of Gorodish where they bond over male connoisseurship of great music, and of top-grade technology that can capture it.

Of Jameson's many insights into *Diva*, the one concerning alliance between Jules and Gorodish is most illuminating, for this is what conjoins the film and its political moment. Together this pair outruns and outwits the two Taiwanese; they then deftly defeat Saporta and his henchmen, who have been trafficking Third World women. The disturbingly familiar theme of female bondage plays out against both the flighty freedom that Alba, an Asian, flaunts and the carefully cultivated independence of Cynthia Hawkins, an African American. Two distinct gangs grow rich by exploiting women: Saporta sells female bodies, and the Taiwanese conspire to exploit the soprano's voice, her soul. This is the state of capitalism as Gorodish understands it, looking down, and as Jules experiences it on the streets, looking up as he delivers mail and flowers.

The most sustained analysis of *Diva* in English puts Jules at the center of a conflicted Freudian family drama featuring two father figures, one good, one bad (Gorodish, Saporta), and two pairs of mother figures (Diva/Alba and Nadia/Karina).[30] But to Jameson, Jules's desperate plight is merely a conventional vehicle to activate the forces and images of the film. What counts is his alliance with

Gorodish; allegorically it joins the distinct voting blocs that brought François Mitterrand and Socialism forward to combat the very capitalist abuses and governmental corruption evident in the film. Jules represents the traditional values of French nationalism against the Taiwanese globalizers, while Gorodish provides a vital new technocratic nationalism, ready to compete with America. Jameson shows this alliance to repeat similar configurations in French political history from the Revolution to the Restoration and then in the 1930s Popular Front. In crucial moments vanguard intellectual elites have supported restive French citizens (the ascendant bourgeoisie of the 1830s, the unions of the 1930s). A similar rhetoric of solidarity brought students and workers together in May 1968 against de Gaulle. Although ploughed under, the husks of that failed event helped form the compost that, over the next decade, fertilized the ground for a socialist victory. Jameson is suspicious of the French reflex to sentimentalize every serious political confrontation since 1793 by calling on Culture (writ large), as he points out the inevitable contradictions these alliances lead to, even when they succeed.

The fantasy of a France rooted in tradition (religious, frankly feudal) while propelled into the future by science gives *Diva* an optimism that is dramatized in the political synthesis of Jules and Gorodish and the spiritual synthesis of soul (the singer) embracing technology (Jules's recording). The diva, Jameson reminds us, is herself a synthesis: her Third World heritage (African slavery) is lodged in the operatic heart of the First World.[31]

This new film and a renovated Parti Socialiste both provisionally solved an endemic contradiction between France's staid affiliations and its futuristic aspirations. *Diva* visibly confounds nostalgia (for 1950s motifs and characters) with a tempo and imagery feeding an appetite for the newest fashion, just as the Parti Socialiste audibly did in election slogans that broadcast a "rhetoric of Utopian urbanism . . . [while] locked into an older French parochial and nationalistic tradition."[32] Jameson was deeply suspicious of a purportedly progressive government barely under way as he wondered how the country could be led toward a high-tech future when its president was "François Mitterrand, himself an elegant traditional stylist . . . periodically returning to his village and donning peasant garb."[33]

In its satisfying pictorial and fictional form, *Diva* presented itself as a "curious mixture of old and new, a mixture about which it is difficult to decide whether it is to be seen as a regressive and conservative recuperation or on the contrary as a historically original 'imaginary solution of a real contradiction' which may be explored for Utopian elements and possibilities, including some whole new aesthetic in emergence."[34] And so while he had already written off the leftist government because it was flawed at its core, Jameson evinces hope that something novel (though hardly revolutionary) might be possible in cinema, thanks to the event of *Diva*.

"Looking Good, Cinematographically Speaking"

In that exuberant notice, celebrating Malraux's approbation of *The 400 Blows*, Godard maliciously called out a litany of older directors for their "false technique," their "ugly camera movements," and their "worthless dialogue," concluding, "In a word, you don't know how to create cinema because you no longer even know what it is." Then, with this unrestrained boast he planted the New Wave flag on the shore of a future that once seemed too far to reach: "Today, victory is ours. It is our films which will go to Cannes to show that France is looking good, cinematographically speaking. Next year it will be the same again, you can be sure of that."[35] What about twenty years hence? What would it take for films to "look good" in 1981? *Diva* was an event because it looked like "a new thing." Jameson realized that, "as with Godard (but the comparison stops there), the novelty would seem to lie in the realm of the image." Despite his focus on characters, Jameson knew these were trumped by the film's stunning visual design.

None of its many "postcard" images may be more freighted than that of the white luxury car silhouetted along a high horizon anchored by the picturesque lighthouse where Jules recovers. Whether taken as a knight's white steed (as Beineix likes to call it) or as a symbol of France's artisanal superiority, the car's brand, a Citroën *traction-avant*, nationalizes this image and the film that delivers it. Jameson writes lyrically about this shot as well as about others such as "the secret blueness of the Parisian night sky, as in the famous Magritte evening cityscape."

The commodity form of such concocted images brings the film under the wide umbrella of postmodernism recently opened at the time. *Diva* arrived slightly before digital technology showed up in film production; but already Betamax and VHS were changing the way films were exchanged and seen. Consumers had begun to collect tapes, to make compilations of clips of favorite scenes, to record stars or shots or advertisements off the air. Like Jules's Nagra, the new Betamax and VHS recorders gave aficionados power for the first time to personalize (or illegally sell) the grandest and most valuable images produced by the culture industry. The "businessmen" tracking down Jules's tape were cast as Taiwanese no doubt because that country was known to flaunt copyright, making it "the pirate kingdom" and a central node in a black market network where grand opera and blockbuster movies could be shrunk to the size of cassettes and sold around the world.[36]

Acknowledging this new economy, *Diva* invests in other attributes of the postmodern. Jameson perceptively recognizes in Beineix's Paris something close to "romantic French photorealism," a species of painting whose postmodernist elements *Diva* shares with De Palma's *Blow Out*, made the same year: a focus on the technology of reproduction, especially the image's relation to the human (painter's) hand, and a "loss of affect" or depth in the subject.[37] Both films mechanize their images as much as their characters, signaling a significant retooling in the culture industry. Postmodern artists in all media react not to the massive machinery of heavy industry as they did in modernism but to tiny silicon chips, thin videotapes, and invisible uranium atoms of nuclear bars that fuel a high-speed economy, built, Jameson says, not for production but for (mechanical) reproduction. No novel or film can represent the miniscule and lightning "processes" of the immeasurably expansive "systems" that sustain postindustrial life. These two words, "process" and "system," are at the heart of the computer age for which *Diva*'s images (like Gorodish's wave machine and Jules's Nagra recorder) are both a symptom and an inevitably inadequate preview.

There is no representing the sublimely intricate network *Diva* asks us to imagine. At best Beineix can show its effects, as in a close-up of a woman's hand dropping a tape into the saddlebag of a moped that happened to be near her as she ran from thugs bent on killing her, or in the baffling sequence in the abandoned Citroën factory where Saporta pays the ransom for the incriminating tape. Saporta delivers a case of cash to Gorodish in the very place where sums of money once were paid for France's proudest manufactured product. Now an equal sum is handed over for a cassette tape, which, when activated, echoes in the empty building. A final irony ensues when Saporta, left alone in the building, pulls out a tiny transmitter of his own, which sets off a bomb meant to blow Gorodish to smithereens when he sits in that white Citroën. But Gorodish, master puzzle solver, had planned the next step and sent the Taiwanese media pirates to the car in his stead. As they burn alive, he opens a nearby garage door and drives away in a duplicate white Citroën. In ways that seem random to all but Gorodish, lines get crossed in the molecular motion of an overheated postmodern economy; plots can easily become interlaced, as when Nadia's desperate voice is heard on a tape that was thought to contain Cynthia Hawkins's soaring song. Both tapes, identically packaged, express the desperation of abused women in an international scheme involving police and gangs alike. If this mirrors Balzac, it does so as pastiche: Saporta is not quite Vautrin, nor is Jules Rastignac.

Yet enough of Paris remains for echoes of *La Comédie Humaine* to rise to the polished city surface: the edge of the Bois de Boulogne where prostitutes saunter, the place de l'Opéra, the cobblestone streets along the canal de l'Ourcq by La Villette (renovated three years after the film), the Pigalle of the opening scenes, and the underbelly of the city. Jameson recognizes the persistence of this romantic quality within *Diva*'s mosaic of Paris. Distinguishing it from the Philadelphia of Brian De Palma's *Blow Out*, a false twin film, he says of the latter that it is just "another well made movie," suggesting that the American city is already a movie set. On the other hand, *Diva* holds, or holds onto, a Paris that has a prior life and will outlast this particular film and this era. Both directors thematize mechanical recording, but De Palma does so with such airtight reflexivity that his own film becomes nothing but a version of that theme. The title, *Diva*, on the other hand, may refer to the city of Paris as well as to the soprano who stands centerstage at the Théâtre de Châtelet.

To distinguish these films and the visual cultures they represent, Jameson came up with a penetrating apercu, writing that *Blow Out* "gleams" like the shiny metal and polished glass of a mall, while *Diva*'s architectural surfaces "glow" from within the celluloid that contains them. Earlier in the essay he used the same term to describe Jules's studio: "glowing with pale colors . . . a dead immobile landscape in which Jules's body has an unearthly pallor with few equivalents in other media: a blanched luminosity, neither that of death, nor of plastic or wax, recalling only, perhaps, that ideal Barthes-Balzac hermaphrodite translucent in moonlight. It is the flesh tone of the more romantic French photorealism (as of Jacques Monory)."[38] *Diva* evokes Monory's signature blue tint that takes over entire scenes.[39] *Diva*'s tremendous success in America can be attributed to the Paris it decks out as romantic as well as ultramodern, nostalgic as well as utopian, fully French as well as international. *Blow Out*'s Philadelphia, on the other hand, looks more like the "gleaming luxury surfaces of Richard Estes's Manhattan"; in these American photorealist paintings even old buildings gleam as framed through windows that also reflect them. Much of *Diva* delivers precisely this look. The silver gown, the accessory jewelry, Alba's plastic wrap, the hoods of taxis are gleaming counterexamples; still *Diva* holds enough warmer shots and motifs to lift it to a different plane in Jameson's view. For him *Diva* and French socialism both succeeded, for a time at least, as compromises between tradition and technology, nostalgia and utopia.

Tarnishing the Look, Demoting the Diva

Jameson did not keep up with Beineix nor with French cinema, aside from Godard. In one sense, *Diva* was nothing more than an unexpected and ready test case that validated his developing thoughts about postmodernism and politics. At the same time, might his ambivalent attraction to *Diva* reveal something that emanated from within himself, perhaps something nostalgic related to the texture of film? *Diva* occasionally displays the feel of the genuine physical world behind its glossy images ("Bazinian," he calls this feel), something that has ceased to play a role in a fully postmodern American film like *Blow Out*. The latter's images are "reflections of reflections," harsh light bouncing from mirrors made of glass and mercury redirected at other mirrors. *Diva* does not go this far. It was not fully postmodern, thus we can see that Jameson's pairing *Diva* and *Blow Out* suggests that he already understood there to be gradations within the postmodern, and that some types of modern postmodernisms were inevitable and inevitably self-contradictory, insofar as they still took account in some way of the past. This dialectic has become clearer thanks to his successive ruminations and the commentaries on them.[40]

Compare the opening scenes of the two films. *Blow Out* starts in the projection room of a studio where silent images of a simulated sex attack are being synchronized to tapes of sounds meant to ground them in "reality." *Diva*, in contrast, begins in an actual and quite antiquated concert hall with the genuine voice of a star soprano—not even an actress—singing an ethereal aria. While we see this art being commercially exploited (Alba wears a skirt with an "opera" pattern), it still serves as a refuge from television (on which much of *Blow Out*'s plot is played out) as well as from the cacophonous and callous commerce of the streets, perhaps like the distant lighthouse where Jules recovers. The glow of sentimental postcard shots like that of the dawn at the lighthouse or of the blue evening spreading over Paris hints at a lost connection to something authentic. We don't need *Midnight in Paris* (2011) to see the capital in the glow of its past, although today it is completely monitored and laid out for maximum commerce.

The films diverge in their conclusions too. Both end with telling images and sounds, indeed with an emphatic separation of image track and sound track (one clear criterion for postmodern cinema). At the end of *Blow Out*, a scream recorded during an actual murder turns out to deliver the best genre effect for the simulated sex attack, while the actual murder loses its place in history. Without the guarantee of this sound, the picture of death becomes innocuous. *Blow Out*, Jameson adds, annuls Antonioni's modernist *Blow Up*, which developed a Heideggerian and Bazinian metaphysical conundrum, when the enlarged blurry photographs of a park—the sound of wind emanating somehow through them—brought the protagonist back to a real moment (and a murder). Jameson could have said that paradoxically Antonioni's images "glow with sound." Like a diver, they sound the "Bazinian" depths of ambiguous reality.[41]

Some of *Diva*'s images faintly echo this, when they signal some attachment to actuality. In its finale, *Diva* glows because its light comes not just from reflections (though plenty of these played into its overall effect) but from an incandescent source, the voice of the diva, her irreplaceable soul. The last scene costs her an innocence she has guarded for a lifetime, but it provides something in return. "It's the first time I've ever heard myself," she says. Hereafter she must co-inhabit the world with her mechanical reproduction; the system will now be able to exploit her commercial value, Beineix being the first to profit. But, as the camera cranes up, accompanying the rising of her voice, we look down on Jules, the perfect listener, holding hands with—coming into physical contact with—the source of what he loves. Its ambiguous ending lets *Diva* float within the realm of the romantic as much as the ironic.

Diva's reputation was quickly tarnished by Beineix's next, overly mannerist film, *The Moon in the Gutter* (*La lune dans le caniveau*, 1983), which he adapted from a moody David Goodis novel (following Truffaut, whose second film, *Shoot the Piano Player* [*Tirez sur le pianist,* 1960], came from the same writer). Disapproval poured in, particularly from *Cahiers du Cinéma*. *Diva* was blamed for spawning an abhorrent "postcard look" that would dominate the eighties, derived from TV ads and suitable only for TV. This observation came from Serge Daney, who stepped down as *Cahiers* editor two months after *Diva* had premiered. In his last issue he agreed in essence with Jameson about the disappointing "Situation of French Cinema" (the title of this special issue). "No big wave, no movement, or school, virtually an aesthetic desert," he wrote.[42] At first Daney did not believe *Diva* had inaugurated a new direction worth pointing to. Indeed he consigned a brief review of the film to a minor critic at *Cahiers*, Guy Saindérichain. Yet, seeing it again in 1988, he realized that he and the critics had missed something, the burst of energy it released: "At the start of the eighties, an unknown director was redefining, in spectacular fashion, Good and Evil at the cinema. Only the audience loved *Diva*, a film the critics shunned, reproaching Jean-Jacques Beineix for having indulged in a fussy exercise in 'applied advertising.' Beineix is the last director about whom anything resembling an 'aesthetic debate' has taken place in France."[43] So Jameson was right; *Diva* had indeed turned French cinema around, inaugurating "a new thing," a postmodern look that is largely still with us today. "Seeing Diva again one Sunday morning on Canal Plus," Daney writes, "is of course a confirmation of just how much the film is in its element on television." He couldn't help but appreciate its insouciance, its popularity, and the fracas he remembered that it had caused among critics, although he rued the "advertising aesthetic" that followed in *Diva*'s wake because it had largely swept genuine cinema off the screens. *Diva* had come out, he said, at a sad moment when "there began to be more stories and desires crammed into sets and objects than into characters . . . when everyone wanted to go back to the studio. Not to build another street but to discover that the word 'studio' now had two meanings: the place where you film (in order to make 'true artifice') and the place where you look at yourself living (in the midst of your 'artificial truth')."[44]

The values Daney espoused all his life were those of the journal that was founded in the high modernist moment of 1951. "L'axiome *Cahiers* c'est que le cinéma a rapport au réel et que le réel n'est pas le représenté."[45] Postmodernism dispenses with this rapport. Images reflect themselves instead of pointing tentatively to something unknown that beckons to be discovered. *Cahiers* considered *Diva* to be both symptom and cause of the postmodernist advertising aesthetic that, along with Hollywood blockbusters, kept genuine films (difficult, modernist ones) off the big screen. Increasingly films in the eighties infiltrated homes like commodities, whether packaged as videotape or sandwiched between commercials on Canal Plus and other channels for the viewer's convenience and comfort. In the living room films are glanced at, not entered.

After *Diva* films even began to look and behave like television. Their images, whether of people, places, or objects (these have become interchangeable), tend to strike poses as if they were ads; moreover, they are literally without consequence. Snippets appear throughout *Diva*, a "thoroughly French but barely sketched thriller," like a day's worth of TV programming "customized for the era of random channel-hopping." In feeding the short attention span of his audience, Beineix disconnected his film from the world and its contingencies, the very thing that made cinema the artform of the century. *Diva* may have been shot on location, but it bears a studio style; "I treated locations as volumes for us to do with as we liked."[46] Had CGI been available Beineix *Diva* would have looked more mannerist still.[47]

Of course its mannerism is precisely what caught the attention of Jameson and everyone else. The title character makes her anticipated appearance on stage, but only as reflected on the lens of a villain's sunglasses. The stately Hotel Royal Monceau where she stays is flipped upside down when seen off the polished fender of a taxi, and so on. Certain throwaway vignettes lighten the drama to allow visual play, such as a busker with an accordion, first shown in reflection from a puddle, then picking from the ground a huge sum that Gorodish has tossed out his window, rejecting the proposed deal with the Taiwanese who sit nearby in their car. Even during a tense life-and-death chase, Beineix throws in snatches of bowling, pinball, and a woman annoyed to have her shooter game disturbed. Among the obvious visual citations is a still life of a coffeepot with cups and apples (à la Morandi), a skyline à la Magritte, and at least two unmistakable film jokes: a réplique of Marilyn Monroe's dress billowing far above her knees when she walks across a subway's vent in *Seven Year Itch* and Michel Piccoli with cigar in a bathtub from *Le Mépris*, a pose that Piccoli himself identifies as imitating Dean Martin in *Some Came Running*. If citation is a modernist technique, then doubling a citation as Beineix does here is postmodern.

While several individual shots are repeated because of their sheer visual interest (the wave machine, the wave puzzle, the Citroën, the lighthouse), the immense mural in Jules's loft comes back because it constitutes an obvious metaphor for the film: vintage red and yellow automobiles, their passengers frozen in melodramatic poses, stand out against the blue urban skyscape across which they are suspended (colors that struck *Diva*'s supporters and detractors).[48] Vivid, incongruous, discontinuous, and unavoidably eye-catching, they provoke Alba to utter, in her cool, placid, but obviously impressed manner, "pas mal." Spectators reacted the same way to *Diva*, and that's precisely what disturbed Daney and the critics at *Cahiers*.

For *Diva*'s look spread. Philippe Rousselot, who shot both *Diva* and *Moon in the Gutter*, went on to film Jean-Jacques Annaud's *The Bear* (*L'Ours*, 1988), a characterless film particularly distasteful to Daney, as would be Annaud's *The Lover* (*L'Amant*, 1992), which, as he was dying of AIDS, Daney found energy to excoriate. *The Lover* was to him the epitome of "non-cinema," a series of advertising clips, hung up as on a clothesline one beside the next, which viewers merely recognize and approve. Cinema had become "virtual tourism" where comfortable spectators validate their tastes, usually doing so in their living rooms on TV, where they appropriate already-made images as "their own," confronting nothing but "the already-seen or the scarcely seen at all . . . in an age of synthetic emotions, in which the chances of an accidental encounter with reality are remote indeed."[49] Imagine what Daney would have said had he lived to review *Amélie*, which begins by introducing each character through an itemization of their "likes" and "dislikes."

Perhaps *Amélie* did not institute a break after all as I initially declared. Perhaps it just updated *Diva*'s formula at the turn of the millennium. A through line can be traced via Claudie Ossard, who served as executive producer for Beineix (*Diva*, *Betty Blue*), and then for Jean-Pierre Jeunet (*Delicatessen*, *City of Lost Children*, and *Amélie*). *Amélie* also pays dubious homage to Beineix's revered model, Truffaut, when it irreverently cites both *Jules et Jim* and *The 400 Blows*.[50] Has there been no deep change, no new phase in French culture or politics over the past forty years? To use Jameson's terms, the postmodern era has withdrawn France from history. No grand narratives, no telos, no real change—just the reshuffling of what is familiar. In the absence of belief—whether Marxist, Christian, or Deleuze's "belief in this world"—both French cinema and French politics appear as abandoned arenas. The show has moved on.

Jameson did not intervene in French debates even when working on *Diva* and on Godard's eighties films. These French instances, instead, helped him recognize the interplay of economics, politics, and cultural production generally, in the era of increasing speed and globalization. Coming to understand *Diva* helped him solidify views he would articulate more systematically and broadly two years later in perhaps the most influential essay of his long career: "Postmodernism; or, The Cultural Logic of Late Capitalism." When that essay became a book, its final chapter before its conclusion was titled "Film." There he again expressed, like Daney, a disappointment over the moribund seventies "whose specificity seemed to consist in having no specificity," though he was writing of America, not France. The two men also shared the sense that things had begun to pick up in the eighties. For Jameson, the novelty *Diva* brought to its dull French backdrop was replicated in 1986 when *Blue Velvet* and *Something Wild* broke free of standard American genre production. Like *Diva* these films showed that cinema could "open space for something else." Like *Diva* their novelty was expressed in a curious "synthesis of nostalgia-deco and punk."[51]

Could there exist today a film about which Jameson could conclude an essay the way he does "On *Diva*," evoking that film's own conclusion: the scene "rapidly recedes from us, suspended, into a distance which leaves the future wide open." *Diva* itself has receded into that distance, perhaps taking the cinema along with it. But a new future for cinema could yet be "wide open," just as has occurred with opera. Let us mention that Jameson is at work on a book about opera. You can bet it won't be nostalgic.

Notes

1 I have omitted the phrase "directed by Jean-Jacques Beneix [*sic*]" because it does not appear in "On *Diva*," the original publication in *Social Text* 4. The reprint, retitled "*Diva* and French Socialism" in *Signatures of the Visible*, is nearly identical to the original, including the frequent use of italics, although on p. 57 "aesthetic" is italicized whereas it is given in standard roman font in the original. A couple

typographical errors crop up in the reprint. Beineix has been shortened to Beneix in the opening, and the character Gorodish is misspelled as Godorosh when first mentioned on p. 55. (François Mitterrand's surname is misspelled as Mitterand consistently in both versions.) Only one misspelling has real consequence for the essay's meaning: in the last sentence of the piece, Jameson surely intends his original "stage" rather than "state," which appears in *Signatures*.

2 Peter Osborne, *The Politics of Time: Modernity and the Avant-Garde* (New York: Verso, 1995), 26–29. Osborne sets these ideas against each other and in relation to several other thinkers of the time. I am grateful to Shaj Matthew for pointing me to Osborne on "conjuncture."

3 Fredric Jameson, "Periodizing the 60s," *Social Text*, nos. 9–10 (Spring 1984): 179.

4 Fredric Jameson, "*Diva* and French Socialism," in *Signatures of the Visible* (London: Routledge, 1990), 61.

5 Jameson uses "realist" in place of "classic" since the first era he deals with is the nineteenth century as studied by Auerbach and Lukács. Realism mutates into modernism later in that century, and into late modernism through the first half of the twentieth century, before starting to give way to the postmodernism of the Nouveau Roman, Borges, Pynchon, and so on. Cinema's equivalent of the realist novel is the classic Hollywood film. Hence my substitution of "classic" for "realist."

6 Deleuze, only a few years younger than Bazin and a budding cinephile, surely knew his views. Deleuze placed his very first publication (on Sartre, like Jameson) in the fall 1945 issue of *Poésie* (vols. 27–28) just after Bazin had published in its summer issue (vols. 25–26), the biggest piece of his young career, "À propos de L'*Espoir* ou du style au cinéma."

7 "Periodizing the 60s," 200.

8 Jameson, "Reification and Utopia in Mass Culture," *Social Text*, no. 1 (1979), reprinted as the lead essay in *Signatures of the Visible*. The paragraph and the essay go on stirringly to conclude: "To reawaken in the midst of a privatized and psychologizing society, obsessed with commodities and bombarded by the ideological slogans of big business, some sense of the ineradicable drive toward collectivity . . . is surely an indispensable precondition for any meaningful Marxist intervention in contemporary culture" (34).

9 Jameson, "Historicism in *The Shining*," in *Signatures of the Visible*, 82–98.

10 She did appear in one televised opera, playing Musetta in *La bohème*, which aired in 1980 on French TV, where Beineix would certainly have seen her.

11 Fredric Jameson, "The Aesthetics of Singularity," *New Left Review* 92 (March–April 2015): 104.

12 Mitterrand, transcript of inaugural address, printed in the *New York Times*, May 22, 1981; Mitterrand interview with James Reston, *New York Times*, June 4, 1981.

13 Modernism, by recent accounts, has not been left behind and indeed is on a comeback. See Michael North's "Afterlife of Modernism," *New Literary History* 50, no. 1 (Winter 2019): 91–112. North explicitly challenges Jameson's characterization of postmodernism in the 1991 book, reminding us that a decade later in *A Singular Modernity*, he "apparently grudgingly returns to the study of modernism." If modernism is equated with "novelty," then even postmodernism—*Diva* included— is modern, it being, as Jameson called it, "a new thing."

14 Jameson, *Signatures of the Visible*, 74–75.

15 Jameson, "High-Tech Collectives in Late Godard," in *The Geopolitical Aesthetic: Cinema and Space in the World System* (Bloomington: Indiana University Press, 1992), 162.

16 Jameson, "High-Tech Collectives in Late Godard," 162.

17 Jameson, "High-Tech Collectives in Late Godard," 165.

18 Jameson, *Geopolitical Aesthetic*, 164–165.

19 Jameson, *Geopolitical Aesthetic*, 163.

20 Jameson, *Geopolitical Aesthetic*, 163.

21 Strictly speaking, neo-romanticism applies to those modernist paintings beginning around 1940 in Denmark, Finland, and Britain that return to nature, spirituality, and the melancholy individual. In *Aesthetics and Neo-romanticism in Film* (London: Bloomsbury, 2012), Susan Hockenhull targets twenty-first-century U.K. films that deal with landscape, finding their sources in Powell and Pressburger's 1940s works.

22 Jean-Jacques Beineix, "personal quotes" in his IMDB biography, https://m.imdb.com/name/nm0000894/quotes.

23 John Kelly., *Diva*, in *Magill's Survey of Cinema, Foreign Language Films*, Vol. 2 (Englewood Cliffs, NJ: Salem Press, 1985), 840. Perhaps an even more apt comparison than given here would be to Jacques Rivette's *Paris Belongs to Us* (*Paris nous appartient*, 1961), for the paranoia of its complicated intrigue played out in the Parisian streets.

24 Trans. Tom Milne in *Godard on Godard* (New York: Viking Press, 1972), 146.

25 Jack Lang was responsible for greatly magnifying the *avance sur recettes* system to finance production and doing so through the CNC (Centre national du cinema).

26 Making good on this promise right away, de Gaulle and Malraux ordered a full steam cleaning of Paris's buildings, its façade, a gesture that restored the old and prepared for the new. You can observe this by comparing the 1959 New Wave films to the much brighter Paris in which Godard set *Masculine-Feminine* in 1966.

27 Jameson, "*Diva* and French Socialism," 59.

28 Jameson authorizes my analogy when, later on p. 59 of his essay, he salutes the way "*Diva* 'manages' the terms of its underlying double-bind or ideological *contradiction*" by generating "an after-image of appeasement, of harmony, and of conflictual reconciliation as, most classically, in the wondrous salvational reversals of late Shakespearean comedy."

29 Jameson, "*Diva* and French Socialism," 56.

30 Phil Powrie, *Jean-Jacques Beineix* (Manchester: Manchester University Press, 2001), 60.

31 Avatars of stolen African women appear in the statuary of the Tuileries and in the guise of a Black prostitute whom Jules engages, and whom he dresses in the gown he took from Cynthia Hawkins's dressing room.

32 Jameson, "*Diva* and French Socialism."

33 Jameson, *Signatures of the Visible*, 62. In an interview just after his inauguration, Mitterrand evoked his long friendship with the Catholic novelist François Mauriac, recognizing in himself a spirituality stemming, he believed, from the provincial region where the two men were raised. See also his interview with James Reston, *New York Times*, June 4, 1981.

34 Jameson, *Signatures of the Visible*, 62.

35 Jean-Luc Godard, *Arts*, April 22, 1959. In writing "Next year it will be the same again," Godard was surely thinking, correctly, of *Breathless*, for which a few weeks before he had signed the contract.

36 Jean Lin, "US-Taiwan Copyright Agreement, Cooperation or Coercion," *Pacific Basin Law Journal* 1992 (1992): esp. 167–171, 169. Also see Andy Sun, "From Pirate King to Jungle King: Transformation of Taiwan's Intellectual Property Protection," *Fordham Intellectual Property, Media and Entertainment Law Journal* 9, no. 1 (1998): 70.

37 Jameson analyzes the paintings of Franz Gertsch, in terms some of which are transferable to *Diva*, in "Towards a Libidinal Economy of Three Modern Painters," *Social Text* 1 (Autumn 1979): 189–199.

38 Jameson, *Signatures of the Visible*, 57. Jameson is at ease reading the formal structures of painting as symptoms of larger psychosocial forces. He had recently written "Towards a Libidinal Economy of Three Modern Painters."

39 A couple scenes may pay tribute to Monory paintings like *Voiture de rêve n.1* or *Meurtre n.10*.

40 See, for instance, David James and Urmila Seshagiri, "Metamodernism: Narratives of Continuity and Revolution," *PMLA* 129, no. 1 (2014): 87–100. Also see the issue "Literary History after the Nation," *Modern Language Quarterly* (December 2019). I thank Shaj Matthew for these references.

41 Jameson, *Geopolitical Aesthetic*, 20. Jameson footnotes his own article, "The Existence of Italy" from *Signatures of the Visible*, 197, where he further explores the rapport between Antonioni, Bazin, and Roland Barthes.

42 Serge Daney, "Le cru et le cuit," *Cahiers du Cinéma* 323–324 (May 1981): 10.

43 The film \ received a brief review by Guy-Patrick Saindérichin in issue 322 (April 1981). Daney's review, called "Beineix Opus 1," appeared in *Liberation*, November 21, 1988. In a footnote he laments how often critics denigrate directors who appeal to the public: Pagnol, Guitry, Jerry Lewis . . . and Beineix.

44 Daney, "Beineix Opus 1."

45 I discuss this axiom in Dudley Andrew, *What Cinema Is!* (New York: Wiley-Blackwell, 2010), 4–11.

46 Beineix said, "Everything was filmed on location. But we considered locations not in relation to their purpose but as volumes for us to do with as we liked." Quoted in Powrie, *Jean-Jacques Beineix*, 32.

47 Powrie, *Jean-Jacques Beineix*.

48 Phil Powrie, *Jean-Jacques Beineix*, is particularly attentive to the color scheme, which he reads allegorically. See also the interview with cameraman Ph. Roussilot on *Diva*'s DVD extras.

49 Serge Daney, "Falling Out of Love," *Sight and Sound* 2, no. 3 (July 1992), 16.

50 Andrew, *What Cinema Is!*, 18–24.

51 Jameson, *Postmodernism; or, The Cultural Logic of Late Capitalism* (Durham, NC: Duke University Press, 1991), 288. The chapter on film was originally published in *South Atlantic Quarterly* 38, no. 2 (Spring 1989).

2

Allegory and Accommodation

Vertov's *Three Songs of Lenin*
(1934) as a Stalinist Film

JOHN MACKAY

Until at least the late 1980s, most film historians in the Soviet Union (if not else-where) would doubtless have identified *Three Songs of Lenin* (1934; silent version 1935; reedited in 1938 and 1970) as Dziga Vertov's greatest and most important contribution to Soviet and world cinema. Although its reputation has now been definitively eclipsed by that of *Man with a Movie Camera* (1929), *Three Songs* was certainly more widely exhibited and unambiguously honored than any of Vertov's other films during his lifetime. After being briefly shelved during the first half of 1934, the film was shown to great acclaim at the Venice Film Festival in August 1934. Prior to its general Soviet release in November 1934, the film was exhibited in Moscow at private but publicized screenings to both Soviet (Karl Radek, Nikolai Bukharin, Stanislav Kossior) and foreign (H. G. Wells, André Malraux, M. A. Nexoe, Paul Nizan, William Bullitt, Sidney Webb) cultural and political luminaries as early as July. Tributes to *Three Songs* by all of these figures were widely disseminated in the Soviet press.

For unknown reasons, the original sound version of *Three Songs* was withdrawn somewhere around November 13 from the major Moscow theaters where it had been playing, although it continued to be exhibited in Moscow and elsewhere, apparently in substandard or fragmentary copies, for some time after that. A silent version prepared especially for cinemas without sound projection capability was completed in 1935 and distributed widely in the Soviet Union; both this version and the original sound *Three Songs* were reedited by Vertov and rereleased in 1938. Vertov never ceased speaking of *Three Songs* with pride, even (or especially) when he was compelled to apologize for his earlier "formalist" works. It was the one Vertov film singled out for attention by Ippolit Sokolov in his 1946 collection of reviews of Soviet sound films.[1] During the Vertov revival of the post-Stalin years, *Three Songs* was apparently the first of his films to be publicly rereleased (together with a very informative book).[2] This new release was part of the 1970 Lenin centenary and took place only after the film was subjected to a most problematic "restoration," carried out in 1969 by Vertov's wife and cocreator Elizaveta Svilova, together with Ilya Kopalin and Seda Pumpyanskaya. It is this film, distributed by Kino Video on VHS and DVD, which most of us know as *Three Songs of Lenin.*

Despite all of this, and notwithstanding its ready availability on VHS/DVD in the United States and Europe, *Three Songs* has attracted remarkably little scholarly attention, at least until recently. Surely this neglect has something to do with the political-ethical embarrassment now attendant upon both the film's ardent rhetorical participation in the Lenin cult and its unabashed celebration of the "modernization" of the Muslim regions of the Soviet Union and hymning of Soviet industrial and agricultural achievement more generally. It would seem that, for many critics, *Three Songs* stands in the same relation to Vertov's earlier films as *Alexander Nevsky* (1938) does to Sergei Eisenstein's experimental work of the 1920s: a clear sign of that regression into authoritarianism and myth that came to compromise both filmmakers as creative artists and Soviet culture as a whole over the course of the 1930s. Meanwhile, the film's fraught history, involving three major reedits and the consequent disappearance of the original sound and silent versions, has no doubt made scholars rightly wary of investing too much interpretive energy in such a dubious text. The three versions coincide with three quite different political moments—specifically, the full-scale inauguration of Stalin's "personality cult" (and the waning of Lenin's) during the Second Five-Year Plan (1933–1937), the complete establishment of the Stalin cult by the purge years of 1937–1938, and the ongoing anti-Stalinist revisionism of the early "stagnation" period (1969–1970). Given that the transition into (and out of) "Stalinist culture" is the real issue here, it is inevitable that the presence or absence of "Stalin" and "Stalinism" in *Three Songs* will figure centrally in any interpretation of the film.

Although many questions remain unanswered about the original 1934 *Three Songs*, archival evidence demonstrates rather clearly that Stalin's image was far more prominent in that original film than in the familiar Svilova-Kopalin-Pumpyanskaya reedit, which can be described, with only the slightest qualification, as a "de-Stalinization" of the versions of the 1930s. Contemporary reviews, for instance, make it plain that Stalin and references to Stalin were conspicuous in the third of the three "songs." A critic who went by the Gogolian pseudonym "Vij," writing about H. G. Wells's viewing of the film (in Moscow on July 26, 1934), indicated that "the writer saw Lenin at the beginning and middle of the film, and Stalin in the middle and the end."[3] Timofei Rokotov, who later became well known as the editor of the journal *International Literature*, praised the film's conclusion in the following terms in his review of November 4, 1934: "It's difficult to imagine a better ending to the film than that image of the super-powered train 'Joseph Stalin,' rushing irrepressibly forward, above which shine the words of our leader: 'The idea of storming [capitalism] is maturing in the consciousness of the masses.'"[4]

The earliest extant versions of *Three Songs* (sound and silent) both contain the image of this well-known train, with "Joseph Stalin" inscribed on the front, near the film's conclusion, and Rokotov's comment strongly suggests that it was in the 1934 original as well. Certainly, the fact that Stalin's then-famous comment— "the idea of storming [capitalism] is maturing in the consciousness of the masses," from his report to the 17th Party Congress (January 24, 1934)—served as the film's concluding slogan is directly confirmed by Vertov's script for *Three Songs*.[5] Rokotov makes an even more intriguing reference in his review to the film's famous prologue, with its image of the "bench" on which Lenin sat: "... A little detail [that] says so much ... here is the same bench, well-known because of the photograph, where the great Lenin and his great student and comrade-in-arms Stalin sat and conversed—not so long ago, it would seem."[6] Similarly, one V. Ivanov, in a review for *Rabochaia Penza* of December 31, 1934, describes the same section of the prologue as follows: "The bench. The memorable bench. You remember the picture: Lenin and Stalin in Gorki, 1922."[7] In contrast to the 1970 reedit, which offers a photograph of Lenin sitting alone on a bench, the 1938 versions present a very famous and widely distributed image of Lenin sitting together with Stalin. Clearly enough, the comments by Rokotov and Ivanov strongly suggest that the portrait of Lenin with Stalin was the one displayed in the original *Three Songs*.

Finally, some of the most telling evidence of Stalin's presence in the 1934 film comes from Vertov's own notes and plans. In a letter of complaint dated November 9, 1934, to Mezhrabpomfil'm administrator Mogilevskii about the poor quality of the print of *Three Songs* being shown in Moscow's Taganka theater, Vertov notes that the shot of "Stalin walking about the Kremlin" is missing, among other absent footage; again, this shot is present in the extant (1938) versions during the third song, though not in the 1970 reedit. Most strikingly, perhaps, a remarkable set of instructions from 1934 compiled by Vertov for the film's sound projectionist indicate not only that Stalin appeared throughout the film, but that Vertov generally intended the volume of the soundtrack to take on "maximum loudness" when the dictator appeared, as (for example) during the funeral sequence. By contrast, the 1970 version mutes the sound almost completely when Stalin appears at the funeral of Lenin—the only appearance he makes in the film.[8]

In truth, one needs to acknowledge that even a cursory examination of the Soviet press in 1934 should have alerted film historians to the improbability of Stalin's absence from the original *Three Songs of Lenin*; Stalin's image was already ubiquitous by this time, and the notion of "the Party of Lenin and Stalin" quite firmly established.[9] Yet the question remains: what effect should this knowledge have on our *reading* of the film, in contrast to our necessary efforts to establish a correct original text? That is, what precise difference does the presence or absence of Stalin make to our considerations of Vertov's artistic evolution and of the structure and ideology of *Three Songs*, apart from what is already apparent from the 1970 version? To be sure, the idea of "Stalin" had become far more central to Soviet culture by 1934 than it had been in 1930, for instance, when Vertov made the film that preceded *Three Songs*, *Enthusiasm: Symphony of the Donbass*. And even the lack of an authoritative version of *Three Songs* has not prevented those scholars who have ventured to write on the film (invariably, the 1970 reedit) over the past twenty years or so to identify it, quite rightly in my view, as marking a crucial turning point in Vertov's artistic career—specifically, the turning point between the "avant-garde" 1920s and the "Stalinist" 1930s—though the evaluations of this watershed moment differ significantly.

The critical consensus on the film—established perhaps first by Annette Michelson, and developed further by Klaus Kanzog and Oksana Bulgakowa— holds that *Three Songs* involves a rhetorical turn to "religious" or quasi "sacred" cinematic discourse (grounded, according to Kanzog's analysis of the film's "internalized religiosity," in deep cultural memories of religious practice), whether conceived as a passage from the "epistemological" to the "iconic" and "monumental" (Michelson), or from the "documentary" to the "allegorical" (Bulgakowa).[10] In an essay that dissents from this "discontinuity thesis" while offering a newly positive evaluation of the film, Mariano Prunes stresses the continuities between *Three Songs* and the 1920s visual practice of both Vertov and his contemporaries in photography and film, arguing that the film incorporates and summarizes all the main streams of photographic visual practice of the preceding decade (constructivist *faktura*, documentary factography, and emergent Stalinist mythography), and in so doing "seriously brings into question the traditional view of Soviet art in the 1930s as absolutely intolerant of previous experimental practices."[11] Accordingly, Prunes does not regard the presence or absence of Stalin in the 1970 version as especially important, suggesting at most that the 1934 film was perceived as paying insufficient homage to Lenin's "Successor" (thus necessitating the 1938 reedit with its "supplementary material on Stalin").[12] For their part, Michelson and Bulgakowa regard the "Stalin" of *Three Songs* as a kind of structuring absence, as prying open "[a] space in which the Beckoning Substitute is now installed" (Michelson), or even as an omnipresent but invisible quasidivinity, "present only in metonymic indicators" (Bulgakowa).[13] But once again,

Stalin was neither a structuring absence in *Three Songs* nor actually absent: he was, simply, explicitly part of the film's message and visual rhetoric.

To determine what that "part" actually consists in will first necessitate a reconsideration of the rhetoric of *Three Songs of Lenin*, both in terms of changes within the trajectory of Soviet culture and in relation to Vertov's artistic response to those changes. In what follows, I show that both the "continuity" and "discontinuity" theses have important merits but need to be thought of in terms of the concrete strategies through which the "avant-gardist" Vertov reacted artistically to the new authoritarian-populist imperatives of early Stalinism. *Three Songs of Lenin* demonstrates that, as far as Vertov was concerned, the most important feature of Stalin-era aesthetic doctrine as it evolved between 1932 and 1936 was its sharp rejection of avant-gardist complexity, antihumanism, and antipsychologism and its concomitant turn toward "character," simplicity, and supposedly popular "folk" sentiment. In this essay, I show how Vertov adapted two related features of the new discourse of the 1930s—attention to individual experience, and textual appeals to "folk sensibility" (or *narodnoe tvorchestvo*, "folk creativity")— in ways that, in *Three Songs of Lenin*, enabled him to fit into the new discursive order while continuing to pursue his old avant-garde concern with the representation of sheer change and dynamism, with material process, and with cinema as a means of reconfiguring perception and spatiotemporal relations. At the same time, I suggest that "folk" poetic materials incorporated in *Three Songs* functioned for Vertov both as publicly verifiable texts that could satisfy the growing institutional need for some preverbalizing of the films and as "sources" to which he could appeal in order to legitimate his own directorial decisions. It was in *Three Songs of Lenin* that Vertov found a way of accommodating the "populist" and centralizing imperatives of the new 1930s cultural order within his already fully formed, fundamentally constructivist artistic worldview and style.

Some of the rhetorical specificity of *Three Songs of Lenin* can be pinpointed through a comparative examination of the stylistic use made by that film of Vertov's own master trope, namely, the great revolutionary passage from the Old to the New—cinematically conceived in his case not primarily as narrative, but rather as sheer movement and sense of movement, the making visible of (as Deleuze put it in his superb discussion of Vertov in *Cinema I*) "all the (communist) transitions from an order [that] is being undone to an order [that] is being constructed . . . between two systems or two orders, between two movements."[14] Vertov was fascinated by the cinematic representation of process, especially processes of long duration, whether natural or historical. While working on *One Sixth of the World* (1926), his film about (among other things) methods of organizing the exploitation of natural resources, he jotted out plans for exceedingly brief film sketches, unfortunately never produced, on themes of process, such as "death-putrefaction-renewal-death." He planned one film that would begin by showing a woman burying her husband, followed by the corpse's consumption by bacteria and worms, the full conversion of the body into soil, and the emergence of grass out of the soil; a cow would eat the grass, only to be devoured in its turn by a human being, who dies, is buried, and then is absorbed into the whole process again, although the eventual addition of manure into the cycle is shown to generate a kind of productive upward spiral. Another Beckett-like four-shot film would show a fresh-faced peasant girl—then one wrinkle on her face—then a bunch of wrinkles—and finally a thoroughly wrinkled old woman.[15] Another featured a man going bald, over the course of three shots.[16]

The fine internal mechanism of any change is, of course, notoriously hard to explain in any non-regressive way. But transition in Vertov's cinema is usually something to be *sensed* rather than articulated or explained; and Vertov tries to generate the required perceptual jolts or shifts by making transition as visually and aurally tangible as possible, as in the opening of his first major feature, *Kino-Eye* (1924). The film is about members of the Young Pioneers organization both from the village of Pavlovskaia and from the proletarian Krasnopresnenskaia area of Moscow, and shows the youngsters engaged in philanthropic and leisure activities in various urban and rural settings. *Kino-Eye* begins, as so often in Vertov, with a sequence representative of the Old: here, the jubilant, besotted dancing of (mainly) women who've had a bit too much to drink during a church holiday. Visually, a dominant circular motif is established gradually but very assertively: circularity links the spinning movements of the women, the circle of the "round dance" itself, and objects like the pot, tambourine, and even the faces of the women themselves. The ecstatic twirling is both exhilarating and enervating, and, after a while, it starts to suggest that the women are trapped within what Russians would call a *zamknutyi krug* (closed circle), although Vertov would resist such aggressive translation of his visual formulas into words. Clearly enough, however, the enormous energy of the women is compelled to inscribe one circle after another, repetition within repetition, creating an image of encompassed and squandered vitality.

The transition to the New—though we are still very much in the village—occurs across a gap, without any "pivot point" whatsoever. Only an intertitle ("with the village pioneers") signals any change. However, the material sense of transition is stressed in classic constructivist fashion by a sudden preponderance of rectilinear shapes and movements: beginning with the siding on the building, then the poster pasted on by the Pioneers, the picket fence, the waterfall (falling, rolling streaks of water is one of Vertov's favorite images of revolution), and the straightforward movement of the marching pioneers. The series culminates with a nearly abstract sequence linking striking overlaps of surging water with the orderly, forward-directed advance of the children, concluding with a demonstration on the main street of the village. Translating again, the message would seem to be that force previously wasted on the inscription of drunken circles is rechanneled (cinematically) into a progressive and architectural rectilinearity; and Vertov hopes to make this "point" by provoking the spectator's perceptual entry into these two differently patterned spaces.

The same topos is found, in a dizzying variety of permutations, in nearly all of Vertov's films. Thus at the end of the prologue to *Man with a Movie Camera* (which contains several such transitions) we see the sudden passage from the stasis of an orchestra—a traditional kind of artistic collective—thrust into a new kind of motion by the activation of the film projector, inaugurating the film (for the audience *in* the film) that we have already started watching. We find a very striking Vertovian transition in the first reel of *Enthusiasm: Symphony of the Donbass* (1930), a film that can be seen as a grandiose rewriting of *Kino-Eye* in a number of respects. *Enthusiasm* begins with a polemical alternation between scenes of drunken behavior and religious devotion—religion as "opiate of the masses" is the intended message—with the camera mimicking both the repetitive motions of prayer and the aimless stumbling of brawling alcoholics. The sense of thudding stagnation intended here is underscored by repeated shots of church bells, shots themselves saturated with repetitive movement and sound. Suddenly, an industrial siren blares, its nearly vertical plume of smoke transected by parallel power lines and garnished by a splash of spontaneous, natural growth.

This siren was apparently shot and recorded using documentary sync sound; thus, the shot serves as a pivot point between old and new, announcing at once the arrival of socialist construction and (on the cinema front) documentary sound film. And once again, this siren blast, seemingly a purely arbitrary cut into the mobile but unprogressive texture of everyday life, is succeeded by the geometrically inflected patterns of a Pioneer parade, now accompanied by documentary sound, with the orderly lines and sharp angles formed by the youngsters matched graphically by the trolley-car tracks across which they march.

Four years after *Enthusiasm*, and ten years after *Kino-Eye*, with the opening of the first of the "three songs of Lenin," we see something new emerging in Vertov's art of transition. The first song opens with what are probably shots taken in a city in Uzbekistan, possibly Tashkent or Bukhara, showing women wearing the *paranji* and *chachvon* veils. It is not unimportant here that it is impossible to tell if the women are looking at the camera or not, and that their gazes are withdrawn. For Vertov, the ability to see is virtually tantamount to the ability to understand and to confront one's oppressor: tantamount to possession of power, in short. It suffices to recall how, in the famous satire on European colonialism in the first reel of *One Sixth of the World*, we get an unforgettable depiction of an African woman "confronting" (though false continuity) her class enemy; or the great sequence in Vertov's next film, *The Eleventh Year* (1928), where at one moment the female "comrade from India" becomes the exemplary witness of the revolutionary collective as a whole. In shaping the rhetoric of *Three Songs*, Vertov could also rely on existing Soviet discourse on the veil—discourse well established even before the *hujum* ("assault" on traditional Central Asian customs and taboos) of 1927—which represented the veil as a kind of imposed blindness. For Soviet agitators (as Gregory Massell puts it), "The implications of freeing a Moslem woman from her veil were far more dramatic than the mere reversal of a physically undesirable condition. It would mean, in effect: to liberate her eyes—'to enable [her] to look at the world with clear eyes,' and not just with unobstructed vision; to liberate her voice, a voice 'deadened' by a heavy, shroud-like cover . . . to free her from [being] a symbol of perpetual 'degradation,' a 'symbol of . . . silence, timidity . . . submissiveness . . . humiliation.'"[17] Thus, although (of course) the veil does not blind its wearer in fact, the sequence clearly links veil wearing to blindness, and therefore (in Vertovian logic) powerlessness.

The second shot seems to be a camera simulation of the motions of prayer, reminiscent of the "drunken camera" in the last reel of *Man with a Movie Camera*, the "praying camera" in *Enthusiasm*, and other moments of camera mimicry in Vertov. The lens inscribes a circular movement of rising and prostration that is intended to elicit the idea and the feeling of dull repetition, entrapment, and mindlessness, an impression retroactively confirmed a few shots later when we get an overhead view of men praying. In some of the succeeding shots, one might read the essentially illegible gestures of the veiled women passing laterally across the screen as evasive, hostile, or indicative of possible interest in the camera. (Historian Sheila Fitzpatrick has shown how important the rhetoric of "tearing off the masks" was during the first twenty years or so of Soviet power; to be sure, Vertovian *kino-pravda* ["film-truth"] participates in its own way in this unmasking project.[18] Yet these particular veils, of course, were masks thought to have been clamped onto the women against their will by a male-dominated Islamic society.) A shot of men apparently leaving some kind of domicile, perhaps taken from an implied female point of view, stuck back in the house, is followed by some classic "associative" montage rhetoric incorporating shots of male prayer and of a blind, half-paralyzed woman stumbling down a road. Taken together, the sequence definitively links the veil with blindness, with ignorance and non-enlightenment, with empty ritual, and with misery.

What happens next is truly remarkable within Vertov's corpus, though it may not appear so at first. The cut to the next shot, accompanied on the soundtrack by a shift from Uzbek music to a proletarian fanfare, yields the hooded face of a young woman jotting something down by a window; she needs the sunlight, for apparently her home has not yet been "electrified." We are now in Baku, not Uzbekistan, and the woman (not named in the film) is almost certainly one Aishat Gasanova, a party activist who worked among women in her native Azerbaidzhan and later in Daghestan. Perhaps not immediately, we realize that the "documents" we have just seen are flashbacks or meditations, "interior" to Gasanova's consciousness, and in the process of being converted into text by the writing hand of Gasanova herself. That we are within the realm of subjectivity is soon confirmed, when the classic Vertovian device of false match shots—in this case, through a window that opens onto a utopian image of young Pioneers marching through a lush forest next to a stream. From imagining the Old in Uzbekistan, Gasanova turns to the New, still figured by marching young people but (importantly) in a pastoral rather than industrial setting. As in *Kino-Eye* and

Enthusiasm, though less assertively, Vertov orchestrates a geometrical contrast with the preceding section. The upright bodies rhyme with the birch trees, even as the panning camera stresses lateral dynamism as well as forward movement: all is linear, lucid, and forward-directed, as opposed to the clutter and repetition of the previous sequence.

What is new here for Vertov is the unobtrusive inclusion of a subjective, psychological pivot linking the two movements of the passage from the Old to the New, as opposed to the raw leaps characteristic of his earlier films. Within the rhetoric of the sequence, that is, Gasanova occupies the same place that the impersonal, mechanical siren did at the beginning of *Enthusiasm*—but not without inflecting the sense of the "Old-New" topos in a new, subjectivizing direction. The activist becomes arguably the closest thing to a "character" to be found in any major Vertov film, inasmuch as we are offered a representation, briefly but powerfully sketched, of her daily and emotional life: we later see her on her way to the Ali Bairamov club for women, still later her intense participation in a Lenin memorial at the club. This new psychologism was noted, not without smugness, by critics at the time of the release of *Three Songs*, who recalled the director's early 1920s comments on the "absurdity" of the "psychological Russo-German film-drama—weighed down with apparitions and childhood memories."[19] At a preview on October 27, 1934, critic V. Bartenev noted how Vertov's old "LEF-type 'thing-ism' [*veshchizm*] was overturned by this film," and that in *Three Songs* "we even see—horror of horrors!—human psychological experience": "from empiricism [Vertov] has moved to a subjective sensation of the world."[20]

To be sure, neither Vertov nor his critics were working within a discursive void; as Sheila Fitzpatrick has shown, the celebration of ordinary "working-class heroes," involving the dissemination of many photographic portraits and interviews, became a major feature of Stalinist culture from the early 1930s onward.[21] And it is no accident that the majority of Vertov's later films (whether produced or not) focus on the life stories of exemplary Soviet citizens (women, mostly), thereby contributing to this large-scale proliferation of biographical celebrations of the "little man and woman." In neither *Kino-Eye* nor *Enthusiasm* is anyone included in the diegesis as a subjective guarantor of the transition from Old to New; the implication is that, by the time of *Three Songs*, there are such guarantors around, people like Gasanova who have "made" or can imaginatively articulate the passage across the developmental gap. Yet it is clear enough that, on the level of style, the insertion of this new psychological "pivot" enabled Vertov to continue his exploration of dynamics—the purely visual materialization of process—in sublimated form.

Much the same can be said about the mediating function performed by the "folk" material utilized in *Three Songs*, although I would argue that this material performed an important institutional function for Vertov as well, inasmuch as it involved the use of written texts. *Three Songs* was apparently the last film on which Vertov was able to work at least part of the time in his notoriously loose, improvisational, "un-scripted" manner. As is well known, Vertov throughout the 1920s took a principled stand against the prescripting of films, usually on the grounds that scripts inhibit some more authentically cinematic approach to the organization of visual and sonic material. This stand arguably led him into even more trouble than his notorious taste for quarrel and polemic: he was famously fired from the Central State Cinema Studio in Moscow (Sovkino) in January 1927 in large part because he refused to present studio chief Ilya Trainin with a script for the "scriptless" film he was then working on—a project that eventually became *Man with a Movie Camera*, ultimately made at the VUFKU (Ukrainian) studio and released in 1929.

With the ascension of the pragmatic anti-avant-gardist Boris Shumyatsky to the top of the cinema ministry in 1929, and the liquidation of semi-independent artistic groupings in 1932–1933 (and the attendant bureaucratization and centralization), it became impossible for Vertov to maintain this principled anti-script position. It was with *Three Songs of Lenin* that Vertov made his last real attempt to produce a "scriptless" documentary or, as he preferred to put it, unplayed or non-acted film. He complained loudly to studio administrators about demands for a script even after finally turning in a scenario at an advanced stage in the production (on August 23, 1933—the film was essentially finished by mid-January 1934):

> This is the first time I've had to explain a montage construction in words. And when it comes to a film like this one, this is a truly thankless task. . . . I have tried to overcome my own objections today, in light of your persistent requests. And so I renounced visuals, sound, the mutual interaction of montage phrases with one another, tonal and rhythmic combinations, expressions of faces and gestures . . . that all develop visually and aurally, organically linking together into an idea without the help of intertitles and words. . . . To write out each shot in detail, one after the other, link after link, montage phrase after phrase, would make sense, except that it's far more time-consuming and complex than actually putting the film together. It's a pity I had to do this.[22]

In truth, Vertov had drafted a variety of plans, if not exactly "scripts," for the film; the early ones had a biographical character and would have brought Vertov to many of Lenin's European haunts (Zürich, Paris, London, and so on) while emphasizing Lenin's role as leader of the international proletariat.[23] As it turned out, improvements in sync sound recording enabled Vertov to incorporate some directly recorded testimonial material by workers, peasants, and engineers, thereby partially circumventing the need for script. At the same time, the core of the scenario that Vertov finally did produce became three so-called "folksongs" about Lenin, selected from among a large number of mostly anonymous Lenin-dedicated verses produced in the Central Asian republics (Tadzhikistan, Turkmenistan, Kirghizstan, and Uzbekistan) in and around 1924.

It is well known that a great deal of "folk" (or "pseudo-folk") culture was generated as the result of official sponsorship in the various national republics, with an intense burst occurring after 1933–1934, after *narodnost'* ("national content" or "folk sensibility") had become a valued dimension of the socialist-realist template.[24] The incorporation of "folk material" along with the sync sound interviews were precisely the aspects of *Three Songs* that made the greatest impression on early audiences. In fact, Vertov began to make recourse to "folk" materials only at the very end of 1932, nearly midway through the production.[25] There was no small irony in this "experimental" filmmaker, previously associated (if only informally) with the Left Front of the Arts (LEF), attempting to make his art more accessible by making it "folksier," since LEF had been deeply hostile to folk art, seeing in it (in Frank Miller's words) "a worthless remnant of a patriarchal society, a cart that should be replaced by a truck."[26] In later years, Vertov repeatedly spoke of folk material as opening up his personal path to socialist realism, with *Three Songs* as his inaugural success in this area. In an unpublished talk "On Formalism" that he gave on March 2, 1936, he identified "folk creation" as the central weapon in the struggle for "the unity of form and content" against "formalism and naturalism." Theoretician P. M. Kerzhentsev was right, Vertov opined, to suggest that "the composer Shostakovich"—recently pilloried in *Pravda* for his *Lady Macbeth of the Mtsensk District*—ought to "travel around the Soviet Union collecting the songs of the people," to discover that "foundation, on the basis of which [he] might grow creatively."[27]

It has been claimed that much of the "folk" writing produced in the Soviet period was more or less pure fabrication, done by professional writers working in Moscow and the republic capitals. Vertov's "songs," however, seem to have a more banal origin: most likely, they were penned in the mid-1920s by young people associated with workers' or women's clubs or the Komsomol (Young Communist Youth League) organization—that is, in settings where Lenin was frequently commemorated, and the production of memorial verses and songs was encouraged (one might look to our own "essay contests" linked to various national or state holidays for an analogue). These poems were collected, and sometimes appeared on the pages of major central newspapers like *Pravda*.

Thus we needn't spend much time worrying about the authenticity of these "folk" productions *as* folk productions; clearly, the important thing is that they were examples of anonymous, "naïve" poetry, and could thus at once be presented as documents of popular sentiment while cohering (inasmuch as they were *documents*) with Vertov's own kino-eye "life-as-it-is" precepts.[28] As scripts or components of scripts, they were texts bearing "folk" legitimacy that could be presented to studio administrators to give them a sense of his direction; they were also collections of images, often (at least in the examples selected by Vertov) images of very physical, elemental, seasonal character, and thus adaptable to his established *faktura* practices. An example is this anonymous "Kirghiz Song," the main text in the third of the three songs: "In Moscow, in a big stone city, Where those chosen by the people gathered, There is a nomad's tent on a square, And in it Lenin lies. If you have great sadness, And nothing comforts you, Go up to this tent, And look upon Lenin, And your woe will disperse like water, And your sadness float away like leaves in an *aryk* [stream or canal]."[29] In *Three Songs* itself, this movement from sadness to "flow" and dispersal occurs in the best Vertov style, as the vast, nearly unmoving expanse of the Kara-Kum desert, rippling with suppressed energy, gives way to motion and flow—catalyzed by Lenin's mausoleum (the "tent"); what was frozen and locked in suddenly becomes a multi-branched stream linking marchers, mass-produced texts (specifically, copies of Lenin's works rolling off the assembly line), and eventually irrigative water as such. Now, however, the formal representation of change is motivated, perhaps even justified, by the "people's" own words.

We have already suggested historical reasons for Vertov's adoption of character and folklore in *Three Songs*. Two final and, I think, related questions concern the respective places of Lenin and Stalin in the film, and how we might account for the film's actual appeal (repeatedly attested by early viewers) to its contemporary audiences. Noël Burch was correct, I think, when he wrote that "among the Soviet masters, Dziga Vertov alone advocated an uncompromising tabula rasa."[30] I interpret this phrase to mean not only that Vertov was (as Malevich saw) drawn to a cinema of near-abstract dynamism in contrast to more theatrically based contemporaries like Eisenstein, but was committed to a translation of politically revolutionary radicalism into cinema, a translation that would require not only a purgation of literary and theatrical dross but a rebuilding of cinema from some presumed ground level of perception. (Perhaps the destruction of the Civil War, leading to very palpable "levelings" of all sorts, helped condition this attitude as well.) In part, this is what accounts for what critics at the time decried as Vertov's "infantilism," his frequent reinventings of the wheel, carried out as though all the established resources of cinema had to be accumulated again and reconfigured. And Vertov seemed truly to believe that these sorts of renovations of vision would have a virtually immediate political effect: "Gradually, through comparison of various parts of the globe, various bits of life, the visible world is being explored. . . . Millions of workers, having recovered their sight, are beginning to doubt the necessity of supporting the bourgeois structure of the world."[31] But with the move to full-scale "socialist construction" in 1929 and the massive production of "Soviet" subjectivities, more efficacious, less implacably corporeal mechanisms for configuring the "revolutionary passage" for Soviet citizens was required. For Vertov, these new mechanisms were precisely the subjective trajectories of biographical individuals and the lure of folk authenticity, into whose vocabularies the raw material-perceptual transitions and leaps of earlier avant-garde *faktura* could be translated. Now, passages between old and new that had previously been represented in a non-"humanist" (or even "non-human") manner were recoded in terms that invited sympathy and subjective investment; the material relationship between the static and the active slowly mutated into a narrative-figural one, like the relationship between promise and fulfillment. If Vertov's work of the 1920s had mobilized material dynamics as both a figure for and a way of effecting (on a perceptual level) revolution, the films of the 1930s, typified by *Three Songs*, insert two additional mediating levels: revolution as a personal, biographical trajectory (or what medieval Christian hermeneutics would call the "moral" level of interpretation), and a new base stratum of presentiment of revolution, as expressed in folksong (or what those same medieval allegorists would call the "literal" level). This new "machinery for ideological investment," to use Fredric Jameson's phrase, is thus arguably more complex as an *ideological* structure than what we find in Vertov's work of the 20s; a diagram of its significant layers, in accord with the four medieval exegetical levels, would look like this:[32]

Anagogical (collective, historical destiny; communism)
Moral (the individual process of becoming "new," "Soviet": psychology)
Allegorical (the perceptual-somatic revolution; modernizing of the senses)
Literal (here, folk poetry and music, with its utopian imagery: *narodnoe tvorchestvo*)

In other words, the desires for change expressed in folk poetry ("your woe will disperse like water": the historically prior or "literal" level) can also *mean* a desire for world-historical socialist transformation (the anagogical level), a desire that can also *be expressed* in terms of individual progress toward revolutionary consciousness (the moral level); and all of these levels can find *representation*, if properly articulated, in the "pure dynamics" of cinema (the allegorical level).

Unsurprisingly, such figurative reading was indeed characteristic of the discourse of the 1930s. We find a rather painful example of Vertov's own allegorizing in an article he wrote about *Three Songs* in 1935, where after noting that he structured one section of the "second song" in accord with the cadences of folk poetry ("through fire / yet they go / they fall / yet they go / they die / yet they go / the masses who won the Civil War / that is Ilich-Lenin"), he goes on to argue that precisely the same passage from defeat to victory characterizes "the revolution in the consciousnesses of the workers on the White Sea Canal."[33] This canal project, in fact a brutal Gulag-style forced labor enterprise built between 1931 and 1933, was widely publicized as—and indeed thought by many to *be*—a grand reform through work venture, a disciplinary mechanism for the creation of Soviet citizens.[34]

These grim motifs bring us back, at long last, to the role of Stalin in the film, and, by extension, that of Lenin. It seems best to assert that the Lenin of *Three Songs* functions as a kind of guarantor of the ultimate mutual intertranslatability of the four levels indicated above. Lenin is at once the exemplary revolutionary person (moral), the great theorist of communism and founder of the Soviet Union (anagogical), and a folk hero to the "people" (literal); as the great "electrifier" or modernizer of the country, he can be assimilated to the more properly

Vertovian "allegorical" level as well. But what of Stalin, who, as we know, was prominently on view throughout the film?

Paradoxically enough, my analysis suggests that "Stalin" was not especially essential to the overall structure and rhetoric of *Three Songs of Lenin*. Judging from the contemporary reviews (whether Soviet or otherwise), he seems in fact to have made very little impression; few mentioned him at all, and very few seemed to regard his role as an essential part of the "meaning" of the film. In truth, this is unsurprising, for Stalin in *Three Songs* neither "replaces" Lenin nor comes to occupy the pole of the "New" (as opposed to Lenin's "Old"). Inasmuch as Stalin is shown "continuing the work" of Lenin, he is like everyone else in the film; inasmuch as he "fulfills" Lenin's directives, he remains decidedly secondary to the primary model (and the original film, I should add, apparently contained no folksong references to Stalin, though it certainly could have included them). Most importantly, the very allegorical structure of the film, fusing folk collective, individuals, historical destiny, and cinematic *faktura* explorations into a single "Leninist" revolutionary paradigm, absolutely precludes a central tenet of the (in 1934, already dominant) Stalin cult: namely, that Stalin was "the intermediary between Lenin and the people," that through "Stalin's works, writings, and person Lenin's spirit was accessible to all."[35] Whether in 1934 or 1970, *Three Songs of Lenin* argues, on the contrary, that "Lenin" is in some sense omnipresent and immanent in discourse, historical action, and artistic practice alike. (Was this the feature that made the 1938 reedit of the film—which includes a speech by Stalin about Lenin—necessary?)

We should not be tempted to think that this rhetorical sidelining of Stalin occurred because of some conscious "dissident" impulse on Vertov's part, of which there is no evidence in any case. Rather, it emerged out of Vertov's effort to preserve a space for his established artistic practice, even while creating an "accessible" and politically useful work. Thus we might see his work on *Three Songs* as a form of preservative figuration or *allegoresis*, a way of saving the old forms, as the Neoplatonist Porphyry did with his philosophical allegory of the Homeric "cave of the nymphs," for example, by rereading them as versions of some newly legitimated brand of knowledge. That an avant-gardist would need to preserve his beloved forms through appeal not to new science or philosophy but to "the folk" and "subjectivities" may be one feature that makes the story of Vertov's own creative passage from the Old of the 1920s to the New of the 1930s a peculiarly Soviet one.

Notes

1 Aleksandr Fevral'skii, "Tri Pesni o Lenine" (reprinted from *Literaturnaia Gazeta* 89 [July 16, 1934]), in *Istoriia Sovetskogo Kinoisskustva Zvuk- ovogo Perioda*, ed. Ippolit Sokolov (Moscow: Goskinoizdat, 1946), 1:67–70.

2 E. I. Vertova-Svilova and V. I. Furtichev, eds., *Tri Pesni o Lenine* (Moscow: Iskusstvo, 1971).

3 Vij, "Pisatel' i fil'ma," *Kino Gazeta* 35 (August 4, 1934); RGALI f. 2091, op. 1, d. 93, l. 24.

4 T. Rokotov, "Tri Pesni o Lenine," *Vechernaia Moskva* 255 (November 4, 1934); RGALI f. 2091, op. 1, d. 93, l. 89.

5 However, the shot of the train "Joseph Stalin" with the slogan was clearly added at a fairly late date in the production: RGALI f. 2091, op. 1, d. 48, l. 17.

6 Rokotov, "Tri Pesni o Lenine."

7 V. Ivanov, "Tri Pesni o Lenine," *Rabochaia Penza* 286 (December 31, 1934); RGALI f. 2091, op. 2, d. 274, l. 22.

8 Much more could be said about the relationships between the various versions, though this is not the place to do so.

9 See, among scores of other examples, the cover of *Pravda* for November 7, 1934 — the seventeenth anniversary of the October Revolution—with its side-by-side portraits of Lenin and Stalin.

10 Klaus Kanzog, "Internalisierte Religiosität: Elemen- tarstrukturen der visuellen Rhetorik in Dziga Vertovs *Drei Lieder über Lenin*," in *Apparatur und Rhapsodie: Zu den Filmen des Dziga Vertov*, ed. Natascha Drubek-Meyer and Jurij Murashov (Frankfurt am Main: Peter Lang, 2000), 218; Annette Michelson, "The Kinetic Icon and the Work of Mourning: Prolegomena to the Analysis of a Textual System," in *The Red Screen: Politics, Society, Art in Soviet Cinema*, ed. Anna Lawton (London: Routledge, 1992), 119, 129; Bulgakowa, "Spatial Figures in Soviet Cinema of the 1930s," 59.

11 Mariano Prunes, "Dziga Vertov's *Three Songs about Lenin* (1934): A Visual Tour through the History of the Soviet Avant-Grade in the Interwar Years," *Criticism* 45, no. 2 (2003): 251–278, 274.

12 Prunes, "Dziga Vertov's *Three Songs about Lenin* (1934)," 272.

13 Michelson, "Kinetic Icon and the Work of Mourning," 129; Bulgakowa, "Spatial Figures in Soviet Cinema of the 1930s," 59.

14 Gilles Deleuze, *Cinema 1: The Movement-Image*, trans. Hugh Tomlinson and Barbara Habberjam (Minneapolis: University of Minnesota Press, 1986), 39. All of Deleuze's comments on Vertov here (especially 39–40 and 82) are of the greatest interest.

15 I am thinking here of a play such as Samuel Beckett's *Breath* (1969).

16 RGALI f. 2091, op. 2, d. 235, ll. 3–6.

17 Gregory J. Massell, *The Surrogate Proletariat: Moslem Women and Revolutionary Strategies in Soviet Central Asia, 1919–1929* (Princeton: Princeton University Press, 1974), 138.

18 See Sheila Fitzpatrick, *Tear Off the Masks! Identity and Imposture in Twentieth-Century Russia* (Princeton: Princeton University Press, 2005), 65.

19 Dziga Vertov, *Kino-Eye: The Writings of Dziga Vertov*, ed. Annette Michelson, trans. Kevin O'Brien (Berkeley: University of California Press, 1984), 5.

20 RGALI f. 2091, op. 2, d. 423, l. 37. The turn to "humanism" was a characteristic of cultural discourse at the time; see the self-critical speech by former LEF-ist Viktor Shklovsky at the first Congress of Soviet Writers: "In the Name of the New Humanism," *Izvestiia*, August 24, 1934, 3.

21 Sheila Fitzpatrick, *Everyday Stalinism: Ordinary Life in Extraordinary Times: Soviet Russia in the 1930s* (New York: Oxford University Press, 1999), 74.

22 RGALI f. 2091, op. 2, d. 423, l. 4. Mezhrabpomfil'm was the studio that produced *Three Songs*. The note was addressed to Mezhrabpomfil'm administrator Babitskii.

23 RGALI f. 2091, op. 1, d. 50, ll. 1–12.

24 See Hans Günther, "Totalitarnaia narodnost' i ee istoki," in *Sotsrealisticheskii Kanon*, ed. Hans Günther and Evgeny Dobrenko (Saint Petersburg: Akademicheskii Proekt, 2000), 377–389; and Frank J. Miller, *Folklore for Stalin: Russian Folklore and Pseudofolklore of the Stalin Era* (Armonk, NY: M.E. Sharpe, 1990), 7–13.

25 Vertova-Svilova and Furtichev, *Tri Pesni o Lenine*, 107.

26 Miller, *Folklore for Stalin*, 6.

27 RGALI f. 2091, op. 2, d. 212, l. 8.

28 Vertov wrote as much in a diary note from 1936: "The same impulse that had once prompted me to collect doggerel verse awoke again within me [during the production of *Three Songs*]. In the first place, these were song-documents; as is well known, I have always had great interest in the arsenal of documentary" (Vertova-Svilova and Furtichev, *Tri Pesni o Lenine*, 107).

29 "Written down in Kirghiz-Kishlak, Fergana region, in February 1926" (RGALI f. 2091, op. 2, d. 422, l. 26).

30 Noël Burch, "Film's Institutional Mode of Representation and the Soviet Response," *October* 11 (Winter 1979): 93.

31 Vertov, *Kino-Eye*, 39.

32 My reading here is based on Jameson's comments on medieval exegesis in *The Political Unconscious: Narrative as a Socially Symbolic Act* (Ithaca, NY: Cornell University Press, 1981), although the anagogical level occupies a somewhat different place in my analysis. Jameson writes, "It is precisely in [the generation of the moral and anagogical levels] that the individual believer is able to 'insert' himself or herself (to use the Althusserian formula), it is precisely by way of the *moral* and *anagogical* interpretations that the textual apparatus is transformed into a 'libidinal apparatus,' a machinery for ideological investment" (30). For medieval exegetes, the literal level is the Old Testament (especially the story of the Exodus); the allegorical is the New Testament (especially the life of Christ); the moral, the tale of the "redemption" of the individual believer; and the anagogical, the eventual historical destiny of all mankind in the Second Coming and Last Judgment. To avoid all misunderstanding, it needs to be stressed that Jameson's analysis is essentially an attempt to understand the ideological effectiveness of certain textual constructs, rather than an advocacy of medieval Christian hermeneutics as an interpretive method. By the same token, my use of Jameson's interpretation is meant to indicate the kind of *ideological* work *Three Songs* is performing, not that Vertov is adopting a "religious" framework in any explicit way.

33 "Poslednii opyt," *Literaturnaia Gazeta*, January 18, 1935, n.p. A well-known "History of the Construction of White Sea-Baltic Canal" was edited by Maksim Gor'kii (1934) and contained contributions by Shklovsky and Zoshchenko, among others.

34 See Mikhail Morukov, "The White Sea-Baltic Canal," in *The Economics of Forced Labor: The Soviet Gulag*, ed. Paul R. Gregory and Valery Lazarev (Stanford, CA: Hoover Institution Press, 2003), 151–162. Vertov actually received permission to film a documentary about the project on February 25, 1934, but this film apparently never got off the ground (RGALI f. 2091, op. 2, d. 247, l. 1030b).

35 Nina Tumarkin, *Lenin Lives! The Lenin Cult in Soviet Russia*, revised edition (Cambridge, MA: Harvard University Press, 1997.)

3

Nostalgia, Melancholy, and the Persistence of Stalin in Polish Cinema

JEREMI SZANIAWSKI

> Is this then to say that even within the extraordinary eclipse of historicity in the postmodern period some deeper memory of history still faintly stirs? Or does this persistence—nostalgia for that ultimate moment of historical time in which difference was still present—rather betoken the incompleteness of the postmodern process, the survival within it of remnants of the past, which have not yet, as in some unimaginable fully realized postmodernism, been dissolved without a trace?
> —Fredric Jameson, "The Existence of Italy"

Can we still assess such recent cinematic productions of what we can call (following David Bordwell's suggestion) "festival pieces"—a late, reified instantiation of the modernist auteur films of the 1950s and 1960s—particularly those whose action is set in the past, in the same way that Fredric Jameson did the productions of the late 1970s and beyond, probing their historicity (or lack thereof), and cinema's relationship to history itself? Two recent Polish films by Paweł Pawlikowski—*Ida* (2013) and *Cold War* (2018)—are perfect examples of this tendency: one that co-opts what were already co-opted reflexes of postmodernism (including of course the movement's favored mode according to Jameson, namely nostalgia). This is very different from the work of resilient and insular late auteurs (Hong Sang Soo, Albert Serra, or the latest Godard), still married to a form close to modernism—transnational, perhaps, but not really "global." Pawlikowski's films are products of cultural politics, and furthermore a bankable commodity, despite their apparent non-commercial aesthetics (parading under the guise of "austerity," but indeed overflowing with the lush and excess of kitsch and melodrama): they are hailed at both the Academy Awards and full-blown global film festivals, and their director is seen as a bona fide global auteur, who emerged from a non-American environment (Poland, then the United Kingdom), before making a return "home" (just as Poland is entering, against the odds, a phase of hegemonic neoliberalism).

The black-and-white cinematography, meant to underscore the films' pastness, collides with a strange sense of perpetual presentness: a fascinating symptom of the working of global capitalism, whose most advanced or latest stage is reflected in their slick, technical perfection. But the latter does not mask entirely a form of longing and the contradictions of its own act of Mephistophelean pact of sorts with the powers that be and the film festival, "quality demographics" market—a tacit rejection of a "vow of poverty" that often characterized the films Pawlikowski references, a gesture that is at one and the same time an acquiescence to the lure of capitalism and a testament to its devitalizing or morbid effects. By the same token, the films, filled with a pronounced sense of lack and longing wrapped in glossy aesthetics, also tell us something about the place of human community, not only in contemporary Polish society but in the West in general—and the impasse that is reached for art when said community has been alienated to such glaring extents. The films then allegorize, on a direct subsurface level, the effects of neoliberal politics in Poland, and, deeper below, the nature of a global phenomenon to which they bring no solution, even of the symbolic kind. I suggest reading the films of Pawlikowski on three levels: their manifest content and reflection on Polish and European history, which is also reinscribed in the recent success on the festival and art-house market; how the manifest political context of their production—which differs starkly from one film to the next—has influenced their content; and in terms of the films' political unconscious proper, which can be detected in their temporal unfolding, chronology, and textures and elucidates what lies behind their deep-seated melancholy and their take on the nostalgia mode. Finally, I will point to what it is they have to tell us about our relationship to history and the Big Other, evoked here in the figure of Stalin and Stalinist Poland.

A satellite communist country at the frontline of the Soviet Union's collapse, Poland has historically served as a case study for neoliberal implementing in a postsocialist country, brutally ushered into market economy. The ground had been prepared by two decades of economic unrest and social disillusionment, with worker's protests in the early 1970s in Gdansk, followed by the Solidarity union movement and martial law of the early 1980s. Steering toward the Western capitalist models, Poland managed to wrest itself off a by then crumbling hand of socialism by the late 1980s (the Soviet Union would promptly follow suit), concomitant to the fall of the Berlin Wall in 1989. It was then rushed into neoliberalism through the "Shock Therapy" planned by Leszek Balcerowicz. The "soaring Polish Eagle" then experienced robust economic growth, just as its gap between rich and poor and staggering unemployment became the worst of any European country, by the late 1990s (a period dominated by the postcommunist leftist party SLD—Sojusz Lewicy Demokratycznej). A huge influx of foreign capital further emboldened the country's newly acquired capitalist ethos, after it joined the European Union in the early 2000s—a moment at which the very texture of its society effected a leap from a communist Poland still deeply attached to its prewar past and tradition, to a full-blown neoliberal Poland of stark contrasts: between new highways, shopping malls, tacky patrimony renovation and urban development, private enterprise, increasing contrast between the cities and their pampered medieval downtowns (Warsaw, Poznan, Gdansk, Cracow), and a countryside and eastern part still entrenched in the habits and drab aesthetic of the communist past and beyond—horse-drawn peasant carriages and nineteenth-century factories (Łódź, Lublin, Białystok).

The 2000s have been dominated in Poland by this continued process of neoliberalization, but in two distinct—apparently contradictory—stages: as Stuart Shields elucidates the critique of austerity measures and score of corruption scandals tarnished and discredited the postcommunist left leadership of the 1990s, leaving room for a distinctly pro–European Union, corporate capitalist side of the doctrine (incarnated by the Donald Tusk–led PO—Platforma Obywatelska), followed in turn by a more nationalist and populist expression (the Kaczyński twins' PiS—Prawo i Sprawiedliwość).[1] While the two parties, their tense cohabitation, their electoral base (the urban, intellectual, and bourgeois voters of the PO against the "B Poland" of the Catholic countryside and disenfranchised voters of the PiS), and their methods have cast them as opposites, Shields rightly points to how the center-right, overtly neoliberal policy of the PO and the populist turn incarnated and enacted by PiS are merely two faces of the continued process of the country's neoliberalization, with only the surface discourse being pushed more to the center or to the right, depending on the formation in power. Coincident to these, of course, has been a dissolution of workers' unions and of leftist political formations across the board (the former ruling party SLD greatly diminished and the Green party basically never taking hold in the country).

We find this historical process and transition from Stalinism to post-Stalinist communism and then neoliberalism clearly reflected in Polish cinema. The country already boasted a robust cinematic production (mostly of a commercial entertainment kind) before the war, and it became one of the most important national cinemas in the communist bloc thereafter—taking the world by storm with the films of the Polish School of Cinema (Andrzej Wajda, Jerzy Kawalerowicz, Kazimierz Kutz, Tadeusz Konwicki, Andrzej Munk) in the late 1950s, enjoying stellar popularity in film festivals and on the international art house market, during the sixties and seventies in the wake of de-Stalinization. The economic slowdown of the 1970s (in spite of heavy-handed attempts by First Secretary Edward Gierek at revitalizing the economy through foreign loans and the massive debt resulting therefrom) only worsened in the troubled 1980s, accounting also for the workers' strikes and the implementation of martial law. So that, upon emerging from communism, Poland was characterized by resilient but impoverished film production structures, an analogon to the sorry spectacle of cities left some twenty-odd years behind their Western counterparts in terms of technological and economic development. The economic recession and precariousness of the country in the 1980s and 1990s particularly left the world of cinema in shambles, even as select ambassadors of cultural politics (Wajda of course, first and foremost, but also an old Kawalerowicz), as easily serving the Capitalist West as they had the Master from Moscow, still enjoyed budgets (albeit more limited and limiting ones) to perpetuate their ideological function—as the concealed voice of the now postcommunist regime. Wajda and Kawalerowicz had started out directing socialist realist fare (*A Generation*, *The Shadow*, both 1955), films that, according to the dogma of the day, represented activists of the Communist People's Army (Armia Ludowa) in a noble light, opposed to the Nazis and soldiers of the Polish underground or Home Army (Armia Krajowa). In 1956, with de-Stalinization, instructions came from Moscow to the Polish boards of filmmaking to introduce a "reconciliatory" corrective to that narrative,[2] showing Home Army soldiers as wayward humans rather than as terrorists. Wajda and others then promptly shifted gear to accommodate the Polish School of Cinema's (post-1956, of course, and of which the beautiful but fallacious *Ashes and Diamonds* [1958] remains the most emblematic picture) program of rehabilitating the beleaguered Home Army up to a point, and of healing or rather muting the nation's wounds (without ever criticizing the crimes of Stalinism, of course). Then, after 1964, came an "apolitical" decade, deeply entrenched in literary adaptations, followed by, in what seemed like a truly subversive turn, the "cinema of moral unrest" of the late 1970s to criticize the ills of an increasingly defunct bureaucracy, which nonetheless started, with a twenty-year delay, its own work of de-Stalinization proper. It came as no surprise, then, that Wajda's films of the 1990s and after espoused the new liberal and/or high Catholic Church doxa, injecting it implicitly into otherwise apolitical films, to a by then increasingly local audience.

It seemed for a moment that Polish cinema, once the toast of the town throughout Europe and even the United States (Coppola's and Scorsese's admiration of Wajda or Wojciech Jerzy Has), would not regain its international visibility. But a growing Polish population and rejuvenated national economy, coupled with a very robust body of technicians and artists still trained at one of the world's best film schools, and the fact that the country did not relinquish its currency (the zloty) in exchange for the pricy euro, proved to be the industry's saving grace. All of a sudden a country much reviled throughout most of the eighties and nineties for its fabled anti-Semitism (and, to some, its underrecognized share of responsibility in the Holocaust), the country of parochial "Polaks"—the butt end of so many anti-Polish jokes in the West—Poland became a new, perfect ground for European film production, following Spielberg's notable stint there filming *Schindler's List* (1993) (itself inspired by Wajda's portrait of the extraordinary Jewish doctor and pedagogue, *Korczak* [1990]), as well as for coproduction schemes, themselves encouraged by the European Union.

It is in this context that Pawlikowski, born in Poland but having spent most of his life in the United Kingdom, returned to his native country as its prodigal cinematic son, at a time when an overinflated pound sterling made film production more difficult for an auteur noted for his aesthetically pleasing (no doubt *My Summer of Love* [2004] is a masterpiece of the use of soft focus) and not quite bankable work (Pawlikowski's attempt at a more commercial genre, the mystery, that is *The Woman in the Fifth* [2011], faltered). Just as Wajda, the old master, was leaving the stage (he would still go on to nominally "direct" two features, *Walesa, Man of Hope* [2013] and *Afterimage* [2016]), the prodigal son and heir apparent turned up. For a fraction of what a film would have cost in Western Europe, Pawlikowski completed two: first came the intimate, low-budget *Ida*, a film whose triumph at the 2014 Academy Awards established Pawlikowski as the most important global Polish auteur, just as this brazen display of formal sophistication and thematic cosmopolitanism incensed the Polish right.[3] Then, in 2018, Pawlikowski acquired the enshrining, "auteur of bankable masterpiece" status with the worldwide art-house hit, *Cold War*.

With beautiful and carefully composed black-and-white cinematography, and a rich palette of grays capturing its melancholy, wintry, misty landscapes, *Ida*—the tale of a nun who discovers that she is in fact Jewish—offers a gripping surface allegory of a country still very much in search of its identity, while tackling a score of taboo issues in Polish culture: anti-Semitism, alcoholism, homosexuality, and, last but not least, the question of "non-Jewish Jews"—people of Jewish descent who, for a variety of reasons, had to hide their true origins, sometimes to the point of forgetting or never knowing about them in the first place, and sometimes shunning the implications of this rediscovered heritage. With such sensitive baggage, it is not surprising that *Ida* should have raised fierce objections among its detractors. While Helena Datner decried the film's backhanded anti-Semitism she perceived in Ida's aunt, Wanda Gruz, a former Stalinist judge,[4] the film otherwise received overwhelming praise in the Polish mainstream media.[5] Datner's criticism, harsh but not without grounds, allows one to probe the film with more nuance, reading precisely the Gruz character on multiple levels. In her functional polysemousness we find a metonym for the film's ambiguity as a whole, casting doubts as to its political message and actual goal, a deliberate act of obfuscation on the part of the filmmaker, perhaps, or a more significant symptom of the contradictions arising in a fraught political context (Poland ca. 2013, that is), on an unconscious level proper.

Indeed, Gruz is at once inspired by and very different from Helena Wolińska-Brus (1919–2008), infamous in Poland for her role in early 1950s Stalinist purges, and who never publicly expressed any qualms about that problematic part of her biography. Pawlikowski, who knew Wolińska (although he admittedly remained unaware of her Stalinist past for many years), described her as a witty and brazenly outspoken elderly lady.[6] Conversely, Wanda Gruz is introverted, sensitive, and wearing the mask of indifference to protect herself (having lost her family to the Holocaust). If she comes across as cold toward her niece at the very beginning of the film, she soon turns out to be a caring, nurturing presence, mellowing in the company of her "Jewish nun."

In an interview for the Polish newspaper *Gazeta Wyborcza*, Pawlikowski made it plain that his wish was, through this film, to rehabilitate all "negative" parties involved: to humanize the "Red Judge," Wanda Gruz, accounting for her idealistic youth that led her to join the communist ranks (instead of the Home Army, associated with the Polish Catholic movement), but also to somewhat justify the actions of the peasants who first hid, and then killed Ida's family. Wanda's suicide, late in the film, can also come across as a form of self-inflicted punishment for her actions as a Stalinist judge, and thus as a symbolic reparation for Wolińska's refusal to show remorse, let alone apologize to the families of Polish officers and underground members she sentenced to death. Pawlikowski's film would thus try to explain the complexities of human character and the factors which led one to perpetrate certain crimes. In doing so, *Ida* would seek to reunite all of Poland in one sweeping gesture of atonement and forgiveness—cinema's symbolic solution to the problem: to come to terms with the traumatic past of both the Holocaust and Stalinism, and participating in an effort of reconciliation between Jews and Gentiles—a fraught issue in Polish culture—no less. Such a tall order is bound to leave any alerted viewer aware of it feeling somewhat uncomfortable, poised between disbelief and slight embarrassment. Can such idealism exist in the realm of commercial filmmaking, and, furthermore, in a system where government funding is indispensable to a project's viability?

While surface allegorical readings of *Ida* have abounded, something is left unspoken in the director's grand conciliatory scheme: in humanizing Gruz, indeed making her the most developed and relatable character of the film (against Ida's muted, quasi affectless stance), Pawlikowski went against the grain of those films reconsidering the war and Stalinism and made during the PiS/Kaczyński twins' reign. During that period, Andrzej Wajda was given free rein to blame the Soviets for the massacre of the Polish officers in *Katyn* (2007), and journeyman Ryszard Bugajski directed *General Nil* (2010), a film that shows the horror of the persecution (and protracted wait on death row) of Polish officers in Stalinist jails.[7] In this latter film it is Wolińska, one of the prime targets of the Kaczyńskis' witch hunt against members of the communist elite, who is represented not as a witty woman, nor as a deep and sensitive tortured soul, but as a coldhearted, primitive, and insensitive bureaucrat, and president Bolesław Bierut as a sociopathic puppet of Stalin.[8] Against this agenda, and seeking to settle old scores with the past, Pawlikowski opts to embrace the rhetoric of "love" promoted by Donald Tusk during the victorious PO election in 2008, which would lead to the uneasy cohabitation with president Lech Kaczyński (until the latter's death in the Smolensk air crash in April 2010), and the PO's stronghold over the country until 2015. Much as "love" was PO's code for ousting PiS, there is a form of dog whistling at work in *Ida*, which ends up not quite including everyone indeed, but rather proposes a more appeased, more glossy engagement with Polish twentieth-century historic tropes in Poland's latest political landscape: one that is allegedly open to everyone, except to the vindictive PiS, and therefore its conservative Catholic constituents—a nonnegligible segment of the Polish population. Indirectly deriding populism and parochialism, Pawlikowski's film may hardly be committing any crime, but it nonetheless meets the demands of realpolitik. This contradiction is also what makes the film stand out and retain value, of course, with the problem—the ideological unease raised by this gorgeously crafted but ambiguous text—remaining intact. Yet if this message is coded, it is not cryptic beyond legibility. The rich ambiguity of the film thus lies elsewhere still—in its political unconscious, this supreme degree of interpretation of a text (Jameson adapting Northrop Frye's take on the anagogical level of Medieval gnosis to Marxist interpretation), going beyond any question of whether or not any "reconciliation" is achieved by the film. We must thus now turn to *Ida*'s form to detect its greater significance, thereby engaging with the cultural history of art cinema and what status "art film" occupies in late capitalism relative to its earlier expressions, and what "community" it gestures toward.

Ida's black-and-white cinematography relates it to Wajda's films of the 1960s (or to Kawalerowicz's nun and convent imagery in *Mother Joan of the Angels* [1961]). I have elsewhere correlated the film to the works of Carl Theodor Dreyer, Robert Bresson, and especially Ingmar Bergman, made in the period depicted in the film—the early 1960s—the heyday of auteurism and cinematic modernism.[9] For Bergman, identity—political, spiritual, sexual, and otherwise—was always a point of contention that led to the characters' conflicts and doubts, reflecting the director's own tortured relationship to faith and sexuality. It is intriguing, in this sense, that Pawlikowski would use such a clear point of reference when trying to tell a story not only about the dialectics of faith and doubt, about skepticism in view of humanity's many lapses, and immanent human goodness and ability for redemption, but also about the questioning of one's identity and the need to revive religion and faith, not as ossified institutions, but as living practices capable of elevating the human soul. This Catholic take on a Lutheran master creates a strange, if seductive mix, one that transforms the (fake) ambiguity of the film's political message into a true formal and philosophical conundrum. But as Jameson taught us, such transcendent or spiritual questions belonged with modernism and became old fashioned or undesirable under postmodernism, and their return in this later context at once rings hollow and is intriguing enough to have us wonder about its meaning and function; the authenticity or truth content of it all can be considered with utmost skepticism only once it is recognized as postmodern pastiche that does not say its name. More interesting to us, then, is not even the story of failed or impossible reconciliation of the narrative, but rather the very adoption of the form of a Western modernist auteur—a gesture of commercial opening up onto the West by virtue of repurposing valuable items of its cultural capital toolkit, and thus not only just meant to "sell" in the West through recognizable aesthetics (digestible high art, as it were), but also in analog with the Polish government's phase of openness onto the West and the EU at the time of the film's production. It is along those lines that the film's closing scene, the only handheld shot of the entire film (a backward tracking shot that precedes Ida, in her religious garment, as she walks a countryside road at night), goes far beyond the modernist "open-endedness" it implies, to the sound of the first and only piece of extra-diegetic music in the film (a piano transcription of Bach's *Ich Ruf Zu Dir Herr Jesu Christ*), thereby gesturing at similar closures in the films of Bresson or Antonioni. What emerges is the importance, in an overtly neoliberal and Europhile context of the PO's rule, of having an international, trans-European Pole retell Polish history through a Western (much more so than "modernist") cinematic lens.

Both form and content here suggest something like a new spin on the nostalgia mode decried by Jameson, which I propose to call melancholy mode: while muddy, gray landscapes were depicted in black-and-white in Béla Tarr's films to represent the abject failure of the late Soviet and post-Soviet project (a sublime of mud and ruins, as it were), Pawlikowski imbues his shots of a drab Thaw-era Poland with so much beauty, summoning the spirit of 1960s high art cinema with such sensuousness, that it is impossible to not detect there a true spirit of longing—as if the spirit of loss of affect of early postmodernism itself had left the place to a blind or merely sensory affect.[10] But longing for what? While the strategy of channeling Western modern auteur cinema in this Polish film has its strategic and commercial value, I also want to suggest that, on the one hand, all the while expressing the smuggling of neoliberalism into the former communist country, the film also points unconsciously to the impossible reconciliation of West and East (the rapprochement yet also the strong contrast between the aesthetic of the films of the French and Polish New Wave, the idiosyncratic accomplishments of Bergman and Tarkovsky, etc.), yet putting the blame of this failure not on capitalism, but on the Cold War itself. This leads to the other aspects of longing, refracted through these Western aesthetics pastiched in *Ida*, and evoked in the film's narrative: Stalin's ghost; and the East/West dialectic that the two replay and that were very much on the minds of Poles at the time— and perhaps, albeit in a dim, hazy manner, still are, as the country scrambles in a schizophrenic reaction to neoliberalism.

This idea of an East-West trade-off (between anomie/freedom and socialization/tyranny) is replayed more literally in *Cold War*, Pawlikowski's sequel of sorts to *Ida*,[11] also shot in lush black-and-white and referencing slices of Polish communist history through the lens of modernist cinema. The film, which spans the years 1949 to 1964, starts out by telling the story of a couple in their late thirties, Wiktor and Irena, who scout the countryside and record Polish folk music in the new communist Poland. The music is then reworked into dance and music numbers by an ensemble called Mazurek (the ensemble's home a repurposed Polish country manor house—as per the practice under collectivization). The story veers off into melodramatic territory when Wiktor meets Zula among the young members of the ensemble.

A summary of *Cold War* makes it sound like a 1920s melodrama (Wiktor and Zula fall in love, he defects to the West but she stays behind, then marries a Sicilian man to obtain the passport that will bring the two lovers back together, away from Stalinist mother Poland. But he neglects her, seduced by the lure of the cosmopolitan Paris intellectual scene, and she cheats on him before returning to Poland, resuming her career, now as a solo pop act. Unable to function without her, he is sent to a labor camp for his defection, she marries his archenemy to get him out, and they commit suicide), yet sans the typical utopian, redeeming element of said fare in Classical Hollywood cinema. Like *Ida*, the film is loosely based on real-life events: Mazurek is the filmic, novelized version of Mazowsze (whose music is used in the lush musical numbers peppering the film), and Wiktor and Irena are tailored in part on Mira and Tadeusz Sygietyński, who started and oversaw Mazowsze until their death. As for Wiktor and Zula's suicide, it bears a distant echo to Stanisław Ignacy Witkiewicz's own suicide, upon finding out that the Soviets had invaded Poland through the East, on September 18, 1939. However, the surface politics of the film are a far cry from the ones that animated *Ida*, produced in the heyday of the PO. The year of *Cold War*'s release, 2018, saw a very different political landscape in Poland. The right wing, Catholic, and conservative PiS was back in the driver's seat, having won the 2015 presidential election and swept an absolute majority in parliament in the 2016 election. One of the party's continued policies consisted in purging Polish culture of texts or narratives unpalatable to its view (for instance by giving the school curriculum a homophobic, anti-intellectual, pro-Catholic bent), stifling any form of cultural expression out of party line. In this context (one symptom of which are the "LGBT free zones" implemented in some parts of the country), it will come as no surprise that Pawlikowski delivered a melodrama with no clear politi-cal message—other than the sterile and negative dialectics pitting capitalist West and communist Poland one against the other, both as nonviable alterna-tives, covertly paying lip service to the PiS's "us versus them" rhetoric. Further in line with realpolitik, the film is also "purged" of all elements unpalatable to the populist party: homosexuals and Jewish characters are basically nonexistent.[12] To be sure, there is a token gesture referring to anti-Semitism in the film, but it is framed as stemming from Stalinism: Kaczmarek, the brutish UB—Urząd Bezpieczeństwa, the Polish communist secret services—crony, who makes sure Mazurek remains politically correct, suggests removing one of the singers of the ensemble who looks stereotypically Jewish. Here it should be noted, however, that Kaczmarek is overall represented as a weak apparatchik, even supine in his post-1956 appearance, who helps get Wiktor out of jail (after Zula marries him and begets him a child). Here, and despite Pawlikowski's rather clear sympathies (he could not be suspected of being a favorite of the PiS or the Polish populist, homophobic, and racist right), one must still conceive of *Cold War* less as a com-promise to the power in place, and rather as yet another expression of the cardi-nal neoliberal values of fluidity and adaptability, and the continuity between the two phases of hegemonization of capitalism in Europe. Seen thus, *Ida* and *Cold War* appear as being in continuity, as a diptych of sorts: *Ida* as an expression of a variegated neoliberal society already contained in the budding liberalization of Thaw-era Poland; *Cold War* as a showcase for one of Poland's cultural export products—the neofolkloristic dance and singing ensemble Mazowsze (once an emblem of communist Poland's ability to modernize its folk tradition and give it a modern social value, and later rebranded and celebrated for its . . . Christ-mas carols). Pawlikowski thus appears to be serving two masters: "fooling" the PiS by delivering an apolitical text that enshrines an important element of postwar Polish culture, recognized and loved by the Polish diaspora world-wide; and at the same time treating his subject in such tone that its apolitical nature bespeaks the director's authentic allegiance. All the while, he just adapts, from film to film, to the flow and requirements of Poland's cultural politics and the art film market.

    While the removal of politically loaded elements turns *Cold War* into an asep-tic product for the neoliberal age (now palatable to a point to the nationalist party, and putting audiences worldwide under its spell at one and the same time), the film remains steeped in history, where its most interesting aspects emerge: the periodization of the narrative is clear, spanning fifteen years of communist Poland's history. The Mazurek ensemble premieres and the characters are sepa-rated in Berlin at the height of the historical Cold War and Stalinism (1951–1952) and are briefly reunited for the first time in Paris, in 1954, following Stalin's death and the first Western tour of the ensemble. Stalin's life and death, in other terms, more so even than the actual end of Stalinism (June 1956) governs the romance of the characters—also marking the end of the romantic possibility between them. We remember (and not least through Žižek's droll reading of the film) how in *The Fall of Berlin* (1949) the love affair between the two protagonists, Natasha and Alyosha, is governed in a triangular mode by the figure of Stalin. At first Stalin recommends that Alyosha read poetry to Natasha, and the two are reunited at the war's end—upon the triumphant (and apocryphal) arrival of Stalin to greet the victorious Red Army in Berlin. It is only once Stalin has given Natasha his blessing that she and Alyosha can be truly together.

In *Cold War*, after Stalin's death, while the lovers reunite, no joy or rapture is any longer possible. The vibrant first thirty-five minutes of the film (the "Stalin" period) make way for the anomie and alienation staged, rehearsed by the Western classics it references: *L'Eclisse* (the black robe and blond hair of Zula, the name of the bar at which Wiktor performs—this is also the "eclipse" of erotic passion under late capitalism, about which Antonioni made his film and wrote in "Sick Eros"), the French *cinéma de la qualité* 1950s classics (the jazz club), and Bergman's films, again. Echoes to the dynamic camera movements of Wajda and the spirituality of Tarkovsky (the church in ruins, the wind sweeping the field after the protagonists commit suicide) are there to enshrine the nostalgic, indeed melancholy, quality of the film—working in a way against the very narrative itself. Melancholy is connected here to the disappearance of the collective, no doubt, from tyrannical but genuine collective efforts under Stalinism to the devitalized alienation and individualism of 1960s capitalism or Thaw-era liberalized communist Poland. All are found echoed in another reference to modern cinema: Zula's marriage to a Sicilian man is a thinly veiled reference to the Lithuanian Karin's marriage to an Italian fisherman (also to escape the communist bloc) in Roberto Rossellini's *Stromboli* (1950). As we know, Rossellini's films engaged with the virtues of more traditional community (*gemeinschaft*) over contemporary society (*gesellschaft*), their neorealist utopia always contained in the former.[13] It is then logical, if surprising and contradictory to the neoliberal logic at work in *Cold War*, that deep within the film's structure, desire and fascination are articulated around this hierarchy that favors the collective (just as did the conservative works of Hollywood cinema of the 1970s Jameson analyzed), its unspoken yet strongly suggested utopia. Here, while on the subject of cinematic references, it should also be noted that Wiktor first becomes captivated by Zula during an audition, as she sings "Serdtse" ("the heart") from the socialist realist musical *Jolly Fellows* (Grigori Alexandrov, 1934). Sung twice by Zula in the first part of the film (the part where the community of dancers and singers recreate the utopia that is Mazurek, soon to be tarnished by the impositions of politics), it seems to embody the pinnacle of the real as it escapes the existence of the protagonists, the glee of brainwashed Soviet citizens who had exposure to only a few select films, all dedicated to the glory of their Big Other: a simpler, politically correct life, desirable insofar as it contrasts with the muddled, complicated, sapped existence of the consumerist West and its entanglements and contradictions.

Jameson has pointed to the Baudrillardian rule of simulacrum, the absence of an original in postmodern society, hence the importance of a mode recycling and re-creating (yet also dehistoricizing) figures of the past in postmodern cinema, now married to the principle of the sequel and repetition. The latter runs like a thread through *Cold War*, but without the playful or deconstructive dimension of earlier postmodern fare, instead tying the film in its tragic narrative of fatality. Another song returns like a leitmotiv throughout, this time taken from Polish folklore: "Dwa serduszka" ("two hearts"), telling the story of a passionate yet forbidden love. It is first sung a capella by a child recorded by Wiktor and Irena, then by the Mazurek ensemble with choir and lush neoromantic orchestration. Finally, the melancholy song is performed solo in a jazz arrangement by Zula, in Polish and then French (and translated by Wiktor's French lover). The poetics at play here are elegant, if not very subtle—the various iterations of the song evoking the stages of the protagonists' relationship, and emphasizing the morose delectation, the amor fati in the inevitable end that any relationship, or life itself, must meet. But by articulating this melodramatic trajectory, *Cold War* also suggests at least two things: on the one hand, that the love affair, which is doomed to failure, is made possible only through some fantasized relationship that involves reviling an Other (Stalin, a metonym for Putin's Russia), which is nonetheless an indispensable element of its constitution. On the other hand, again, it presents a past that appears somehow more ideal than the present, demonstrating textbook nostalgia.

But it is a strange form of nostalgia that Pawlikowski's films instantiate: just as in *Ida*, the image, however glossy and beautiful, seems devitalized (even as the more muted shades of gray of *Ida* seem to bespeak a more complex reality, against the sharp high contrast of *Cold War*), and memory itself of the events is all but short-circuited by the interpolation of historical accuracy (the props, costumes, sets) and contemporary reimagining (Pawlikowski's rewriting of Wolińska-Brus into Gruz, the stuff of impossible melodrama between Wiktor and Zula—culminating, both times, in suicide). One may wonder, also, what kind of nostalgia is possible when the events depicted do not call for a knowledge of history proper. Writing about the nostalgia films of the 1970s, Jameson observed: "Such epic durations mean in any case that only sample probes of the various historical moments they include can be given, and that great gaps and leaps will necessarily be negotiated by our own historical stereotypes. The matter of prior knowledge in fact offers at least one useful way of distinguishing between older historical representations (such as the historical novel . . .) and this newer type. . . . 'Experiencing history' in these novels was therefore a kind of thirst for presence and perception, ultimately gratified by the view of what such a renowned personage 'really was like.'"[14] Indeed (and here Fontane, who insisted that the historical novel was conceivable only for action taking place within just two generations removed from the reader, comes in handy), anyone who spent time in Poland and interacted with people of Wiktor or Zula's generation (people born in the 1920s or 1930s) would feel the postmodern at play, with the actors' attitudes, mannerisms, affectation (or even physiognomy!) having little in common with the appearance, speech, or behavior of their historical counterparts. This does not generate estrangement exactly, nor is it meant to—least of all in Western, non-Polish-speaking viewers—but it does account for a sense of the irretrievability of the past, a function of the vanishing of a socioeconomic system and the knowable community attached to it, now sensed not only in terms of nostalgia (utopian longing for a better past), but also in terms of melancholy (and its corollary traits, legible as well in Marxist as in psychological terms: apathy, depression, and, of course, alienation). This melancholy also has to do with a pastiche or postmodernism that does not any more speak its name, almost subconsciously deploying its formal processes.

This strange new mix of acquired postmodern reflexes and (lack of) self-awareness is captured from *Cold War*'s outset, in the pseudo-ethnographic image that opens the film: the vacant stare of a Polish man singing a folklore tune, as his music is consigned onto magnetic tape for processing and reification, under the mysterious, uncomprehending gaze of a child, placed there with rehearsed precision—like a pastiche of Kieślowski's documentary that lapses into constructed and controlled unreality (we find something similar with so many of the perfectly placed props in Alfonso Cuarón's *Roma* [2018]) that undermine these films' claims to any form of spontaneity, and let alone historical reality, when the real itself loses any hold, having become a perfect image completely subject to control. Perfectly captured, too, is the relegation of the collective—the Mazurek ensemble's creation and work—to peripheral status, expressed through snippets of its rehearsals and end result, the performance itself, on various stages across the Eastern bloc—Warsaw, Moscow, Berlin, Split, like so many mausoleums, and history is flattened and reduced, in strict postmodern fashion, to images ready for consumption.

This is where the question of the aesthetic as such becomes unavoidable: the images of the film, their texture, are nothing short of gorgeous, eye-gouging, as Jameson would put it. But they do so not without anesthesia: sedating beauty (straight out of a Studio Harcourt photo session!) pervades *Cold War* through and through, and after aimless meandering (in *Ida*) resignation becomes the main mode of the protagonists and the viewer faced with the mannerisms deployed here. But why, may one ask, should this kind of beauty give way to the spectator's "resigned" attitude? This is already rehearsed in the characters' own *Bovarysme*, their perpetual weltschmerz and desire to be elsewhere in space and/or time, or to literally be somebody else (it is useful to remind here that Flaubert's Emma's biggest crime was attempting to solve the problem of her bourgeois alienation precisely by injecting the aesthetic in her otherwise dissatisfying provincial existence.). Pitted against their excess of aesthetics, the morbid, melancholy disposition of the films evoke the erstwhile graceful tiger, now dead and taxidermized, in the glass cabinet of a museum: we do lament the killing of the animal, but we do not any more yearn for its liberation. Political resentment and dissent gives way, in neoliberalism, to melancholy contemplation.

Jameson identified a form of "magic realism" in Polish communist cinema. Characterized by a lush use of color, a "perforated take on history," and a focus on violence and the body, these films proposed a vibrant socialist response to the nostalgia mode of Western postmodernism. But *Ida* and *Cold War* are Polish only by means of their locale and language, having nothing left in common with the texts Jameson writes about. Their black-and-white cinematography is a function, of course, of their historical setting, of the pastness they gesture to all but overdeterminedly, and the contemporaneous high art classics they reference. In this sense, it is a doubling of the pastiche mask, the transparent mask covering the more visible one—a mask of modernist, black-and-white sadness. But since the last moment of legitimate use of monochrome (dictated by the aesthetics of paucity of those committed to shooting on film—of what Jameson termed, following Bernstein, the "restrictive codes" of postethnic, punk, or minority films—"real" but never hegemonic),[15] the use of black-and-white in the twenty-first century is no longer a technological imposition to transcend (the glorious photography of Sven Nyqvist that responded to the lush Technicolor and Cinerama of American productions, themselves a response to the rise of the TV set in American households!), in the digital age, nor a marker of budgetary constraints. Black-and-white no longer bespeaks limitation but instead takes on a new, historically specific meaning and function. In Pawlikowski it not only singularizes or marks the text as "art" or "auteur" cinema, but also smoothens the heterogeneity of color (and, beyond, the contradictions of history and a more authentic reality), which would otherwise betray a less than perfect historical reproduction. By the same token, it flattens history, by glossing over the heterogeneity of the whole and, again, anesthesizing our political nerves.

Clearly such aesthetic choice of the monochrome carries its ethical weight. Somewhere between the moral quality with which Michael Haneke endowed monochrome in his tale on the origins of evil, *The White Ribbon* (2009), and the full-on lowbrow silent film aesthetic pastiche of another Oscar winner, *The Artist* (2011), or of the messy pastiche *The Lighthouse* (2019), the black-and-white of Pawlikowski, like that of his good friend Cuarón (the two men cross thank each other in their films' credit scenes) is meant as a marker of the exact opposite to "the junk and garbage landscapes, and of deliberately shoddy . . . black-and-white stock, mark[ing] the will to inauthenticity as the sign of a now socially marginalized Real and as the only true space of authenticity in a spurious image culture dominated by a hegemonic postmodernism,"[16] namely: good taste in Bourdieu's sense. Every shot screams painstaking composition, elaborate lighting, blocking, and artifice—the artifice that is increasingly that of an untenable neoliberal ideology as a "natural" mode of human society. It is no longer the kind of aesthetics that would have the Impressionists, as Jameson put it, throw their arms up in the air and shutting down their paintboxes, but rather one that leaves the dulled and tyrannized viewer wanting but incapable of ripping the screen apart, of screaming in anger against the manifest "tasteful" expression of a multifarious fallacy—the aesthetic arm of neoliberal ideology, and its echoes to its totalitarian nature, a kind of (even darker?) double of Stalinist totalitarianism (suggesting yet another function served by the figure of Stalin in these films).

In a far more recent piece, Jameson restated this perennial concern: "Who will deliver us from this reign of beauty and its disreputable ideology, aesthetic philosophy? In a society in which the near-total commodification of the world, linked with the already looming world market, can be glimpsed, beauty is [...] the law of the land. For the existential support of universal commodification [...] was always aestheticization. One may see it as an addiction, halfway between drugs or pornography and the mania of the pathological collector."[17] And indeed the reaction that Pawlikowski's films lead to—one of unease as though experiencing a mild form of withdrawal accompanied at the same time by the dulling effect of a sedative—this is where we find, or feel, the deep contradiction at play in *Ida* and *Cold War*, between their morbidly overaestheticized, dulling cinematography and the aesthetic in praxis, which seems always connected, legible in Freudian and Marxist terms, with death (or, following Jameson, a pathological and fatal addiction, as in Wanda Gruz's alcoholism): think of the scene where Wanda displays family pictures of her dead relatives to Ida (where the actress playing Ida also incarnates her young dead mother in the photograph); the stained glass "uselessly" or absurdly arranged by Ida's mother in the barn, to bring beauty even to cattle; or the classical music Wanda listens to before jumping to her death. Think also of the trajectory of *Cold War*, which is also that of an increasingly reified musical realm, moving through its folk iteration to its neoclassical version (Mazurek) to the vinyl onto which Zula's solo version of "Dwa serduszka" are consigned, all the way to the exotic pop song she performs before throwing up at the sight of a ravaged Wiktor. But is this to say that Pawlikowski knowingly performs his autocriticism (in pure Soviet fashion!), atoning for the overlay of the gorgeous and the glossy he injects his films with? One may doubt this, considering how the music of Bach (and the humming of Glenn Gould over the Goldberg variations), which closes both films, reinstating the aesthetic as a supreme value, hints at the most important teaching of all: that it is community that is the key to art (which the latter must connect and strengthen), and that art without community is a morbid object.

Cold War thus floats as a purely aesthetic object, embodying this aforementioned new genre or category of "festival film," indeed a pure mass culture artefact parading as high art, albeit of a devitalized, dumbed-down kind, in this uncanny valley between pure kitsch, self-knowing pastiche, and shadows of modernist gestures, whose postures it imitates, in an otherwise desert of the human *gemeinschaft*, leaving each spectator entranced or exasperated in their bubble of incommunicability. What this reveals or suggests further is the lack that inhabits it through and through. Indeed the church in ruins is an important symbol, beyond its Tarkovskyan echoes: while its destruction may be imparted to the German bombings, it was also part of Stalin's project to not only bring about a materialist atheistic society, but to raze down the temples of the erstwhile faith. The recurrence of the symbol seems to point to a circular position, reinforced by the seasonal pattern (the church is first seen in the dead of winter, and then in the end on a summer day—even as the footage of the open dome come from the same shooting session apparently, with the tops of the trees lining the building still bare). The melancholy here is that of a commodified realm, one without a first time. There is nothing to return to, no prewar capitalist Poland any more than Stalinist Poland. The utopia that was the Mazurek ensemble was corrupted from the get-go by Stalinist surveillance, but the regime and its ideology of the collective were its condition of existence and enabler in the first place. So that, if the film's narrative articulates all those threads and is inhabited by this sense of lack and melancholy, if it mourns the lost precapitalist Poland still contained in the folk songs, or the passing of one more liberal model in Poland into a more national populist one, its contradiction no doubt is in the longing for history and it actor, the people (here alluded to through Stalin), while being a pure product of a medium that has been through reification and commodification the exact neutralizer of any drive toward a genuine collectivity.

It is here that the films' blind spot (following Macherey) is revealed: the figure of Stalin, associated with Wanda's time as a powerful judge sending Polish home army officers to their deaths, as well as with the vibrant initial collective creative effort of Mazurek. While Pawlikowski's scripts endeavor to mark these moments (the 1950s) as fraught with totalitarian violence, they nonetheless still associate them with élan vital—of the same kind that animated Pawlikowski's youth in Thatcher's Great Britain and Poland's postcommunist heyday and capitalist growth in the early 2000s. In the most surprising and contradictory way (which however is not any more contradictory if we accept the hypothesis whereby the two echo the PO/PiS "evolution" in neoliberal Poland), then, Stalin is equated with neoliberal capitalism (antihumanist ruthlessness and vitality they share) and history (Stalin as the steward of the people) at the same time as they are pitted as polar opposites to one another (vibrant totalitarianism in the East vs. devitalized capitalism in the West). It is this lack ("le peuple manque" to summon Deleuze) that, in the end, accounts for the films' strange melancholy, now in this new instantiation of a postmodernism in its latest expression—that is, one that is the antithesis of both realism and modernism, yet all the while poaches from their territories (the false, re-created real of realism, the alienated subject mystique of modernism). The nostalgia mode of the period piece is thus redoubled with the melancholy desire for the authentic, the vibrant, the unadulterated libidinal drive and rush linked not with individualistic consumerist frenzy, nor even with high art, but with a true collective—of which high art is a result and a cement, not a source.

It is thus that the films restore Stalin as a force animating the dead (or as melancholy nostalgia for the fear and trembling of the people under Stalinism—and it is hardly a stretch to conceive of such vitality under neoliberalism as a kind of pleasure in being tyrannized), all the while morbidly revisiting modernist works different from the ones previously considered, in which we might find another such vital surge, equally ambivalent, namely those Polish and Soviet films of the late 1950s and 1960s, where rewriting history with one hand while erasing Stalin as the manifest victorious protagonist of the war with the other first occurred. Think of Thaw cinema's ambitious set pieces, disturbing violence, and baroque camera movements (the latter all the more glaring in Kalatozov's *I am Cuba* [1964] due to its displacement to a locale where the revolution was still recent and vibrant), which one might see as an expression, of a formal kind, for the surge of sublime and outright libidinal impulse generated by the removal of the figure of Stalin and the resulting lack of any libidinal object that would serve as a substitute. A dual process was at play: on the one hand, a release and surge of impulse at this point due to a relaxation of totalitarian measures and terror imposed on millions of people. But on the other hand, this libidinal impulse, previously directed toward Stalin, now lacked an object—a situation echoed in the petty individual concerns of Pawlikowski's romances strewn with absence, whether the absent bedfellow or the departed and cannibalistic father (Zula's gesture of stabbing her own incestuous father here acquires a less psychologizing resonance).

Stalin, of course, had just a few years earlier featured front and center across the Soviet Union and the satellite countries, not only in films paying tribute to his glory, but in the press, in literature, and in pictures in every school and administrative office. Even after his removal, the communist regime did not come to terms with his legacy and significance, nor did the doctrine fill the void he left. The gap between the Bolshevik Revolution (Lenin) and Thaw-era communist life had left the trace, the cutout, of Stalin's profile in the fabric of society. But whereas Stalin was associated in the Soviet Union with terror but also major accomplishments (not least the victory against fascism, celebrated to this day in Russia), in Poland he represented an almost integrally dark presence, of an invader who deprived the country of its autonomy and retained his grasp over it for decades after the end of the war. Stalin, in other words, was inscribed in Polish culture, cinema, and the traumatized postwar Polish subconscious in the form of the "Big Other" and the Gaze. He left his imprint on the capital, Warsaw—the Palace of Culture and Science (today a popular attraction for tourists), erected in the late 1940s in the middle of a city still in rubble, as a "gift of the Soviet Union to the people of Poland." Stalinist judges, magistrates, policy makers, film-makers, and intellectuals—hard-line communists who had spent the war in the Soviet Union and returned to a Poland stripped of its anticommunist elites—imposed the tone of the country's doctrine onto a silenced majority.[18] In short, Stalin never left Poland's communist intellectual and political landscape, obsessing it through the late 1980s, when Mikhail Gorbachev declassified the Katyn file, which incriminated Stalin for the summary execution of forty thousand Polish officers, for which Nazi Germany had been blamed hitherto. After the end of communism, one would have expected the figure of Stalin to recede into the background and terminally vanish through the 1990s, but the trauma and corollary fascination were deep: he made a resounding return in the twenty-first century, in part due to the renewed tensions between the West and Vladimir Putin's Russian Federation, but also due to attention in Anglo-American academia (Boris Groys's work and Stephen Kotkin's gigantic three-volume biography in the making are cases in point; also the popular graphic novel turned into a lurid comedy, *The Death of Stalin*), and because of this strange and surface contradictory analogy between Stalin and capitalism—a dialectic still at play in Poland against the odds.

While on the surface level, the Holocaust and the war are no doubt in part to blame for the melancholy and *weltschmerz* of the protagonists of *Ida* and *Cold War*, its ripple effects leading them to suicide, it seems clear also that their lives are a whole lot more vibrant under Stalin, whereas they become parodies (of Wanda's work as a judge, of Zula's career as a performer) in the "mediocre" Thaw years, aligned with the tedium of neoliberalism itself, which the current populist turn in Poland seems to replay. In the end, at the deeper level, what the films seem to suggest is that in a devitalized, global market economy, no spirit of the great past can even be revived, the solution to this problem being these films— as beautiful on the surface (the wrapping of the commodity) as they are hollow inside, like cold, windy voids.

This is where it is of the utmost importance to underline that the figure of Stalin is not a nostalgia ploy ("the past"), nor even a twisted allegory for the nationalist populist turn of neoliberalism, or neoliberalization in general, of the country. Stalin or "Stalin" is also a trace, or double, or marker, for that which cannot be spoken about in the present. Stalin still represents the persistent need for the Big Other (now as great as ever, but in a more diffuse way than before— just like history itself), not just to represent "history" or the people, not merely as a figure of strong leader and power that European liberal democracies seem to be lacking, not just to authorize or prohibit romance, but to enable subjectivity and its neoliberal counterpart, "identity," themselves. But this desire to put oneself together again, to find a self or self-identity at all (whether individual or national) by way of the Big Other cannot just be seen as a kind of acquiescence to or irresistible desire for totalitarianism of one kind of another; while (at least in this case) the absent force that would allow both self and collective to exist is still only registered in the form of a single "person" (however much we must render that term elastic to speak of Stalin's existence as concept and spectacle—his sublime as it were), the longing for the collective itself perhaps still lies behind it, however blocked or self-thwarted by the straitjacket of a postmodern aesthetics that struggles to reach past a position of pure contemplation. Thus Pawlikowski's films express a larger dynamic at work in our relationship to the past and to history: we yearn for the past, but we have been (and perhaps cannot help but be) complicit in its liquidation and its irretrievability in any truly historical sense. This sobering and degraded reality is what accounts, beyond their sheer aesthetic "triumphs" for the deep melancholy which inhabits *Ida* and *Cold War*, "auteur" films, a concept now retrieved from the ash can of history, dusted, and sold as dashing and exciting one (final?) time, but in fact more disheartening and impotent than ever.

Notes

1 Stuart Shields, "Opposing Neoliberalism? Poland's Renewed Populism and Post-communist Transition," *Third World Quarterly* 33, no. 2 (2012): 359–381.

2 In the Soviet Union, this "humanist" accent, meant to move away from the monolithic, psychologically simplistic sotsrealist idiom, and to emphasize the plight of humans during World War II, found its expression in films such as Kalatozov's *The Cranes Are Flying* or Tarkovsky's *Ivan's Childhood*. In Poland, Wajda delivered *Kanal* and *Ashes and Diamonds*; Andrzej Munk, his *Eroica*; Tadeusz Konwicki, his *Last Day of Summer*.

3 One could not tell what enraged it more—the film's redeeming of a Stalinist criminal, its favorable representation of a lesbian, or its mitigated but clear pointing at the responsibility of Poles in murdering Jews during the war.

4 "Co Polacy chcieliby myśleć o Żydówce, budującej powojenny socjalizm? Że to k*rwa i alkoholiczka" (What would Poles like to think of a Jewish woman, building postwar socialism? That she is a sl*t and an alcoholic), quoted in Rojek, http://natemat.pl/80843,ida-pelna-antysemickich-stereotypow.

5 The film was acclaimed across the mainstream media, from *Rzeczpospolita* to *Gazeta Wyborcza*.

6 "A fun, unabashedly jovial loudmouth of a lady" ("Fajna, dowcipna pani z niewyparzoną gębą"), Pawlikowski, interviewed by Tadeusz Sobolewski in *Gazeta Wyborcza*, September 17, 2013.

7 When asked during a Q&A in New York in the summer of 2010 whether the political situation in Poland had any bearing on the choice of topic and financing of the film, Bugajski did not provide a straight or clear answer.

8 History surely will remember Bierut as such, who in March 1956 died in murky circumstances while on a visit to Moscow, which led to the rather cheerful quip in Polish "pojechał *w* futerku, *a* wrócił *w* kuferku" ("he went in a cute fur coat, and came back in a cute casket").

9 See my text on *Ida*: https://www.academia.edu/11032531/Benefits_of_the_Doubt_Pawlikowski_s_Ida_and_the_taste_s_of_ambiguity.

10 For a revisiting of Jameson's theory on postmodernism and (absence of) affect, see of course Eugenie Brinkema, *The Forms of the Affects* (Durham, NC: Duke University Press, 2014), or Pansy Duncan, "Once More with Fredric Jameson: Affect, Emotion and the 'Euphoric Intensity,'" *Cultural Critique* 97 (Fall 2017): 1–23.

11 Here one can add another black-and-white film—closer to straight-faced pastiche, the political satire *The Reverse* (Borys Lankosz, 2007), in which a woman is raped by a Stalinist agent, whom she poisons and dismembers, giving birth to a child who, in his postcommunist adulthood, appears as the epitome of the European liberal subject: worldly, fully fluent in English, and casually gay.

12 While the French musical producer played by Cédric Kahn can be read as Jewish, as can be the character played by Jeanne Balibar (Étienne Balibar's daughter), Wiktor's French mistress until Zula's return, nothing beyond the actors' real-life ethnicity can even remotely substantiate this reading.

13 Rossellini implemented this distinction clearly as of *Rome Open City* (1945), where a community of resistors (the Catholic priest, the communist underground activist, the mother courage), is opposed to fascist Italian society, a society that was rendered all the more nefarious and unjust as it was essentially ruled by Nazi Germany.

14 Fredric Jameson, "The Existence of Italy," in *Signatures of the Visible* (London: Routledge, 1992), 221.

15 See Jameson, *Signatures of the Visible,* 168–169.

16 Jameson, *Signatures of the Visible*, 218.

17 Jameson, 'Suffocating Kinesis', in *The Global Auteur: The Politics of Authorship in 21ˢᵗ Century Cinema*, Seung-hoon Jeong and Jeremi Szaniawski, eds. (London, New York: Bloomsbury, 2016), 227.

18 Unlike in the Soviet Union, there was a measure of possibility of evoking Stalin in Polish culture. Jerzy Skolimowski did this with his visual gag (a poster of Stalin with four eyes) in *Hands Up!* (1967), after which he went into exile for several decades.

4

Jameson, Angelopoulos, and the Spirit of Utopia

PAUL COATES

> Au fond de l'Inconnu pour trouver
> du nouveau!
> —Charles Baudelaire, *Les Fleurs du mal*

Blank Spaces on the Cognitive Map

In the early pages of "The Existence of Italy," the long essay in *Signatures of the Visible* that takes as its epigraph the statement by Adorno and Horkheimer that "not Italy is offered, but proof that it exists," Fredric Jameson argues that "the development of silent film from some inaugural realism of Griffith into the extraordinary modernisms of Eisenstein and Stroheim, cannot be dealt with further here";[1] remarks apropos the question "how to escape from the image by means of the image?" that "nor will the present essay pursue those answers further, although the presence of the unasked question—and the mystery of photography itself—haunts the following pages with welcome persistence";[2] and states that "nor can we deal here with other crucial preconditions for realistic narrative, such as the emergence of social mobility and the formal effects of a money economy and a market system."[3] In each case, a question is broached, as if discerned on the horizon, but placed beyond the horizon of expectation, of a voyage heading elsewhere by a captain cognizant nevertheless of its significance within the totality of reality and honor-bound therefore to register its presence; but it is stated that no effort will be made to answer it, perhaps because his individual attention to it could be only partial. And although this repeated move may frustrate the reader, and the frequency of the gesture may be taken as a signature manifestation of Jameson's authorship, it is one that resists commodification, for—despite the title of the volume in which the essay appears—it is rather one of the invisible than the visible. It is argued here that the move recurs because it follows necessarily from the intersection of an effort both to pursue totalization and to acknowledge its impossibility. For although these three questions' pursuit might have become possible through the opening of another of the many parentheses studding the essays, as a matter of tact and awareness of the inevitable limitation of one's own individuality or moment Jameson recognizes the potentially problematic quality of an imperative to advance steadily across a terrain sown with rabbit holes. It is argued further that these gaps in the argument correspond to the aporia of all totalizing efforts registered in Gödel's famous denial that a system can be both consistent and complete: in other words, his realization that one level of discourse cannot but open up onto another in what we might call a hierarchy of discourses or, at best, a set of discourses in solidarity comparable perhaps to the allocation in Godard's *Vent d'est* (1970) of necessary cinematic tasks to other directors such as Bertolucci and Glauber Rocha.

The process of advance and continual suspension just described is paralleled in this article with that of the films of Theo Angelopoulos, whose repetitions set up chain reactions with potentially nearly infinite extensions the director seeks to arrest, consciously or unconsciously, by corralling them in successive trilogic structures that represent locks in the trajectory of the voyage to which he likens his filmmaking: structures whose pervasively tripartite form might also be compared to what many would term the master framework of Jameson's dialectically periodizing thought, that of realism, modernism, and postmodernism. The impulse to totalize may be described as inherited from Lukács, while its periodic interruptions might be aligned with the recognition of nonidentity in Adorno, whose melancholy logic of disintegration Jameson's spirit of hope may embrace only reluctantly. If Angelopoulos could describe his work as falling into two phases, that biphasality is for Jameson the dialectical movement of and within individual exercises of thought. It is as if the urge to totalize activates a set of stylistic and thematic ripples whose backwash of mutual interference becomes apparent at these points, where issues are raised yet deliberately not pursued, a suspension (Angelopoulos's suspension of the step of the stork) whose conclusion can be only the Adornian recognition of the negative quality of a dialectic that precludes arrival, as has the history in which the moment for the actualization of Marx's final thesis on Feuerbach was missed somehow.[4] The openness is that of a nonsystematic method that reflects the breadth and speculative scope of Jameson's mode of argumentation. If Angelopoulos could be termed "the last modernist" of cinema,[5] could the same be said of Jameson, his admirer and in many respects kindred spirit, for all the centrality to his thought of the idea of the postmodern? In each case, the prototypical Ulysses is not Homer's but Dante's, the one drawn to the end and edge of the world (a world that for Jameson would end positively in a utopia that for Angelopoulos corresponds to the mythical, poetic, folkloric space that adds a day to eternity, in a new prototype of Greek mathematics, though each attends the birth of a new collectivity): to that which lies beyond the horizon, including the horizon of individual thought.

Some New Contexts for Film Studies

One might begin again, however, by following Jameson's own injunction to historicize, at the same time suspending and backtracking in the manner of both Angelopoulos and Jameson himself, by recalling the particular value to film and cultural studies of his work's intervention. Hospitably unwilling to view novel cultural formations as merely fashionable, as events may have a species of necessity not to be confused with an older Marxism's "laws of history," he delves into them for their positive, even utopian, "seeds of time,"[6] albeit ones sometimes welded to chaff. For instance, he will not simply combat poststructuralism in the name of a Marxism it largely abjured, but, referencing the early work of Barthes, find in Barthes's denunciation of the transformation of the historical into the natural a point of contact with his advocacy of Brecht and the discernible basis for what otherwise might seem an almost oxymoronic "properly Brechtian poststructuralism."[7] One might seek therefore to correct any problematic features of the often salutary theorization inspired by May 1968 by "going behind" it—historicizing it—to the earlier theorizers of estrangement who often inspired that moment: primarily, the ones addressed in his *Marxism and Form*. The subsequent "turn to the visual" Perry Anderson identified in Jameson's work of the 1980s may begin even earlier,[8] in his statement of 1977, when summing up the New Left Books anthology of debates between these German and mostly German-Jewish Marxists, that "the increasing importance . . . of film in artistic production since the time of these debates (witness the frequent juxtapositions of Brecht and Godard) likewise suggests that structural differences in medium and in genre may play a larger part in compounding the dilemmas of the Realism/Modernism controversy than its earliest participants were willing to admit,"[9] though he does not yet consider whether, and in what way, consideration of the new medium adds to the array of "all the logical possibilities"[10] generated by these opposed aesthetic movements. They are positions one could imagine him mapping both spatially, using the semiotic square of Greimas (whose introduction into English-language criticism and theory has been one of his major contributions), and temporally, through his call for film studies to display a greater awareness of cinema's embedding within the large-scale succession of such movements as realism, modernism, and postmodernism, and the historically shrinking and lengthening ideological shadows they cast.

Film itself, of course, could clearly claim an alignment with materialism, even before its stunning mobilization by such early Soviet figures as Eisenstein, Pudovkin, Vertov, and Medvedkin, as its adherence to the surface of the real and emergence through scientific discovery chimed well with the Marxist project of employing science to illuminate reality, the demystification of whose appearances would enable the proletariat clearly to perceive its exploitation and rise up against it. Thus Benjamin's denunciation of "mystery" as a keyword of bourgeois discourse concerning art, in his "Artwork in the Age of Mechanical Reproducibility" essay,[11] is classically Marxist, and perhaps even (Adorno would say, lamenting Benjamin's effort to demonstrate where he stood amid the perils of the 1930s by imitating "das plumpe Denken" of Brecht) vulgarly so. In this respect, Jameson's willingness, in the quotation given in my first paragraph, to speak of "the mystery of photography" indicates his willingness to avoid hidebound associations, a sign perhaps of sufficient realism to recognize the effects of the photograph's dissociation of the image from its context: a disconnection he might wish to remedy, like Brecht complaining of the silence of a photograph of the Krupps armaments factory regarding the networks of supply and policy converging upon it, by inserting it into the narrativity that is a key category of his thought. Jameson's retention of the word "mystery" is one reason why his criticism can illuminate the films of Angelopoulos, which could be seen as answering Jameson's unanswered question in "The Existence of Italy" concerning the apparently Münchhausenian project of saving the image through the image. Angelopoulos's squaring of this circle can be discerned paradigmatically in two moments in *Topio Stin Omichli* (*Landscape in the Mist*, 1988): in the emergence from the sea churning before Orestes of a grayish object whose enigmatic abstraction resolves itself into a statue's hand; and in the final image of the two children clutching the tree, a destination that cannot be in the Germany they are seeking, as the Greek border they have just crossed (but whose river crossing may be that of Lethe) is not adjacent to it. Each of these images is a transcendence of narrative that in fact sublates it, incorporating it as the temporality required both for the image to emerge and for its contemplation. The image is revolved, be it on screen, like the hand swung round by the helicopter, or in the mind of the spectator, as in the cryptic ending. Some useful reflections on such enigmas have been formulated by Andrew Horton, who remarks, "Commentators are swift to suggest it represents a classical past that no longer 'connects' with the Greek present . . . yet the *experience* of watching the hand emerge and rise creates something of a feeling of awe, of mystery, of potential."[12] Among other things, Angelopoulos is intent on restoring a sense of experience that juxtaposes disconnected images as pointers to an archipelago, island dots joined at some deep, invisible level, utilizing long shots, long takes, and pans to permit an ingathering of the various elements of a scene and spectators to contemplate their interrelationship, be it one of static tableau (the figures standing outside as snow falls in *Landscape in the Mist*), shifting mass (the motorbike mart in the same film), or a range of intermediate possibilities. Such filmic devices highlight film's ability to produce the temporality required for experience (the German *Erlebnis*), to—as Tarkovsky would have put it—"sculpt in time," during which a static image, be it a fragment inherently difficult to decipher, such as the statue's hand or the strip of film Orestes finds in the trash can, or the disjointed, reclining Lenin statue on the barge in *To Vlemma Tou Odyssea* (*Ulysses' Gaze*, 1995), can be contemplated meditatively from various sides. Through all this it remains an open possibility whether these images have the mystery of the fetish, cherished to ward off the trauma of death or dismemberment, mourning life as it was before the interventions of such ruptures as that of the Greek Civil War or the colonels' seizure of power in 1967, amid the underlying tonality of the director's melancholy science and the cold color schemes that privilege black, pale blue, and dark green, in wintry landscapes, or, as I will suggest later, display an unreadability in which an Adorno would discern artistic resistance to exchange.

The long groundswells of thought in Jameson, like the long takes of Angelopoulos, enable a breadth of contextualization of sociocultural phenomena characteristic of that rare thing, a genuinely dialectical procedure. Much of the generous breadth of this embrace reflects Jameson's mining of the utopian in the spirit of Ernst Bloch, whose thought's fundamental impulse he describes as involving "detecting the positive impulses at work within the negative ones, in appropriating the motor force of such destructive but collective passions as reactionary religion, nationalism, fascism, and even consumerism."[13] (Thus the "reactionary religion" mentioned here elsewhere dialectically displays another face Jameson describes as having "value ... for revolutionary activity":[14] the "conjunction of absolute belief and collective participation" that "distinguishes the force of religion from the less binding, more contemplative play of art proper.")[15] Thus a consideration of "the ideological functions of Mafia narratives" can then ask "what can be said to be their transcendent or Utopian function?,"[16] with *The Godfather* (1972) being deemed "to perform an urgent ideological function at the same time that it provides the vehicle for the investment of a desperate Utopian fantasy."[17] If Jameson's analysis of *The Godfather*, as well as the essay that contains it, "Reification and Utopia in Mass Culture,"[18] surprisingly leaves Bloch unmentioned, he stands behind the titular quotation of his keyword, "Utopia," along with his equally unnamed and dialectically necessary adversary, Lukács, whose own keyword "reification" also has a titular presence (the firm opposition between the two being one of the things documented in their exchange anthologized in New Left Books' *Aesthetics and Politics*). Jameson's nuanced analysis is a salutary, if unfortunately little-heeded, corrective to film and cultural studies' habitually simple derogatory use of the word "ideology," a move also available for correction through historicization, as Lenin did not accord it a negative connotation (it became so only when it was the one opponents propagated), while the philosophy of that assiduous student of Lenin, Althusser, with which Jameson is intimate, maintains that ideology will always be with us.

Reflecting on the legacy of Thomas More's *Utopia*, Jameson distinguishes between "two distinct lines of descendency from More's inaugural text: the one intent on the realization of the Utopian program, the other an obscure yet omnipresent Utopian impulse finding its way to the surface in a variety of covert expressions and practices."[19] This second, Blochian line of descent characterizes Jameson's own theorization, whose urge to totalize is subordinated to the imperative always to consider the history that blows a hole in the would-be systems to which his intimacy with the great German traditions of Marxist thought renders him nevertheless sympathetic. It also defines the constitutionally incomplete work of Angelopoulos, who told Gideon Bachmann that "if you look carefully . . . my films never really end. To me they are all "works in progress." Like building sites."[20] As Horton notes, "His ability to leave things out has the . . . effect of opening his films up for us to complete in our own minds."[21] What is more, this stimulation of and respect for addressees, a hallmark for Barthes of the text that is *scriptible*, leaves minds open to the constitutive incompleteness of the real, the above-mentioned Gödelian necessity of another system arising out of, and against, the consistency of any particular one.

In this context, therefore, Jameson's willingness to retain a word such as "mystery," in the incidental mention of photography quoted at the outset, escapes the strictures directed against that word in the opening section of Benjamin's "Work of Art" essay, while the late work of Angelopoulos, to which mystery is central, can also, as we will see below, have a value that might qualify some of Jameson's own reservations about it.

"Late Angelopoulos" and the Afterlives of Modernism

Since Jameson's contributions to film studies include cinema's contextualization in terms of his career-long reflection on the interrelations of realism, modernism, and postmodernism, and given his initial acceptance of Andrew Horton's designation of Angelopoulos as "the last modernist," it is no surprise that his consideration of the director's later work, particularly *Ulysses' Gaze*, invokes the last two of those periodizing categories. Early in that essay Jameson identifies "the eclipse of style" as a marker of the passing of modernism.[22] In this context, his mention of the "'non-synchronicity' of the history of cinema with respect to the neighboring histories of literature and painting"[23] allows one to ask whether this eclipse might apply more to the literary and painterly modern, inasmuch as there "le style c'est l'homme même," in the sense of depending to an unquantifiable degree on biological and other unconscious dimensions and motives: one plausible definition of modernism being the swamping of realism by the un- or semiconscious, the corresponding style being stream of consciousness (a stream flowing sometimes underground, sometimes above). In cinema, conversely, Astruc's *caméra stylo* is more a metaphor intended to elevate the prestige of a medium in which the link between its stylistic possibilities and a specific individuality is weakened by their mediation through the filmmaking collectivity and a technology available to others and imitable to a degree that can and should strip the idea of the auteur of some of its afflatus. "Style" may be seen therefore as fading with the advent of cinema itself, flaring up in high modernism in the arts in general as if in unconscious response to the strength of the threat to it associated with that very medium's emergence. Cinema's partial later replaying of the thematics and formal displacements of modernism, meanwhile, is muted not only by its inherent multiauthorship but also by the shadow realism casts over the medium through its photographic nature, a shadow dispelled only partially by digital technology, as audiences monitor screens for disparities between the digital images and the realities they simulate and to some extent still rest upon—as the industry is well aware.

If the historical space traversed by the narratives of "late Angelopoulos" possesses a new form of spatiality corresponding to their transnationality, as Jameson suggests,[24] it matches the director's production situation. Thus the clumsiness Jameson also discerns arguably results from the lack of any single audience as an addressee, itself the persistence into a moment he would call postmodern of an inherently modernistic feature.[25] It condemns auteurs to a deeper isolation than the one mitigated earlier by their embedding within national cinemas that provided audiences as unified as any could be, through intimate awareness of the contradictions structuring their own societies.

Moreover, whereas previously national cinemas offered counterweights to a text's internalized "Americanization," understood as menacing coherence through the need to enlist the largest possible audience to bankroll star salaries, unrivaled production values or cutting-edge special effects, and generate commensurate profits, the new European coproduction imperatives threaten coherence through the need to respond, if only with the bad faith of tokenism, to the desiderata of various national sponsors. The cooking of the artistic books that yields the notorious Europudding renders this no empty threat. The transnationalization of cinema cannot therefore simply be celebrated. The situation of the traveling players in *Landscape in the Mist* thus allegorizes that of Angelopoulos himself, conscious lateness anticipating possibly imminent demise: the *argathini* ("very late at night")[26] that is one of three keywords for *Mia Eoniotita Ke Mia Mera* (*Eternity and a Day*, 1998). The alternative offered by the outdoor screening in *Ulysses' Gaze*, unlike that in the simply nostalgic *Nuovo Cinema Paradiso* (*Cinema Paradiso*, Giuseppe Tornatore, 1988), is marked as utopian, in the colloquial sense of not really viable, by the opportunity it also extends to opponents well able also to take to, and take, the streets to frustrate it.

Geist der Utopie: Mist, Music, Shores, Emergence

Maybe it's only in our injuries, he said, that the future can take root.

—Rachel Cusk, *Transit*

The Sarajevo of *Ulysses' Gaze* is both place and non-place, real and imaginary at the same time.

—John Orr, *The Art and Politics of Film*

Although Jameson's two essays on Angelopoulos lay greater stress on the early films—particularly the 2015 "Collective Narrative" essay loosely based on his 1997 one[27]—I will argue below that the later films pursue most insistently what may be the great central theme of Jameson's work, that of utopia, which ceases to be defined primarily by negation through documentation of the political conditions that murder hope,[28] but appears periodically in a network of what T. S. Eliot would have called "hints and guesses":[29] in an imagery of mist; in a modified use of music; in an new interest in early cinema (in *Landscape in the Mist* in particular, in the expansion of imagination and cinema's birth); in moments explicitly presented as poetic; in the resonance of fragments of ancient statuary; and in a solidarity with the stranger in our midst.

Jameson's prioritization of narrative may cause him to ignore the importance of these largely nonnarrative elements. His apparent disquiet over the status he sees *Ulysses' Gaze* as having achieved, that of having, "for a non-political age," "replaced" *The Travelling Players* as "the most legendary cinematic icon of the Left,"[30] as well as his definite "mixed feelings" regarding the later work in general,[31] seem also to reflect a belief that it displays, and is vitiated by, an attenuation of the political. I would argue however that the development it unfolds is genuinely dialectical, not so much denying the political as assuming it into more complex, open structures, interweaving a Brechtian modernist method with tragic and existential motifs and strategies and superimposing a closer attention to the individual, and his or her membership of a couple, upon the earlier one to the larger collectivity. And if old and new levels fail to fuse completely, or even exemplify an Adornian "logic of disintegration," this surely indicates a clear-eyed registration of the power of contradiction. Should this be the case, an aphoristic line from the Austrian modernist poet Georg Trakl may be relevant: "Wie scheint doch alles Werdende so krank!" (How all that is becoming seems so sick!).[32] Conversely, it may simply be that a great artist's evolution is always potentially disconcerting (Kieślowski's after *Dekalog* [*The Decalogue*, 1988] was so for me at the time);[33] one may not discern its necessity at first. Admirers of one phase of an artist's work may wish to see new ones cast from the old mold, particularly when that earlier strain of work has convinced them, as it had Jameson, that the films of Angelopoulos "are clearly better than anyone else's."[34] The reaction to the transformation may therefore even involve a certain grief. The following section will argue however that although the voyage of "Late Angelopoulos" takes him beyond the earlier films, because they were in a sense its precondition, it remains in dialogue with them (most explicitly so in the case of the relationship between *The Travelling Players* and *Landscape in the Mist*).

If a Blochian leitmotif of the utopian pervades Jameson's thought, it is because of Bloch's concern for the future,[35] logically paired therefore with meditations on science fiction in Jameson's own *Archaeologies of the Future*. The importance of Angelopoulos for Jameson lies not just in their sharing of socialism's commitment to collective life, but in the adumbration in the Greek director's work of possible future forms of filmmaking and perception in a world of increasingly pervasive crossings of borders, be they in necessary flight from underdeveloped or disaster-stricken communities, in search of a lost homeland, or in quest of an exit from the increasing authoritarianism of a more developed world intent on forestalling any crossings of its own borders. Thus, despite his worries about the strands of an individualistic existentialism in the late work of Angelopoulos, not to mention an increasing organization of works around such well-established actors as Marcello Mastroianni, Harvey Keitel, and Bruno Ganz or "the flaws and clumsiness of aspects of this convulsive effort,"[36] Jameson's 1997 essay on the director concludes that "it is at the very least an extraordinary destiny for a filmmaker, who already achieved a distinctive oeuvre at the end of the modern period, to have been sufficiently receptive to the deeper swirling currents and trends of history after postmodernity itself to have projected his artistic language into a work such as *Ulysses' Gaze*, whose active prophecy of new and future forms will not be its least and most negligible achievement."[37] Some of the forms of that prophecy are manifest in the often-interlocking features of the late films enumerated in my previous paragraph. Where Angelopoulos's move away from nonprofessionals is concerned, however, it is worth recalling his stated purely technical motive: "When I first started making films, I didn't like professional actors much. Their performance seemed false to me. I preferred to work with nonprofessionals, but I found out that they aren't always sensitive to the pace of a scene and they tend to overplay the dramatic moments."[38] He is in no sense another Visconti, moving from *La Terra Trema* (*The Earth Trembles*, 1948) to *Morte a Venezia* (*Death in Venice*, 1971). The clumsiness meanwhile may be that of a human repetition of the suspended step of the stork, or of the new in general: the new as "the yearning for the new, hardly that new thing itself," for "the Utopia that feels itself to be such remains a negative of the existent, and in bondage to it."[39] Meanwhile, if *Ulysses' Gaze* envisages a condition that is beyond postmodernity and this can be parsed to mean one that is aware of history in a way in which Jameson deems the postmodern not to be, its cardinal feature may be the sense of an ongoing woundedness by history that not only fueled the Balkan Wars of the 1990s but underpins the self-legitimations of such Eastern-Central European nationalist governments currently in power as those of Hungary and Poland.

One of the late films' figurations of a future form, necessarily halting in the light of a twentieth-century Greek history scarred by the traumatic legacy of the Civil War of 1945–1952 and then the suppression of democracy by the colonels' seizure of power and subsequent junta rule between 1967 and 1974 would come from more distant pasts that include the classical one and whose preexistence reignites hopes that hope can indeed assume material form, resurrect lost possibilities, and restore those either thought dead (Orestes, Ulysses) or exiled and pronounced dead in public discourse, even if not, tragically, the actual dead themselves. When A. says what will happen, in the Homeric monologue he utters at the end of *Ulysses' Gaze*, he leaves its occurrence to the imagination-stimulating offstage whose importance for Greek tragedy Angelopoulos has noted.[40] These events' futurity may be figured by their separation from the film itself, as it extrudes its original planned ending, a simulation of the apocryphal fifty-two-second early Manakis brothers' film of Ulysses' landing on Ithaca's shores that would have matched its opening commitment to early cinema: an ending then located elsewhere, in the multiauthorial homage to those other founding brothers of early cinema, the Lumières, in *Lumière et compagnie* (1995). *Ulysses' Gaze* wonders whether viable "new and future forms" will indeed emerge from the depths to which it shows national cultures sinking, whether in moving through them A. may be only alphabetically and ironically the first, while actually that protagonist of science fiction, "the last man." For even if Greek culture may retain traces of a lost, viable world in a DNA either hidden underground or buried in that signifier of the unconscious, water, a border crossing into the past may well not escape the attendant dangers of the utopia known as time travel, as in *Ulysses' Gaze* A. hears the execution and exile orders against the Manakis brothers read against himself.

Contrastingly, a resonant utopian image, in which the constitutive nonexistence of the genre's object is in a sense *aufgehoben* (rising mist a curtain carrying upward the idea of the screen behind it . . .) is offered by the last image of *Landscape in the Mist*. Just as the film "began" abstractly, after its pre-credit sequence, with darkness and the voice of Vuola recounting to her younger brother Alexander the creation myth of light's separation from darkness, so it seems to "begin again" beyond the darkness of the river we see them begin crossing in search of the father they believe is in Germany. What supervenes is a grayness instinct with possibility and reminiscent of that of the strip of film Orestes, the only survivor of Angelopoulos's earlier traveling players with whom they interact at length, had found in a trash can and given to Alexander. As he held up the frames up against a screen-like white background, Orestes had asked what Alexander could see there, responding to his statement "nothing" with "Behind the mist, in the distance, can't you see a tree?" When Alexander maintained he still could not see anything, Orestes, both artist and congenial companion, said "Me neither. I was kidding." Irrespective of whether he too saw nothing, the film's conclusion suggests he has sown in Alexander's mind a seed that will indeed blossom as a tree

drawn quasi-magically out of "nothing," out of thin air, offering the children shelter, in a possible veiling or acceptance of the father's irremediable absence. It is
as if the mist has erased the landscape as a prelude for reinscription. When Orestes
describes the children as "going somewhere and going nowhere," the phrase could
define any trajectory toward utopia, the word "nowhere" having served either to
"English" utopia, as in Morris's *News from Nowhere*, or been reversed to match
utopia's overturning of current orders, as in Samuel Butler's *Erewhon*. The blank-
ness of the film image may belong to a nowhere incubating a somewhere
indeed, one whose status as elsewhere renders it adjacent to a science fictional
consciousness, in an alternative history or dimensionality, perhaps a Deleuzian
"any-place-whatever," where Germany borders Greece. Meanwhile, if the landscape's erasure creates the nowhere of utopia, within it the tree extends the
missing father's protection in a displaced, metaphorical, or mythical form, as if
a Greek deity had metamorphosed him into a tree. The centrality to Norse
mythology of the ash tree Yggdrasill, the world's axis, renders its presence also
implicitly plausibly representative of the Germany they are seeking. It stands in
a utopian space beyond a river that has become the equally utopian form of the
River of Death. If its poetic multivalence renders it akin to the Tree of Life, as
Horton has noted,[41] its placement beyond the river aligns it also with the German *Totenbaum* (tree of death); and given Jung's reading of the *Totenbaum* as
indicating that *"the dead are delivered back to the mother for rebirth,"*[42] it may
betoken oneirically a return to the mother that cannot be acknowledged, for
the absent father is the primary conscious object of desire.

As in the work of Bloch, to whose utopia music is central,[43] a privileged space
of absent presence is also shaped by the plangent scores of Eleni Karaindrou, the
advent of whose musical collaboration with Angelopoulos coincides with what
he declares the beginning of his work's "second phase," in *Taxidi Sta Kithiri (Voyage to Cythera,* 1983) and may be read as ushering it in. After all, if the question
"How many borders do we have to cross before we can get home?" is a recurrent
one, formulated in *To Meteoro Vima To Pelargou (The Suspended Step of the Stork,*
1991) and reiterated in *Ulysses' Gaze,* music itself presides over, and enacts, a border crossing, floating over and around barriers. Karaindrou's is in a sense "meta-
music," at least in relation to the diegetic short folk, popular, and partisan tunes
that shaped individual scenes in the earlier works; crossing the borders of scenes,
it suggests possible access to a level of unspoken synthesis. The way an invisible
tenant of the opposite building continues playing music heard by Alexander in
Eternity and a Day when he himself switches it off creates a unity of spirit across
the unbreached space between them, as if anticipating the singing engaged in
by Siennese on their balconies when COVID-19 self-isolation prevented physical closeness. And it may be appropriate to consider here Jameson's statement that
Ulysses' Gaze allows one "to posit the possibility of some new narrative form of
regional mapping, over against the world system," one "reaching out beyond the
older national allegory in order to invent a cultural politics commensurable with

the new world system."[44] Rather than any attempt at delineation of a world system of markets whose intricacies, uneven development, and staggered time scales (among other things) render it all but unrepresentable, that reaching out might be figured in music's creation of solidarity, it being an equally abstract and possibly therefore well-matched counterweight to that system's abstraction, becoming as it were the modern form of the "universal language" once discerned in the silent cinema haunting *Ulysses' Gaze* (the opening early film of weavers allowing one to imagine really seeing Penelope with Ulysses' eyes). In each case the passage is one beyond the confines of the language that renders allegory national. This passage may be one into silence, into waving at inaudible others on a far shore or massing to become visible, and silent cinema may be an art of the future inasmuch as it shows, as if through a telescope, those we cannot hear, whose place, blessed or cursed, might become ours, though we might just catch the distant strains of their music, or the pianist accompanying most films might just do so, rendering the cinema an auditorium indeed.

Considered in this context the repetitions Andrew Horton deems Faulknerian,[45] such as the recurrence of the traveling players in *Landscape in the Mist*; the name of Alexander in film after film; or such images as the yellow-clad travelers crossing the protagonists' paths in *Landscape in the Mist*, *The Suspended Step of the Stork*, or *Eternity and a Day*, also become musical. When Alexander, the poet protagonist of *Eternity and a Day*, says his one regret is never having finished anything, he echoes Angelopoulos's own confession of the constitutive incompletion of his own works, as if any claim to round them out would be tantamount to the transgression classical Greek thought patterns identified as hubris. When Ted Hughes states in his poem sequence *Crow*, apropos the Oedipus myth, that one of the two human responses to "what you cannot understand" is to sing to it (the other abandoning it on the royal road to the unconscious, like Oedipus himself, as one sleeps on it),[46] he locates the birth of art in the spirit of music, as Angelopoulos seems to come to do in his late works. The image of that incomprehension, that Adornian recognition of the nonidentity of the object, is standing staring on the shore, as Alexander does in the final shot of *Eternity and a Day*, as spectators stare similarly at the back of the head that withholds revelation of the face. At the shore's edge one plays as if to solicit the unknown reality the sea secretes. And it is there that, according to a fragment of Heraklitos alluded to by Angelopoulos in the child's definition of time given at the film's outset, one encounters time, which adds to eternity the day that spoils its completeness and opens it up magically to the new. And so this film's title preserves the collective speech of folklore under the auspices of an avowal of love and a utopian temporality.

For Angelopoulos, the look to the future is one at and across water, or the mist whose shifting suggests a coming unveiling of new forms, such as the tree, to music playing in celebration or pronouncing the spell that makes it happen. Mist, which so often arises at shores, as the different temperatures of land and sea converge, may therefore be called both a marker and unmaker of borders. The "meditation on everything dialectical about the border" Jameson's most recent essay on Angelopoulos discerns in these later films should logically include mist, particularly if the border is conceptualized, as Jameson does so memorably, as "a space somehow beyond the world itself even though subject to everything that happens on either side of it."[47] Its importance to *Landscape in the Mist* lies in its creation of the image of an absence from which something may emerge, and this key signifier of Angelopoulos's late works may powerfully enrich Bachelard's typology of the transformations of water (the Greek tutelary philosophical spirit of Angelopoulos's late works surely being Thales).[48] The image found in the ash can by Orestes, duplicated in the mist beyond the river at the work's end, is one whose emptiness and unwantedness allows space for all those history has discarded or victimized, becoming the place of pure possibility where Alexander sees the tree described by Orestes, who thereby becomes a father to the fatherless, figuring embodiment of Bloch's principle of hope. Mist's formlessness, potentiality, and ambiguity lend it particular importance for a Bachelardian typology of the relationship between the elements and dreams. And yet it is also Homeric, recalling the mist deities throw around heroes to hide them from foes. As if recalling this device of the Homeric deities, *Ulysses' Gaze* shows fog unfolding a cloak of invisibility over the inhabitants of Sarajevo during the Balkan Wars, preventing snipers from picking them out. Music's floating quality matches that of the mist that enables the unmolested playing of the Youth Orchestra of Sarajevo. Similarly, in *Eternity and a Day* mist envelops the Albanian refugees standing by and clinging to the border fence, as if complicit with their desire to shed an old identity.

For Angelopoulos mist effects a modernist estrangement and renewal of vision like the one seen/unseen in the English poet John Clare's "Mist in the Meadows":

Mist in the hollows reaks and curdles up
Like fallen clouds that spread—and things retire
Less seen and less—the shepherd passes near
And little distant most grotesquely shades
As walking without legs—lost to his knees . . . [49]

Mist, that agent of disappearance and hence imminent symbolic death or loss, also becomes utopian through a blurring of borders, including temporal ones, that renders them passable. One may be on the far side already and not even know it yet. And here Angelopoulos's imagery and thought intersect with those of Tarkovsky, whose *Nostalghia* (1983) shares a number of features with *Ulysses' Gaze*, whose poetics of the elements accords pride of place to water, which is sublated as mist. Mutable as it is, water either gives birth to separate material entities, like the statue or the tree in *Landscape in the Mist*, or conceals a lost world, like the ancient, earthquake-destroyed city of which Alexander's unseen child-companion speaks in *Eternity and a Day*, which comes out of the water every once in a while, significantly at a moment of nostalgia, "when the morning star is homesick for the earth." Angelopoulos also locates his scenarios in northern Greece because an awareness of this climatically other Greece reinforces awareness of the country's politically defeated other identity, driven to and beyond its margins, and because mist so often lines and limns the shores dotted by loved ones hoping for their return, from exile or prison. It consoles with the thought that its very presence may be the reason why one cannot see them yet.

In addition to this, mist also activates a Bressonian aesthetic, allowing sound (music in particular) to come into its own as and precisely *because* the image fades. This too is utopian, cinema's practice of a self-denying ordinance: the music of the Sarajevo youth orchestra strikes up and couples dance as mist descends on the war-torn city, permitting a rebirth of a benign collective life amid the tribalist collectivism of war. Mist veils the killings of Ivo's family near the end of *Ulysses' Gaze*, re-creating the offstage that is the structuring absence of Greek tragedy. A utopian gaze would be answered by a world where no one had to see such things.

The frame full of mist in *Landscape in the Mist* is like a developing tray. One does not know what may emerge from it, and it is similarly unclear what will come of, or befall, the voyaging children of this film or *Eternity and a Day*. Likewise, the statue emerging from the sea in the former film seems at first possibly the beginning of the appearance of a monstrous sea creature. That suggestion of a sea monster is one of a rewritten *La Dolce Vita* (Federico Fellini, 1960), running backward from the beached fish of its end to the bearing away by helicopter of the quasi-sacred image of its opening sequence: this echo of Fellini's film, noted by Vassiliki Kolocotoni,[50] concatenates end and beginning in a manner that may be quite deliberate, as T. S. Eliot's "in my end is my beginning" is quoted by A. near the beginning of *Ulysses' Gaze*, the concern with time echoing that of Eliot's *Four Quartets*. The sea's surging suggests the first stirrings of the undersea city invoked at the beginning of *Eternity and a Day*. The fluidity of the image is that of an emerging out of the cinematic dark that is a writing large (consider the size of the statue's hand . . .), a macrocosm, of the darkroom and its developing fluid. The shores of rivers and seas are sites of nostalgia, memory, and aspiration, for internal or imminent exiles, but also of the primal separation of the elements themselves: places from which one looks toward those who have left, like Alexis in the boat in *To Livadi Pou Dakryzei* (*The Weeping Meadow*, 2004), after the dropping away of the tangible thread linking him to the shore, as the sweater knit for him by Eleni unravels. Angelopoulos's pans suggest a dialectically countervailing, because utopian, crossing of borders, as when, in *Eternity and a Day*, the camera moves from the poet Alexander to the nineteenth century's Dyonisios Solomos, the thread of the pan being dropped or cut in this case as and when its movement can stop, this time *happily*, upon attachment to a past usually considered lost, to which the present can be moored. And here there is a point of difference with Jameson, whose most influential reading of nostalgia couples it with a postmodern depthlessness and commodification,[51] though he too might discern in mist a venue for the mysterious brewing of new matter, and not necessarily a cosmetic applied to the existent. Bloch, of course, endorses the linkage of nostalgia and utopia under the aegis of music, quoting approvingly Jean Paul's rhetorical question whether "the higher attribute of music" might be "its power of nostalgia, a nostalgia not for an old country we have left behind but for a virgin one, not for a past but for a future."[52]

The natural inhabitant of the utopia whose other name is "nowhere" is no-man. That was of course the name wherewith Ulysses identified himself to Polyphemous, whom his fellow cyclops mocked when he cried out that no-man had blinded him. The protagonist A. is aligned explicitly with Ulysses-as-no-man when the barge he has boarded reaches a tripartite border control and the captain answers the enquiry about possible passengers by stating "nobody." In a similar spirit, the disappeared politician of *The Suspended Step of the Stork* once made a taped statement denying that we can call anything our own, not even our names. No wonder the names or identities of Ulysses and Penelope or Alexander undergo reincarnation in film after film, slipping from one character to another. The runaway bride of *The Weeping Meadow*, Eleni, may bear a different name, but she becomes Penelope by knitting her husband Alexis a sweater that unravels as he holds it while sitting in the boat taking him to the ship to America, and the Manakis brothers' short film shown at the beginning of *Ulysses' Gaze* pointedly records women weaving, as if to show the descendants of Penelope known to the brothers and give them primacy ahead of a still later incarnation of Ulysses, Harvey Keitel's A. Thus the other natural inhabitant of nowhere is no-woman. That epic namelessness and constant companionship render the late works of Angelopoulos not simply regressive, because "organised around an individual protagonist."[53] The apparently individualistic *Ulysses' Gaze* breathes a constant yearning for soulmate, family, and community, while reducing the protagonist's name to A. lends him a prototypicality that counteracts the specificity of the filmed individual, whose identity in this case as Keitel may be a Brechtian estrangement (as so much in this film is Brechtian) appropriate to a supposed Greek emigrant. His actual Romanian-Polish Jewish descent may even reinforce the film's search for a position beyond identities set in conflict. The focus is not individualistic but underscores the protagonist's quest to rediscover the possibilities of relationship, association and commitment traduced by local tribalisms and threatened by a world system that values only transient attachments and frequent relocation. Couplings across ethnicities oppose the former, while pairings of any kind become germs of the alliance that resists the latter. Similarly, in *Eternity and a Day* the poet soon finds himself accompanying and protecting the young Albanian refugee and has long doubled the nineteenth-century poet Dyonisios Solomos, while his dog's constant presence indicates a desire for the "best friend" it symbolizes conventionally, and like A. in *Ulysses' Gaze* he continually encounters groups. Even the echoes of Bergman's *Smulltron-stället* (*Wild Strawberries*, 1957) can be read as asserting solidarity with a fellow artist, their arguable overinsistence deliberately underlining the debt and possibly exemplifying Adorno's contention that the greatest artworks are those that are lucky or successful ("Glück haben") even at their most dubious points.[54]

At one point in *Landscape in the Mist* Vuola writes to the absent father that sometimes they forget him and do not know if they are going backward or forward, thinking that they are lost. It is surely significant that being lost is often represented metaphorically by being in mist. The film's title suggests such a loss of direction not only by mentioning mist but through its very first word, "topio," which may have the specificity of "landscape" but is also shadowed, through the poetic displacement mechanism of echo and the difference of a mere letter or two, by the abstraction and vagueness of "topos," "place," whose plural is of course "topoi." When the film finally arrives at one, in the rural and utopian (even Edenic) space whose axis is a tree, its emergence follows the logic of a phrase by Rilke, "nur wo du bist, entsteht ein Ort" (only where you are does a place arise),[55] as if the fact of relationship threw down a bridge across the abyss looming at the center of modernity, be it Baudelaire's version of Pascal's one, "avec lui se mouvant," or the Nietzschean one that returns its viewer's gaze. Rilke becomes particularly appropriate through the film's explicit entry into the orbit of his work just after the emergence of the statue's hand, which precedes Orestes's quotation of the famous opening of the *Duino Elegies*, "Wer, wenn ich schriee, hörte mich denn aus der Engel / Ordnungen?" (Who, if I screamed, would hear me among the angel orders?).[56] His subsequent slumping forward onto his motorbike's handlebars may activate recollection of another work by Rilke, his reaction to the fragment of classical sculpture resembling the Rilkean one to the archaic torso of Apollo, which although headless seemed to see and speak and exhort "Du mußt dein Leben ändern" (You must change your life).[57] As the hand, raised by a helicopter, points toward Orestes and the children, subsequently moving away as if to trace the trajectory of a voyage to be imitated, its ambiguous import even enfolds a suggestion of the pointing hands of recruiting posters, singling him out on the eve of his military service. Its dreamlike pointing, all the more mysterious for the fragmentation of the finger, suggests equally well the power of a militarized, alienated state and that of an otherworldly, now fragmented religious past. (In the context of possible manifestations of those powers, its emergence anticipates that of the head of Apollo from another element, the earth cracking open, described by A. in *Ulysses' Gaze*.) Considered in the Rilkean context of Orestes's words, the hand he sees might also be Rodinesque.

Over Angelopoulos's career, the poetic identity whose dissolution permitted his turn to filmmaking persists, sublated, in works whose charged imagery resists the easy exchange of "the administered world" with the intensity Adorno ascribed to the least readable of modern works, those of Beckett and Celan.

Thus Angelopoulos himself would remark that "the symbolic elements are a means of escaping the confines of the simple narrative, explorations of a surreal world. They are inserted into the fabric of the script, though quite often I am not sure what they mean. For instance, I couldn't really tell you the significance of the stone hand pulled out of the Thessaloniki harbor."[58] Given Walter Benjamin's sympathy with surrealism, these insertions—particularly the combination of helicopter and ancient statue in *Landscape in the Mist*—might seem to enact his proposed "blasting" of objects "out of the continuum of history's course" through the maximal tension inherent in "dialectical images," though the multiple questions bedeviling that concept, and summarized in part by Susan Buck-Morss,[59] may render this speculation moot. The importance of these moments, however, which arise most often when forward movement encounters a barrier of some kind, may be underplayed in any analysis committed primarily to mapping narrative (in Jakobson's terms, to metonymy rather than metaphor), such as that of the Lukács whose project Jameson defined as involving "a continuous and lifelong meditation on narrative."[60] Thus the threat to "genuine narration" is not one of "static poetry,"[61] as poetry represents the antidote narrative needs to evolve (as it does in modernism) to counter its own temptation to flatness, to the horizontality of the merely contiguous, to naturalism's mortgaging of narration to the triteness (skewered most acidly by Karl Kraus) endemic in the discourse of the burgeoning mass media. In this sense, modernism reacts more to naturalism than realism. The image may be anything but static but rather whirl up in what Pound called a vortex, mining both depth and height, teeming with life and multiple meanings, a waterspout in one of the rivers contemplated or traveled by one of Angelopoulos's protagonists. At such points in the "late" films the immersion in materiality Jameson deems a signal and exemplary feature of Angelopoulos's earlier work (for instance, the bus whose wheels churn the mud in *Anaparastasis* [*Reconstruction*, 1970]) expands into an unresolved potentiality of form and meaning, be it that of such indeterminate matter as the water whose depths or far shore may harbor something of uncertain import, or a determinate object grown hauntingly mysterious, like the statue of Lenin wrenched from its functional context and strapped to a barge in *Ulysses' Gaze*. There therefore ceases to be a felt need, such as Jameson describes,[62] to emerge from the moment, as most would wish to from mud, but rather a suspension of the imperative to progress that can suspend narrative itself and the often ruthless forward impulsion of late modern society. It may perhaps appear most stunningly at the film's actual end, like the tree in *Landscape in the Mist*, but also, more mutedly in ceremonies, many of them what Jameson calls the films' "set-pieces,"[63] or the icon-like, frontal images that cause Horton to invoke Byzantine art.[64] Angelopoulos's commitment to escape narrative may also represent one able to elude the form of fatality known as teleology, and it renders his protagonists' stares at and across water ones at an unconscious that is not simply political, though it is that too, as the far side may be dotted with members of a community that has been impressed to stand for the Other, and bodies may lie beneath the waters. But he also explores it like an archaeologist, an explicitly poetic, political, and hence corrected Freud even, hoping not just for recovery, reemergence, and, where persons are concerned, return, but for the fragment offering a clue to the future. The clue may be as small and yet weighty as a name, and naming's magic may usher in a return of Orestes or Alexander or provide a space for occupation by a future carrier of those names. It might be an earnest of the return of elements of the past that have acquired through burial and oblivion the power of germs of new possibility, like the body whose immersion ("sea-change") renders its parts "rich and strange" in that other late work, *The Tempest*,[65] the above-mentioned statue's hand, or the Manakis brothers' lost, first film. What might emerge however is mostly unseen or not yet seen, like the absent body of the statue. In this context, one of the things to which its hand points is the tree's emergence at the film's end, as if Orestes's imagination, in priming the seeing of something where there seems to be nothing, had rendered Alexander a younger (future) version of the poet who stands center stage in *Eternity and a Day*.

Conclusion

A collective identity free of tribalism is often deemed utopian in the colloquial sense of impossible. So too might an escape from the alternative possible outcomes of crossing a border mentioned by the Greek colonel in *The Suspended Step of the Stork*, who lifts his foot as if to breach the Albanian one: "If I take one more step, I will be somewhere else. Or die," the latter alternative indicating his possible shooting by border guards. Utopia means being somewhere else without the deadly danger of a border-crossing; it may therefore be the fruit of imagination indeed. As Adam Cichoń remarks of this film, "Lifted from the ground, the foot remains for a moment without territory. It is between places, does not belong to the earth, is without status, undefined."[66] The principle of hope in Jameson and Angelopoulos, as in Bloch, coupled with an awareness of the ruses of history's reason and the vicissitudes of a dialectic whose work is one of transformation, forestalls the widespread identification of "utopian" and "impossible," however. The difficulty of landing in such a place, of the arrival in Ithaka Angelopoulos sure-footedly leaves unrepresented in *Ulysses' Gaze*, is spelled out in the final question excerpted from the vanished politician's book titled *Despair at the End of the Century* in *The Suspended Step . . .* : "What are the key words we could use in order to make a new collective dream come true?" The explicit and implicit invocations of Rilke in *Landscape in the Mist* noted above may be taken in this context as correcting the subjectivity of that poet's recipe for healing, the subsuming of religion into art that confounded the necessary distinction between them in the Jamesonian passage on Bloch and religion quoted earlier. In other words, unlike Rilke, Angelopoulos may be taken as recognizing utterance's need for the answering and sustaining collectivity travestied in the unheavenly order of the army that will soon swallow Orestes up. A true one would preserve the camaraderie of the traveling players and supply them with times and places hospitable to their performances, allowing them to finish (as *Golfo the Shepherdess* never does in *The Travelling Players*), not punctuating them with warfare or a bursting onto the stage of political factions. The life of the players, like that of the musicians Alexis joins in *The Weeping Meadow*, posits a utopia that is beyond tribalism because, like the raised foot as described by Cichoń, it lacks territory, and so never needs those armies and militias whose ravaging of his native Greece and Balkans Angelopoulos mourns. The shape of his career, which began with an aspiration to be a poet but issued in filmmaking, may be taken as his deeply communal innermost spirit's correction, though not repudiation, of that initial lyric ambition. Filmmaking would itself be a utopian, productive resolution of the contradictory demands of individual expression and the recognition of the collectivity upon which any expression, not just so obviously any film, depends, requiring immediate collaborators and the audience that will justify its shaping.

The way the repetitions within Angelopoulos's work point to a deliberate, Gödelian recognition of the incompleteness of any system, including his own artistic one, to a Blochian Open System, breathes an openness that strips utopia of its aspirations to totalize and enclose, as the genre has tended to do from the outset and as the would-be realizers of political utopias have done in practice, creating airless, often deadly totalitarian spaces. The drift of mist is that of a spirit, its placelessness utopian. The incompletion of the space over which it hangs, whose borders it problematizes, is a suspension of the step less easy for humans than for storks, which stand one-leggedly with aplomb. With their Bloch-like openness to the future and their dialectic of incompletion, Jameson and Angelopoulos adopt a similar stance, one demanding more effort than that expended by a philosophical bird one might set over against, and prefer to, Hegel's owl. It may do so postmodernistically, for its flight does not betoken the imminent ending of any grand narrative, or indeed of anything at all. There can always be hope, that supremely Blochian principle, as one waits, awkwardly, energy held in reserve, one foot upraised, teleology suspended, for a next step in history that could also be historic. . . .

Notes

1 Fredric Jameson, *Signatures of the Visible* (New York: Routledge, 2007), 217.
2 Jameson, *Signatures of the Visible*, 223.
3 Jameson, *Signatures of the Visible*, 225.
4 T. W. Adorno, *Negative Dialektik* (Frankfurt am Main: Suhrkamp, 1966), 13.
5 Andrew Horton, ed., *The Last Modernist: The Films of Theo Angelopoulos* (Westport, CT: Greenwood, 1997).
6 Cf. Fredric Jameson, *The Seeds of Time* (New York: Columbia University Press, 1994).
7 Fredric Jameson, *Brecht and Method* (London: Verso, 1998), 40.

8 Perry Anderson, *The Origins of Postmodernity* (London: Verso, 1998), 53.

9 Fredric Jameson, "Reflections in Conclusion," in *Aesthetics and Politics* (London: New Left Books, 1979), 197.

10 Jameson, "Reflections in Conclusion," 196.

11 Walter Benjamin, "The Work of Art in the Age of Its Technological Reproducibility: Second Version," in *The Work of Art in the Age of Its Technological Reproducibility and Other Writings*, ed. Michael W. Jennings, Brigid Docherty, and Thomas Y. Levin (Cambridge, MA: Harvard University Press, 2008), 20.

12 Andrew Horton, *The Films of Theo Angelopoulos: A Cinema of Contemplation* (Princeton, NJ: Princeton University Press, 1997), 12.

13 Jameson, *Signatures of the Visible*, 96.

14 Fredric Jameson, *Marxism and Form: Twentieth-Century Dialectical Theories of Literature* (Princeton: Princeton University Press, 1971), 157.

15 Jameson, *Marxism and Form*, 156.

16 Jameson, *Signatures of the Visible*, 43.

17 Jameson, *Signatures of the Visible*, 44.

18 Fredric Jameson, "Reification and Utopia in Mass Culture," in Jameson, *Signatures of the Visible*, 11–46.

19 Fredric Jameson, *Archaeologies of the Future: The Desire Called Utopia and Other Science Fictions* (London: Verso, 2005), 3.

20 Gideon Bachmann, "The Time That Flows By: Theo Angelopoulos in Conversation with Gideon Bachmann," *Film Comment* 34, no. 4 (July–August 1998): 49.

21 Horton, *Films of Theo Angelopoulos*, 10.

22 Fredric Jameson, "Theo Angelopoulos: The Past as History, the Future as Form," in Horton, *Last Modernist*, 79.

23 Jameson, "Theo Angelopoulos," 81.

24 Jameson, "Theo Angelopoulos," 78.

25 Jameson, "Theo Angelopoulos," 92.

26 Bachmann, "Time That Flows By," 51.

27 Fredric Jameson, "Angelopoulos and Collective Narrative," in *The Ancients and the Postmoderns: On the Historicity of Forms* (London: Verso, 2015), 131–148.

28 For more on the Greek history of most immediate relevance to Angelopoulos's work, see the informative long footnote by Dan Georgakas quoted at the beginning of Jameson's "Angelopoulos and Collective Narrative," 131–132.

29 T. S. Eliot, *Four Quartets* (London: Faber, 1970), 44.

30 Jameson, "Angelopoulos and Collective Narrative," 133.

31 Jameson, "Theo Angelopoulos," 88.

32 Georg Trakl, *Das dichterische Werk* (Munich: DTV, 1974), 29.

33 See, for instance, my "Metaphysical Love in Two Films by Krzysztof Kieślowski," *Polish Review* 37, no. 3 (1992): 335–343, and for some later reactions to *La double vie de Véronique* (*The Double Life of Véronique*, France/Poland, 1991), my *The Red and the White: The Cinema of People's Poland* (London: Wallflower, 2005), 207–208, and *Doubling, Distance and Identification in the Cinema* (Basingstoke: Palgrave Macmillan, 2015), 76–88.

34 Jameson, "Theo Angelopoulos," 89.

35 Jameson, *Marxism and Form*, 116–159.

36 Jameson, "Theo Angelopoulos," 92.

37 Jameson, "Theo Angelopoulos," 94.

38 "*Landscape in the Mist*," interview with Serge Toubiana and Frédéric Strauss, in *Theo Angelopoulos: Interviews*, ed. Dan Fainaru (Jackson: University Press of Mississippi, 2001), 62.

39 T. W. Adorno, *Ästhetische Theorie* (Frankfurt am Main: Suhrkamp, 1974), 55.

40 Adorno, *Ästhetische Theorie*, 206.

41 Adorno, *Ästhetische Theorie*, 159.

42 C. G. Jung, *Symbols of Transformation: An Analysis of the Prelude to a Case of Schizophrenia*, trans. R. F. C. Hull (Princeton: Princeton University Press, 1976), 233, emphasis original.

43 Jameson, *Marxism and Form*, 143.

44 Jameson, "Theo Angelopoulos," 94.

45 Horton, *Films of Theo Angelopoulos*, 15.

46 Ted Hughes, *Crow: From the Life and Songs of the Crow* (London: Faber & Faber, 1970), 65.

47 Jameson, "Angelopoulos and Collective Narrative," 133.

48 Gaston Bachelard, *L'Eau et les rêves: Essai sur l'imagination de la matière* (Paris: Librarire José Corti, 1942).

49 John Clare, "Mist in the Meadows," in *Selected Poems and Prose of John Clare*, ed. Eric Robinson and Geoffrey Summerfield (Oxford: Oxford University Press, 1978), 154.

50 See Vassiliki Kolocontroni, "Monuments of Time: The Works of Theo Angelopoulos," in *Post-war Cinema and Modernity: A Reader*, ed. John Orr and Olga Taxidou (Edinburgh: Edinburgh University Press, 2000), 406n2.

51 Fredric Jameson, "Postmodernism, or the Cultural Logic of Late Capitalism," *New Left Review* 146 (July–August 1984): 53–92.

52 Ernst Bloch, *Essays on the Philosophy of Music*, trans. Peter Palmer (Cambridge: Cambridge University Press, 1991), 132.

53 Jameson, "Theo Angelopoulos," 89.

54 T. W. Adorno, "Rede über Lyrik und Gesellschaft," in *Noten zur Literatur* (Frankfurt am Main: Suhrkamp, 1975), 1:102.

55 Elizabeth Barrett-Browning, *Sonette aus dem Portugiesischen*, trans. Rainer Maria Rilke (Leipzig: Insel Verlag, 1908), 9.

56 Rainer Maria Rilke, *Werke in drei Bänden, Erster Band*, ed. Horst Nalewski (Leipzig: Insel, 1978), 579.

57 Rilke, *Werke in drei Bänden*, 467.

58 Toubiana and Strauss interview, 63.

59 Susan Buck-Morss, *The Dialectics of Seeing: Walter Benjamin and the Arcades Project* (Cambridge, MA: MIT Press, 1989), 219–22.

60 Jameson, *Marxism and Form*, 163.

61 Jameson, *Marxism and Form*, 176.

62 Jameson, "Theo Angelopoulos," 87.

63 Jameson, "Theo Angelopoulos," 84.

64 Horton, *Films of Theo Angelopoulos*, 27–30.

65 William Shakespeare, *The Tempest*, act 1, scene 2, lines 401–402.

66 Adam Cichoń, "*Korfulamu*—podróże przez czas w kinie Theodorasa Angelopoulosa," *Kwartalnik filmowy* 107 (Jesień 2019): 145.

5

Jameson and Japanese Media Theory

A Virtual Dialogue

NAOKI YAMAMOTO

Fredric Jameson has been recognized not only for his theoretical rigor but also for his keen interest in cultures and regions beyond the West. He has written on figures such as Lu Xun in China, Ousmane Sembène in Senegal, Humberto Solás in Cuba, Edward Yang in Taiwan, and Kidlat Tahimik in the Philippines, while collaborating in the form of interview with a group of local scholars he met during his frequent visits to non-Western countries. Given such a wide range of coverage, Perry Anderson offers a plausible narrative about the successful out-come of Jameson's own *geopolitical aesthetic*. In Anderson's view, Jameson's increasing interest in non-Western cultural products was indispensable from his concurrent theorization of the postmodern condition. Jameson repeatedly defined postmodernity as a situation in which the process of modernization has been completed on a global scale, to the point where no one in this world is given any opportunities to get out of this encroaching situation. Because Jameson pro-vided a new language to articulate the lived experience of this ongoing shift without failing to acknowledge subtle, but no less significant, differences found in each location, his theory of postmodernity "has won a growing audience in countries once of the Third or Second world." This, in turn, also helps us insti-gate a radical reconfiguration of the hegemony of the West as embodiment of the logic of the second or imperialist stage of capitalism. "With this break-out from the Occident," says Anderson, "the idea of the postmodern has come full circle back to its original inspiration, as a time when the dominance of the West would cease."[1]

Perhaps one could endorse this apparently optimistic account by looking at, say, the positive reception of Jameson's writing among Chinese readers where "'cultural criticism' is primarily a Jamesonian notion, first brought to them by your visit in 1985."[2] But I'd like to complicate this same account by inserting another non-Western country that Jameson frequently visited and commented on: Japan. It is true that Jameson's writings on non-Western novels and films tend to privilege those from the Third World. And his schematic division between the First and Third Worlds was strategically employed. In an interview with Sabry Hafez, Abbas Al-Tonsi, and Mona Abousenna, he explained his approach to Third World cultural production as follows: "In my opinion, the new interest in the culture fully as much as the literature of the third world comes into being simultaneously with postmodernism. . . . This also has something to do, I think, with the impoverishment of culture in a kind of standardized media society like this first world one, which is therefore tempted to reinvigorate itself perpetually and to restore its vitality by infusions of a more vital culture from the outside."[3]

The paradox here is that Jameson has always treated Japan, despite its non-Western background, as part of the First World, given the country's exceptional entry in the ranks of Western imperialist powers in the early twentieth century as well as its persistent visibility and influence on the world market today. Indeed, Jameson himself recognized the marked difference of Japan from the majority of other non-Western countries by saying, "I myself speak from a perspective in which the relative sterility of the cultures of the three great first world or late-capitalist zones (Europe, the US, Japan) is acknowledged, and therefore in which the more vital cultural production of the other areas now affords us possibilities of analysis we cannot find in our own literatures."[4] Around the time when he was diligently writing about Third World cinemas and literature, Jameson also published essays on the work of the Japanese literature giant Natsume Sōseki and of the Japanese literary critic and philosopher Karatani Kōjin. But following his own conviction that only cultures of the Third or Second Worlds could provide us a refreshing understanding of our postmodern condition, he deliberately included those two essays on Japan in his *Modernist Papers* (2007).

Jameson's dissociation of Japan from his theoretical inquiry into postmodern also illuminates relative indifference given to Jameson's postmodern theory by local Japanese intellectuals. It is true that in Japan Jameson has been one of the most famous American Marxist literary scholars. Starting with the 1980 translation of *Marxism and Form* (1971), Japanese publishers have made constant effort to introduce Jameson and his work to their local readers. As a result, Japan remains one of the most productive countries in terms of translating Jameson's monographs into its own local language.[5] But when it comes to Japanese intellectuals' own reaction to the emergence of postmodern culture in their local context, Jameson's name was usually mentioned only in passing, or simply ignored. Indeed, in an encyclopedic entry for "postmodernism" published in 2011, the aesthetician Tasaki Hideaki omitted Jameson from his account and instead provided detailed exegeses of European commentators on the topic including Jean-François Lyotard, Jean Baudrillard, Jacques Derrida, Michel Serres, and Friedrich Kittler.[6] This miscommunication appears alarming since Japan, especially during the 1980s, unabashedly promoted itself as a country filled with numerous examples of the culture of postmodernism. To speak only of Jameson's favorite media objects, Japan in this decade produced a variety of consumer-oriented novels (Tanaka Yasuo's *Somehow Crystal*, 1981), pastiche films (Itami Jūzō's *The Funeral*, 1984), cyber-punk films (Ishii Sōgo's *Crazy Thunder Road*, 1981), anime with apocalyptic or "end-of-history" themes (Ōtomo Katsuhiro's *Akira*, 1988), techno music (Yellow Magic Orchestra), postmodern architecture (Isozaki Arata's Tsukuba Center Building, 1984), and unceasing commodification of knowledge production and consumption at large.[7]

What then did create such a disparity between Jameson and Japanese intellectuals in their mutual attempts at elaborating a theory of the postmodern? And what could we gain by speculatively reconstructing the misplaced, scattered, and even nonexisting dialogues between these two camps equally located at the forefront of late capitalism and its ongoing shift to the so-called postindustrial and information society? In what follows, I answer these questions by offering a comparative reading of three different theorizations of postmodernity by Japanese thinkers that emerged and developed in parallel with Jameson's own investigation. In executing this mission, I challenge the efficacy of the "positivist" or "empirical" approach. I say this because it not only privileges the visible—but equally very limited and selective—traces of actual interactions but often ends up confirming the centrality or even transcendentality of Jameson as the originator of discussion, compared to the secondary or passive status given to his non-Western readers. Therefore, the approach I adopt here would be more "speculative," always foregrounding through my own interpretation of the things or correlations that are not visible or represented as they are on the surface of given texts. The goal of this chapter is to come up with a better discursive framework to deal with theoretical inputs from the non-West in the age of full postmodernity. But before addressing this central concern, let us first look at how Jameson and his postmodern theory was introduced to Japan around the turn of the 1990s.

A Misguided Encounter

In August 1991, Jameson made his second visit to Japan. During his short stay, Jameson participated in a roundtable titled "After the Gulf War: The Third Stage of Imperialism and Postmodernism."[8] The impetus behind this meeting was to announce Jameson's recent joining of the advisory board of *Critical Space* (*Hihyō kūkan*), a bimonthly academic journal edited by Karatani Kōjin (1941–) and Asada Akira (1957–), his Japanese interlocutors at the roundtable. This now largely forgotten episode in Jameson's long career tells us about the increasing visibility in Japan of Jameson as a leading Marxist literary scholar, but also the shared recognition of postmodernism as a global phenomenon on both sides of the Pacific. Indeed, Jameson, Karatani, and Asada had much in common in their diagnoses of postmodernism, as they agreed that the task of intellectuals in this so-called post-historical period is to offer a sober and reflexive analysis of the present from a strictly historical (and not "historicist") perspective, rather than to make moralistic judgments on the values of various cultural and aesthetic practices. Nevertheless, at the very end of their discussion, they came to a disagreement about how to address the problematic of the postmodern in the Japanese context. Karatani argued that Japan, along with other Asian countries, still retained traces of the "matrilineal society," and that this apparently non-Western social system must deserve our critical attention insofar as it began to threaten the world via Japan's intensive economic growth during the 1980s. But Jameson rejected this statement by arguing that "if the characterization of the Japanese postmodern you disclosed at the end were correct, then your task as an intellectual would be distanced from ours and thus we would again witness the point of difference."[9]

Jameson's negative reaction here stemmed from his profound doubt about the concept of so-called "alternative modernities." To him, this concept implied that "there can be a modernity for everybody which is different from the standard or hegemonic Anglo-Saxon model," and henceforth it seems to help decenter and pluralize the experience of modernity by foregrounding indigenous or culturally specific aspects of the modernization processes that took place differently in each non-Western context.[10] But Jameson didn't impart any positive meaning to this undeniably cultural articulation of non-Western modernity because he thought it would lead "to overlook the other fundamental meaning of modernity which is that of a worldwide capitalism itself."[11] Thus, for Jameson, if the Japanese economy and some of its cultural products became prominent on the global market, they must be analyzed as a symptom of this third or late stage of capitalism, and not as the result of the alleged alterity of Japanese society and its unique process of modernization. What one could infer from this signaling gesture is Jameson's profound doubt about cultural pluralism, which, he thought, would transform into a sheer confirmation of the alleged singularity of a given *national* culture.

Jameson was not alone among American scholars who detected in Japanese discourse on postmodernism a general tendency toward cultural exceptionalism. Masao Miyoshi and Harry Harootunian, editors of *Postmodernism and Japan* (1989), referred to this same problem as a combined result of "Japan's latecomer experience" to modern statehood and its concomitant efforts to "make Japan appear as something more than a pale double of the Western ratio." What then came to fill in the gap was a conception of Japan "as signified, whose uniqueness was fixed in an irreducible essence that was unchanging and unaffected by history." Moreover, they continued, it is "this sense of Japan as signified, unique and different from all other cultures, that is promoted by the most strident and, we should say, shrill spokesmen for Japan's postmodernity."[12] The editors also added that such a willful equation of Japan's pre- or nonmodernity with the antihistorical nature of postmodernity had recourse to Alexandre Kojève's notion of "the end of History," discussed in a footnote added to the second edition of his *Introduction to the Reading of Hegel*. According to Kojève, there are two distinct forms of society that have already made a transition to "the post-historical period" with their irreversible cancellation of the very idea of humanity in its "European" and "Historical" sense. The first is "the American way of life," whereby postwar prosperity and unceasing pursuit of consumption brought humans back to their "animality." The second is Japan, which he believed to have already lived in the post-historical world for almost three centuries by reducing all "human content"—including religion, morals, and politics—to "totally formalized values" in the form of snobbism.[13] Needless to say, the irony here, as Miyoshi and Harootunian would add, was the frequent use of this very Eurocentric discourse of "the end of history" by Japanese postmodernists to differentiate Japan from the West.

This ruthless criticism, however, was not only aimed at a group of Japanese apologists for postmodernism such as the novelist Tanaka Yasuo and the advertising copywriter Itoi Shigesato who deliberately conflated the recent economic success of Japan with the supposed superiority of their own national culture,[14] but also addressed to Karatani and Asada who served in this same edited volume both as contributors and the very objects of analysis by other American contributors. This means that in context of 1980s Japan, Karatani and Asada played an indispensable role in introducing postmodernism to their local readers. In 1975–1976, Karatani stayed at Yale as a visiting scholar and became acquainted with deconstruction under the tutelage of Paul de Man. He then elucidated what he learned there in studies such as *Origins of Modern Japanese Literature* (1980), *Architecture as Metaphor* (1983), and *Criticism and the Postmodern* (1985).[15] On the other hand, Asada made his foray into the world of criticism with his first monograph, *Structure and Power* (1983), published when he was just twenty-six.[16] Although the book was a scholarly exposition of the work of Jacques Lacan, Michel Foucault, and Gilles Deleuze and Félix Guattari, it became a huge best seller (selling more than 150,000 copies) and thereby made Asada an icon of the emergent cultural movement known as "new academism."[17] Moreover, since Asada made frequent media appearances and seemed to celebrate the arrival of a mass consumer society, another American contributor of *Postmodernism and Japan* sardonically described him and his campaign of new academism as disseminating "a defense of knowledge as 'play' (*tawamure*; *yūgi*), a game suitable for the generation that has been labeled apathetic and superficial."[18]

Of course, Karatani and Asada were aware of this type of criticism. And this created another layer behind the disagreement that appeared at the end of the aforementioned roundtable. When Karatani and Asada launched *Critical Space* in 1991, they intended to make a shift from being mere symptoms of Japanese postmodernism to being more critical, self-reflective agents who tasked themselves with clarifying the negative aspects of Japan's recent craze about postmodernism. In this respect, it is unsurprising that Jameson's 1984 essay, "The Politics of Theory: Ideological Positions in the Postmodern Debate," appeared in the inaugural issue of *Critical Space*.[19] Anticipating Jameson's later investigation into the false postmodern antinomies or what he called "the identity of identity and non-identity," this essay provides a chart that put major commenters on postmodernism—Tom Wolfe, Christopher Jencks, Manfredo Tafuri, Jean-François Lyotard, Hilton Kramer, and Jürgen Habermas—into the four categories comprising the twin dyads of "anti-modernist/pro-modernist" and "anti-postmodernist/pro-postmodernist."[20] Judging from this perspective, Karatani and Asada recognized the potential of Jameson's theoretical writings as a useful guide for approaching the problem of postmodernism in the Japanese context.[21]

That said, Karatani and Asada's intention was more than to follow Jameson's footsteps. It is because they observed the global spread of the postmodern condition as a result not just of "Americanization" but also of "Japanization." Indeed, what bothered Karatani and Asada the most at the time of the roundtable was a perceptible similarity between the 1930s and the 1980s. The 1930s, or more precisely, the decade known as the Shōwa teens (1935–1945) in the Japanese era calendar scheme, saw the emergence of a particular local, ultranationalist discourse called "the overcoming of modernity" (*kindai no chōkoku*). This discourse placed Japan in a quasi-postmodern position at which a series of the former hegemonic dichotomies between the West and the non-West, the modern and the premodern, and the colonizer and the colonized could be dialectically synthesized by Japan's historical engagement with both positions, as well as by its ongoing commitment to the creation of a "new world order" that would have appeared with the victory of the Axis countries in World War II.[22] The 1980s, or, to be precise again, the last decade of the Shōwa era (1926–1989) in turn witnessed the uncanny revival of this disturbing local discourse about Japan's imperialist invasion of Asia through the economic, cultural, and technological domination of the region. For this very reason, Karatani and Asada came to critically designate the 1990s as marking the end of "the end of history," a period in which Japan would finally get the opportunity to fulfill its unaccomplished mission of overcoming Western modernity and the Western domination of the world at large.[23]

Retroactively, Karatani and Asada's anxiety about the Japanization of the world turned out to be a pipe dream due to the burst of the Japanese asset price bubble in the early 1990s and the following economic recession that lasted for the next two decades. And yet their negative assessment of Japan's recent post-modern boom as a mere historical recapitulation—perhaps as "farce," as Marx might call it—remained very influential among the Japanese throughout the decade. This, for one, led to the resurgence of academic interest in the history of Japanese modernity and modernization that now contained two distinct post-modern moments as constitutive parts. But it also involved the parallel decline of general interest in postmodernism, as most Japanese intellectuals in the 1990s began to reject it as a signifier of or even a proper noun for cultural ethos of the bygone decade. One could also find the direct impact of this discursive turn in the reduced pace of translating Jameson's writings into Japanese. Of the three books on postmodernism and postmodernity, only *The Seeds of Time* was trans-lated during this post "post-historical" decade. After this, *The Cultural Turn* did not become available until 2006, whereas *Postmodernism; or, The Cultural Logic of Late Capitalism* still remains untranslated.[24]

Does this mean that Jameson's work did not yield any perceptible effect or trace on Japanese debates on postmodernism? According to the majority of Japanese intellectuals of the period, the answer must be yes, as succinctly demon-strated in the complete omission of Jameson's contribution to the topic in the aforementioned encyclopedic entry. But my own answer does not reach such total denial. It is true that if one were to look for evidence of interaction, the result would most likely be unfruitful given the lack of *positive* data available. There-fore, the strategy I propose here must be something akin to what Jameson con-ceptualized as "cognitive mapping" in that it no longer presupposes one-to-one correspondence between the sign (Japanese texts) and its referent (Jameson's ideas). In other words, my inquiry below offers an imaginary reconstruction of the dialogue that never happened, the dialogue that comes into view only through a careful but inventive interpretation of Japanese theoretical texts on the post-modern. Since this approach does not grant Jameson the place of origin—again, he cannot serve as the referent of those Japanese texts—it also prevents us from reproducing a hegemonic narrative of Western "influence," which has long justi-fied systemic ignorance of the value of non-Western critical discourse in general.

As a tentative demonstration of such a speculative reading, I have chosen to examine the work of the two younger Japanese thinkers, Ōsawa Masachi (1958–) and Azuma Hiroki (1971–). The reason behind my selection is threefold. First, Ōsawa and Azuma came out of the same intellectual circle I have described above—they were both frequent contributors to Karatani and Asada's *Critical Space*, for instance—and this makes it easy to track how Japanese debates on postmodernism and postmodernity took a different direction in the 1990s and beyond. Second, they distinguished between postmodernism as a cultural move-ment in the 1980s and postmodernity as an overarching living condition of the present. Consequently, their stance toward the postmodern condition became akin to that of Jameson, that is, treating postmodernity as "a periodizing con-cept" to track and articulate various and interrelated symptoms of a whole new world economic system called late or a third-stage capitalism. Third, both Ōsawa and Azuma presented their own diagnoses of postmodernity in the form of media theory. This last point would be a useful amendment to Jameson's own postmodern theory, which seldom takes into account the significance of new media platforms emerging after video.

The Narrative Return of the Repressed

Ōsawa began his career as a theoretical sociologist specializing in Niklas Luhmann's systems theory and in a wide variety of philosophical traditions ranging from German idealism (Immanuel Kant, G. W. Hegel), modern mathematics (Kurt Gödel, G. Spencer-Brown), and analytical philosophy (W. V. Quine, Ludwig Wittgenstein) to French poststructuralism (Jacques Lacan, Jacques Derrida). In his earlier works such as *Comparative Sociology of the Body* (*Shintai no hikaku shakaigaku*, 1990) and *Meaning and Otherness* (*Imi to tashasei*, 1994), Ōsawa challenged the Cartesian notion of the cogito as a singular and self-contained being by redefining our bodies as a *mediating* space where both imaginary and physical communications between the self and the other take place, or more precisely, as a *reflexive* space where an individual subject could encounter and reflect upon his or her own innate alterity.[25] This, for one, reminds us of Rimbaud's famous line "Je est un autre" and its theoretical elaboration in Lacanian psychoanalysis. But Ōsawa's intention was to offer an alternative account of the constructedness of subjectivity beyond the then dominant linguistic model. And this became the central concern of his 1995 monograph, *On Electronic Media* (*Denshi media ron*).

To begin with, Ōsawa defines modernity as a historical period or condition demarcated by the establishment of subjectivity as a unified and discrete unit. The term "subjectivity" here means a state in which the condition for each individual's behavior and cognition process belongs to himself or herself. Thus, under this presumption, anyone making decisions according to God or any external faculty must be rejected as either "non-subjective" or "non- or pre-modern."[26] However, Ōsawa argues that this idealist notion of subjectivity has never been realized in full, and he explains it by referring to Kant's notion of "apperception." In Kantian philosophy, human cognition always operates at two levels: empirical and transcendental. On the first level, it is a combination of what Kant called "a priori representations" in sensibility (i.e., space and time) and the "pure concepts of understanding" (i.e., categories) that gives the raw data of sensation, or the effects of external objects by which we are affected, a certain unity and form to be cognized by the subject.[27] But on the second level, there should be a higher principle that constitutes a priori the condition on which those various empirical cognitions are ordered and unified as the experience of the one and same subject. Kant called this transcendental principle apperception, and it has since served as a theoretical backdrop for the unity of ego or self-consciousness that is a prerequisite for the successful establishment of a modern subject.

After introducing this argument, Ōsawa asks whether apperception as defined this way could really reach its proclaimed transcendental status. For if the main function of apperception is to confirm the identity of a cognizing subject via the same subject's a posteriori assemblage of inner experience, then it must remain within the realm of the empirical as a delayed or secondary perception of the already perceived objects. Moreover, one can also find this same paradox at work in Kant's conception of the "antinomy," as it refers to the incapability of pure reason to make any logical judgment on the two antithetical propositions that are in themselves true and reasonable. Drawing on these observations, Ōsawa amends his initial remark by stating that modernity is rather marked by and sustained through the impossibility of the subject to be a real possessor of the pure and universal form of transcendental apperception.[28]

Ōsawa then discloses his main working hypothesis—that is, the hitherto unaccomplished idea of transcendental apperception would come into being in full postmodernity. In the modern period, he argues, there were at least two technical problems that had prevented apperception from being both universal and transcendental in their strict sense: the first is the lack of a functional database that can register and accumulate all the possible behavioral patterns made by each single person on the globe; the second is the time lag between perception (input) and cognition (output) in the unifying act of apperception, a problem that had always pushed our cognization process back into the empirical realm. These old problems, however, can easily be solved with the use of the Internet and other network-based information technologies that can translate the raw and unorganized data accumulated from all over the world into a cognizable representation.[29] To put it differently, what has been called "subjectivity" can fulfill its presupposed role—the integration of empirical and transcendental apperceptions—only in this digital age.

However, Ōsawa is far from a technocrat or media guru who would eulogize the arrival of digital utopia. His diagnosis of modernity lies rather in its *programmed* incapability of granting the subject an absolute control and self-formation of transcendental apperception. Just like the ancient people's trust in the alleged almighty of God, people living in the modern period—defined roughly as a period after the Enlightenment and the Industrial Revolution—still needed and utilized the notion of the transcendent(al) Other who preemptively delimits the condition of each individual's experience from above or outside. This novel Other, however, no longer needed to be personified. Rather, it took the form of what Lacan called the "symbolic order," a web of dominant cultural, ethical, and sociopolitical discourses that always precedes and determines the formation of ego and superego.[30] According to Ōsawa, what then characterizes postmodernity is not the entire effacement of the symbolic order as such, but the latter's radical fragmentation and reconfiguration caused by the emergence of a well-nigh perfected form of transcendental apperception in this new media environment.

It is here that one could find some intriguing affinities between Ōsawa and Jameson. First of all, they both employ Kant's notion of "antinomy" in their theorizations of postmodernity. As we have seen, Ōsawa speaks of the resolution of the modern antinomies, which Kant himself defined as a product of the paralogisms of pure reason, by the ongoing externalization or de-humanization of transcendental apperception though digital media. Jameson, on the other hand, singles out what he calls "four distinct postmodern antinomies"—time (change and permanence), space (variety and homogeneity), naturalism (nature and human nature), and utopia (totality and monism)—and discusses how in a postmodern or late capitalist society these presupposed oppositions came to designate the one and same phenomena through "their ceaseless alternation between Identity and Difference."[31] In addition, unlike Lyotard's famous rendering of the postmodern condition as marked by the end of grand narratives, Ōsawa and Jameson do not accept such a radical break to begin with, and instead share a recognition that "postmodernity is what obtains under a tendentially far more complete modernization" on a global scale.[32] Equally important in this regard is their mutual interest in the persistence or recurrence of the "narrative" in the seemingly anti- or nonnarrative nature of postmodern cultural production. In fact, Ōsawa's postmodern theory aims to scrutinize the ideological implications of what Jameson calls the "narrative return of the repressed" in the period in which all the former and "modern" examples of grand narratives—rationalism, nationalism, socialism, class-struggle, and history—have already been repudiated under the overwhelming triumph of capitalism.

To see the actual effect of "the narrative return of the repressed" in the Japanese context, Ōsawa draws attention to the emergence of a particular type of consumers called *otaku*. Often equated with "geek" or "nerd" in the English lexicon, otaku refers to those "who fanatically consume, produce, and collect comic books (*manga*), animated films (*anime*), and other products related to those forms of popular visual culture and who participate in the production and sales of derivative fan merchandise," as Jonathan E. Abel and Shion Kono summarize.[33] Although the term *otaku* itself was already in use since the early 1980s, it became widely recognized around the turn of the 1990s, especially after the arrest of twenty-six-year-old serial killer Miyazaki Tsutomu, who between August 1988 and June 1989 kidnapped and murdered four little girls between four and seven years old. Miyazaki was said to be a huge collector of anime and horror films and almost always confined himself in his room in isolation. It is true that his apparently abnormal personality helped circulate a very negative image of otaku as antisocial and potentially dangerous. This stigmatization intensified in 1995, when members of the new religious cult called Aum Shinrikyō conducted a terrorist attack on the Tokyo subway and killed twelve people using poisonous sarin gas. Like Miyazaki's incident, the media coverage stressed that this incident was a by-product of the burgeoning otaku culture as its apocalyptic imaginations seemed to stem directly from anime, sci-fi, and other forms of sub- or popular culture.

As a sociologist, Ōsawa aims to give a credible account of these interrelated social events. And what he discovers in both cases is the decline of a concrete sense of the actual existence of reality. In full postmodernity, he contends, reality might appear before us a mere assemblage of simulacra due to the excessive influx of information and the concomitant malfunction of the symbolic order. It is as if everything has now regressed into the realm of the Imaginary, where the relationship between the self and the other is no longer defined by their traumatic recognition of absolute difference but rather by their primordial desire to become one with each other through mimesis or sympathetic identification. Of course, this can explain why otaku people prefer to form a semiclosed community based on their shared knowledge about very specific but seemingly unimportant objects such as the designs of mechas and giant robots in TV anime, bugs or cheating techniques in video games, and mediocre and unrecognized teenage idols.[34] But Ōsawa also reminds us that Japanese otaku culture in general has an equally strong desire for "historicization." Or to quote Jameson's words again, it "cannot not periodize" its own genesis and evolution in the form of a quasi-historical narrative.[35] This was also the case for the Aum's terrorist attack insofar as its perpetrators intended to rewrite Japanese history as such by subverting the status quo and declaring the coming of Armageddon.[36]

But what underlies this almost parallel movement between the dissolution of grand narratives and its unceasing replacement with small or more personalized narratives? Or, why do people in postmodernity still pursue the shadow of the transcendent(al) Other that is now imagined either as a globalized computer network and database or as very secularized icons like new cult leaders and media celebrities? Ōsawa's answer appears to be "Jamesonian" to the extent that it associates these recent postmodern phenomena with the transformation of capitalism itself. In the age of modernity, he argues, it was the imperialist expansion of territories that guaranteed the creation and accumulation of surplus value owing to the unequal development of the world economy. But once this spatial movement reaches its limit with the arrival of postmodernity, capitalism now generates surplus value by exploiting the temporal difference between the future and the present.[37] As Ōsawa indicates, the most profitable mode of production in this temporalized capitalism must be the one that constantly changes its norms and conditions for consumption. This, in the end, provides a logical explanation for the return of the repressed in the postmodern age: the saturation of small narratives in today's media outlets is nothing but a very symptom of our age's relentless search for highly flexible and disposable *others*.

Database Animals and Reified Antinomies

If my reading of Ōsawa represents a positive side of Jameson's virtual dialogue with his Japanese counterparts, this section reflects its negative side. Like Asada in the previous decade, Azuma Hiroki became another media "star" in the late 1990s with his first monograph, *Ontological, Postal: On Jacques Derrida* (*Sonzaironteki, yūbinteki: Jakku Derida ni tsuite*), published when he was twenty-seven.[38] However, he is now better known as a leading scholar of anime, video games, "light" or fantastic adolescent novels, and many other forms of on- and offline Japanese subculture, thanks to the international success of his 2001 book, *Otaku: Japan's Database Animals*. What bridges these two seemingly disparate interests in philosophy and subculture is his theoretical take on the postmodern and media.[39] Indeed, as Takeshi Kadobayashi points out, Azuma was planning to publish yet another monograph that would encompass his "grand theory of media in the postmodern age."[40] However, he later abandoned the idea, having written the major part of the planned book. According to Azuma, this was because of the shift in his own understanding of postmodernity as well as of his growing doubt about the relevance of "theory" to readers of the new millennium.[41] But my attention here goes rather to a certain tendency that seems to penetrate his critical inquiries in general.

Azuma's theoretical writing shows a strong inclination toward dualism. For instance, Azuma rebukes Karatani and Asada for their failure to distinguish postmodernism from postmodernity. For Azuma, postmodernism signifies a proper noun for dominant cultural currents and styles in the late 1970s and 1980s, with the help of such delegatory terms as pastiche, schizophrenia, and deconstruction. Postmodernity, on the other hand, encompasses more fundamental shifts in both epistemology and modes of production and consumption engendered by the emergence of so-called postindustrial, consumer, and information societies.[42] In this regard, it can be said that whereas postmodernism as a movement had already lost its impetus after the turn of the 1990s, postmodernity as a situation became more imperative and omnipresent from this new decade onward and thus cannot be overlooked as a mere transitory phenomenon. Azuma also draws a clear-cut demarcation—or "epistemological break," to use Gaston Bachelard's terms—between modernity and postmodernity, rather than treating the latter as a continuation or acceleration of the former.

In Azuma's view, the specificity of postmodernity as a situation lies in its total negation of grand narratives, which includes people's shared "respect for authority, patriotism, the ideal of the family, obedience to the law" and their proclaimed role as a sole provider of universal norms.[43] Like Ōsawa, Azuma ascribes the liquidation of grand narratives to the malfunction of the Lacanian symbolic order. As a symptom of this ongoing shift, he refers to the emergence of what he calls the "interfacial subjectivity," a virtual but no less denotative identity that one assumes in the cyberspace, or whenever he or she communicates with others through the Internet and other digital and electronic devices. This new subjectivity, he continues, tends to take everything it encounters online at "face value," for it understands through experience that what lies behind the image or text-based information appearing on the computer screen is not an ideology in its reified forms but the combination of an unceasing accumulation of data and a series of protocols and applications to run the programs.[44] Therefore, the deterioration of the symbolic order in postmodernity heralds the end of the Foucauldian concept of disciplinary society and the Althusserian model of interpellation: no longer able or required to respond to interpellations by the invisible "Other," the postmodern interfacial subject now seeks for temporary and interchangeable small narratives by way of "an imaginary simulation of symbolic identification."[45]

To discuss the Japanese experience of postmodernity in more detail, Azuma introduces a new mode of consumption that he saw emerging among the devoted fans of Japanese anime. According to Azuma, anime fans or *otaku* tend to decide the object of their viewing activities by means of *moe*, a set of visual features of anime characters that arose their affection or sexual desires, including "bells," "cat ears," "maid costumes," "hair sticking up like antennae," and so on.[46] What is remarkable here is that *otaku* often prioritize those superficial features of their beloved characters over main stories of each anime or video game, developing the database that stores the information they want. This Azuma calls the "database consumption," and it helps elucidate working hypotheses for his inquiry into the postmodern condition.

First, the database consumption tells us postmodern subjects' specific consumption patterns after the demise of grand narratives. As Azuma writes, "After having failed to grasp the significance of a 'god' or 'society' supported by tradition, otaku try to fill the void with the subculture at their disposal."[47] In other words, in this postindustrial, information society it is the database that serves an ad hoc substitute for Kant's notion of "transcendental apperception" by offering and renewing temporary guidance for people's perceptual and cognitive behaviors. Second, it also designates a shift in the very function of signs and representation. In the modern period, he argues, signs were divided into either the symbol or the image. But in our current age, we witness the total collapse of such a schematic division. Drawing upon this observation, Azuma declares that all signs in postmodernity become not only simulacra but also *écriture* (writing), insofar as the latter allows us to assess the aesthetic, rhetorical, and stylistic features of visual representation without confining ourselves to their symbolic meanings. Finally, Azuma promotes his concept of database consumption to call for a more serious, unbiased treatment of *otaku* or subculture in general,[48] criticizing both traditional scholars and *otaku* themselves for their incapability to address this recent local phenomenon as constituting an essential part of what we call the postmodern and its global dissemination.

While Azuma's conscious rejection of moralizing judgments on *otaku*'s seemingly trivial and illogical obsession with *moe*-elements is admirable, his overall recourse to the modern/postmodern dichotomies remain unsatisfactory. Take, for example, his discussion of signs. Despite his emphasis on the schematic division between the image and the symbol in the modern period, semioticians such as C. S. Peirce and Peter Wollen always argued that the three basic types of signs—the icon, the index, and the symbol—are not mutually exclusive but interchangeable with each other.[49] It is thus not the ontological difference of each given sign but its actual usage in varying contexts that determines how we use and interpret its meaning and communicational value. Azuma also employs Derrida's concept of *écriture* to illuminate our age's general retreat from the symbolic to the imaginary and the concomitant decline of the relevance of ideological criticism. Yet, unlike Azuma's treatment of ideology as a sole product of the invisible symbolic order, Althusser defined ideology as "the representation of the subject's *Imaginary* relationship to his or her *Real* conditions of existence."[50] Furthermore, as Jameson reminds us, the main objects of Marxist analyses—class consciousness, the metamorphosis of commodity into money, and the logic and actual function of capitalism in its totality—are neither representable nor given in direct experience *as they are*. As a plausible solution for this problem, Jameson adopts what he calls the "cognitive mapping," always stressing the importance of our speculative interpretation of given texts or phenomena as an *imperfect* figuration of those unrepresentable entities.[51]

In addition to the database consumption, Azuma argues that animality, or people's regression into their primordial state, constitutes the predicament of postmodernity in general and of *otaku* culture in particular. He borrows this term from Kojève's earlier discussion of the end of history, although he adds that Japanese snobbishness, a term that captures *otaku*'s compulsive obsession with meticulous details, now serves as a more recent and globalized form of the "animalization" which Kojève associated with the rise of hyperconsumerism in 1950s America.[52] As another point of reference, Azuma also discusses Hannah Arendt's elaboration of the same issue. Following Arendt's identification of work and action with humanity and of labor and consumption with animality, Azuma argues that postmodernity, thanks to its overt reliance on information technology, admits the coexistence of these two contrasting modalities and expands the disparity between them. "The advent of information society," he writes, "makes humans more humanistic while at the same making humans more animalistic."[53] With this statement Azuma concludes that postmodernity must be scrutinized through its peculiar "double-layered structure" (*nisō kōzō*), reaching a position similar to Jameson's inquiry into the antinomies of postmodernity.[54]

However, Azuma still differs from Jameson in his lack of concern about the totality of postmodernity as a materialization of late or third-stage capitalism. For Azuma, the disparity between humans and animals is a given, and thus the postmodern or interfacial subjectivity in his account is destined to vacillate between these two poles at his or her will. Indeed, Azuma asserts that the human-animal divide stems directly from our innate mode of existence: "We do not always live our lives as a *humanistic, subjective,* and *active* 'citizen.' Rather, most part of our life is filled with time in which we serve as a *nonsubjective* and *passive* 'consumer' who *animalistically* take care of the tasks that await us out of habit and in some way quench our thirst with given products and media."[55] Ultimately, Azuma's theoretical intervention aims at throwing a positive light onto the creative energy that he detects in the realm of animalistic labor and consumption. He thus pays special attention to the enduring influence of Japanese *otaku* culture on the rise of *prosumers* and participatory culture in the United States and beyond. Nevertheless, his real fascination goes to those works that offer a sort of "metacommentary" on the current situation, showing his hesitation in deposing the humanist notion of *poiesis* altogether.[56]

Azuma's discussion here gives us some reservations. If, as Azuma argues, animality were an a priori condition for what we call humanity, then his marked emphasis on the separation between the two must be both tautological and ahistorical because what he provided in this account was nothing but a sheer affirmation of the basic human condition that had already been in place since the emergence of ancient civilization. And if the notion of animality as an intrinsic feature of humanity becomes more and more apparent in postmodernity, then it must be imperative for us to examine what makes the reinstallment of such an age-old antinomy possible and sustainable in our times. Needless to say, this is exactly what Jameson did with his concept of "postmodern antinomies." He argues that the postmodern condition establishes countless antinomies only to confirm the ultimate identity of these opposites. To Jameson, this bidirectional— at once centripetal and centrifugal—movement is of particular importance because it espouses capitalism's totalizing effect that makes profit through the discovery and creation of different (meaning "local," "cheaper," and "manipulatable") value systems and the forceful integration of the latter into the globalized, yet singular, logic of market economy. This last point reveals the enduring relevance of Marxism even to Azuma's dualistic reasoning. In the Marxist tradition, nothing is more fundamental than the realms of labor and consumption, and one could easily prove it with Marx's remark that "the human being is in the most literal sense a political animal, not merely a gregarious animal, but an animal which can individuate itself in the midst of society."[57]

Conclusion

The conclusion I would like to offer after providing my speculative reading of Jameson's virtual dialogues with his Japanese counterparts is intentionally dogmatic. That is, "Only Marxism can give us an adequate account of the essential *mystery* of the cultural past."[58] This provocative statement from Jameson's *The Political Unconscious* offers us at least two lessons for further research on Japanese postmodernity and its theorizations. On the one hand, it impels us to reaffirm the necessity and importance of socioeconomic analysis in the 2000s and beyond when the term *otaku* has changed its connotation from a synonym for obscure Japanese subculture to that of one of the most profitable and influential cultural products that Japan has ever exported to the world market. This does not simply mean the saturation of "Japan-made" media platforms such as manga, anime, and videogame in both our households and classrooms; it also involves an unabashed exploitation of this specific cultural form both by top-notch contemporary artists (e.g., Murakami Takashi's collaboration with Louis Vuitton) and by local government officials (e.g., the former prime minster Abe Shinzō's promotion of "Cool Japan," a state-funded campaign to enhance Japan's "soft-power").[59] One might say that we need a *post*-Marxist theory, which ought to a more positive light on our daily commitment to affective labor and consumption, to address our age's wholesale concession to mass commodification. However, what this popular *postmodern* discourse implies is not the deficiency of Marxist thought per se. Rather, it exposes our lack of imagination to read Marx not as a prophet for the end of modern capitalist society but as a shrewd commentator on the oxymoronic nature of capitalism and its ever-shifting strategies for survival.

The second lesson is more directly related to the discursive constitution of Anglo-American film and media studies as an academic discipline. As I have argued elsewhere, what we call "theory" in our discipline has historically been demarcated by its systemic exclusion of critical inputs originally written and presented in non-European languages.[60] Thanks to the exegeses above, we can now understand that this symptomatic absence (or "erasure") of non-Western theories in our current curricula faithfully traces the trajectory of the second or imperialist model of capitalism whose main profits stemmed from the perpetual creation of exploitation of the *others* belonging to a different world system or temporality (hence the commonplace identification of the non-West and the pre- or nonmodern). In contrast, postmodernity is a condition in which those preexisting spatial and temporal divides are being forcibly cancelled due to late capitalism's totalizing logic. This new geopolitical (and historical) setting therefore makes it mandatory to pay more critical and close attention to previously neglected non-Western theorizations of the present and its dominant cultural forms. As Jameson once stated, "This new system of globalization really is a system in which intellectuals from different national situation can talk much more directly to each other. They can answer back, and they do answer back."[61]

The last point I want to add is that we should not treat this proposition as a mere confirmation of multiculturalism. Instead of treating non-Western media and postmodern theories as a credible empirical account of the cultural specificity of given national contexts, we must use them creatively, highlighting their epistemological potentials to enhance and complicate our imperfect understanding of late capitalism and its inherently global nature. Such a revisionist, *post*-postcolonial approach to non-Western knowledge production would require a radical alternation of the traditional division between *theoria*, *praxis*, and *poiesis*, as well as of our commonplace presumption of theory as a universal and ahistorical discourse. But as far as the legacy of Marxism is concerned, we don't need to overwhelm ourselves with this pressing methodological challenge. Indeed, Marx was among the first to make explicit the necessity of developing theory through practice (and vice versa) in his "Theses on Feuerbach" and elsewhere. In the Marxist lexicon, moreover, the term "universal" means less an unassailable account of a given situation than our well-nigh impossible "utopian" efforts to capture, inspect, and ultimately overcome capitalism without disregarding the totality of its fluctuating and self-contradictory mode of existence.

Notes

In this chapter, Japanese names appear in the Eastern name order, with the family name first and the given name second, unless the person cited—including myself—deliberately adopted the Western name order in their non-Japanese publications.

1 Perry Anderson, *The Origins of Postmodernity* (London: Verso, 1998), 75. Despite Anderson's optimistic account, Jameson's very schematic division between the First and Third Worlds became the subject of criticism by intellectuals working in those former Third World countries. See, for instance, Aijaz Ahmad, "Jameson's Rhetoric of Otherness and the 'National Allegory,'" in *Marxist Literary Theory*, ed. Terry Eagleton and Drew Milne (Malden, MA: Blackwell, 1996), 375–398. Jameson was also aware of the increasing negative reactions given to him from his non-Western readers, saying: "I was sorry to say that after the publication of *A Singular Modernity* (2002), in which the very concept of 'alternative modernities' was dismissed, my Chinese and Brazilian readers seem to have parted with me, accusing me of being yet another Western or first theorist preaching to the rest of the world and seeking to impose Western theories on it." Fredric Jameson, "Introduction: On Not Giving Interviews," in *Jameson on Jameson: Conversations on Cultural Marxism*, ed. Ian Buchanan (Durham, NC: Duke University Press, 2007), 7.

2 Fredric Jameson, "Interview with Xudong Zhang," in Buchanan, *Jameson on Jameson*, 196. To endorse Zhang's comment here, seven monographs by Jameson had been translated into Chinese by 2007. Also, Jameson tested his theorization of postmodernism in a lecture series he gave in 1985 at University of Beijing, and it was immediately published in Chinese that same year.

3 Fredric Jameson, "Interview with Sabry Hafez, Abbas Al-Tonsi, and Mona Abousenna," in Buchanan, *Jameson on Jameson*, 103.

4 Jameson, "Interview with Sabry Hafez," 112.

5 As of 2020, fifteen monographs, and several essays by Jameson have been translated into Japanese.

6 Tasaki Hideaki, "Posutomodan" [The Postmodern], *Gendai shisō* 29, no. 15 (November 2011): 46–51.

7 Jameson never talked about these Japanese postmodern media products except for Isazaki's architecture. See Fredric Jameson, "Interview with Michael Speaks," in Buchanan, *Jameson on Jameson*, 123–134.

8 Fredric Jameson, Asada Akira, and Karatani Kōjin, "Wangan sensō igo: Teikoku shugi no dai-san dankai to posutomodanizumu" [After the Gulf War: The Third Stage of Imperialism and Postmodernism], *Hihyō kūkan* 4 (January 1992): 6–35.

Before this encounter, Jameson had also participated in another roundtable organized by Karatani in 1989.

9 Jameson, Asada, and Karatani, "Wangan sensō igo," 35.

10 Fredric Jameson, *A Singular Modernity* (London: Verso, 2002), 12. For more on Jameson's critique of alternate modernity, see "In the Mirror of Alternate Modernities," in *The Modernist Papers* (London: Verso, 2007), 281–293. This essay was originally published as the foreword to the English translation of Karatani's *Origins of Modern Japanese Literature*, ed. and trans. Brett de Bary (Durham, NC: Duke University Press, 1993). As for alternative modernities as a concept, see Dilip Parameshwar Gaonkar, ed., *Alternative Modernities* (Durham, NC: Duke University Press, 2001).

11 Jameson, *Singular Modernity*, 12.

12 Masao Miyoshi and H. D. Harootunian, "Introduction," in *Postmodernism and Japan*, ed. Masao Miyoshi and H. D. Harootunian (Durham, NC: Duke University Press, 1989), xvi. This edited volume was first published in 1987 as a special issue of *South Atlantic Quarterly*, and its Japanese translation appeared in *Gendai shisō* 15, no. 15 (December 1987).

13 Alexandre Kojève, *Introduction to the Reading of Hegel: Lectures on the Phenomenology of Spirit*, ed. Allan Bloom, trans. James H. Nichols Jr. (Ithaca, NY: Cornell University Press, 1980), 159–162.

14 For a critical analysis of their "postmodern" work, see Norma Field, "*Somehow*: The Postmodern as Atmosphere," in Miyoshi and Harootunian, *Postmodernism and Japan*, 169–188.

15 Karatani Kōjin, *Nihon kindai bungaku no kigen* [Origins of Modern Japanese Literature] (Tokyo: Kōdansha, 1980); Karatani, *Inyu to shite no Kenchiku* [Architecture as Metaphor] (Tokyo: Kōdansha, 1983); Karatani, *Hihyō to postomodan* [Criticism and the Postmodern] (Tokyo: Fukutake Shoten, 1985).

16 Asada Akira, *Kōzō to chikara* [Structure and Power] (Tokyo: Keisō Shobō, 1983).

17 On the "new academism" and Asada's activities in the 1980s, see Marilyn Ivy, "Critical Texts, Mass Artifacts: The Consumption of Knowledge in Postmodern Japan," in Miyoshi and Harootunian, *Postmodernism and Japan*, 21–46; Alexander Zahlten, "1980s *Nyū Aka*: (Non)Media Theory as Romantic Performance," in *Media Theory in Japan*, ed. Marc Steinberg and Alexander Zahlten (Durham, NC: Duke University Press, 2017), 200–220.

18 Ivy, "Critical Texts, Mass Artifacts," 28.

19 Fredric Jameson, "Riron no seijigaku: Posutomodanizumu ni okeru ideorogīteki tachiba," trans. Suzuki Satoshi, *Hihyō kūkan* 1 (April 1991): 118–130.

20 Fredric Jameson, "Theories of the Postmodern," in *The Cultural Turn: Selected Writings on the Postmodern, 1983–1989* (London: Verso, 1998), 29.

21 Karatani and Asada differ regarding how to assess postmodern culture in general and the intellectual legacy of Marxism in particular. Still, their standpoints overlapped during their terms as coeditors of *Critical Space* (1991–2002). See Karatani Kojin and Asada Akira, *Karatani Kōjin Asada Akira zentaiwa* [A Complete Collection of Dialogues between Karatani Kōjin and Asada Akira] (Tokyo: Kōdansha, 2019).

22 Chiteki kyōryoku kaigi, ed., *Kindai no chōkoku* [Overcoming Modernity] (Tokyo: Sōgensha, 1943). For detailed accounts of this debate, see Sun Ge, "In Search of the Modern: Tracing Japanese Thought on 'Overcoming Modernity,'" trans. Peter Button, in *Impacts of Modernities*, ed. Thomas Lamarre and Kang Nae-hui (Hong Kong: Hong Kong University Press, 2004), 53–75; Harry Harootunian, *Overcome*

by Modernity: History, Culture, and Community in Interwar Japan (Princeton: Princeton University Press, 2000), esp. chap. 2.

23 See, for instance, Karatani Kōjin, *"Senzen" no shikō* [Thought in the Prewar Era] (Tokyo: Bungei Shunjū, 1994); Asada Akira, *"Rekishi no owari" to seikimatsu no sekai* [The End of History" and the World of the Fin de Siècle] (Tokyo: Shōgakukan, 1994). Asada's book is composed of his interviews with Francis Fukuyama, Edward Said, Slavoj Žižek, Jean-François Lyotard, and Jean Baudrillard.

24 Jameson's 1982 lecture titled "Postmodernism and the Consumer Society," which later developed into the first chapter of *Postmodernism*, was translated in 1987 along with other essays included in *The Anti-Aesthetic*, edited by Hal Foster.

25 Ōsawa Masachi, *Shintai no hikaku shakaigaku* [Comparative Sociology of the Body], 2 vols. (Tokyo: Keisō Shobō, 1990), *Imi to tashasei* [Meaning and Otherness] (Tokyo: Keisō Shobō, 1994). Ōsawa often spells his last name as "Ohsawa," but in this chapter I follow the traditional Hepburn romanization in transcribing Japanese words.

26 Ōsawa Masachi, *Denshi media ron: Shintai no mediateki hen'yō* [On Electronic Media: Body's Mediatic Transformation] (Tokyo: Shinyōsha, 1995), 12.

27 Immanuel Kant, *Critique of Pure Reason*, trans. and ed. Paul Guyer and Allen W. Wood (Cambridge: Cambridge University Press, 1998), 219–244.

28 Ōsawa, *Denshi media ron*, 15–17.

29 Ōsawa, *Denshi media ron*, 19.

30 In addition to "the symbolic order," Ōsawa uses the phase "the Instance of the third person" (*dai-san sha no shinkyū*) to refer to the same transcendental Other.

31 Fredric Jameson, "The Antinomies of Postmodernity," in *The Seeds of Time* (New York: Columbia University Press, 1994), 70.

32 Jameson, *Singular Modernity*, 12.

33 Jonathan E. Abel and Shion Kono, "Translators Introduction," in Hiroki Azuma, *Otaku: Japan's Database Animals* (Minneapolis: University of Minnesota Press, 2009), xv.

34 Ōsawa, *Denshi media ron*, 259–271.

35 Jameson, *Singular Modernity*, 29.

36 Ōsawa, *Denshi media ron*, 305–309.

37 Ōsawa, *Denshi media ron*, 218–228.

38 Azuma Hiroki, *Sonzaironteki yūbinteki: Jakku Derida ni tsuite* [Ontological, Postal: On Jacques Derrida] (Tokyo: Shinchōsha, 1998).

39 Azuma Hiroki, *Dōbutsuka suru postomodan: Otaku kara mita Nihon shakai* (Tokyo: Kōdansha, 2001). This book is translated into English as *Otaku: Japan's Database Animals* and is also available in Korean and French.

40 Takeshi Kadobayashi, "The Media Theory and Media Strategy of Azuma Hiroki, 1997–2003," in Steinberg and Zahlten, *Media Theory in Japan*, 82.

41 Azuma Hiroki, "90-nendai wo furikaeru: Atogaki ni kaete 2" [Looking Back at the 1990s: In Place of an Afterword], in *Saibā supēsu wa naze sō yobareruka +: Azuma Hiroki ākaibusu 2* [Why Is Cyberspace Called So? +: Volume 2 of the Azuma Hiroki Archive] (Tokyo: Kawade Shobō Shinsha, 2011), 453–454.

42 Azuma Hiroki, "Posutomodan saikō: Sumiwakeru hihyō 2" [Reconsidering the Postmodern: Segregated Criticism 2], in *Yūbinteki fuan tachi β* [Postal Anxieties β] (Tokyo: Kawade Shobō Shinsha, 2011), 38–39.

43 Fredric Jameson, "Class and Allegory in Contemporary Mass Culture: *Dog Day Afternoon* as a Political Film," *College English* 38, no. 8 (April 1977): 851.

44 Azuma Hiroki, "Saibā supēsu wa naze sō yobareruka," in *Jōhō kankyō ronshū S* [Essays on the Informational Environment S] (Tokyo: Kōdansha, 2007), 278–279.

45 Azuma, "Saibā supēsu wa naze sō yobareruka," 276.

46 Azuma, *Otaku,* 43.

47 Azuma, *Otaku,* 28.

48 Azuma, "Saibā supēsu wa naze sō yobareruka," 295.

49 See Peter Wollen, "The Semiology of the Cinema," in *Signs and Meanings in the Cinema,* new and enlarged ed. (Bloomington: Indiana University Press, 1972), 116–154.

50 Louis Althusser, "Ideological State Apparatuses," in *Lenin and Philosophy and Other Essays* (New York: Monthly Review Press, 1972), quoted in Fredric Jameson, "The Cultural Logic of Late Capitalism," in *Postmodernism; or, The Cultural Logic of Late Capitalism* (Durham, NC: Duke University Press, 1991), 51.

51 See, for instance, Fredric Jameson, "Cognitive Mapping," in *Marxism and the Interpretation of Culture,* ed. Cary Nelson and Lawrence Grossberg (Urbana: University of Illinois Press, 1988), 347–357.

52 Azuma, *Otaku,* 66–74.

53 Azuma Hiroki, "Jōhō jiyū ron" [On Information Freedom], in *Jōhō kankyō ronshū S,* 150. Arendt's discussion of animality is found in *The Human Condition,* 2nd ed. (Chicago: University of Chicago Press, 1998).

54 Azuma, "Jōhō jiyū ron," 83.

55 Azuma, "Jōhō jiyū ron," 149.

56 Toward the end of *Otaku,* Azuma discussed a PC-based visual novel titled *Yu-No* (1996) and expressed his admiration of this work's "metacommentaries" on *otaku* or postmodern culture as follows: "With words such as 'postmodernity' or 'otaku culture' many readers might imagine the play of simulacra cut off from social reality and self-contained in fiction, but this kind of engaged work also exists. This book was written to create a moment in which great works such as these can be freely analyzed and critiqued, without distinctions such as high culture versus subculture, academism versus otaku . . . and art versus entertainment" (Azuma, *Otaku,* 116).

57 Karl Marx, *Grundrisse,* trans. Martin Nicolaus (London: Penguin, 1993), 84.

58 Fredric Jameson, *The Political Unconscious: Narrative as a Socially Symbolic Act* (Ithaca, NY: Cornell University Press, 1981), 19.

59 For more detailed accounts of the global dissemination of Japanese "soft power," see Anne Allison, *Millennial Monsters: Japanese Toys and the Global Imagination* (Berkeley: University of California Press, 2006); Cristine R. Yano, *Pink Globalization: Hello Kitty's Trek across the Pacific* (Durham, NC: Duke University Press, 2013).

60 See my *Dialectics without Synthesis: Japanese Film Theory and Realism in a Global Frame* (Oakland: University of California Press, 2020).

61 Fredric Jameson, "Marxism and the Historicity of Theory: An Interview by Xudong Zhang," in *The Jameson Reader,* ed. Michael Hardt and Kathi Weeks (Malden, MA: Blackwell, 2000), 163.

6

Where Jameson Meets Queer Theory

Queer Cognitive Mapping in
1990s Sinophone Cinema

ALVIN K. WONG

It has almost been thirty years since Fredric Jameson published his 1992 book *The Geopolitical Aesthetic*, which pioneered the spatial turn in film studies and introduced provocative concepts such as cognitive mapping, urban totality, and conspiracy as allegory as means to consider the otherwise unmappable world system of postmodernity. Rather than developing his theories through the works of a mainland Chinese filmmaker such as Chen Kaige or Zhang Yimou, Jameson instead turned his attention to Edward Yang, whose 1986 Taiwanese New Wave film *The Terrorizers* illuminates for him "some generally late-capitalist urbanization ... that one finds everywhere in the First and Third Worlds alike."[1] By mapping the city of Taipei through the ruins of alleyways, the confinement of domestic space, and the generic space of hotel rooms, *The Terrorizers* expresses the uneven globality of postmodernism and late capitalism in a way that provides an exemplary demonstration of Jameson's theory of cognitive mapping and its relationship to postmodern urbanity. The film scans the unevenness of the world system, from the most traditional space "all the way to the *national* space of the hospital, the *multinational* space of the publisher's office ... [and finally to] the equally *transnational* anonymity of the hotel corridor with its identical bedrooms."[2]

Subsequent scholarship on East Asian cinema and Jameson's spatial turn in film studies, however, has called Jameson to task for his lack of attention to the specificity of urban totality in the Sinophone world as well as his lack of acknowledgment of his own positionality vis-à-vis the Chinese and Taiwanese young intellectuals to whom he exported Marxist theory of postmodernism. Catherine Liu's critique of Jameson's reading of *The Terrorizers* and his prior intellectual encounters with students in Mainland China is revealing: "When he went out, he was accompanied by an entourage of young male admirers. He was searching for Third World, Communist authenticity on the one hand, but welcomed by intellectually starved Chinese students as a voice from the West on the other."[3] Similarly, in her book on the citationality of China in world cinema and postmodernism, Gina Marchetti writes, "As Jameson cited 'China' to develop his ideas about postmodernity, Chinese intellectuals absorbed Jameson on the postmodern."[4] In short, Jameson could be charged with imposing his own theories of postmodernism, developed largely in a Western context, upon the realities of a Sinophone world whose specificities thus run the risk of being obscured. At the same time, though, Jameson's theories can be reworked and reapplied in such a way that such specificities of both place and experience are maintained, adding depth and nuance to a still-totalizing account of postmodern urban life. While previous debates on Jameson, the spatial turn, and the reception of his theories of postmodernism in the Sinophone world have highlighted the global dynamics of the travel and dissemination of theory as well as his tendency to overgeneralize or abstract the urban materiality of Taipei, my work here takes another tack, at once examining the specificities of urban locations in Sinophone cinema and queering the concept of cognitive mapping altogether. In what follows, I propose that one of the recurring but overlooked figures of the Taiwanese cityscape and a key figure in the allegorical staging of the conspiracies of postmodernism in Sinophone cinema is the gay male youth and urban roamer. The cinema of queer Taiwan art-house filmmaker Tsai Ming-liang powerfully visualizes the entrapment of gay male urban subjects within the spatial unevenness of Taipei's postmodernity in the 1990s, thus offering an opportunity to stage a meeting between Jameson's approach and specificities that it did not itself engage with.

The 1990s was also an era of intense acceleration in both urbanization and the development of LGBT and queer movements in Asian global cities. In particular, cities like Hong Kong and Taipei both underwent drastic processes of urbanization entailing gentrification, increasing cross-border and global migrations from Mainland China and Southeast Asia,[5] and the development of real estate hegemony that buttressed foreign investments and corporatization. It is therefore not surprising that one of the recurring figures of 1990s queer Sinophone cinemas from Hong Kong and Taiwan is a gay male urban subject feeling lost and trapped within the dystopia of rapid urbanization.[6] This chapter explores the intricate intersection of urbanization and queer sexuality within the films of arguably the most important queer Taiwanese filmmaker, namely Tsai Ming-liang. Conceptually, it places Fredric Jameson's theorization of postmodernism in relation to questions of affect, queer theory, and the cinematic expression of what I will call queer cognitive mapping. Overall, I aim to reconsider the role of affect in Jameson's theory of postmodernism and how the question of affect gets taken up in the later affective turn in queer theory. By exploring the cinematic aesthetics of queer cognitive mapping, using Tsai as our example, we can remap the relationship between queer theory, Marxism, postmodernism, and global film studies.[7] By examining queer Sinophone films within the context of the temporal and spatial compression of global postmodernity, my work here points toward a horizontal method of comparison that emphasizes the co-contemporaneity of time, space, and desire. By expanding Jameson's work into the domain of queer Sinophone cinema and reassessing the implication of Marxist thinking about totality in transnational cinema studies, we can gain a critical understanding of postmodernity beyond its Jamesonian characterization as an aesthetic of pastiche, spatial compression, the death of the subject, or waning of affect. Queer theory, in its critical encounter with Jameson's work and global film studies, allows us to discern the very uneven situatedness of gender, sexuality, and desire within world systems and calls for new modes of queer cognitive mapping to express and understand the experience of queer subjects within the postmodern context.

If cognitive mapping calls for human subjects' need for heightened sense of awareness of the world system as they inhabit new temporal and spatial mutations in late capitalism, queer cognitive mapping daringly gestures toward alternative modes of survival and minoritarian performativity that must likewise grapple with such temporal and spatial disorientation. As evident in the films of Tsai Ming-liang, queer subjects are rather resourceful in their playful rearticulations and inhabitation of spaces such as the domestic home, the bathhouse, and even the multinational space of the shopping mall, precisely because queers *must* learn to inhabit these spaces in new ways in order to cope with new regimes of gentrification, gendered discipline, and class segmentation in postmodern urban totality.

First, a brief sketch of the overlooked centrality of affect in Jameson's theory of postmodernism is in order. If in Lyotard's work, the concept of the postmodern constitutes an "incredulity towards metanarratives,"[8] for Jameson postmodernism marks a radical shift in the dominant logics of art, history, and cultural politics. No longer are we as individual workers, consumers, and urban subjects simply dealing with the modernist logics of alienation and shock resulting from the suffocating effects of industrial work, but instead we face a new set of experiences and problems. For Jameson, postmodernism and related postmodern artwork, literature, and films in general mark "a new depthlessness," a "weakening of historicity," and a new kind of emotional flatness that he calls "the waning of affect in postmodern culture."[9] Feminist and queer theorists writing about postmodern culture have since taken issue with Jameson's point about the waning of affect. For instance, Rei Terada's book *Feeling in Theory* can be read as a general defense of the centrality and persistent relevance of emotional categories even after the "death of the subject" proclaimed by poststructuralism.[10] Jack Halberstam, meanwhile, is more explicitly critical in his appraisal of Jameson's work and its relevance to gender and sexuality studies. Halberstam argues that "queer work on sexuality and space, like queer work on sexuality and time, has had to respond to canonical work on 'postmodern geography' by Edward Soja, Fredric Jameson, David Harvey, and others that has actively excluded sexuality as a category for analysis precisely because desire has been cast by neo-Marxists as part of a ludic body politics that obstructs the 'real' work of activism."[11]

In revisiting these debates, it becomes clear that while some feminists and queer critics engage in a theory war with neo-Marxist theorists of the postmodern, the two camps nonetheless concur that the conditions of postmodernity have resulted in new individual and collective experiences of loss, dystopic feeling, emotional flatness, and new modes of affective intensities and disorientations as we enter into postmodern temporality and spatiality. This mutation in time and space constitutes what David Harvey termed "time-space compression," which marks "another fierce round in that process of annihilation of space through time that has always lain at the center of capitalism's dynamic."[12] One useful way to enliven the debate on postmodernism, queer theory, and Sinophone studies is to *queer* Jamesonian conceptual categories and his concept of cognitive mapping in particular. For Jameson, postmodern entrapment in a space like the Westin Bonaventure Hotel in Los Angeles necessarily calls for a radical politics of "cognitive mapping" in which the individual trapped in postmodern geography needs to regain "some new heightened sense of its place in the global system" in order to grasp their imaginary relationship to the social totality.[13] In his subsequent work on cinema and space in the world system, Jameson applies cognitive mapping to cinematic analysis, examining how representations of postmodern spatiality constitute "the conspiratorial allegory of late capitalist totality."[14] Totality for Jameson is "very precisely that gap between form and content,"[15] and cognitive mapping provides one mode to think the unthinkable time-space of late capitalism. While neo-Marxist thinkers like Jameson may only "read" sexuality and queerness as part and parcel of the collective fantasy and allegory of conspiracy expressed in postmodern cinema, queering the concept of cognitive mapping would demonstrate that queer characters who roam around the urban spaces of Hong Kong, Taipei, and other Asian global cities are very much part of the allegorical script of late capitalism, but not necessarily in the same way as other subjects; in other words, queer theory offers a way to add nuance and questions of affect to Jameson's key theorizations. In proposing the concept of queer cognitive mapping, I point to the specific ways that representations of nonnormative sexualities and queer subjects in Sinophone cinemas visually exemplify the lived experiences of urban dystopia, spatial compression, and claustrophobia. In particular, I show how queer Sinophone cinema's articulations of queer desire evince visual optics of disidentification and divergence from normative spatial ordering of kinship and the gendered division of the private and the public.

The emphasis on queer Sinophone cinema here is also meant to redress the lack of focus on gender and sexuality in existing research about the global city, urbanism, and urban inequality in the Sinosphere.[16] While existing urban studies draw largely on data of urban density, GDP per capita, and Gini coefficient that characterize high rate of urban polarization in global cities like Hong Kong and Taipei (e.g., Hong Kong's Gini coefficient increased from 0.476 in 1991 to 0.525 in 2001),[17] these statistics do not always tell the whole complex story of how gender and racial minorities bear the brunt of real estate hegemony, spatial inequality, and gender and sexual discrimination.[18] Even fewer studies address the intersection of queer sexuality, cinematic aesthetics, and space within the context of globalization and late capitalism in Sinophone cinema. One key concept through which we can begin to consider the experience of queer individuals in both actual urban contexts and the representations we find of them in films is that of claustrophobia. In his book *The Geopolitical Aesthetic*, Jameson notes the claustrophobic character of Hong Kong and Taipei, noting their "all-encompassing closed urban space" and their "anthology of closed dwellings." For the queer residents of these cities, claustrophobia of course takes on an even deeper meaning, on both physical and emotional levels, which can be unpacked through an analysis of queer Sinophone filmmakers.

I argue that the films of Tsai Ming-liang both express the existing logics of queer claustrophobia while self-reflexively providing alternatives through queer cognitive mapping. Queer cognitive mapping provides a cinematic language to express how queer subjects in Sinophone films navigate time-space compression, gentrification, and the heteronormative gendered division of the public and the private. While the postmodern urban totality is ultimately unmappable and can be grasped only as a theoretical abstraction, queer cognitive mapping offers a specific means to understand how queer subjects in cinema make do with and at times subversively queer unlivable social space, what Jameson calls the "unevenness or inequality of the world system."[19] The dominant logic of postmodern queer claustrophobia is evident in two films by Tsai Ming-liang that focus on 1990s Taipei, namely *Rebels of the Neon God* (1992) and *The River* (1997). They imagine queerness within the context of materialist pressures of postmodern spatial compression yet move beyond the conspiratorial script of claustrophobia.

The films of Tsai Ming-liang are highly attuned to postmodern reconfigurations of time and space. Taipei's urban mapping has remained a main concern in almost all of his films since his 1992 debut, *Rebels of the Neon God*. It is this consistent interest in urban maps, street scenes, and queer male subjects' entrapments in 1990s Taipei that makes Tsai's urban aesthetics an inviting case to compare with other Sinophone queer cinema (for instance, Yonfan's sentimental look at 1990s Hong Kong in films like *Bishonen*, or more art-house-oriented films like Wong Kar-wai's *Happy Together*). Whereas a filmmaker like Yonfan sees queer death as brought about through logics of surveillance, the resanctification of the domestic home, and the relegation of queer subjects to the perverse public scenes of cruising that are at odds with normative kinship spaces, Tsai's films are rife with elements of playfulness, reversal, perversity, and even campiness. In other words, Tsai's cinematic approach gives queer cognitive mapping a more positive and radical spin that is missing in Yonfan's or Wong's work.

In what follows, using Tsai's *Rebels of the Neon God* (1992) and *The River* (1997) as examples, I explore various queer cognitive mappings of sexuality and space that lend themselves to an aesthetic of "overlapping territories." As a cinema in which heterosexual desire overlaps with a latent gay male erotic desire (as in the case of *Rebels*) and where the order of kinship is not only overlapped with incest but queered from the inside out (as in *River*), Tsai's work allows viewers to read the heterogeneity of urban space. In other words, these films map queer male subjects' relation to spaces where social power is most dominant, where the possibility of queerness seems laughable and impossible (kinship), and where sexual subjects may connect through intermediary, liminal spaces within urban Taipei. I pay especially close attention to the intertextual use of Lee Kang-sheng as the main character in each film in order to tease out his overlapping relationship with other characters in the films.[20]

In *Rebels of the Neon God*, Tsai offers a novel vision of urban Taipei by highlighting the queer affect of urban alienation that is central to all his other films as well. However, moving beyond conventional discussions of Tsai's films as mainly concerned with the feeling of alienation,[21] I will also show how the affect of alienation as such is mediated through intersubjective relationships, in which the alienated queer subject, Hsiao Kang, seeks to explore urban pleasure but ends up disappointed, while those who seem to partake most wildly within the city, Ah Tze (Chen Chao-jung), Ah Bing, and Ah Kuei (Wang Yu-wen), end up finding themselves alienated, marginalized, and spatially trapped with nowhere to go in a ruined and flooded apartment by the end of the film. In other words, I argue that there is no "spatial exit" as such in *Rebels*: liberation and sexual pleasure outside of home within the city is one side of the same coin as the boxed-in interiority of the domestic home. Therefore, the narrative does not privilege the space outside the home as one of freedom, urban pleasure, and liberation; rather, different sexual subjects (heterosexual, queer) are trapped within urban territories differently. My reading of this film emphasizes the spaces of the apartment and the video arcade as ones where the possibility of sexual freedom and urban entrapment overlap through intense affect. An aesthetic of queer cognitive mapping can demonstrate how queer subjects navigate and often disrupt the division between the public versus the private, the licit versus the illicit, and the normative versus the queer within the spatial unevenness of urban Taipei in a way that differs from heterosexual subjects.

How does Tsai visually convey these elements of overlapping spaces, affect, and sexuality? One way to probe deeper into this cinematic aesthetic of queer cognitive mapping is to think through his use of spatial coincidences or doublings in the film. In the opening sequence of *Rebels*, we are introduced to the visually alluring image of two preppy looking young men, Ah Tze and Ah Bing. They are soaked by the heavy rain outside, squeeze into a little telephone booth, and smoke a joint. We are tempted to think of them as an obvious pair of gay lovers, but are then surprised by their actions as they take out an electric screwdriver, open up the coin storage compartment of the telephone, and steal a large number of coins. This combination of a tight space and the naughty, campy, and comic insinuation of homoeroticism and homosociality strategically overlaps with the situation of the alienated young man Hsiao Kang, who is trapped within a domestic home. While the first shot of Ah Tze and Ah Bing frames them as parasitic urban subjects, whose means of survival are dependent on liquid capitalism, the informal economy of the global city, and illicit commerce, Hsiao Kang, the latent gay young man trapped within the home, turns out to be just as much of an urban parasite as these two men, as a close reading of the next several shots demonstrates. The cognitive map that Tsai's film draws is thus one that insists that all places are alike, at least in some senses, to the queer subject.

The next sequence moves from a medium shot to a close-up of Hsiao Kang's back as he is moving his studying chair back and forth due to boredom as a result of excessive studying (or not studying?). Out of nowhere, a cockroach (the quintessential urban pest, suggesting a kind of parasitism as it feeds on detritus left behind by human beings) sneaks into his room. Hsiao Kang, provoked by the insect's intrusion into his space, uses the pointy needle of a compass to stab its body. The insect, struggling on the desk, cannot move. Hsiao Kang then throws the cockroach out of his window. The next shot shows Ah Tze and Ah Bing entering a local video arcade, where many other young urban parasites are seeking audiovisual electronic entertainment, suggesting that the two spaces are in some way doubles of one another. The next shot comes back to Hsiao Kang's room. Surprised by the magical survival of the cockroach, which is now lying on the middle of his window outside in the rain, Hsiao Kang slams the window twice, only to break it and injure his hands. His blood then drips drop by drop onto his high school textbook; the page tainted with blood shows the map of Taiwan itself.

While these scenes of urban overlapping strike one as particularly mundane (raining, video store, and cockroach), and cinematically they are modest in production (dirty old room, any telephone booth in Taipei, etc.), they are nonetheless visually striking in their linking of different urban subjects through the logic of overlapping territories: young rebels and lawbreakers, a young student who doesn't want to study, and a cockroach are juxtaposed early on in the narrative. Moreover, such a logic of spatial coincidence foreshadows the social locations of these urban parasites through the figure of the cockroach. The cockroach that is crushed by Hsiao Kang may represent Ah Tze and Ah Bing, who will be captured by competing gangsters and mafia groups whose territory of power is violated by their other acts of theft. The cockroach also functions as a sign pointing to the intersubjective relation between Ah Tze and Hsiao Kang, with the latter following every move of the former who is the young, charismatic, and virile heterosexual object of desire that the cockroach-like Hsiao Kang can never possess. As such, through the visually ugly cockroach, Tsai beautifully maps the overlapping territories of late capitalist above-ground and underground commerce, sexual desire, heterosexuality, and male homoeroticism through logics of spatial compression and coincidence.[22] Cinematic spatial overlapping thus stands out as a key signature of queer cognitive mapping, where urban density and spatial unevenness both separate and conjoin diverse urban subjects. In one of the first books in Taiwan on Tsai's cinema, Wen Tianxiang reads the cockroach and the blood on the map of Taiwan as alluding to Hsiao Kang's symbolic death at the hands of its Taiwan's educational system."[23] Here, I further extend Wen's insightful reading of the insect by suggesting that Hsiao Kang's blood, literally tainting the map of Taiwan, marks "the mapping of urban desire" as intersubjectively queer. By linking personal pain and frustration, the dripping of blood, and the geopolitical map of Taiwan, Tsai connects the personal space of the home to the geopolitical "space" of the nation and the urban city, again, through the logics of spatial coincidence, yet all spaces remain equally confined and thwart efforts to claim or exist within them, to the point of being deadly.

The specific example of the video arcade as a site where desire, underground commerce, law, and crime coexist elucidates the queer cartography of confinement and overlapping urbanity in Taipei. In what is probably the most claustrophobic scene in the film, Ah Tze and Ah Bing are playing the big hammer game. They continue until the closing of the store, when both men hide behind a corner in the bathroom to make sure that the security guard has left. With the electric door sliding down, the "real game" has begun. The men engage in yet another illicit form of economic activity as they open up the back sides of all of the video game booths, unscrewing the green decoding video chipboards. In this scene, Hsiao Kang is also hiding in the store. But exhibiting his usual clumsiness, he fails to leave before the two men lock it up following their crime. Hsiao Kang is literally trapped in a space where he thought he could get a glimpse of urban desire and liberation from his home. His pursuit of freedom and latent sexual desire for Ah Tze reinscribes him into yet another space of compression, boredom, and restraint. Queer cognitive mapping here evinces a form of mapping in which one can find no space in the totality in which one desire could be satisfied or where one could "belong" in a different way, but one that seems only to reflect or extend the immediate conditions of confinement and frustration outward.

We might think further about how Tsai uses generic or familiar spaces in order to insist on the idea that confinement exists everywhere, particularly for the queer subject, even if there may still be certain marginal spaces in which different subjects and territories overlap. In the geospatial imaginary, the video arcade is a commonplace in cities across the globe to the point of being what Ackbar Abbas calls a nondescript space in his global cosmopolitan comparison between Shanghai and Hong Kong. Abbas's remark provides a characterization that can easily describe 1990s Taipei as well: "Beyond a certain point, there is a blurring and scrambling of signs and an overlapping of spatial and temporal grids, all of which make urban signs and images difficult to read. . . . This means that the anomalous is in danger of turning *nondescript*, in much the same way that the more complex the city today, the more it becomes a city without qualities."[24] Abbas's acute analysis of the global city as engendering "an overlapping of spatial and temporal grids" of nondescript spaces calls for an analysis that appreciates the overcomplexity of spaces and overhomogenization of Taipei and other world cities, as well as the specificity of local and translocal spaces that contain within them not only overlapping territories but overlapping desires as well. To illustrate this, we can look to how the local video store serves several visual typologies in the film. It is at once a space of masculinity, where Ah Tze shows off his great skill in winning the latest Japanese video games in front of his girlfriend Ah Kuei, and a space of high-level, visualized, and electronicized liquid capitalism, where money (coins) and pleasure (visual pleasure) are mediated and exchanged at an accelerating rate.[25] Finally, it is also a space of claustrophobic queerness, as Hsiao Kang literally stalks Ah Tze and his friends. The overlapping of desires (to perform a certain type of masculinity, to make money, to satisfy sexual urges, to escape) adds an additional layer of depth to the common theme of urban alienation in Tsai's films. Here though it is not only alienated desire that deserves our attention—it is also the way that Tsai maps desire both multidirectionally and nonreciprocally that makes his practice specifically queer. At one moment in the narrative Ah Tze misses out on a date with Ah Kuei because of his need to make money, whereas Hsiao Kang also attempts to meet Ah Tze, misses the opportunity, and ends up boxed and reentrapped again. Therefore, straight, heteronormative urban desire is coincidentally and disorientingly aligned and linked with queer desire.

While *Rebel* illustrates the nuanced ways that the overlapping, translocal, and highly claustrophobic spaces of the apartment and video game store both constrain, enable, and induce overlapping forms of desire within Taipei's postmodernity, *The River* abandons the apartment and the video arcade to explore the subculture of bathhouse. While an easy argument can be made that this film is all about exploring this gay male subcultural space as a new postmodern space that is comparable to other bathhouses in the global queer urban hubs (for example, those in San Francisco, Los Angeles, and large European cities), I want to locate the specific potentiality of queerness in Taipei's postmodernity by calling for a reading that examines the breakdown of private versus public spaces, especially the queering of the oppositional spaces of the domestic "private" home and the "public" bathhouse. This queer cognitive mapping of postmodern space moves beyond *Rebels* insofar as it suggests how the domestic itself might be queered. *The River*, through the incestuous relationship between the father (played by Miao Tien) and the son Hsiao Kang (Lee Kang-sheng), publicizes, commercializes, and scandalizes the normative kinship between father and son while, paradoxically, reestablishing the "normative" bonds of father-son through intense intimacy in "public" spaces.

More than implying the proximity between heterosexuality and homo-sexuality, in *The River* Tsai provocatively marks the Kuomintang (KMT)-identified patriarch as queer. Gina Marchetti goes so far as to argue that the film potentially reasserts neo-Confucianism and political conservatism, despite its queer message, by having the KMT-identified father figure have sex with his son, who can be seen as the new Taiwanese youth figure that is identified with post–Martial Law native Taiwanese identity.[26] While such an allegorical reading is very suggestive in terms of rethinking the geopolitical significance of the film, the allegorical reading risks reducing the materialist significance of social spaces themselves to mere political abstractions. That is not to say that a highly politi-cal reading of the father figure does not produce a radical queer reading, and indeed other allegorical readings are possible: one might assert that the queer father, as a Mainland perpetual exile in post–Martial Law Taiwan and as a gay man stuck with a patriarchal duty, mirrors the status of Taiwan on the political world stage as doubly marginalized, a concept that Ping-hui Liao theorizes in another context. Liao describes the historical and global rejection of Taiwan by world politics from the time of Nixon's visit to China in 1972 to that of a new political democratization in 1978 in the following way: "By the time Chiang Ching-kuo took over as president in 1978, he was ready to declare himself a 'Tai-wanese' and, unlike his father, gradually accepted the historical effects of Tai-wan's relocation from China's *pien-tsui* (periphery) to the world's *pien-yuan* (margin), of a tiny island-state being twice removed from the global culture map."[27] If one conceives of the father's symbolic role in this way, he is doubly abandoned by the failed KMT's desire to reconquer the mainland as well as abandoned by the vibrant queer youth culture that has emerged since 1987 Taiwan post–Martial Law sexual liberalization.

However, Tsai's film's overwhelming images of the postmodern shopping mall, of overlapping spaces between the familial and the commercial, of the com-partmentalization of family members into subjects almost unknown to one another, and of McDonald's as a sign of global capitalism, produce an altogether overwhelming array of meanings that resist allegorical analysis and call instead for a more materialist analysis of postmodern spaces. Rey Chow reads *The River* as engendering "a production of discursivity, one that is not exactly geared toward a centralizable and thus summarizable logic but that operates in the manner of an archaeological excavation."[28] My reading asks how the postmodernity of social spaces is mediated through the destabilization of the private and the public by showing how Tsai's film "empties out" and makes questionable the privacy of the home and the publicness of public sex through a representational strategy that I have called "overlapping territories." A cinematic aesthetic of queer cognitive mapping illustrates how spaces can double one another in a way that goes beyond representing homogeneity and confinement. Instead, it shows how space itself can be transformed, unraveling the ways in which queerness disorientingly traverses these overlapping urban spaces while disrupting the gendered division of spaces of normative kinship versus spaces of queer public sex.

Tsai destabilizes the kinship-family-home equivalence by representing familial subjects as coincidentally related, rather than naturally and intimately tied by blood or the coherence of domestic space; the private, in other words, has been stripped of its previous functions and leads to the same kind of atomization and isolation that one finds in other urban spaces. The absence of traditional structures of kinship is doubled by the isolation of individuals from one another in public space. The opening scene in which Hsiao Kang rekindles his friendship with an unnamed female friend (played by Shiang-chyi Chen) on the two-way escalator rising up and down to the entrance of Shin Kong Mitsukoshi Department Store suggests the fragility and contingency of relationships in a city marked by postmodern dystopia and overlapping spaces. First, the young woman almost passes by Hsiao Kang, and only after a moment does she recognize her old friend. The escalator in public space, however, could just as easily have led to a missed encounter. In a crowded situation, they would probably be pushed to the side of each escalator and would surely miss one another; at a non-busy daytime hour, however, when the opening sequence takes place, the escalator's built-in structure makes the avoidance of the gaze almost impossible and thus links urban subjects through their visual-spatial-temporal recompartmentalization within boxed-in, inescapable moments, even when, contradictorily, such moments happen in an "open" space.

While the meaning of Shin Kong Mitsukoshi Tower remains puzzling in the film, I would argue that the compartmentalization of the building's activities, in the supremely multifunctional sites of shopping (on its first twelve floors and two underground floors) and life insurance business, makes the division between consumption, production, pleasure, and work obsolete.[29] The postmodern overcoming of distinct social spaces suggested by the tower parallels the representation of Hsiao Kang's social identity as well, as the "chance" encounter between him and the woman leads him to be involved with her work as part of a film production crew. He is introduced to a film director (played by renowned Hong Kong filmmaker Ann Hui) who asks him to play a human corpse floating on a dirty river because the fake prop is simply not convincing enough. The staging of a heterosexual encounter between friends (or strangers?) in an early sequence of a film about queer incest troubles any definitive reading of Hsiao Kang's identity as stable in social and sexual terms, and the dummy scene further suggests this instability. By having Hsiao Kang stand in for a dummy, an object that is supposed to closely resemble an actual dead human body, Tsai playfully depicts human subjects as interchangeable, and the real and the imagined as malleable. The nonhuman dummy does not capture the authenticity of a dead body, yet, ironically, it is the "alive" human body of Hsiao Kang that simulates the true realness of a "dead" body. By inference, Tsai shows that "real" human relationships like that between father and son may be more malleable than they seem. Just as a human can be turned into a dummy, the authentically alive body into an authentically dead body representationally, normative kin relations can turn queer.

If human subjects can be recompartmentalized within postmodern space, kinship structure can also be decompartmentalized into barely related encounters between postmodern subjects. Such is the picture of Hsiao Kang's family presented here. One intriguing but easily overlooked sequence of the film makes such deprivatizing of the family clear. Family drama surrounds the neck pain of Hsiao Kang, which his parents try to cure through various methods such as Taoist medicine, acupuncture, and physical therapy to no avail. Aside from their concern for their son's pain, the parents and the son live in the home behaving as if they were mere tenants and strangers, and each is more concerned with their public lives and extrafamilial affairs than their kinship roles. For example, one sequence shows mother, son, and father, separated from one another in the apartment and each going about their own business (the mother watching pornographic films, the son using his mother's vibrator to massage his neck, the father tossing sleeplessly in bed, likely due to his sexual desire for young men). The home here is decompartmentalized, depersonalized, and deprivatized through a cinematic depiction of each in their rooms doing their own deeds in an intersecting montage sequence. The next shot shows the father sitting inside the glossy McDonald's in the morning as he fixates on a young male hustler (played by Chen Chao-jung, the actor who plays the straight young man Ah Tze in *Rebels*). The film thus playfully links the space of kinship to what exists outside the home, namely the cruising activity of the father and public commercial sex in general. In this way, the film practices queer cognitive mapping through visually linking local and translocal spaces like the home, video rental store, and shopping mall, suggesting the erasure of the public/private distinction and the existence of "different" or "outside" spaces. At the same time, these spaces themselves can be queered, or serve as sites in which kinship itself is both subverted and reaffirmed. In a very campy way,[30] through a scene of public sex, the son and the father reunite in the public bathhouse.

The scene in question accentuates the major issues that I have examined thus far, namely the configuration of claustrophobic sexuality in postmodern space and the queer cognitive mapping envisioned by Sinophone filmmakers. Specifically, I contend that it would be too simplistic to argue that the film privileges the opposition between commercial sex versus private relationships; more critically, the film debunks any assumptions about private and public life by depicting a possible utopian, salvational, and interlocking relationship between kinship and public sex, between the intimate and the commercial, and between father and son as both strangers and lovers. The film moves beyond a simple elevation of public sex as queer, because even the male hustler does not satisfy the desire of the father (in one scene in the bathhouse, the hustler refuses to perform fellatio on the old man). Conversely, in the incest scene, the father is waiting in the dark room in the bathhouse while the son, after walking through many rooms, happens to come into the dark room where the father lies. Both, unknown to each other, engage in mutual affection, with the father selflessly helping the son masturbate instead of forcing Hsiao Kang to perform oral sex on him. After pleasuring the young man, the father enjoys affection by holding him from behind. The morning after, recognizing that it was his son with whom he just engaged in a sexual encounter, the father slaps his face hard. The same day, returning to the motel room (they were on a journey to find medicinal cure for the son's neck pain), the father makes a call to the religious master Mr. Liu, only to find out that the master has instructed them to return to Taipei to find a doctor. The father goes out to buy breakfast for the son, while the son, opening the curtains in the room, gazes toward the bright sky.

Critics have performed different readings of these queer representations of "kinship trouble" in Tsai's film; while some comment on the possible neo-Confucian message of the father as reestablishing his role as paternal, most agree that the film's ending urges a queering of the family. Gina Marchetti reads the film's ending as an optimistic call for sexual liberation in Taiwan: "The father's slap can be read as a wakeup call to Chinese gays that the closet cannot continue and that it is time for all homosexuals to come out of their dark cubicles and face the light of the day as Hsiao Kang does in *The River*'s closing image."[31] Fran Martin's reading seems a bit more aligned with my attempt to locate spaces of sexual possibility even within the most claustrophobic, all-enclosing context of postmodern urbanism. Martin writes, "What these shots represent are perhaps paradoxically *situated* utopias: new spaces of possibility opening up within the constrained conditions of everyday life in the dystopian cities of Taiwanese (post)modernity—the spaces of love re-imagined."[32] By reordering the discursive limits of social spaces in urban Taipei, *The River* turns the claustrophobic space of interiority and postmodern dystopia into a kind of perverse social space. Through this perverse remapping of claustrophobia, Tsai's cinematic aesthetic also allows for the possibility of a new temporality—a queer futurity yet to come, as pictured by the gesture of Hsiao Kang looking up to the sky. If cognitive mapping provides a framework to realign oneself in the new space of multinational capitalism and unevenness across the world system, the aesthetic of queer cognitive mapping in the case of Tsai Ming-liang's queer Sinophone cinema daringly imagines a new queer utopia within the cracks of time-space compression and global postmodernity.

Notes

1 Fredric Jameson, *The Geopolitical Aesthetic: Cinema and Space in the World System* (Bloomington: Indiana University Press, 1992), 117.

2 Jameson, *Geopolitical Aesthetic*, 154.

3 Catherine Liu, "Taiwan's Cold War: Geopolitics in Edward Yang's *The Terrorizers*," in *Surveillance in Asian Cinema: Under Eastern Eyes*, ed. Karen Fang (London: Routledge, 2017), 115.

4 Gina Marchetti, *Citing China: Politics, Postmodernism, and World Cinema* (Honolulu: University of Hawaii Press, 2018), 2.

5 For studies on international migration of domestic workers to Hong Kong and Taiwan, see Nicole Constable, *Maid to Order in Hong Kong: Stories of Migrant Workers* (Ithaca, NY: Cornell University Press, 1997), and Pei-Chia Lan, *Global Cinderellas: Migrant Domestics and Newly Rich Employers in Taiwan* (Durham, NC: Duke University Press, 2006).

6 For a study that examines Taiwanese gay male literature in light of urbanization and gentrification, see Hans Tao-Ming Huang, "From Glass Clique to *Tongzhi* Nation: *Crystal Boys*, Identity Formation, and the Politics of Sexual Shame," *positions* 18, no. 2 (2010): 373–398.

7 For the most recent scholarship on queer theory and global film studies, see Karl Schoonover and Rosalind Galt, *Queer Cinema in the World* (Durham, NC: Duke University Press, 2016).

8 Jean-François Lyotard, *The Postmodern Condition: A Report on Knowledge* (Minneapolis: University of Minnesota Press, 1984), xxiv.

9 Fredric Jameson, *Postmodernism; or, The Cultural Logic of Late Capitalism* (Durham, NC: Duke University Press, 1991), 6 and 10.

10 Rei Terada, *Feeling in Theory: Emotion after the "Death of the Subject"* (Cambridge, MA: Harvard University Press, 2001).

11 Judith Halberstam, *In a Queer Time and Place: Transgender Bodies, Subcultural Lives* (New York: New York University Press, 2005), 5.

12 David Harvey, *The Condition of Postmodernity* (Malden, MA: Blackwell, 1990), 293.

13 Jameson, *Postmodernism*, 54.

14 Jameson, *Geopolitical Aesthetic*, 22.

15 Jameson, *Geopolitical Aesthetic*, 22.

16 For a definition of the Sinophone as one that critiques the Mainland-centric discourse and linguistic essentialism of Chineseness, see Shu-mei Shih, *Visuality and Identity: Sinophone Articulations across the Pacific* (Berkeley: University of California Press, 2007); for a queer Sinophone approach to Hong Kong cinema, see Alvin K. Wong, "Postcoloniality beyond China-centrism: Queer Sinophone Transnationalism in Hong Kong Cinema," in *Keywords in Queer Sinophone Studies*, ed. Howard Chiang and Alvin K. Wong (London: Routledge, 2020), 62–79.

17 Claudio O. Delang and Ho Cheuk Lung, "Public Housing and Poverty Concentration in Urban Neighbourhoods: The Case of Hong Kong in the 1990s," *Urban Studies* 47, no. 7 (June 2010): 1392.

18 One study that does include gender in the analysis of urbanization through a comparison of Singapore, Hong Kong, and Taipei might be the exception that proves the rule of heteronormativity. While the study draws from data sampling such as median age of first marriage, total fertility rate, and divorce rate, it overlooks questions of sexuality, single-parent families, and nonheterosexual desire. See Po-Fen Tai, "Gender Matters in Social Polarisation: Comparing Singapore, Hong Kong and Taipei," *Urban Studies* 50, no. 6 (May 2013): 1148–1164.

19 Jameson, *Geopolitical Aesthetic*, 154.

20 My interest in intertextuality in Tsai's film is mostly concerned with Lee's character Hsiao Kang by illustrating the overlapping territories of desire; for a more in-depth discussion of intertextuality in Tsai's films, see Song Hwee Lim, "Positioning Auteur Theory in Chinese Cinemas Studies: Intratextuality, Intertextuality, and Paratextuality in the Films of Tsai Ming-liang," *Journal of Chinese Cinemas* 1, no. 3 (2007): 223–245.

21 See Woei Lien Chong's essay "Alienation in the Modern Metropolis: The Visual Idiom of Taiwanese Film Director Tsai Ming-liang," *China Information* 9, no. 4 (1995): 81–95.

22 On reading capitalist commerce and personal, intersubjective relationships in transnational Chinese films, see Gina Marchetti's essay "Buying American, Consuming Hong Kong: Cultural Commerce, Fantasies of Identity, and the Cinema," in *The Cinema of Hong Kong: History, Arts, Identity*, ed. Poshek Fu and David Desser (Cambridge: Cambridge University Press, 2000), 289–313.

23 Wen Tianxiang (聞天祥), *Guang ying ding ge: Cai Mingliang de xin ling chang yu* (光影定格: 蔡明亮的心靈場域) (Taipei: Heng xing guo ji wen hua shi ye you xian gong si, 2002), 77.

24 Ackbar Abbas, "Cosmopolitan De-scriptions: Shanghai and Hong Kong," *Public Culture* 12, no. 3 (2000): 769–786, 772.

25 See Zygmunt Bauman, *Liquid Modernity* (Cambridge: Polity, 2000).

26 Gina Marchetti, "On Tsai Ming-liang's *The River*," in *Island on the Edge: Taiwan New Cinema and After*, ed. Chris Berry and Feii Lu (Hong Kong: Hong Kong University Press, 2005), 117.

27 Ping-hui Liao, "Postmodern Literary Discourse and Contemporary Public Culture in Taiwan," in *Postmodernism and China*, ed. Arif Dirlik and Xudong Zhang (Durham, NC: Duke University Press, 2000), 81.

28 Rey Chow, *Sentimental Fabulations, Contemporary Chinese Films: Attachment in the Age of Global Visibility* (New York: Columbia University Press, 2007), 187.

29 For a brief reading of the building as postmodern, see Ping-hui Liao, "Postmodern Literary Discourse," 79.

30 For a reading of Tsai's cinema as practicing camp aesthetics, see Emilie Yueh-yu Yeh and Darrell William Davis, *Taiwan Film Directors: A Treasure Island* (New York: Columbia University Press, 2005), 217–248.

31 Gina Marchetti, "On Tsai Ming-liang's *The River*," 126.

32 Fran Martin, *Situating Sexualities: Queer Representation in Taiwanese Fiction, Film and Public Culture* (Hong Kong: Hong Kong University Press, 2003), 180.

7

A Jamesonian Reading of
Parasite (2019)

Homes, Real Estate
Speculation, and Bubble
Markets in Seoul

KEITH B. WAGNER

Communities mean very little in the cinematic worlds devised by Bong Joon-ho. The world system, however—faulty, corrupt, and often inscrutable—is a thing perceived as far greater than national unity, families, and even the individual protagonist; each unit, large and small, becomes expendable in Bong's storytelling, secondary to the larger systems at play. The place of the world system in Bong's cinema can be usefully illuminated via Fredric Jameson's film theory, as elaborated in 1992's *The Geopolitical Aesthetic: Cinema and Space in the World System*. It might seem incongruous to bring back a thirty-year-old theory by Jameson, but his understanding of large-scale changes under late capitalism is impervious to time. In his chapter "Remapping Taipei," Jameson argues that Edward Yang's masterpiece *The Terrorizers* (1986) no longer indicts any one class for the city's harsh realities, but rather depicts a system-specific phenomenon, where "the various forms which reification and commodification and the corporate standardizations of media society [come to] imprint on human subjectivity and existential experience."[1] This was quite an astute move by Jameson to shift to a scope greater than that of any one national cinema, and he was right to pinpoint the effects of a certain standardization of market forces on every facet of life; this is not only present in East Asia, as Yang shows us, but also demonstrated in other chapters dealing with Europe, North America, and Southeast Asia, and these art cinemas taken together offer an illuminating global perspective.

Tragically, however, three decades later the system-specific problem of global capitalism that Jameson identified still persists and the deregulation of markets continues to impact urban infrastructure and renovation in other ways. Different to what Jameson identifies as Yang's filmic penchant for "depressing signs of urban squalor" in Taipei,[2] there has been an emergence since the 2010s of new wealthy districts in East Asian cities brought to screen by other directors (contrasting the older urban squalor): Eva Jin's doll house cosmopolitan-styled Beijing in *One Night Surprise* (2013), about Fan Bingbing's character's workplace romances and career aspirations at an advertising firm in the capital's creative industry district; or Sion Sono's *Anti-Porno* (2017), about the unglamorous life of a Japanese adult video star, where the wealthy Ginza district of Tokyo becomes a luxurious backdrop to this provocative film. These ritzy residential districts are sprouting up across Asia (and globally) and should not be completely denigrated given the financial opportunities and investment potential they bring to the country. But these areas also create a different kind of urban condition: allusions to a neoliberal utopia of gated and exclusive communities, these new (and old money) milieus come to serve mostly an elite class and, to borrow from Aihwa Ong, "become centres to be invoked, envied, and emulated as exemplary sites of a new urban normativity."[3]

Bong's most recent orchestration of the world system can be found in the depiction of the residential housing struggle in Seoul in *Parasite* (2019), which reflects fictionally on "speculative assets and spectacular spaces."[4] On the one hand, Bong's treatment of the subject is specific to Korea and Korean citizens because he shows Seoul as being not all high-tech skyline but also full of affluent districts of growing world renown, places that have also become unlivable for nearly every social class in Korea. On the other hand, and simultaneously, *Parasite* invokes the global in such a way that real estate is likewise relevant and applicable to those around the world, and Bong's local-to-global perspective allows him to grapple with urban instability resulting from the market forces that many of us now face. Bong uses the luxury home—characterized not as dwelling or abode but as property and real estate—to serve as a compelling figure through which to scrutinize the financialized organization of society, and the residential property's role in it, in such a way that a single limited location, the home itself, becomes a way to speak about a larger financialized world system that is not directly depicted. How we see what lies beneath the infinite expansion of the market through a series of events that happen within a luxury home in *Parasite* is my focus in this chapter.

The film portrays three Korean families—the nouveau-riche Parks, the precariat Kims, as well as the other precariat married couple, Moon-gwang and Geun-sae (never given a surname in the film)—who are each layered upon one another in the Parks' luxury home. Although the characters and their hierarchical arrangement are similar to the social subjects found in George Cruikshank's etching *The British Beehive* (1867), Bong's film diverges from the Victorian metaphor and its stratified lower classes through the privileging of property over pedigree and class disposition. The Park home becomes a contested space, a miniature Koreanized beehive of activity, work, and the escapades of different social classes, yet the great aspiration and equalizer in Korea is the affective component—the sense of the home—of its market appeal that finds relevance across all classes. *Parasite* comes to "acknowledge the fallibility of any sense of home," and devises scenarios of "empowerment and control"[5] wielded not by any one class but by the market itself. From the very beginning of the film, the Kim family is shown to enter into service of the Park family, and their "infiltration,"[6] like that of Moon-gwang and Geun-sae before them, their worship of property, and the status of the property's location in affluent Seongbuk-dong form the basic structure around which the plot unfolds.

Despite never wishing to speak fully and directly about Korea's own real estate bonanza, Bong's film nonetheless can tell us something quite specific, and indeed different from the other media texts that will be discussed below, even if they deal with similar issues. I use a Jamesonian allegorical reading to methodologically assist in the task at hand: to unpick the different ways that the home and the household is culturally, economically, and psychologically seen as speculative asset. For Jameson, allegory is an "amphibious formation, whose essential structural characteristic may be described as its possibility to manifest itself either as a pseudo-idea—a conceptual or belief system, an abstract value, an opinion or prejudice—or as a protonarrative, a kind of ultimate class fantasy about the collective characters which are the class in opposition."[7] *Parasite* speaks to such fantasies by giving allegorical figuration to the fundamental experience of poor living standards under Seoul's neoliberal urbanization, driven by real estate speculation and, the film suggests, giving rise to a looming housing bubble about to burst. What legitimizes any Marxian interpretation of *Parasite* is not only one's apprehension of this larger allegory, but more importantly the way in which one can classify Bong as a forecaster of such a possible and tragic socioeconomic event, allegorized through the more local tragic moments of home invasion and a backyard killing spree during a birthday party toward which the film builds. This is one way to revise Jameson's notion of allegory, insofar as it can be conceived of not only as the expression of a fixed social totality, but also as a way to gesture toward something that has not yet occurred but seems imminent.

The primary concern of this essay, however, is how these issues revolve around the figure of the home itself. The chapter does a number of things: First, Jameson's work on neo-noir film proves useful here. I expand on Jameson's notion of aesthetic signs in *Body Heat* (Lawrence Kasdan, 1981) with my own theories pertaining to how the large estate in the Hollywood film registers as a sexualized and financialized space, quintessential to film noir's rejection of the nuclear family and the home. Not unlike *Body Heat* (although not necessarily a neo-noir film), *Parasite* builds on other Korean films of the past that center on the simulacrum of the home. Like Rem Koolhaas's "generic city," the Seongbuk-dong home takes on a generic architectural form, appearing like a "museal home" in the capital. Such generic cities and generic homes are thus like any others around the world, susceptible to turbulent markets, and *Parasite* is a cautionary tale about seeing property as safe haven or as home. Second, this chapter shows how the figure of the home reflects inhospitable conditions in Seoul, but also how these conditions are connected to larger dynamics, specifically real estate speculation and bubbles in other countries, thus linking the local and global. And third, it aims to understand the function of allegory in Bong's depiction of bubble markets as "trends and forces in the world system"[8] and to consider how his film makes evaluations that are built out of formal elements of storytelling and aesthetics rather than simply prescriptive readings of actual material conditions. Jameson would view this as a strength, a means through which the "text reorganizes the subtexts,"[9] but I would also argue that *Parasite*'s global success owes much to its careful placement of social classes as independent from one another, as the film presents an "oppositional culture which will, often in covert and disguised strategies, seek to contest and to undermine the dominant 'value system.'"[10] In Korea and for Bong this dominant value system is not the exploitation of classes, as it would be in a Marxist account, but rather the grotesque speculative value placed on the home. However opaquely Bong goes about it, the film ultimately ends by meditating not only on the "cultural hegemony of property"[11] in Seoul but also on how homes or apartments connote a new sense of placelessness under a real estate market concerned exclusively with their surplus value.

From Jameson's Neo-noir Home to Bong's Museal Home

Although Jameson has been noticeably silent on the cinematic appearance of the home under late capitalism, his use of the neo-noir film allows us to begin to see the home as no longer *longed for* but now *financially coveted*, a change that has occurred in genre cinemas from both the United States and South Korea. Using *Body Heat*, a remake of Billy Wilder's *Double Indemnity* (1944) (part of the first cycle of noir films), as an example, Jameson reminds us that the way architecture is depicted in this film is "exceedingly polysemous,"[12] and it connotes both the past and present. One could argue that *Body Heat* coincided with the opening of the neoliberal era (in my view)[13] and postmodern era (in Jameson's conception), which is why the specificity of the way Kasdan treats the home can be clearly connected with *Parasite*. Because *Parasite* heralds the end of an era, not for neoliberalism but rather for anyone wishing to reverse property / real estate's seductive association to pure asset, the home becomes a postmodern form in the 2010s. Bong's creation of the home becomes another example of what Jameson calls the "glossy mirage" in *Body Heat*.[14] The home itself in *Body Heat* is viewed along with other settings such as a dive bar, a low-rate law firm, and the seaside boardwalk as if they "were set in some eternal thirties, beyond real historical time."[15] Moving from the South of the United States and a filmic depiction of "the growing economic power of the region"[16] alongside an assortment of white-collar crimes (e.g., land speculation, tax evasion, embezzlement for the mafia), Bong's use of the luxury home in *Parasite* is different, in that it shows an increasingly homogenized and globalized form, "a mesmerizing new aesthetic mode,"[17] one catering to the tastes of transnational elite found both in Seoul and in other elite enclaves across the globe. While the luxury home is a key figure in both diegetic worlds, the two homes depicted belong to different eras as regards the functioning of the property market and the culture of home. In *Body Heat*, dirty money flows in from offshore accounts in the Cayman Islands and from crime families in New York, and this gives several characters access to multiple properties across Florida and elsewhere in the world. For Bong, the home in *Parasite* is the domain of figures emblematic of a later stage of capitalism, namely the internet mogul, Mr. Park, or the white German transnational family who later move in.

The plot of *Body Heat* is based around an insidious plan to use a large estate as honey trap for a lawyer named Ned Racine (William Hurt). Ned's knowledge of commercial real estate law, a type of practice he is disinterested in and doesn't practice very competently, captures the attention of a femme fatale, who sees his legal ineptitude as a means to future financial gain. As Ned becomes infatuated with the alluring Matty Walker (Kathleen Turner), her luxury home becomes a site for his seduction and the duo's planning of Matty's husband's murder. They camouflage his murder as accident in an act of arson to collect insurance money and claim the property. As neo-noir devalues the sanctity of the home, the large estate (or commercial property in a portfolio) in *Body Heat* located in suburban Florida, a few hours from Miami, can never return to being a place of shelter for these two lovers. On the contrary, Matty's large estate is a type of property that John David Rhodes calls "fungible and alienable; thus whatever is promised by the house is radically susceptible to violation, displacement, and loss."[18] Gone, one might say in *Body Heat*, is the quaintness of Bachelard's iconic home as sanctuary or sacred dwelling.[19] Instead, under a new logic of carnal lust, venality, and murder, the older lyrical exploration of such domestic spaces in our past has now given way to the primacy of their transactional value: something must happen in or to the home for it to hold social value under neoliberalism.

Like Kasdan's homage to Wilder, Bong's film creates what Jamesonian scholar Carl Freedman would call a "revisionary relationship" to the home today.[20] *Parasite* can be productively contrasted with Im Song-soo's luxury home film *The Housemaid* (2010), a remake of Kim Ki-young's 1960 film of the same title, which tells a tale about the class anxieties and dispossession in the context of a lower-middle-class family's home.[21] Different from the original film, Im's remake focuses on a luxury property in Seoul that reveals a precariat housemaid's vengeance that triggers, presumably, the loss of such property. Eun-yi (Do-yeon Jeon), the precarious domestic servant, is pushed to her psychological breaking point after Hoon, the patriarch, initiates an affair with her. Later Hoon's wife and mother-in-law discover the tryst and poison a pregnant Eun-yi; this leads later to her dramatic suicide, hanging herself from a chandelier, after losing her unborn child. Aesthetically, *The Housemaid*'s "pristine yet decadent images of the home punctuate languorous moments in the film: Im's use of black reflective surfaces and lowlighting give the film a neoliberal atmosphere of unrestrained consumption and lust. These shimmering dark surfaces become portraiture that provides fake posturing or the notion"[22] of the venal upper class who reside in these palatial enclaves. Another important film about real estate, *Gangnam Blues* (Yoo Ha, 2015), and a precursor to *Parasite*, stands out as an excoriating cultural history of Seoul's dubious real estate speculation, transpiring in the 1970s. The film focuses on illegal evictions and demolition of shanty homes needed to make way for modern-day Gangnam—a form of "urbicide"[23]—as it sheds important light on the violent dislocation and corrupt government actions used to redevelop farmland into expensive condominiums. As Jameson correctly sees *Body Heat*'s camerawork eluding "the high-rise landscape of the 1970s and 1980s,"[24] *Parasite*'s visuality also bypasses these larger structures, no longer fixated on the apartment building or condominium. Darting up like gray and white concrete wildflowers (or Lego stacks of colored bricks), often twenty-five to forty stories high, apartment buildings and skyscraper condominiums ("sky villas") remain signs of hyperdevelopment in Seoul under dictatorial and democratic regimes, the luxury home in Bong's film however takes our eye from a city of verticality to one of opulence, up on the mountainous hills of the capital.

In other ways, Bong's reappropriation and neutralization of the traditional notions associated with the home—as representational strategy in Korea and by Hollywood—come through his decision not to shoot on location in Seungbuk-dong and to deny any particular social class direct control of this property for any sustained period of time. To put things somewhat differently, we might consider Bong's "museal vision" of the Park home: it was built by Bong's film crew and does not actually exist in the district of Seungbuk-dong (and thus cannot wholly hold the status of its referential counterparts), and could almost be seen as a kind of reconstruction of the locale, like the home, as speculative, something I will elaborate on in detail in the third section of the essay. For now, we can say that this move creates a type of simulacrum, fabricated and made legible via the filmmaker's impressions and memories of the district. Therefore, Bong continues the art cinema tradition of expressing urban experience (and in this case a very exclusive one) through aestheticized form, transcending its literal referents by creating a cinematic construct that reworks and draws out their meaning.

Parasite's luxury home is thus not simply the visual representation of a luxury home, but carries manifold connotations through its design and the ways in which it is presented. My use of the term "museal home" is a riff on Andreas Huyssen's "other cities" paradigm, which argues that the "museal dimension" of cities leads them to become places that depend "on 'cultural engineering' more than ever to attract capital, business, and power."[25] Indeed, the Park home exhibits an architectural hybridity similar to real museums found in Korea, both globally modern and Korean in style. It is seemingly inspired by the Pitch's House by Iñaqui Carnicero Architects, and its hypermodern reference to Internationalism's past (of, say, Le Corbusier); the other architectonic impulse it displays is a specifically Korean monumentality of form, taking inspiration from the design of the Jeju Provincial Art Museum and the National Museum of Modern and Contemporary Art (MMCA) in Seoul. This mash-up of architectural forms—neither unrecognizably foreign nor distinctly Korean, and perhaps not primarily the ones we would normally associate with residential homes—allows viewers from all backgrounds and locations in the world to see the Park home as a transnational dwelling, one evoking neoliberal urban dislocation: the home, particularly this type of luxury home in Seoul (or elsewhere in the world), is a site to be inhabited briefly, not held on to. Furthermore, the "museal" quality of the home this design connotes (constructed, spectacular, instrumentalized as a tool of capital) underscores how deeply it refuses any identification with feelings of belonging, safety, or community.

The layered significance of the Park home is also owed to the film's sumptuous set design and mise-en-scène. Mostly emptied out of creature comforts associated with living spaces and very different from the Kims' apartment, the Park home's expensive Scandinavian furniture, fitted kitchen appliances, and recessed lighting, even the jars of red kimchi in the basement, stacked like ancestral ceramics, only begin to seem more valuable when the Kims infiltrate about halfway through the film. These furnishings and décor resonate as coldly rational and not covetable in the traditional sense; this luxury property can never be made into a home, not for the Parks and definitely not for the Kims. Despite the fact that, to the lower classes, the district of Seongbuk-dong serves as a signifier for an elite place of wealth and pleasure, characterized by the highest concentration of art collectors in the country, the Park house betrays its emptiness: unlike the museum as repository of art, it sits nearly empty, with no cultivation of artifacts, a mere auction house bereft of refinement or "sensuous nobility."[26] Instead, its lifeless, clinical aesthetic suggests a state in which the house has become nothing more than an image, a signifier for wealth rather than a home, and thus in turn stands in for the unpresentable real estate market itself, and the way that has made its citizens beholden to a new speculative visuality.

Despite its seeming emptiness (or even undesirability), the Parks' home in *Parasite* is clearly connected with the "museal dimension" of cities discussed by Huyssen, which one can of course find across the globe: the Park house has equivalents in other old-moneyed districts in cities across the world (for example, Mayfair in London, the Upper East Side in New York, or the Peak in Hong Kong). Indeed Seongbuk-dong's association with a cosmopolitan worldliness, particularly due to its history as residence for foreign diplomats and *chaebol* CEOs, each jet-setting across the world, is also conveyed in the narrative and culturally engineered by Bong to orchestrate Seongbuk-dong's "acclamatory cultural scripting."[27] In contrast, the Kim family's apartment, said to be located in the impoverished and centrally located Ahyeon-dong district in Seoul, stands in stark contrast to the spectacular homes of Seongbuk-dong and their tourist-drawing potential. Bong draws attention to the dilapidated housing, presenting it not so much as slum porn but as a sinister dwelling, saying: "Cinephiles may be reminded of Akira Kurosawa's *High and Low*. In that case, the structure is simpler and stronger. The Japanese title is 'Heaven and Hell.' On the top of the hill is a rich guy and in [*sic*] the bottom [of the hill], there is the criminal kind of structure. It's basically the same in *Parasite*, but with more layers."[28] The Kim family's slum apartment indeed doubles Kurosawa's menacing dugout down the hill, yet it is also more meticulously rendered than the Park home, free of its cold, museal quality. In contrast with the Parks' house, the Kims' basement apartment is brimming with references to their work-life routine and half-baked schemes. So desperate is its squalid appearance, it feels lived in and made theirs, a portrait of blue-collar living albeit one tinged with indigent markers. We find signs of wear-and-tear everywhere: one notices how the Kims use their cramped apartment as both living quarters and workshop, filled with folded pizza boxes and other reminders of odd jobs done in the past. The Kims' family photos, kitschy scholar rock, comics, trade manuals, school workbooks, magazines, newspapers, recyclable items stacked up and strewn about, soda, green soju empties, and Cass beer bottles fill up the mise-en-scène. In the scenes shot at their apartment, we find out-of-date, garish wallpaper patterns from a different predemocracy era, Hangul characters on book spines and food stuffs littered around, leaving one feeling as though they are visiting a Koreanized Richard Billingham photo documentation of the artist's working-class family not in Birmingham, England, but in Seoul, South Korea. Both film and photos are somehow excessive in their blue-collar/precariat home life décor but also visually powerful testaments to a kind of "squalid realism," whether this is Billingham's parents' "dreary, drunken existence"[29] or the Kims' reliance on a bare life of convenience store goods, cheap alcohol, and fast food, with both families equally dependent on libations to get them through the day.

Elsewhere, the visual effect of this kind of layering of objects or urban forms through Bong's cinematography beyond the Kims' apartment needs attention: the interior levels of the home as rectangular stacks of polished concrete or worn concrete, the private entrance leading up to the Parks' home or the public steps leading down to the Kims' dwelling all culminate in a contemporary piling tableau, but this time in aesthetic homage to postwar Korean cinema. The stair-cases are striking in *Parasite* because they hark back to Kim's *The Housemaid*, released in 1960. Kim's use of the staircase showed the possibility for a new middle class—a home built during the colonial period having fallen on hard times, with falling plaster and wobbly, warped steps, a kind of "fixer-upper" for its new family, that like the social class newly living there, the home too could be repaired after the Korean War to ensure future prosperity. Like Bong's decision to build the Park home as set piece, Kim also built the home as set piece and showed the real danger came not from falling ceilings or broken steps but from materialism and sexual perversity that ultimately led to the disintegration of the Confucian family that lived here. The piling up of images of characters ascending and descend-ing the staircase is a plentiful and dark motif in Bong's film as well: the staircase to the bunker meant isolated freedom for Geun-sae but also an unforgiving mate-rial surface as Moon-gwang will learn, as she breaks her neck from being violently pushed down the concrete steps to the bunker during a scuffle.

Sumptuous building material aside, even so, the piling of rubbish and knick-knacks in the Kims' apartment has far more of the "home" about it than the Parks' house, and much of this has to do with the way that the material fabric of their daily life, and indeed of history itself (in the outdated decorations and accu-mulated ephemera), is woven into their dwelling. At the same time, this kind of living situation is presented as no longer sustainable, and the Kims themselves seem far more drawn to a life of luxury that may ultimately prove sterile, per-haps a suggestion that desire for acquisition and luxury has supplanted any sense of class identity or pride that might have existed in earlier times.

The Park Home's Anticipated Liquidity and the Kim Family's Revanchism

We can deepen our reading of Bong's film by turning in more detail to the reali-ties that at once ground it, giving it its truly global meaning, and remain largely off-screen. If Seoul was once hailed a city of sustainable growth and equitable possibilities for housing, it has since gone mad for real estate. Yet throughout Seoul's different housing epochs, a process "of space given over to commodity value"[30] has driven up market value for those wishing to rent and buy property in the capital. The paradoxical pressures of overaccumulation by some and insta-bility for everyone else frame Seoul's rise as a megacity. Hyun Bang Shin's impeccable research puts real estate price inflation into stark empirical terms:

The average price of land in Korea increased by 2,976 times between 1964 and 2013, whereas the price of daily necessities (e.g., rice) grew by only fifty to sixty times. As of 2013, real estate assets reportedly accounted for about 89 percent of national assets (N.-H. Ha 2015). In this context, with the industrial restruc-turing, it can be said that the post-1980s period has seen the reversal of the relationship between urbanization and industrialization, whereby the highly speculative nature of urbanization (real estate investment in particular) becomes more important for asset accumulation. That is, the investment in the built environment has come to focus more on expanding speculative real estate assets than the expansion of productive investments.[31]

Property inflation at these levels, an increase of more than three thousand times since 1964 (derived from 2020 statistics), is cause for serious concern. These statistics speak to untenable conditions for a vast majority of Koreans living in Seoul and the intensification of such practices after the IMF bailout in the late 1990s. Bong's film fictionally imagines the outcome, by way of revanchism, that will result from unchecked and rampant asset accumulation through the home. His forecast that lower-class families will attempt to take back the city (in this case, by temporarily occupying the Park home) is clearly connected to exorbitant home prices. In other words, the Kim family's siege of the Parks' palatial home comes about not simply because of class resentment but also because of the impossibility of living a dignified life in Seoul's housing system.

It is important to note how much Bong's film, however indirectly, thus pushes against dominant representations of the real estate market, just as it shows us characters—the Kims—who have likely bought into them entirely. With lavish brochures and real estate offices now giving way to property buying television programs, the reified qualities of over-valuation and the promotion of the fantasy that anyone, as long as they are savvy and entrepreneurial, can afford homes in luxury locales is a seductive and misleading message. Incarnated in Britain as a reality television genre, property-themed shows such as the long-running *House Doctor* (Channel 5, 1998–) and newer programs like *Homes Under the Hammer* (BBC One, 2003–) and *Building the Dream* (More4, 2013–), among others, all present homeownership as a financial adventure, with cliff-hangers about families or individuals worried about being approved for loans and mortgages. After tense scenes in almost every episode, the money always comes through, as no cast member is ever denied credit on these programs. These shows then encourage the indebted to sell, rent or "flip" newly acquired properties, with a hefty profit in mind. Korea has recently found their own national niche in film and reality television about property value and luxury apartment and home hunting. In *Yurang Market* (JTBC, 2020) and *Hyori's Homestay* (JTBC, 2017) celebrities are found in search of new apartments in swanky parts of the capital. As the real estate market is repackaged as hassle-free and housing insecurity is nonexistent in these productions, these two popular series disingenuously show gaining a foothold in Seoul's very expensive property market to be an easy task; like those in the British incarnations before them, the cast members never meet with barriers in their acquisition of homes.

Parasite, however, offers the novelty of showing us how modern-day precariats in a global, neoliberal Seoul that approach residential properties and the concept of "home" with a paradoxical blend of desire and *ressentiment*. Throughout the film, it is largely from the Kims' perspective that we see Seoul in general and the Parks' house in particular, and this is one way in which the city itself takes on a rather new cast. For the Kims, the city is "rendered a wilderness, or worse, a 'jungle,'"[32] and the laws of the jungle mean that if one wants a property, one needs to lay siege to it. The city and the Parks' home are no longer "tame and domesticated," but become something akin to a frontier space, full of conflict. The Kims' partying—we find them camped out in the Parks' living room, with empty beer and soju bottles lining the glass coffee table and sofa, a scene very much class coded for Koreans but also exemplifying, honestly, how the stress of life is released through "heavy drinking" by precariats as well as stable blue-collar workers—at this exclusive enclave is understandable despite the revanchist undertones: they have gotten away with their scam (though not for long) and want to celebrate their deception in luxurious surroundings. Such disregard for their employers—duped or not—is a form of righteous indignation, a "screw you" to the offensive and snobbish nouveau-riche Parks, who exemplify the colossal pecking order in Korean society. Fantasies of wish fulfilment dominate the film, from the squatting by the Kims and Moon-gwang and Geun-sae to Mr. Kim attacking Mr. Park in one of the final scenes. At the same time, it is unclear whether or not the viewer is expected to "enjoy" or endorse the fantasies, particularly given their unpleasant outcome and their almost-certain failure, and the Kims' ruthless cunning, characteristic of depictions of Korean precariats, may also give us pause; while we will return to the question of this outcome shortly, we might note for the moment that *Parasite* differs from many other labor-conscious films insofar as the precariats are not shown to be an ennobled class, with Bong instead establishing the Kim family as duplicitous and revenge prone.

But perhaps how we judge the Kim family is less important than what happens to the house—which is after all the meeting point of classes, and more indirectly of local and global levels—and their relationship to it. Up to this point, I have discussed the iconic and neoliberal elements of the luxury home and apartment in *Parasite*; however, the film reaches another point of no return after the Native American–themed birthday party. It turns into a gruesome crime scene, one that unfolds after a vicious fight between the Kims and Moon-gwang and Geun-sae in the underground bunker a scene earlier that spills out into the backyard birthday party the next day. We can infer that both families know their crimes will catch up to them and stare down the barrel of certain imprisonment and destitution, or both. The slow-motion attack by Geun-sae in a fit of bloodlust after his wife dies of her neck injuries leaves viewers stunned. Yet it is the next few scenes that require some unpacking first before returning to the birthday party in detail.

Some months later in the narrative after the precariat families attack one another and kill Mr. Park, we see Ki-woo, Mr. Kim's son, gazing down on the Park family home from a hilltop behind the property. It is winter, and Seoul's bleak dusk milieu is captured with a melancholic serenity, compounded by the home's stoic and hard concrete lines, which give it the feel of a mausoleum to a great many things in the film (as well as the extra-diegetic culture it is based on): it is a grim site of death for young and old; a cultural battleground for a dehumanizing urbanism; a reminder of failed housing security and precarious employment in this megacity; a vicinity where gentrification or razing of properties happens significantly less in this wealthier neighborhood; most importantly, it is a home that survives the doomed lives of the three families that worked and lived there. The home once owned by the Parks will never be demolished as it sits defiantly in a viceroyalty area of Seoul—its imperviousness to gentrification and devaluation establishes the indestructibility of an idea: a warped craze for property. We find in the final scene new homeowners, a white family from Germany, members of a foreign transnational class that keeps speculation alive as the home, like the property market itself, is now more open to foreign direct investment in Korea—a clever message from Bong to show that luxury real estate is the world's new currency.[33] As such, the anticipated value and the liquidity of this property itself live on in the scene, while human compassion and class consciousness wither from memory.

The house is an important site to Ki-woo, a place where he lost his sister and his father vanished and that he was taught to admire and envy as a lower-class Korean. From a prior courtroom scene, we learn Ki-woo was convicted of fraud and is out on parole, and he is shown in a wishful daydream that he will one day be successful enough to purchase the Park family home. We learn that his fugitive father is still hidden away in the home's secret bunker, a subterranean space that is unknown to the police. Not unsurprisingly, he notices the outdoor lamp, once controlled by Geun-sae, and now operated by his father using Morse code, signaling to his resourceful son that he is tucked away safely beneath the concrete façade of the home, presumably subsisting on the barest essentials of life in self-isolation. Yet the wistful discovery is interrupted by the German family who slide open the floor-to-ceiling glass door and enter the back garden, attesting to the cyclical process of property exchange and speculation that eradicates any form of obligation, sacredness, or lineage of families to the home; it is now considered simply an investment and changes hands like erratic capital. Property like the Park home exists to be populated by a speculative dream, unsustainable by its very nature, and yet Ki-woo still longs for the possibility of it becoming a home. Dealing with the concept of home in more psychological terms, Bong's depiction of the Park home casts it as the site of financial longing; the Park home is objectified for its zip-code worth and even motivates the Kims to kill. In other words, real estate speculation has molded its own cultural realm, laden with not just social class issues but also a psychic dependency on anticipated liquidity, as opposed to the longing for a lost and idealized home. The Park home to Ki-woo is reduced to nothing more than a speculative asset, although we might add that it is only as such that he can even begin to imagine it (erroneously) as a future site of security. While Kim's conception of home in *The Housemaid* changes by the end of the film, the postwar director expresses an ideal of community that would be just as unfamiliar to Ki-woo as his concept of home as anything other than a material asset is. Where Kim's creation of the home is the dream of a Korean middle class desperate to have anything right after the war, Ki-woo refuses to let the property go and return to a life of rent tenure in post-IMF Korea. Thus Ki-woo is fixated on executing the "long con"—on figuring out how to securitize this high-risk "(pipe) dream" home in the future for what is left of his family. Thus, we can understand him as unrepentant and determined to get a foothold in this luxury market, deluded by the Parks' "super prime real estate."[34] Nothing else matters, it would seem, as the liquidity attached to property outstrips the reunion with his fugitive father.

Real Estate Speculation, Property Bubbles, and Custard Cakes in *Parasite*

Now we can turn to *Parasite*'s climactic birthday party scene in detail: here, the bursting of speculative bubbles is given figuration through an outburst of tragic violence, and Bong's allegorical forecast stands in for a coming collapse that we cannot yet see, but that certainly has its antecedents. The value of place-based location has multiple effects on real estate, some more major than others. Since 2000, appraisals of property in certain sections of Seoul have often been inflated by real estate speculation, allowing property portfolios to appreciate at exponential rates and driving up prices for renters and those seeking mortgages in other, usually lower value locations in the city.[35] When there is a "distortion in pricing introduced by risky traders," this culminates in volatility of pricing, which can lead to strains on banks and the domestic economy. The excessively high real estate prices also trigger a bandwagon effect, leading to price bubbles. In *Parasite* one finds not only a specific commentary on the "anti-social elements of luxury property"[36] rooted in decades of real estate speculation, but also a synthetic figuration of this process itself and the ways that it is experienced through different classes, creating images that stand in for the larger, nonrepresentable whole. Never is this more the case than when the film draws to a close and Bong places the viewer at the Parks' Native American–themed birthday party for their son in the manicured backyard of their opulent home. Here the birthday party becomes an allegorical expression of the inflection point of a real estate bubble, ready to implode at any moment.

The Parks and the many wealthy families invited to their daytime party can be likened to real estate speculators in Seoul who have appropriated most areas of the city, with the lower classes, literally on the fringes of this market/backyard, waiting their turn for whatever opportunities come their way. While an opportunity to get on the property ladder seldom comes for many of the lower classes, when it does arrive, the precariat and the working and lower-middle classes are sometimes defrauded or financially murdered by corrupt speculators and property developers. In reality and outside of Bong's Seoul, even acquaintances from the office or church all seem to offer advice on how to get rich through the new financialization of property and monopoly rents. Many stories of Seoul-based investors swindled out of money through Ponzi schemes connected to the property market or the outright theft of huge deposits supposedly used for land development fees continue to make national headlines. In most cases, the lower classes turn a blind eye to any risks attached to speculative property investment but still end up losing substantial amounts of money, even to the point of going insolvent. Because of such unchecked speculation the Geun-sae character, a victim of his own "inexperienced restauranteurism" and unethical franchising practices in Korea, has lost his home by the time we meet him in *Parasite*. As we learn, he was forced to live illegally in the Parks' underground bunker in order to hide from debt collectors. His character represents a common lower middle class turned precarious Korean citizen, fed up with their socioeconomic abuse and lack of rights to property. Earlier in the film we hear the story of his ramshackle operation that sold Taiwanese custard cakes or "king castella cake."[37] Most Koreans (and this author) are familiar with the food scandal that serves as a backstory in *Parasite*.[38] Bong hammers home this real-life reference to a dessert craze not only to trigger empathy for those who have experienced misfortune due to failed investments but also to point to many Koreans' overzealous belief in this type of practice. Geun-sae goes all in and loses big. Thus overinvestment for Geun-sae led to bankruptcy when the cake trend quickly went out of style—as trends so often do in Seoul—and he is made to rely on loan sharks to infuse cash into a doomed business. Here we can take one bubble, the Taiwanese custard cake fad, as standing in for another, the Seoul housing bubble. Often investment in franchises or residential property is cunningly presented to would-be investors, and the speed of Korea's consumer and property market, driven by trends in a homogenous and internet-saturated vacuum, leads to fickleness and unwise investment. The result is clouded judgment, a belief that trends will last longer than they usually do—whether in dessert choices or property investment in the capital—leading, on occasion, to desperate behavior. While Mr. Kim waits in the bushes dressed as a Native American warrior for Mr. Park's son and the other children, Geun-sae emerges from the underground bunker in a manic and homicidal state. He is set to kill any member of the Kim family in reprisal for the murder of his wife at the Kims' hands. One could say he is reacting to "increasingly perilous conditions faced by those living on the margins or at 'city's end,' spaces in which urban futures, often without development, are being negotiated through dispossession."[39] His underground bunker thus represents where one ends up once bubbles burst; however, the trouble here is no one knows how long the *real* bubble in Seoul will stay inflated, and thus Bong is forecasting a tragic outcome that has yet to occur while at the same time gesturing toward past outcomes like Geun-sae's desperation.

Put another way, the film is allegorizing a Korean society that is walking on a tightrope, with the impending bubble ready to burst. This is the power of the film's use of allegory: it renders the intangible bubble visible, seen from below or through the lower classes' eyes, however unsuspecting they may be. Like the underground bunker itself, they stumble upon it or perhaps can see it dangerously inflating in front of them, day by day, week by week, year by year, for decades on end. Rather than imagining any possible solution, Bong allegorically *predicts* that there will be riots in the streets if this goes on. Forced to act, Geun-sae wreaks havoc on a scene of Boy Scouts hunting Native American Indians (itself evoking the relationship between oppressed and oppressors), but his violence is directed toward Ki-jung, the daughter of the Kim family: just as in the real world, the precariats attack other precariats, as the wealthy are rarely directly targeted for their speculation and the resulting residential alienation.

A prediction like this is not unreasonable, and the allegory about actual real estate speculation occurring all around the three families and the two properties is a very sound account of the situation. Jameson can support this by pointing to different reactions to things when homes are dispossessed by various socioeconomic forces and thus lead to various "anarchist gestures, to the sole remaining ultimate protests of the wildcat strike, terrorism and death."[40] Revanchism becomes the anarchist protest by the Kims in *Parasite*, and this quickly devolves into domestic violence and people being murdered in otherwise safe neighborhoods in Seoul. "In order to start to imagine resistance in the era of Nasdaq [and real estate speculation], it is crucial to construct a genealogy of contemporary finance that takes into account the coevolution of technical infrastructure and mechanical subjugation."[41] But lessons have not been learned globally about financial encroachment into property. Korea seems very unbothered by what happened not too long ago in the United States. The U.S. subprime mortgage crisis (2007–2009) may be a distant memory for some, but the targeting of lower-income first-time home buyers through predatory lending practices resulted in a disproportionate number of African American and Latino buyers losing their homes. This came about because of impossible repayment options offered to these homeowners and the structural racism of these individuals in the finance and real estate industries not caring about these communities' financial well-being. What made this so unethical is that brokers and real estate agents knew that many of these first-time buyers would be unable to afford the homes they were talked into buying and that their debt could be repackaged and sold when properties were repossessed, with the unintended outcome of such repackaged debt eventually leading to a global recession. In light of this history, I believe that Bong understands real estate bubbles and that when they burst they bring forth sudden, devastating, and violent consequences in their wake (e.g., dead capital and real fatalities for desperate families mourning the loss of their home/asset), but also that these bubbles shape the entire world, and not simply Korea. The film thus comes to esoterically address what Jameson would label "two distinct publics at once": all of Korea's social classes with a warning about overvaluation and the dangers of real speculation leading to a possible crash in Seoul (a well-known public fear in the country) and regional and global audiences who have already lived through speculative bubbles in the past: the Chinese property bubble (2005–2011), the Irish property bubble (1999–2006), the asset price bubble in Japan (1986–1991), and the Spanish property bubble (1985–2008). *Parasite* gives us no reason to believe that what has happened elsewhere is not imminent in South Korea as well.

Conclusion

In the context of this kind of real estate dystopia in which the bubble could burst at any moment, it becomes apparent that the Parks' opulent home is imbued with a fake or even magical perfection, like that of a booming real estate market: both appear to be smooth-running and efficient safe havens from a *retracting middle class* and their lamentations about "rights to the city" (protection from the Kims and other lower-class families) and *bust cycles* (imperviousness to market fluctuations).[42] In other words, the home is not just a home, nor even a particular kind of residence, but stands in for the larger spectacle of which real estate is a primary part in neoliberal society. Bong does not, however, attempt to counter that fake perfection or spectacle through a "realist" corrective in the vein of Ken Loach or Park Kwang-su's depictions of working-class life in cities and towns afflicted by urban restructuring and dislocation. Instead, *Parasite* attempts to give figuration what Jameson calls the "experience of anomie,"[43] allowing the pristine and perfect physical dwelling itself to stand in for the absence or impossibility of "home." What unites the characters turns out to be not, as it first appears, a home that could theoretically be owned by any of them, but rather an allegorical figuration of a system that has negated the concept of home as such.

Bong's stroke of genius here is to let go of what Jameson calls ideological closure, which would transform the film into an affirmative or cathartic experience. *Parasite* does not try "in vain wholly to control or master"[44] the repressive relationships built around property and ownership or to suggest that there is any reason we should not be troubled by them. At the same time, this means that it fails or willfully refuses to consider how we overcome the destruction of housing rights and the financialization of property. Perhaps it is because the invisible force of real estate speculation is just another part of an unjust system—one that is heavily mediatized and propagated through television shows like the ones described above. *Parasite* complicates and challenges perceptions about urban development and urges us to consider public housing rehabilitation alongside the "trendification"[45] found in much media representation today. If no resolution is proposed or even allegorically imagined here, it is perhaps because one cannot be conceived of in the real world, or even perhaps because when caught up in the frenzy of the spectacularized market, no one can any longer resist. My reading here of class tensions caused by dangerous shifts in housing in Seoul and refracted through *Parasite*'s cultural logic is more than just an "allegorical decipherment … in which the concept of class interest supplies the functional link between superstructural symptoms or category and its 'ultimately determining' reality in the base."[46] Jameson showed the utility of such an approach throughout *The Political Unconscious*; but allegory is "by no means the end of the story" to put it in his own words. We can also see the Kims' fantasies or delusions as representing the limitations of class consciousness in the present. The deeper subjective fantasy enacted by the Kims expresses the desire for prosperity and enjoyment of luxury by any means necessary, the inability to let go of the link between home and commodity and the decision to "wait for it," the belief that eventually one will be able to conquer it and own it, all of which are shown to be delusions by the film's violent outcome, and to have become a kind of pathology or obsession (Ki-woo looking down at the house) that detaches one completely from reality. The Kims' fantasies about wealth and property are not really different from those of other classes; they lack any class consciousness because they completely identify with the Parks; they are seen not as ontological others with their own separate class way of thinking but simply as rivals for the same prize: the luxury home. At the same time, the Parks' home doubles as a kind of mobile or unstable capital—money, like the home, becomes elusive and intangible—making "cross-class alliance"[47] impossible. With decades of tenants forced to pay into the unfair *jeonse* rental system, displacement from districts because of increased rents and property made largely unaffordable to buy, many like the three families in *Parasite* could be seen as turning away from housing activism to instead participate in covetous actions to obtain a status symbol in Seoul: the luxury home.[48] Ultimately, however, the Park home becomes nothing more than a grift, a battleground, and, ultimately, a graveyard to equitable housing in Seoul.

Notes

1 Fredric Jameson, *The Geopolitical Aesthetic: Cinema and Space in the World System* (Bloomington: Indiana University Press, 1992), 131.
2 Jameson, *Geopolitical Aesthetic*, 117.
3 Aihwa Ong, "Worlding Cities, or the Art of Being Global," in *Worlding Cities: Asian Experiments and the Art of Being Global*, ed. Ananya Roy and Aihwa Ong (Oxford: Wiley-Blackwell, 2011), 14.
4 Ong, "Worlding Cities," 20.
5 Elizabeth Bronfen, *Home in Hollywood: The Imaginary Geography of Cinema* (New York: Columbia University Press, 2004), 26.
6 Bong cited in Chris O'Falt, "Building the 'Parasite' House: How Bong Joon Ho and His Team Made the Year's Best Set," *IndieWire*, October 29, 2019.
7 Fredric Jameson, *The Political Unconscious: Narrative as a Socially Symbolic Act* (Ithaca, NY: Cornell University Press, 1981), 72.
8 Jameson, *Geopolitical Aesthetic*, 5.

9 Jameson, *Political Unconscious*, 82.

10 Jameson, *Political Unconscious*, 85.

11 For more on the cultural hegemony of property, see David Ley and Sin Yih Teo, "Gentrification in Hong Kong? Epistemology vs. Ontology," *International Journal of Urban and Regional Research* 38, no. 4 (2014): 1286–1303.

12 Ley and Teo, "Gentrification in Hong Kong?," 1286–1303.

13 Jyotsna Kapur and Keith B. Wagner, eds., *Neoliberalism and Global Cinema: Capital, Culture and Marxist Critique* (London: Routledge, 2011).

14 Fredric Jameson, *Postmodernism; or, The Cultural Logic of Late Capitalism* (London; Verso, 1991), 21.

15 Jameson, *Postmodernism*, 21.

16 Derek Nystrom, *Hard Hats, Rednecks, and Macho Men: Class in 1970s American Cinema* (Oxford: Oxford University Press, 2009), 72.

17 Jameson, *Political Unconscious*, 21.

18 John David Rhodes, *Spectacle of Property: The House in American Film* (Minneapolis: University of Minnesota Press, 2017), viii.

19 Gaston Bachelard, *The Poetics of Space* (New York: Beacon, 1992).

20 Carl Freedman, "The End of Work: From *Double Indemnity* to *Body Heat*," in *Neo-Noir*, ed. Mark Bould, Kathrina Glitre, and Greg Tuck (London: Wallflower Press, 2009), 65.

21 For a relevant essay on dispossession, see Chris Berry's "The Housemaid (1960): Possessed by the Dispossessed," in *Rediscovering Korean Cinema*, ed. Sangjoon Lee (Ann Arbor: University of Michigan Press, 2019).

22 Keith B. Wagner, "Endorsing Upper-Class Refinement or Critiquing Extravagance and Debt? The Rise of Neoliberal Genre Modification in Contemporary South Korean Cinema," *Critical Arts* 30, no. 1 (2016): 130.

23 Iain Watson, "(Re)Constructing a World City: Urbicide in Global Korea," *Globalizations* 10, no. 2 (2013): 310–319.

24 Jameson, *Postmodernism*, 20.

25 Andreas Huyssen, "Introduction: World Cultures, World Cities," in *Other Cities, Other Worlds: Urban Imaginaries in a Globalizing Age*, ed. Huyssen (Durham, NC: Duke University Press, 2008), 9.

26 Pierre Bourdieu, *Distinction: A Social Critique of the Judgment of Taste* (London: Routledge, 2010), 23.

27 Neil Smith, *The New Urban Frontier: Gentrification and Revanchist City* (London: Routledge, 1996), xvi.

28 O'Falt, "Building the 'Parasite' House."

29 Tim Adams, "Richard Billingham: 'I Just Hated Growing Up in That Tower Block,'" *Guardian*, March 13, 2016, https://www.theguardian.com/artanddesign /2016/mar/13/richard-billingham-tower-block-white-dee-rays-a-laugh-liz.

30 Annie McClanahan, *Dead Pledges: Debt, Crisis, and Twenty-First-Century Culture* (Stanford, CA: Stanford University Press: 2016), 123.

31 Hyun bang Shin, "Urban Movements and the Genealogy of Urban Rights Discourses: The Case of Urban Protesters against Redevelopment and Displacement in Seoul, South Korea," *Annals of the American Association of Geographers* 108, no. 2 (2018): 360.

32 Smith, *New Urban Frontier*, 7.

33 Peter Marcuse and David Madden, *In Defense of Housing: The Politics of Crisis* (London: Verso, 2016), 36

34 Madden and Marcuse, *In Defense of Housing*, 36.

35 Even the Moon Jae-in center-left government, which came to power in 2017, was determined to reform real estate speculation, left largely unchecked and unregulated by prior conservative governments. See Reuters, "S Korea Tightens Housing Rules to Curb Price Surge," *Business Times*, December 17, 2019.

36 Madden and Marcuse, *In Defense of Housing*,, 38.

37 See 기생충과 대만카스테라 ("Parasite and Taiwan Castella"), *ChosunBiz*, June 27, 2019, https://biz.chosun.com/site/data/html_dir/2019/06/27/2019062701049.html.

38 S. Nathan Park, "'Parasite' Has a Hidden Backstory of Middle-Class Failure and Chicken Joints," *Foreign Policy*, February 21, 2020, https://foreignpolicy.com/2020/02/21/korea-bong-oscars-parasite-hidden-backstory-middle-class-chicken-bong-joon-ho/.

39 Joshua Akers and Eric Seymour, "Instrumental exploitation: Predatory property relations at city's end," *Geoforum* 91 (May 2018), 127. Also see Saskia Sassen, *Expulsions* (Cambridge, MA: Harvard University Press, 2014).

40 Jameson, *Political Unconscious*, 91.

41 Morgan Adamson, "Markets without Subject: Nasdaq and the Financial Interface," *New Formations* 88 (2016): 86.

42 See Jung Min-kyung, "Korean Investors Turn to Real Estate, Less Interested in Stock Market," *The Investor*, December 8, 2019, http://www.theinvestor.co.kr/view.php?ud=20191208000148; David Harvey, *Rebel Cities: From the Right to the City to the Urban Revolution* (London: Verso, 2012), 17.

43 Jameson, *Political Unconscious*, 42.

44 Jameson, *Political Unconscious*, 49.

45 Smith, *New Urban Frontier*, 33.

46 Jameson, *Political Unconscious*, 33.

47 Shin, "Urban Movements," 366.

48 The barricading-in of one lower-class family along with their physical attacks on another is a shadowy reminder of the tragic 2009 incident in Yongsan, Seoul. This small business tenants' protest over their eviction saw them barricade themselves in; by the end five protestors and one policeman had died due to a SWAT team "carrying out military style suppression of small business tenant protesters," a reminder of how violent and unjust property development can be (see Shin, "Urban Movements," 361–365).

8

Strategies of Containment
in Middle-Class Films
from Mexico and Brazil

MERCEDES VÁZQUEZ

The first decade of the twenty-first century witnessed an unprecedented rise of the middle classes in Mexico and Brazil due to neoliberal developments in both countries and, in Brazil, attests to the legacy of the "Lula era" and the turn to the left.[1] This transformation toward *países clasemedieros* (middle-class countries), in Calle and Rubio's terms,[2] is reflected in the cinemas of Mexico and Brazil, which increasingly create "a sympathetic portrait of the contemporary middle class in Mexico"[3] and record "the lives and inhabited spaces of the upper middle class" in Brazil.[4] Acknowledging these unprecedented changes since the 2000s, film scholars and filmmakers have identified a shift toward a predominantly middle-class audience and new articulations of textual politics in Mexican and Brazilian cinemas, even though Brazil was one of the countries of the turn to the left where the working class made spectacular social advances.[5] Moreover, the use of cinematic space exposes these widespread and ongoing class transformations in the twenty-first century. As film scholars Cacilda Rêgo and Carolina Rocha note with regard to contemporary Latin American cinema, "Space in neoliberal times redefines social relations."[6] Other recent studies, meanwhile, have applied notions of place and urban space to examine shifting class relations in contemporary Brazilian films.[7]

This chapter identifies a middle-class perspective through *strategies of containment* found in the use of filmic space and cinematography. Fredric Jameson uses the term "strategies of containment" to denote the artistic and theoretical limitations to which middle-class intellectuals and artists are constrained due to their social position. Referring to Marx's *contention that* petit-bourgeois intellectuals "are ... driven, theoretically, to the same problems and solutions to which material interest and social position drive the latter politically,"[8] Jameson suggests that "such an approach posits ideology in terms of *strategies of containment,* whether intellectual or (in the case of narratives) formal."[9]

Despite the fact that filmmaking has been a predominantly middle-class profession in Latin America,[10] in the past socially engaged middle-class directors of the New Latin American Cinema and Cinema Novo demonstrated a predilection for popular revolutionary art, whose potential and limitations have been pointed out by scholars such as Vicki Mayer and Carlos Estevam.[11] In the twenty-first century however, middle-class filmmakers have increasingly turned their gaze toward their own class. Rather than perceiving it as a *limitation*, this new awareness is better understood as a *liberation* that embodies the filmmakers' acknowledgment of their own constraints and interests. This perception was already occasionally present in Latin American literature but has gained further traction in contemporary cinema. Jorge Luis Borges, an upper-middle-class writer, serves to illustrate this awareness in his 1970s short story "Juan Muraña," where he writes a brief dialogue between the writer's fictional alter ego and a hoodlum called Trápani:

> Then, abruptly, Trápani said to me, "Someone lent me your Carriego book, where you're talking about hoodlums all the time. Tell me, Borges, what in the world can you know about hoodlums?" He stared at me with a kind of wonder.
> "I've done research," I answered.
> Not letting me go on, he said, "Research is the word, all right. Personally, I have no use for research—I know these people inside out."[12]

Contemporary Mexican and Brazilian filmmakers exhibit a similar awareness through their narratives, which I demonstrate through the analysis of the Mexican drama *Post Tenebras Lux* (Carlos Reygadas, 2012) and the Brazilian social comedy *Que horas ela volta?* (*The Second Mother*, Anna Muylaert, 2015). Though both films exhibit skepticism about middle-class philanthropic attitudes, their cinematography and framing of space constitute formal and specifically middle-class strategies of containment that unveil the filmmakers' limitations. Reygadas and Muylaert are not alone. On the contrary, they are part of a group of Mexican and Brazilian filmmakers including Kleber Mendonça Filho, Beto Brant, Gary Alazraki, Alfonso Cuarón, and Fernando Sariñana, among others, who situate their own class concerns at the center of their narratives. Mendonça

Filho, for instance, underlined this attitude when he noted that it was absurd to film in spaces that members of the middle class are unfamiliar with.[13]

The correlation between the growth of the middle classes in Brazil and Mexico and a cinematic production geared toward narratives set in middle-class milieus thematizing an interaction between social classes as employers and employees justifies labeling this cinema as *cine clasemediero* (middle-class cinema). *Cine clasemediero* reflects spatial developments linked to the effects of neoliberalism in Mexico and Brazil, such as spatial segregation and class lines that limit opportunities for social interaction in public spaces.[14] Another equally common urban development associated with neoliberalism that has severely affected the lower classes is the displacement of the urban poor from city centers in order to make space for middle-class residential developments.[15] While this phenomenon has barely caught the attention of filmmakers,[16] despite being linked to class conflict in both Mexico and Brazil and indeed worldwide,[17] narratives where house cleaners work for the middle class (*Que horas ela volta?*) or stories in which middle-class individuals fear the invasion of their private space by the lower classes (*Post Tenebras Lux*) abound.

Before proceeding to a close analysis of the spatial dynamics in these two films, a discussion of the notion of space is required. Fredric Jameson's definition of space's relationship with class fits within the conceptual framework of the present analysis insofar as, for Jameson, "the land is not only an object of struggle between the classes, between rich and poor, it defines their very existence and the separation between them."[18] Furthermore, Doreen Massey views space as a relational notion intimately entwined with time and unavoidably political.[19] Not only does space construct relationships, but also "these relationships themselves . . . *create/define* space and time."[20] Massey convincingly argues that space and time cannot be viewed as separate entities but are inextricably interwoven and that "the spatial is integral to the production of history, and thus to the possibility of politics."[21] Notwithstanding their differences regarding the politics of time, whose discussion is not necessary for the present study, Massey's and Jameson's conceptualizations can shed new light on the politics of contemporary films, which will be the point of departure for my analysis of *Post Tenebras Lux*.

Political Spaces and Fragmentation in *Post Tenebras Lux*

The dominance of spatial explorations in "the narrative discourses of contemporary Mexican cinema" is a trend that Miriam Haddu identified already in the 1990s.[22] Vinicius Navarro, on the other hand, identifies space as key for understanding cinema's "concern with social inequality" and the consequent revitalization of Brazilian political cinema.[23] Yet with regard to Reygadas, studies seem to neglect that in his texts space is intricately interwoven with social and political issues. Ignacio M. Sánchez Prado, for instance, observes that the "re-signification of cinematic spaces" in Reygadas's films works toward "the deliberate undermining of the marks of the national,"[24] and Cynthia Tompkins's analysis highlights the filmmaker's concentration on "feelings and states of mind" in narratives that stress "ideological differences."[25] Reygadas himself seems to confirm this view. In describing his approach to *Post Tenebras Lux*, he noted that "reason [would] intervene as little as possible, like an expressionist painting where you try to express what you are feeling through the painting rather than depict what something looks like."[26] This fits with Tiago de Luca's contention that Carlos Reygadas's films are best understood within Rancière's "aesthetic regime" of art.[27] As de Luca argues, "More than representations of social issues, these films are sensory explorations of realities yet to be properly understood. Averse to didacticism and univocal messages, they reveal the bewildering complexity of local and global events while producing unexpected configurations of the sensible that contravene the logic of the world."[28] Without contradicting these approaches to Reygadas's multilayered texts, the following analysis takes into account Jameson's contention that a Marxist analysis subsumes these "self-sufficient" critical operations and expands on the politics of Reygadas's use of space and cinematography in *Post Tenebras Lux*.[29]

Arguably because of its disregard for a structured narrative, its use of computer-generated images and what might be called the home video approach of some of the scenes, *Post Tenebras Lux* met a mixed reception. Released in 2012, it was selected for the Cannes Film Festival, where it won the prestigious Best Director Award despite being booed by the audience when it was screened. The main plot of Reygadas's film deals with the daily life of a family of four, Juan (Adolfo Jiménez Castro), his wife Natalia (Nathalia Acevedo), and their two children, living in a house in rural Mexico. A secondary plotline concerns the relationship between Juan and his employees "el Jarro" (José Alberto Sánchez) and especially "el Siete" (Willebaldo Torres), who had been previously employed by Juan. Juan attempts to befriend el Siete by helping to reunite him with his battered wife and children, but el Siete shoots Juan when the former is caught burgling the latter's house. Juan dies as a result of this attack, an outcome that, together with other traumatic personal problems, will drive el Siete toward self-decapitation.

The film displays a preference for patterns of incoherence and discontinuity, whether temporal—the ages of the two children vary in different scenes without any apparent reason and Juan is present at a Christmas dinner that would have logically happened several years after his death—or narrative—there are scenes of a rugby match and a bird hunt that are unrelated to the plot. Most scenes are set in Mexico, where the characters speak Spanish, but there are also scenes in the United Kingdom (the rugby match), where the characters speak English, and in France (a swingers' sauna), where French is spoken. Underscoring this disjointed style, *Post Tenebras Lux* does not contain establishing shots or exterior images aimed at providing spatial orientation to the viewer. The main space,

Juan's home, is located in a mountainous rural environment, but the landscape shots do not help orientate the audience. Spaces seem disconnected from one another in the manner of a postmodern pastiche, or possibly connected only through the logic of dreams, and the blurred edges of the camera lens used to shoot many scenes support this surrealistic effect. The first sequences are set, consecutively, in an improvised soccer field with grazing cattle in the mountains, Juan's upper-middle-class home surrounded by a similar landscape, a forest with a woodcutter, el Siete, going about his work, the middle-class home of Juan again, a shack covered with a corrugated metal roof where Alcoholics Anonymous members meet, and the aforementioned rugby field.

Tellingly, Juan's middle-class home is in reality Reygadas's own residence in the suburbs of Mexico City, but in the film there is no reference to any urban center or neighboring communities that would allow the viewer to locate the area. Just a few details suggest that this house with an open design, which allows easy access from the outside, is in fact within a gated community. In *Post Tenebras Lux* only Juan's employee el Jarro and some dogs oversee the house. This scenario induces a certain fear of invasion that is a common trope in other Mexican films. Yet the absence of fences or security cameras contrasts markedly with other contemporary films set in gated communities, where we see security devices and overtly conspicuous security staff.[30] In this sense, Juan and Natalia's home temporarily serves as a heterotopia: a "counter-site" that is "outside of all places."[31] More specifically, it is a "heterotopia of compensation" for the insecurity of urban centers in the way that its "role is to create a space that is other, another real space, as perfect, as meticulous, as well arranged as ours is messy, ill constructed, and jumbled."[32] The invasion of Juan's residence by el Siete, however, will prove that his heterotopic home is not immune to attacks from the outside.

The disorienting effect in Reygadas's film that is produced by insufficient spatial mapping is aggravated through a compartmentalization of space that appears to separate social classes from each other. The scenes in interiors organized around a bed, a table, a courtyard, and a lectern are generally depicted with static shots, which makes them seem photographic. This is the case in one early scene when the children wake up. The camera remains static, focused on Rut, while the mother, out of frame, picks up toys and talks to her daughter. In her study of Reygadas's first feature, *Japón*, Laura Podalsky explains that this use of space does not correspond to that of "a 'container' through which the human subject moves; indeed, off-screen sounds often remind the viewer of the limits of the frame."[33] In some cases, Alexis Zabé, the cinematographer of *Post Tenebras Lux*, uses a wide shot that allows us to situate the characters within a particular space, but often, particularly when the characters in front of the camera are from the lower classes, information about the locations in which they move is limited. The medium shots and close-ups used in lower-class settings reduce the field of vision and fragment bodies. There are a number of scenes that document this approach. When Juan and his family are at a village party, there are such shots of people eating at tables. Sometimes the camera appears static and the characters face it. This also occurs when the alcoholics share their substance abuse experiences with each other. The medium and extreme close-ups of these lower-class characters prevent us from seeing them within the context of a broader visual context.

In contrast with this use of the camera, which produces the effect of lower-class characters "performing" while being scrutinized, the upper-class Christmas party, swingers' sauna, and rugby match are filmed with long shots and with considerable camera movement. In the Christmas party scene, for instance, a hand-held camera travels through the rooms among different characters, which reflects Reygadas's familiarity and comfort with this more upper-class setting. Conversations between members of this same social class are fluid and rich in detail, whereas the lower-class characters in the film appear mainly in exchanges between Juan and the locals and do not interact among themselves often, suggesting that Reygadas shoots from a middle-class perspective and primarily for a middle-class audience.

This choice of cinematography reflects Reygadas's distrust of collectivism. Indeed, he claims to see characters as individuals, not as members of a social class. In a 2010 interview, the director stated that for him "community is nothing but the sum of individuals" and that "declaring . . . a social truth will turn it into dogma and therefore will prevent it from being experienced as real."[34] This claim ought to be understood in the context of a general distrust for Marxist ideology and, in cinematic terms, a distancing from the left-wing ideology of New Latin American Cinema and Cinema Novo. Reygadas's ideas conform to a wider trend in line with what Leslie L. Marsh observes in the Brazilian Film *O som ao redor* (*Neighbouring Sounds*, Mendonça Filho, 2012), namely "the contemporary urban experience of being distanced, isolated, and disconnected from one's surroundings."[35] However, in *Post Tenebras Lux*, the produced spatial limitation and bodily fragmentation seem more apparent in depictions of members of the lower classes.

This shift from political filmmaking of previous times, and a focus that has moved from community to isolated individuals, is undoubtedly related to the effects of neoliberalism, such as the disintegration of unions, the fragmentation of society, and the precarization of the labor force. Neoliberalism is, as David Harvey observes, "in the first instance a theory of political economic practices that proposes that human well-being can best be advanced by liberating individual entrepreneurial freedoms and skills within an institutional framework characterized by strong private property rights, free markets, and free trade."[36] In Mexico, neoliberalism can be traced particularly to the implementation of the North American Free Trade Agreement (NAFTA) between Mexico, the United States, and Canada in 1994, which has arguably "destroyed the country's industrial and agricultural productive structure as well as its public social institutions,"[37] while in Brazil it was introduced in the same decade and continued even during the successive governments of the Workers' Party.[38] The inability of filmmakers to map the whole social environment is related to the rejection of "totalities" described by Jean-François Lyotard and has been identified by Jameson as part of the "cultural logic of late capitalism."[39] This is a reflection of the way neoliberalism has infringed on societies both culturally and socially, replacing class solidarity with individualist desires.

The framing in the climactic scene when el Siete shoots Juan conveys a somewhat ambivalent social message. Juan and Natalia are en route to the airport with their children when they suddenly remember that Natalia has left the baby stroller behind. They decide that Juan should return home to collect it while Natalia and the children wait at a restaurant. Upon arriving at his house, Juan discovers his friend and former employee's intrusion. From a distance the audience hears el Siete shoot Juan, through a static long shot that obscures the men's faces, the weapon, and the wound inflicted on Juan. Juan does not turn el Siete over to the police for his crime and will eventually die, but Reygadas's condescending gesture to avoid criminalizing lower-class characters like el Siete is barely enough to muffle the echoes of the common narratives of fear middle-class characters have of members of lower social classes. At the same time, as Michael Cramer has observed,[40] this kind of condescension toward or insistent "othering" of the working class in Reygadas's films can be seen as the projection of a kind of desire on the part of the bourgeois filmmaker to become more "innocent," and we might even read Juan's death as the fulfilment of a masochistic fantasy in which the bourgeoisie is liquidated by its others, albeit in a way that reduces the latter to sites of projection for the fantasies of the former, thus confirming Reygadas's resolute situation as a middle-class filmmaker.

Political Spaces in *Que horas ela volta?*

Anna Muylaert's *Que horas ela volta?* was sold for distribution in more than twenty-two countries. In France alone, it was shown in 122 theaters, nearly reaching the box-office success of *Cidade de Deus* there.[41] This considerable interest in narratives about class conflict in Latin America, however, was not so evident in Latin American theaters.

As in *Post Tenebras Lux*, the middle-class domestic space is the setting and theme in *Que horas ela volta?* The narrative takes place for the most part in the Morumbi district of São Paulo, a middle-class neighborhood that is a referent for the living spaces of its affluent urban middle class. *Que horas ela volta?* depicts the relationship of two mothers from different social backgrounds, a fashion/television celebrity, Bárbara (Karine Teles), and her domestic helper, Val (played by the Brazilian star Regina Casé), with their children.[42] Bárbara is married to Carlos (Lourenço Mutarelli), a member of the Brazilian rentier class (living on income from inherited properties) who is also a frustrated artist. One day Val receives a call from her estranged daughter Jéssica (Camila Márdila), to tell her that she is coming to São Paulo to take university entrance exams. Because of a conflict with Jéssica's father, Val has not seen her daughter for more than a decade and the relationship between them is strained. Nevertheless, Val picks Jéssica up from the airport and arranges for her to stay at her employer's home, and because Jéssica does not abide by the implicit rules established in Bárbara and Carlos's household, which confine her to a lower social status, a series of conflicts arise. Ultimately, Jéssica moves to a rented apartment in the much poorer district of Embu-Guaçú. She passes her first exam, and her mother, socially and emotionally transformed by her daughter, quits her job to finally take care of her daughter and her (newly discovered) grandson.

Que horas ela volta? initially invites a reading through the prism of affect. "Que horas ela volta?" (What time does [mother] come back?) is the question uttered by countless children the world over to express resentment toward the absence of the mother from the gendered role of caretaker and domestic matriarch. Affect and social mobility are key terms for understanding *Que horas ela volta?*[43] Leslie L. Marsh notes that in Anna Muylaert's films, "domestic space frequently becomes the context for examining issues such as motherhood and cross-class relationships,"[44] but focuses exclusively on gender, rather than space.

I argue that in *Que horas ela volta?* space has centrality as a marker for the division of social classes. Unlike *Post Tenebras Lux*, however, space does not generally appear fragmented. For instance, when Val walks the dog, one of the few exterior scenes, we get a glimpse of the Morumbi neighborhood through a traveling shot. The first scene of the film is set in an emblematic part of the house that is charged with class overtones: the swimming pool. The pool is reserved for Carlos, Bárbara, and Fabinho; that is, it is a place of pleasure restricted to the upper middle class and off-limits to Val and Jéssica. As the family's house cleaner, Val would never dare to enter such a place, as she conforms to the rigid class separation that keeps her out. It is not until later when her daughter plays in the pool and challenges her mother that she contemplates and eventually uses this space for her own enjoyment. Bárbara has the swimming pool emptied with the excuse of having seen a rat (Jéssica) in order to curtail the young woman's brazen occupation of what she sees as her space. At the end of the film, when Jéssica has already left, Val, having decided to quit her job, finally enters the water. In this scene her figure occupies the central position in a long shot. Lights in the background surround Val as if she were a star in a theater show, a visual trope that signifies her desire for social mobility.[45] Her daughter's forceful, even truculent character at times charismatic, and indeed less haughty than Bárbara, challenges old class divisions in Brazil and has motivated Val to at least aspire to climb the social ladder.

A similar significance attached to the swimming pool in *Que horas ela volta?* is highlighted in Lucrecia Martel's *La ciénaga* (2001). The opening scene of this Argentine film depicting the malaise of a middle-class family also takes place at a swimming pool. In her analysis of *La ciénaga*, Amanda Holmes argues that

Martel "draws attention to spatial order and categorization" and that "the construction of spatial representation reflects questions about the formation of social and personal order in the complexity of contemporary Argentine society."[46] In other words, the swimming pool in *La ciénaga* takes part in social categorization and class division. The same applies to space in *Que horas ela volta?* with regard to contemporary Brazilian society, but while the swimming pool in *La ciénaga* evokes the "passivity, almost despondency"[47] of the Argentine middle classes, in *Que horas ela volta?* it symbolizes both the upward social mobility of the lower classes and the fear of traditional middle classes for the *new* middle class that emerged in the twenty-first century as a result of the policies to address social inequality that the governments of the Brazilian Workers' Party put into place, namely Lula da Silva's Bolsa Família (Family Allowance), a conditional cash transfer program that played an important role in the reduction of poverty and the reconfiguration of higher education toward inclusion that both Lula and Dilma Rousseff promoted.[48] Hence, the pool is fraught with social conflict.

Jéssica is depicted as an ambitious character who uses space to push class boundaries. From the moment this student from the Northeast, who aspires to study at the university, enters Bárbara's home, her movements and her body language display an irreverent attitude toward established house rules and more general social conventions. When Bárbara's husband shows her the guest room, she sits on the spacious bed and jokingly suggests that she occupy this comfortable bedroom instead of sharing the cleaner's confined room. Carlos, who likes Jéssica from the beginning, asks Bárbara whether Jéssica can be accommodated in the guest room. Bárbara feels forced to agree, but this moment is visually conveyed as the realization of a class conflict. A close-up of Bárbara looking at Jéssica is followed by an eyeline match of Jéssica looking at her, with Carlos in the middle. Carlos will gradually fall in love with Jéssica, later asking her to marry him.

The cinematography in *Que horas ela volta?* emphasizes social conflict within neoliberal parameters, according to which Jéssica and Val should interact with Bárbara's family, members of the middle class, only insofar as they provide a service to them. Unable to stand a dangerous situation in which Jéssica clearly takes advantage of every opportunity to live comfortably in Bárbara's home, Bárbara requests first that Jéssica vacate the guest room and later that she remain within the limits of the helper's room. Jéssica's entrance into the domestic helper's area is visually rendered as Jéssica's occupation of an animal's space. A bird's-eye view of the space in this scene allows the audience to perceive Jéssica's confinement to the lowest floor of the house and her gaze at the sky, a visual metaphor for her current social position and her aspirations alike. The staircase inside the home next to the guest room is another space symbolizing social mobility. There are several eye-level shots of the empty staircase, the camera zooming in to invite the viewer to contemplate this possibility.

Spatial arrangements in the house also underscore the social segregation that neoliberalism promotes. The kitchen doorframe is unquestionably the most important space in the film as it represents the boundaries between classes. The original title of the film was, in fact, *The Kitchen Door*, a door that, in this film, serves as a threshold between the worlds of employer and employee. Many scenes are filmed from Val's point of view from the kitchen sink, from where she sees the dining room through the doorframe. The kitchen is not only Val's workplace but also the family's breakfast room. In her first morning in São Paulo, Jéssica wakes up before her mother and finds Bárbara in the kitchen making juice for breakfast. In this scene, Bárbara stands next to the sink usually occupied by Val while Jéssica sits at the table. In just one night, Jéssica has shaken up the social order of the household. Jéssica is now symbolically occupying Bárbara's space in the house, something that Bárbara quickly realizes and resents. In another scene, Carlos invites Jéssica to eat with him in the dining room. Whereas Val's view of and access to the dining room has always been limited, Jéssica's is now unrestricted.

Anna Muylaert's depictions of the protagonists Val and Jéssica in connection to Bárbara's home and the relationship between Bárbara and Val as employer and employee are part of a *cine clasemediero*. Another example that allows us to classify this film as *cine clasemediero* is the reluctance to represent a favela in the film. *Que horas ela volta?* revisits the common favela/sertão theme only toward the end of the film, the poverty-stricken districts in Brazilian cities that are a reminder of uneven growth and urban development. Jéssica and her mother are originally from Pernambuco, the Northeast, and the land of the sertão. When Val visits her daughter right before resigning and moving in with her, we see them arguing in the small apartment rented by Jéssica. The favela of Embu-Guaçú appears in the background, seen through the apartment door. Parallel to the framing of the family dining room in Bárbara's middle-class kitchen from Val's perspective, the framing of the favela from Jéssica's new apartment suggests that Val and Jéssica do not belong to this space either.

The favela has enjoyed a long tradition of cinematic representation. Igor Krstić has identified a general transition from a referential to a symbolic representation of the favela on the Brazilian screen between the first films set in the favelas in the 1930s and those of contemporary cinema.[49] Throughout the decades, the favela has been approached as a romanticized setting, a location for stories about struggling characters, a politicized space, and, in more contemporary films, a place associated with extreme violence (Ivana Bentes's "cosmetics of violence") as in *Cidade de Deus* and *Tropa de elite* (*Elite Squad*, José Padilha, 2007), and a space for creativity, as in *Orfeu* (Carlos Diegues, 1999).[50] Despite this long history of the favela on screen, director Anna Muylaert keeps the favela "outside." Just as Val was incapable of crossing the boundaries to the dining room table, so is director Anna Muylaert reluctant to enter the favela, a territory that she, as a member of the Brazilian middle class, does not seem to know well. For this reason, she remains in the safety of the interior of Jéssica's home and frames/contains the favela as a lit picture in the distance.

Concluding Remarks

Post Tenebras Lux and *Que horas ela volta?* exhibit a similar emerging awareness of the filmmaker's social position and the ensuing *limitations* in trying to depict the lives of the members of the lower classes. The films' strategies of containment are made evident through several means. At a narrative level, members of lower classes are presented as service providers for the middle classes.[51] Cinematography and the depiction of space demonstrate Reygadas's and Muylaert's strategies of containment. Last, both films exhibit a fear of the lower classes. The "fear of violence and anxiety about security"[52] is palpable in *Post Tenebras Lux*. In the case of *Que horas ela volta?*, we find the traditional middle-class fear of downward social mobility combined with a fear of the rise of the lower classes. The most interesting aspect of both films is the combination of an awareness of the limitations concerning knowledge about "the other" and a critical view toward the middle class that might be construed as a creative liberation.

Spatial representation in these two films is tied to the effects of neoliberalism in Mexican and Brazilian societies. In *Post Tenebras Lux*, the innovative connotation of the rural space as a setting for class segregation and class conflict leaves behind earlier associations of the countryside with innocence and virtue,[53] backwardness, and even spirituality.[54] Anna Muylaert's *Que horas ela volta?* is a more positive spin on social mobility, which might be attributed to the effects of sociopolitical policies aimed at reducing inequality in Brazil between 2003 and 2016, when the Workers' Party was in power. In any case, the camera has turned its attention from underprivileged to middle-class characters and sees working-class people as their employees.

A relational approach to space allows us to identify the social position assumed by filmmakers and cinematographers. In *Post Tenebras Lux* and *Que horas ela volta?*, the camera films from a middle-class "position" even in shots that are from the point of view of working-class characters. The construction of middle-class spaces in contrast to the spaces traditionally associated with the lower classes clearly indicates that the fear of invasion in *Post Tenebras Lux* and the anxiety toward the new middle-class upward social mobility in *Que horas ela volta?* are central to the understanding of these films as political in Fredric Jameson's terms.

Notes

1   See Francisco H. G. Ferreira et al., *Economic Mobility and the Rise of the Latin American Middle Class* (Washington, DC: World Bank, 2013); Jorge Castañeda, *Mañana Forever? Mexico and the Mexicans* (New York: Vintage, 2011). There is a consensus about the rise of a new class that most scholars identify as a middle class, although Brazilian sociologist Jessé Souza prefers to call it *os batalhadores* (the fighters): Uirá Machado, "É um erro falar que existe nova classe média, diz sociólogo," *Folha de São Paulo*, February 13, 2011, http://www1.folha.uol.com.br

/poder/2011/02/874777-e-um-erro-falar-que-existe-nova-classe-media-diz-sociologo
.shtml. These references illustrate differing views about the causes for this rise.

2 Luis de la Calle and Luis Rubio, "Clasemedieros," *Nexos*, May 2010, http://www
.nexos.com.mx/?p=13742.

3 Kathleen Newman, "A Different Mexican Postcard: Fernando Eimbcke's *Lake Tahoe* (2008)," *Studies in Spanish & Latin American Cinemas* 12, no. 2 (2015): 159.

4 Leslie L. Marsh, "Reordering (Social) Sensibilities: Balancing Realisms in *Neighbouring Sounds*," *Studies in Spanish & Latin American Cinemas* 12, no. 2 (2015): 155. Newman's and Marsh's studies refer specifically to the Mexican film *Lake Tahoe* (Fernando Eimbcke, 2008) and the Brazilian film *O som ao redor* (Kleber Mendonça Filho, 2012), not necessarily to a group of films.

5 Misha MacLaird, *Aesthetics and Politics in the Mexican Film Industry* (New York: Palgrave Macmillan, 2013); Ignacio M. Sánchez Prado, *Screening Neoliberalism: Transforming Mexican Cinema 1988–2012* (Nashville, TN: Vanderbilt University Press, 2014). See also the statements of one of the most prominent Brazilian filmmakers, Lúcia Murat, in Alain Arias Barreto, "Lucía Murat y el cine," *La Jiribilla. Revista de cultura cubana* 397 (December 13–19, 2008).

6 Cacilda Rêgo and Carolina Rocha, eds., *New Trends in Argentine and Brazilian Cinema* (Bristol: Intellect, 2011), 9.

7 Vinicius Navarro, "Local Filmmaking in Brazil: Place, Politics, and Pernambuco's New Cinema," *Studies in Spanish and Latin American Cinemas* 14, no. 1 (2017); Marsh, "Reordering (Social) Sensibilities."

8 Karl Marx, *The Eighteenth Brumaire of Louis Bonaparte* (New York: International, 1963), 50–51.

9 Fredric Jameson, *The Political Unconscious: Narrative as a Socially Symbolic Act* (London: Routledge, 2002), 37.

10 The renowned Argentine director Lucrecia Martel declared in an interview that cinema's weakness worldwide is that it is only in the hands of the upper-middle class (Iván Pinto Veas, "Lucrecia Martel," *La fuga* 17 [2015], http://2016.lafuga.cl/lucrecia -martel/735); film scholar Lúcia Nagib noted earlier, "There is still an economic cleavage which reserves cinematographic activity for the middle and upper classes" (*O cinema da retomada. Depoimentos de 90 cineastas dos anos 90* [São Paulo: Editora 34, 2002], 15).

11 Vicki Mayer, "For the People and by the People: TV Maxambomba's Regeneration of Popular Cinema," *Studies in Latin American Popular Culture* 17 (January 1998): 223; Carlos Estevam, "For a Popular Revolutionary Art," in *Brazilian Cinema*, ed. Randal Johnson and Robert Stam (New York: Columbia University Press, 1995), 58–63.

12 Jorge Luis Borges, "Juan Muraña," in *Doctor Brodie's Report*, trans. Norman Thomas di Giovanni (New York: E.P. Dutton, 1972), 82.

13 Paul Dallas, "Culture Wars: Talking Brazilian Cinema and Its Discontents with Director Kleber Mendonça Filho," *Filmmaker*, January 28, 2013, http://filmmaker magazine.com.

14 Michael Janoschka and Axel Borsdorf, "Condominios Fechados and Barrios Privados: The Rise of Private Residential Neighbourhoods in Latin America," in *Private Cities: Global and Local Perspectives*, ed. Georg Glasze, Chris Webster, and Klaus Frantz (London: Routledge, 2006), 105. Néstor García Canclini has aptly observed, "Latin American elites . . . live in gated communities and consume in the segregated shopping centers of their cities." *Imagined Globalization* (Durham, NC: Duke University Press, 2014), 73.

15 Michael Janoschka, Jorge Sequera, and Luis Salinas, "Gentrification in Spain and Latin America: A Critical Dialogue," *International Journal of Urban and Regional Research* 38, no. 4 (July 2014): 1244, 1245, 1247, 1248; Ermínia Maricato, "The Statute of the Peripheral City," in *The City Statute of Brazil: A Commentary*, ed. Celso Santos Carvalho and Anaclaudia Rossbach (São Paulo: Cities Alliance and Ministry of Cities, 2010), 31–32; Teresa P. R. Caldeira, *City of Walls: Crime, Segregation and Citizenship in São Paulo* (Berkeley: University of California Press, 2000), 251.

16 Mexican filmmaker Iria Gómez Concheiro had a project titled *Los inquilinos* about this forced gentrification at the time of writing, but attention to this urban and social phenomenon is not yet common.

17 Fredric Jameson, "The Aesthetics of Singularity," *New Left Review* 92 (2015): 130.

18 Jameson, "Aesthetics of Singularity," 130–131.

19 Doreen Massey, "Politics and Space/Time," *New Left Review* 1, no. 196 (November–December 1992): 66–67.

20 Massey, "Politics and Space/Time," 79.

21 Massey, "Politics and Space/Time," 84.

22 Miriam Haddu, *Contemporary Mexican Cinema 1989–1999: History, Space and Identity* (New York: Edwin Mellen Press, 2007), 9.

23 Navarro, "Local Filmmaking in Brazil," 70.

24 Sánchez Prado, *Screening Neoliberalism*, 201.

25 Cynthia Tompkins, *Experimental Latin American Cinema: History and Aesthetics*, (Austin: University of Texas Press, 2013), 160.

26 John Hopewell and Emilio Mayorga, "Reygadas Looks to 'Lux,'" *Variety* 418, no. 2 (2010): 8.

27 Tiago de Luca, *Realism of the Senses in World Cinema: The Experience of Physical Reality*, (London: I.B. Tauris, 2014), 90–91. De Luca concentrates on Reygadas's first three features, not on *Post Tenebras Lux*.

28 De Luca, *Realism of the Senses in World Cinema*, 240.

29 Jameson, *Political Unconscious*, x.

30 In contrast to *Post Tenebras Lux*, in some Mexican and Brazilian crime dramas about the invasion of middle-class homes or neighborhoods, the protection of middle-class residents is foregrounded and "safe" and "dangerous" spaces are often visually rendered as interdependent with each other (*O som ao redor*, Kleber Mendonça Filho, 2012; *La zona*, Rodrigo Plá, 2007; *Redentor*, Cláudio Torres, 2004; *Era uma vez . . .* , Breno Silveira, 2008; *Amar te duele*, Fernando Sariñana, 2002; *O invasor*, Beto Brant, 2002; *Os inquilinos*, Sergio Bianchi, 2009).

31 Michel Foucault, "Of Other Spaces," *Diacritics* 16, no. 1 (1986): 24.

32 Foucault, "Of Other Spaces," 27.

33 Laura Podalsky, "Landscapes of Subjectivity in Contemporary Mexican Cinema," *New Cinemas* 9, nos. 2–3 (2011): 168.

34 José Castillo, "Carlos Reygadas," *Bomb* 111 (2010): 72–73.

35 Marsh, "Reordering (Social) Sensibilities, 151.

36 David Harvey, *A Brief History of Neoliberalism* (New York: Oxford University Press, 2005), 2.

37 Asa Cristina Laurell, "Three Decades of Neoliberalism in Mexico: The Destruction of Society," *International Journal of Health Services* 45, no. 2 (2015): 246–64.

38 Alfredo Saad-Filho, "Varieties of Neoliberalism in Brazil (2003–2019)," *Latin American Perspectives* 47, no. 1 (January 2020): 9–27.

39 Jean-François Lyotard, *The Postmodern Condition: A Report on Knowledge* (Manchester: Manchester University Press, 1984), 7; Fredric Jameson, *Postmodernism; or, The Cultural Logic of Late Capitalism* (Durham, NC: Duke University Press), 55–57.

40 Michael Cramer, "Battle with History: Carlos Reygadas and the Cinema of Being," in *The Global Auteur: The Politics of Authorship in 21st Century Cinema*, ed. Jeremi Szaniawski and Seung-Hoon Jeong (New York: Bloomsbury, 2016), 235–252.

41 This is according to data gathered by Thiago Stivaletti shortly after the film's release in 2015 ("*Que horas ela volta?* é vendido para 22 países," *Filme B*, July 17, 2015, http://www.filmeb.com.br), but the popularity of the film continued growing after 2015.

42 For more on Casé's performance as a "Brazilian style" star, see Randal Johnson, "Television and the Transformation of the Star System in Brazil," in *A Companion to Latin American Cinema*, ed. Maria M. Delgado, Stephen M. Hart, and Randal Johnson (Malden, MA: John Wiley, 2017), 29–31.

43 Lígia Lana, "'Da porta da cozinha pra lá': gênero e mudança social no filme *Que horas ela volta?*," *Rumores* 19, no. 10 (January–June 2016): 121–137; Rui Fernando Correia Ferreira and Lívia Almada Neves, "O conceito do ócio vicário no filme 'Que horas ela volta?': Revisitando Thorstein Veblen em uma nova perspectiva dos fenômenos socioeconômicos" (paper, XL Encontro da ANPAD, September 25–28, 2016).

44 Leslie L. Marsh, "Women's Filmmaking and Comedy in Brazil: Anna Muylaert's *Durval Discos* (2002) and *É Proibido Fumar* (2009)," in *Latin American Women Filmmakers: Production, Politics, Poetics*, ed. Deborah Martin and Deborah Shaw (London: I.B. Tauris, 2017), 151.

45 Anna Muylaert felt the need to reflect on her own social class when asked in an interview about the swimming pool's symbolism. For her, in addition to being "the place for leisure and for the privileged," it is also the place for *machismo* (male chauvinism), and in this sense Muylaert would identify with both Jéssica and Val in such a place, even though she "belong[s] to the other social class." "Director Anna Muylaert Interviewed by French Journalist Pierre-Michel Meier" (DVD extra features, 2016, Oscilloscope Pictures).

46 Amanda Holmes, "Landscape and the Artist's Frame in Lucrecia Martel's *La ciénaga / The Swamp* and *La niña santa / The Holy Girl*," in Rêgo and Rocha, *New Trends in Argentine and Brazilian Cinema*, 131, 133.

47 Holmes, "Landscape and the Artist's Frame," 134.

48 See Eduardo Santos and Manuel Tavares, "Desafios históricos da inclusão: Características institucionais de duas novas universidades federais brasileiras," *Arquivos analíticos de políticas educativas* 24, no. 62 (May 2016). As Lima has noted, "Fifteen years ago, a work dealing with the relationship between a wealthy Morumbi family and its maid, played by a well-known and charismatic actress like Regina Casé, would hardly have resonated in the same way as *The Second Mother* does today." Bruna Della Torre De Carvalho Lima, "Criticism and Condescension: The Triumph of the Poor in *The Second Mother*," *Latin American Perspectives* 211, no. 6 (November 2016): 141.

49 Igor Krstić, *Slums on Screen: World Cinema and the Planet of Slums* (Edinburgh: Edinburgh University Press, 2016), 196.

50 Krstić, *Slums on Screen*, 196, 202.

51 There is a significant number of films on domestic and security services in contemporary Latin American cinema, such as *Doméstica* (*Housemaids*, Mascaro, 2012), Benjamín Naishtat's *Historia del miedo* (*History of Fear*, 2014), Rodrigo Moreno's *El*

custodio (*The Bodyguard*, 2006) and *Réimon* (2014), and Jorge Gaggero's *Cama adentro* (*Live-in Maid*, 2004), but the Chilean-Mexican coproduction *La nana* (*The Maid*, Sebastián Silva, 2009) is probably the best known internationally. The growing number of films about domestic helpers has led film scholar Deborah Shaw to classify them as a genre (Deborah Shaw, "Intimacy and Distance—Domestic Servants in Latin American Women's Cinema: *La mujer sin cabeza* and *El niño pez* / *The Fish Child*," in Martin and Shaw, *Latin American Women Filmmakers*, 124).

52 Teresa P. R. Caldeira, "From Modernism to Neoliberalism in São Paulo: Reconfiguring the City and Its Citizens," in *Other Cities, Other Worlds: Urban Imaginaries in a Globalizing Age*, ed. Andreas Huyssen (Durham, NC: Duke University Press, 2008), 52.

53 Haddu, *Contemporary Mexican Cinema*, 213.

54 Sánchez Prado, *Screening Neoliberalism*, 205.

9

The Neoliberal Conspiracy

Jameson, New Hollywood, and
All the President's Men

MICHAEL CRAMER

Fredric Jameson's writings on Hollywood films of the 1970s, particularly "Total-ity as Conspiracy," cast them as grappling with the difficulty of giving figura-tion to a global, information-based capitalism, of "cognitive mapping" within such a context, and of conceiving of individual agency within such a seemingly incomprehensible and unrepresentable totality. Many of Jameson's readings of the films of this period are bound up with his formulation of the "postmodern" as a type of cultural production specific to late capitalism, and indeed, if we assume that all fields of culture are subject to large-scale economic/material devel-opments, what happens in the field of cinema cannot be read as isolated or sepa-rate from what happens elsewhere. Even so, there may be some use in situating Jameson's analyses of 1970s films not in respect to the broader phenomenon of postmodernism but rather in a more local context, namely as part of what is com-monly referred to now as "New Hollywood." Doing so allows us to see how the films usually placed in this category, characterized by a breakdown of many ele-ments of the "Classical Hollywood" formula (the motivated protagonist, goal-oriented narrative, effective action and overcoming of obstacles, clear conclusion or "happy ending," all in the support of an affirmative ideological function), register transformations of capitalism and ideological shifts in a way specific to the Hollywood film.

New Hollywood films question and often negate the conventional narrative, actantial, and generic structures of Classical Hollywood, but in some cases, particularly by the mid-1970s, seek to revise them or develop new ones. These alterations to the Classical Hollywood formula function as attempts to offer allegorical solutions to the difficulties raised by a rapidly mutating and increasingly incomprehensible totality. As Jameson puts it, "The social context (including the history of forms themselves and the condition of the vernacular language) is to be grasped as the situation—the problem, the dilemma, the contradiction, the 'question'—to which the work of art comes as an imaginary solution, resolution, or 'answer.'"[1] Here, I examine how the New Hollywood represents an attempt to develop just such a solution, not simply to the crisis of the Hollywood film industry but to the failure of Hollywood cinema during the 1960s and 1970s to replace or update the Classical model with new ways of representing plausible, navigable worlds in which the individual could still exercise agency and obtain success.

While the New Hollywood phenomenon—that cycle often identified as beginning in 1967 with films like *Bonnie and Clyde* and *The Graduate*, and ending with the advent of the big-budget spectaculars (*Jaws*, *Star Wars*) that would define the paradigm for 1980s Hollywood cinema—was of course highly overdetermined (the product of industrial crisis, a waning of faith in social institutions, and a growing detachment of Hollywood production from the concerns and experiences of its spectators, among other things), we might, at least in part, define it as a major instance of the posing and attempted resolution of what Jameson identifies as a fundamental "form-problem" of cinema under late capitalism: how can a film resolve the incommensurability between "the individual subject of the protagonist" and "the collective web of the hidden social order" in a way that will retain some sort of "reality-effect" and be accepted as plausible by the viewer?[2] The particular relevance of this problem to the Hollywood film lies in the fact that a commensurability between subject and world had long been its central premise or even condition of possibility (with, of course, some moments of crisis, such as those found in film noir), one permitting the construction of narratives that allowed protagonists to successfully navigate the world, act effectively within it, and ultimately achieve their goals. This form-problem, of course, is not merely formal or aesthetic but is itself an attempt to resolve a larger tension raised by the rapid transformations that result in subjects failing to "keep up" or falling out of sync with the world around them, or suffering from the absence of a symbolic system that would allow them to function within it. The allegorical resolutions offered by films are, of course, not necessarily "real" or applicable to what lies outside of the film in any direct way, but nonetheless hold the potential to fulfill an important cultural function, enabling cognitive mapping and offering models that implicitly illustrate how subjects can operate within the world. However one chooses to judge them, Classical Hollywood films were often successful in fulfilling this task, and on a far larger scale than earlier forms (for example, novels).

What I propose here, drawing on Jameson's insights while also putting them into closer dialogue with work undertaken by scholars working more specifically within the field of film studies, is that the films of the New Hollywood period move through a dialectical process that begins as the negation of many elements of Classical Hollywood form and then proceeds to the "negation of the negation," through which the very terms laid out by the New Hollywood films that function in a purely negative manner are taken up and worked through in such a way that what initially seemed to be a questioning or negation ends up being a solution in itself, or is at any rate subsumed into a solution.[3] This solution, when it does occur, is of course formal-allegorical, but it can be more or less convincing, more or less articulated, more or less dense in ideological content. It is not, however, one that is necessarily conscious or localizable to one individual subject, and indeed the superficial content that any film may think it is "working through" often registers far fewer traces of the deeper ideological and material processes at stake than the work being undertaken on the level of form.

My particular interest here is the "solution" offered by Alan J. Pakula's *All the President's Men* (1976), in which the resolution of the surface-level problem would seem to almost entirely match with that of the form-problem: on both levels, we might identify a restoration of faith, first in "traditional" American institutions and ideology, and second in the Classical Hollywood model, with its motivated protagonists who operate effectively within the world, setting things right in a way that obtains a balance between the individual and the social. Like most restorations, though, this one considerably revises what it restores. The film depends heavily on alterations of the narrative and actantial structures of earlier Hollywood films, a characteristic that Jameson has noted,[4] yet it also appears to restore the successful goal-oriented narrative typical of Classical Hollywood. What appears to be a restoration in fact requires a redefinition of agency and success as well as of the protagonist function, not to mention a very different framework of values than we would have found in the pre–New Hollywood era. Formally and ideologically, the film thus proposes a way to salvage many of the attributes of Classical Hollywood while revising them in such a way that they "catch up" with the contemporary world that 1950s and 1960s Hollywood largely had to liquidate in order to keep its narrative machine working (for example, by favoring films set in the past or in fantasy settings and populated with stock characters),[5] and whose appearance in New Hollywood narratives of passivity and failure (often conceived of as a "realist" response to an escapist Hollywood) had thrown a wrench into that machine.

Similarly, the film's implicit ideology has little to do with the affirmation of the foundational American values one might expect to see in older Hollywood products, or even with the freedom of the press (which here instead functions as an allegory for a very different kind of circulation of information, as we will see). As Jameson notes, the film *seems* at first glance to be one of the most unallegorical and literal representations of broader historical shifts that we could possibly imagine: it is "a political film that looks deceptively like a political film, a representation that seeks to convey some conception of political relations by way of overtly political material."[6] He goes on to observe, however, that it dispenses with much of the "overtly political content" that one might expect, which allows for the narrative to develop more abstractly, "as the struggle between two conspiracies, two collectives, two suprapersonal organizations."[7] While this observation will remain central to my analysis, I argue that the "content" here, namely a preexisting, "real life" narrative ending in *success* (so rare in the preceding New Hollywood films, including Pakula's own), acts as something like the raw material through which a new way of conceiving of and representing agency and effective action can be developed. In other words, it would be a mistake to read the film as merely a representation of the series of events through which Nixon and his cronies were brought to justice; what matters more here is *how* this occurs and *who* does it, in other words, how the job gets done, as producer/star/uncredited coauthor Robert Redford himself has repeatedly noted in respect to the film ("what interested me . . . was the really hard work they'd done")[8]—even though its emotional payoff depends to a large extent on the sense of triumph or restoration of integrity to American institutions that the real-life events would connote.

All the President's Men is in fact an exceptionally allegorical film: its deepest political significance lies not in its representation of the deliverance of America from Richard Nixon, the restoration of democratic institutions or proof that they function effectively, or the triumph of the freedom of the press, but rather in the way that it gives figuration to or maps a social totality and demonstrates how the individual can best work effectively within it. This was of course a function of many Classical Hollywood films, yet the way *All the President's Men* accomplishes these tasks is radically different from how they would be dealt with in Classical Hollywood: many aspects of the conception of labor we see here, and the particular way that it relates the protagonist to the social whole, align considerably with what we would now call neoliberal ideology, with the caveat that the latter is not some unified, coherent thing, and that the film is not without its contradictions or reservations. I focus here on the specifics of the film itself, rather than attempting to identify it with any particular account or definition of neoliberalism (itself subject to stages and contradictions and also referring to multiple spheres such as economic policy, discourses, conception of state and government, etc.), and most of these specifics can indeed be quite easily connected with broader historical shifts occurring in the 1970s, particularly insofar as the film implies that the success it depicts represents an overcoming of the political discord and loss of faith in "the system" characteristic of the sixties and early seventies. In this sense, it positions itself as "problem solving" much in the way that neoliberal economic policy, conceptions of government/state, and the ideologies associated with these were posited as the solution to the crises of capitalism and the state that came to a head in the 1960s and 1970s, particularly in the rhetoric of Ronald Reagan and Margaret Thatcher.[9] The film remains, however, a fantasy and an allegorical resolution (and hence subject to the operations of what Jameson would call the "political unconscious"), rather than one to be taken literally or at face value, but this is precisely what allows it to give voice to the contradictions of and ambivalence toward the very solution that it proposes.

While the characteristics of this solution and the new world to which it will lead are most visible in the film's representation of how its reporter-heroes operate, they are also palpable in its fixation on information (a central motif for the new era of capitalism, not just as a means to allegorically represent unrepresentable connections, a usage that Jameson notes, but as a "field" that will need to be mastered to succeed)[10] and in its representation of a process through which "the government" as a discrete institution and primary ordering force of society is supplanted by something more nebulous and diffuse as non- or paragovernmental entities become the dominant forces in our lives, and "governance" replaces it.[11] Pauline Kael once remarked that Redford's films all operate as "how to" manuals,[12] and *All the President's Men* is no exception: it is less, however, about how to be a successful journalist than about how to navigate the emerging order, what sorts of beliefs and values it requires and rewards, and how one can maintain within it something like (but also very different from) the kind of agency in the world that was the staple of the very Classical Hollywood films that early New Hollywood seemed to throw into doubt. This allegorical depth, however, will be much more apparent if we first situate the film specifically within the New Hollywood context.

New Hollywood as Crisis

The usual account of the New Hollywood casts it as the response both to a financial crisis in the Hollywood film industry and to the shifting sociopolitical landscape of the 1960s. On an industrial level, the stage for New Hollywood was set by the changing shape of the industry itself (the impact of the Paramount Decrees, the purchasing of studios by conglomerates, the increasing power of talent agencies), but also changing habits of consumption linked to suburbanization, the rise of TV, preferences for other forms of leisure, and so on.[13]

This financial crisis, however, surely had at least something to do with the content of films themselves. Part of the problem with Hollywood production of the 1950s and 1960s stemmed from a disconnect with audiences, signaled through films that had absolutely no connection to the quotidian experience of their spectators, but focused instead on the foreign and the exotic, or the distant, mythic past, rather than on anything more concretely linked to American life in the way that the films of the 1930s and 1940s had been. This phenomenon stemmed from a larger lack of social consensus, the impossibility of constructing a world that could be agreed upon and comprehended by a mass audience, to which fantasy (not in the sense of depicting our world in defamiliarized terms, but rather that of fleeing any effort to represent it altogether in favor of a schematic, cliché framework) offered one possible solution, one that is of course even more pronounced today. As I suggested above, one might see this flight into fantasy as not only necessary to appeal to a broad audience but also the only way to construct a world in which the triumphant heroes and happy endings of Hollywood would still be at least somewhat plausible (although of course the financial failure of so many of the films in this category suggests that this was not a viable solution).

Film's inability to create a consensual, plausible world can be seen as a symptom of a broader loss of faith or belief; as Michael Ryan and Douglas Kellner put it, the films that emerged in the late sixties "transcoded a growing sense of alienation from the dominant myths and ideals of U.S. society."[14] As they note, this does not occur simply on the level of content (i.e., depicting skeptical or rebellious characters) but instead necessitates the critique of existing formal models.[15] This critique often took the form of a kind of staged failure, in which the protagonists who might have succeeded in earlier films can now only either fail or die, as though turning the mechanisms of Classical Hollywood storytelling and genre into occasions to represent a broken machine. This often appears in conjunction with the "demythification" or negation of genre, for example in Altman's *McCabe and Mrs. Miller* (1971), in which the harsh realities of frontier capitalism supplant the allegorical forms of the Western. The "real world," in other words, is shown to be one in which the heroic narratives of Hollywood cannot in fact function. This failure to function usually entails the figuration of a split between subject and world discussed above, as though the world that the former expects to act within has become unknowable or unnavigable, or simply inhospitable to the subject who is out of sync with it. One thinks here of *Easy Rider* (1969), in which freedom and the frontier are revealed as foreclosed possibilities (again, recalling and negating the Western), and a series of possible ways of existing in the world (that of the yeoman farmer, the commune member, or the ACLU activist) are in turn rejected. There are of course many more examples, such as *Five Easy Pieces* (1970), in which the protagonist rejects his bourgeois identity but fails to find anything to replace it with (one of the rare instances in which class comes into the picture, as though to call for an overhaul of class identity), or *Two-Lane Blacktop* (1971), in which any end or goal rings hollow and there seems to no longer be any world outside of the moving car itself, the bubble inside which the alienated protagonists enclose themselves. Not only agency but morality and values as well (one thinks here not only of the drug-dealing heroes of *Easy Rider* but also of *Bonnie and Clyde*, who seem to spit in the face of a black-and-white old Hollywood morality in which good guys and bad guys are clearly discernable) seem to be evacuated from this world, in which the only possible heroes are antiheroes.

The unresolved or failed narratives characteristic of New Hollywood are thus fundamentally negational in character, operating on the level of genre, protagonist, narrative structure, and morality/values all at once; gone is the model in which, as Thomas Elsaesser puts it, "the image or scene not only pointed forward and backward to what had been and what was to come, but also helped to develop a motivational logic that functioned as an implicit causality, enveloping the hero and connecting him to the world."[16] Elsaesser identifies this failure of action and narrative with a sense of the closure of historical possibility more broadly: "One might call them films that dramatize the end of history, for what is a story, a motivated narrative (which such movies refuse to employ), other than an implicit recognition of the existence of history, at least in its formal dimension—of driving forces and determinants, of causes, conflicts, consequence, and interaction?"[17]

This end of history, however, is something more like a pause, a moment for culture and ideology to catch up with the development of capitalism. For Jameson, conspiracy is a useful trope in this context insofar as it offers a means to overhaul narrative in a way that strives toward understanding a seemingly inscrutable world. This amounts to revealing history not to be over, but simply hidden from view, or no longer representable. Conspiracy narratives call for the figuration of "a potentially infinite network, along with a plausible explanation of its invisibility; or in other words: the collective and the epistemological."[18] This of course would explain why conspiracy narratives might surface at any juncture in which the legibility of the world and the possibility of cognitive mapping are called into question (as, for example, in Balzac and elsewhere in the nineteenth century). It is thus no coincidence that the wave of conspiracy films of the early seventies (*The Conversation* [1974], *The Parallax View* [1974], *Chinatown* [1974], *Three Days of the Condor* [1975]) appear after the cycle of "alienated" films mentioned above, as though providing an explanation for what preceded them. Such narratives are inevitable in a historical moment marked by regular political assassinations and a loss of trust in government, among other things, but their deeper symptomatic value and their function as "problem-solving" texts lie on a more abstract level. In the first films of the conspiracy cycle, conspiracy too seems to lead only to failure: one can gain knowledge and ultimately understand, at least to some extent, what is going on, but one cannot do anything about it. The breadth of the conspiracy and the figuration or lack thereof of who is behind it vary drastically between films in which failure still appears to be inevitable. *Chinatown*, for example, gives us the satisfaction of putting a face on evil as well as of explaining its motivation, reverting to an older narrative paradigm in which a single individual comes to stand for a larger network; in this sense it is a regressive film that can map the world only by reverting to earlier forms of representation (and indeed to mythic ones), even as it expresses an angst that is certainly of its time. The agents behind the conspiracy in *The Parallax View* and their motivation, meanwhile, remain entirely unknown, placing it more squarely in the negational camp of the New Hollywood. But in both films, in any case, knowledge of conspiracy fails to lead to an ability to act; indeed, any presumption to do so is shown to be futile and foolhardy, as the heroes of each are brought down by an Oedipal hubris that can result only in death or castration, in which drawing too close to the conspiracy can ultimately reveal only one's subordination to it.

Even so, the conspiracy narrative presents an opportunity to pass beyond the pure negativity of the earlier films and toward the construction of new narrative forms and new conceptions of agency that would be commensurate with the world that it "discovers." We might also think of this step in terms of genre: if the first wave of New Hollywood films draw upon the Western as a way to spatialize the idea of limitation and inability to act, to show the lack of a frontier or of any *place* one might successfully exist, the conspiracy films turn to film noir and other detective narratives, in which connections between spaces and characters are more abstract and inscrutable, less strictly topographical. Although the detective film too is subject to negation or reduction to the real (as in Altman's *The Long Goodbye* [1973] or Penn's *Night Moves* [1975]), it can also, particularly through the conspiracy motif, be revived as a means to find the formal structures that will be required for the depiction of a real that can be represented only through allegory. While the "real" in the earlier New Hollywood cycle is thus primarily negative, a way to represent the outmodedness of Hollywood convention, realism in a deeper sense turns out to be attainable only through a repurposing of those conventions, insofar as the world of global information-based capitalism cannot be represented directly and requires mediated, allegorical representation. Furthermore, the conspiracy motif allows for a revision of actantial structure, creating, as Jameson puts it, "a situation in which what is wanted is as absolute a collectivization of the individual functions as possible: no longer an individual victim, but everybody; no longer an individual villain, but an omnipresent network; no longer an individual detective with a specific brief, but rather someone who blunders into all of this just as anyone might have done."[19] Finally, it requires the positing of some sort of relationship between the individual and this broader framework, some formal device through which the "two poles" of the detective and the crime/conspiracy can be forced "into a common world."[20] While this may result in yet another staging of the impossibility of action, it also introduces a new way of conceiving of agency and the connections between actants that opens the door to solutions to the form-problem that the earlier New Hollywood films could not resolve.

Within this context, *All the President's Men* is significant for Jameson insofar as it allows the protagonist and antagonist functions to both take the form of a conspiracy/collective, with the *Washington Post* pitted against the White House.[21] However, this alone is not what makes Pakula's film so illuminating:

what matters here is not simply an alteration of the actantial structures of Classical Hollywood narrative and the new forms of representing agency it might allow, but also the ways in which this alteration is employed in the service of an ideological project that attempts to resolve the crisis of incommensurability between subject and world. This resolution entails a dialectical transformation of both the negational elements of the earlier New Hollywood films (a lack of clear motivation, a fuzzy or mediated sense of agency, endings that seem arbitrary or open, lack of clear moral universe) and the corresponding fatalistic or emptied-out ideology (or refusal to live within ideology that can result only in the negation/death of the subject). In short, the film is one in which these attributes, through a radical change in the representation of totality and agency, are transformed into virtues, into the conditions of possibility for the emergence of a radically new world that nonetheless looks reassuringly familiar, as though there had been no change at all but simply a return to the days of the successful protagonist and the happy ending.

Two Conspiracies

To begin with, we might say that the kind of moral "grayness" characteristic of the earlier New Hollywood films is here a necessary starting point for a new conception of the protagonist, one that changes the hero's role from that of a morally marked "good guy" into a kind of value-neutral actor, one who is effective but who does not succeed due to some inherent moral goodness or just cause. The protagonists of most New Hollywood films evade easy moral categorization, yet in most cases this ambivalence is posed as a problem, or at least foregrounded as a novelty. In *All the President's Men*, it is simply rendered irrelevant: we know next to nothing about the two protagonists (who in many cases, whether intentionally or not, appear rather unsympathetic, an issue I will return to below), but more importantly the film is evacuated of any kind of political or moral criticism, so the clash between protagonist and antagonist loses any melodramatic charge. Those working for Nixon are not demonized and in some cases (for example, that of Donald Segretti) appear quite sympathetic; Pakula describes them as people with "rational thinking" and notes that "some of them weren't bad people."[22] This means that the antagonists we find here are far different from those we might expect; the problem with them is not that they are morally or even politically wrong or bad (although they are marked as negative in a different way, insofar as they have been "found out"). There is thus, as Jameson notes, no "villainy" in the film,[23] although this does not necessarily mean that there is no meaningful opposition between the reporters and the Nixonians; it simply has to be cast in other terms, ones that are neither ethical nor political. Jameson is thus right to say this is not a film about "practical politics,"[24] but we might even go so far as to say that its depoliticization symptomatizes the dissolution or subsumption of the sphere of the political proper characteristic of neoliberalism (both in terms of its increasing indistinguishability from other spheres and in terms of its seemingly nonideological or apolitical character),[25] as though it no longer mattered as a way to motivate or guide actions or to construct a convincing and reassuring worldview.

This liquidation of moral and political antagonisms is also a necessary precondition of the narrative form that is adopted here, insofar as this is what allows the protagonists to function as the representatives of a "second conspiracy." For the conventional actantial structures of the Hollywood narrative to be replaced by "conspiratorial" ones, highly negative characterizations of conspiracy as something that victimizes, that is primarily associated with a kind of pervasive menace or powerlessness that negates the individual, have to be overturned; if we presume that conspiracy in its negative form conveys a fear of a faceless, delocalized capitalism that acts in ways invisible to the average individual, then it is precisely this mode of deindividualized and diffuse action that must be made acceptable. We have to move from a model like *Chinatown* (in which the hero's virtue is perhaps present only insofar as he is a victim rather than a participant in the conspiracy) or *The Parallax View* (in which the character who enters the conspiracy and tries to match it unwittingly becomes part of it, losing his own agency and identity and having them replaced by the ones the conspiracy has prepared for him) into one in which conspiracy becomes an admissible form of agency, something that one can control or navigate successfully, cleansed of its ethical connotations and the sense that it negates the individual. Subjects have to accept that they do not and cannot act alone, that within the complex world depicted here, individual agency is no longer sufficient and must be subordinated to something larger, must renounce its self-motivated character in order to be exercised at all; the self-contained protagonist typical of Classical Hollywood film must be turned into something else, something less independent and autonomous, yet still appearing to be so. *All the President's Men* achieves this by situating the individual (or rather, two individuals, although they carry out a single actantial function) as an agent of a larger institution who nonetheless operates with considerable freedom. While the individuals benefit from the resources and protection of that institution, that institution does not instruct or guide their action. The film thus conveys the terms of a kind of bargain with the conspiracy that strongly resonates with the neoliberal bargain (which admittedly perhaps only amplifies a dynamic already present and observed by Marx in the nineteenth century) in which relative autonomy in many spheres (and indeed more autonomy than would have been available under the old liberal order, characterized as stifling and bureaucratic) is offered in exchange for a radical sacrifice of independence on a more fundamental level.

Here we can begin to see the utility of the journalist as protagonist: with the shift from the private detective / investigator seen in films like *Chinatown* and *The Conversation* to the journalist heroes of *All the President's Men* comes the ability to connect the impotent individual to larger conspiratorial structures while still presenting him as relatively autonomous (Warren Beatty's journalist/ detective character in *The Parallax View* fails, at least in part, because he works for a small-town newspaper that is a far cry from the *Washington Post*, because he is too far from the institution, still too much the antiestablishment rebel). While the film's journalist-heroes may share much with the private investigator figures that long populated Hollywood films, they diverge from them in that they are no longer free agents, standing at arm's length from a questionable institution (i.e., the police), but rather part of a different, less immediately visible and structured institution (here incarnated in the press, although something other than the press could conceivably serve this purpose as well).[26] They are exemplary neoliberal figures insofar as, as Pierre Dardot and Christian Laval characterize labor under neoliberalism, they "work for enterprises as if they were working for themselves, thereby abolishing any sense of alienation and even any *distance* between individuals and the enterprises employing them."[27] Woodward and Bernstein carry out a form of labor in which institutions are still necessary but have become flexible, and individual or entrepreneurial initiative is seen as preferable to structured management. Here we might pause over the way that the film depicts the relationship between the two reporters and the *Post*'s executive editor, Ben Bradlee: Bradlee is there to support and protect his employees and to give his final authorization to their stories, but he does not in any way direct or interfere with their work. In this sense, he is the permissive father standing in contrast to Nixon's control freak patriarch, the director of a looser, more flexible conspiracy. In contrasting the heads of these two conspiracies, we can begin to see how the *Post* / White House binary functions not so much as an ethical opposition but as a means for representing two contrasting ways of doing similar things. The relationship between these two terms is therefore not one of moral or political antagonism but one based on a model of the market in which the primary relationship between agents is that of competition (identified by Foucault as the core of neoliberalism's conception of the market, replacing the primacy of exchange in classical liberal thought).[28] The Nixonians are the losers in this relationship, representing a failed attempt at the mastery of information necessary for the transformation of capitalism, a kind of prototype or beta version (and a very "buggy" one at that) of more or less the same kind of enterprise that Woodward and Bernstein attempt to undertake.

Here, furthermore, we find, as Jameson notes, that the distance between the crime and its resolution "has been reduced to an absolute minimum by the positing of a 'crime' as informational and media-centered as its own solution."[29] Nixon's conspiracy stands not only for tight, even pathological control often associated with an outmoded management style, but also for the blocking of the flow of information, whereas Bradlee's gentle hand facilitates the unblocking of that flow, a key opposition that transcends the conflict between a secretive government and the free press and instead provides two mirroring images of how best to gather information and conduct surveillance. The "president's men," at the same time, clearly stand for "the establishment," broadly conceived, whereas the press appears to be the realm of the antiestablishment rebel, now fairly domesticated and reconciled with a more flexible establishment, and thus identified less with antagonism toward the system than with a new conception of labor and management. As Drehli Robnik notes, "The young rebel protagonist of the earlier countercultural cycle seems to be displaced [in later films] into the figure of the liberal investigator (often a not-so-young, but long haired journalist)."[30] Woodward and Bernstein do not retain the negativity or antisocial character of these earlier protagonists, but their contrast with Nixon, particularly in their commitment to "transparency" (not to mention Bernstein's long hair), allows the film to position them in a way that recalls such figures, who now are shown to be easily subsumable into the social.

The most important problem with the Nixonians is not that they represent "the system," but simply that, as Deep Throat puts it, they are "not very bright guys": like Bernstein and Woodward, they are called upon to obtain information and to undertake surveillance, but their efforts to do so are thwarted. Their ineptitude, however, is also associated with a kind of outmoded, overly politicized ideology, as suggested by Bernard Barker's response of "anti-communist" when asked his occupation at the arraignment of the Watergate burglars. In the order heralded by *All the President's Men*, old political oppositions like those between communists and capitalists are no longer relevant: "Modernity or efficiency," as Dardot and Laval put it, "is neither left-wing nor right-wing, in the formula of those who 'don't do politics.' The main thing is that 'it works,' as Blair often repeated."[31]

Bureaucracy and old, overly politicized ideologies are precisely what prevent the government agencies in the film from being more efficient and successful. While Reagan's version of neoliberalism would of course rely heavily on the revival of Cold War antagonisms and ethical oppositions (the "Evil Empire")—and for this reason we might consider what is on display here to fall more in line with the less politicized "second wave" of neoliberalism represented by Clinton and Blair, possible after the collapse of the Soviet Bloc—specifically Reaganite/Thatcherite resonances are apparent: the government is simply not very good at what it does, and the private sector is more efficient, flexible, tolerant, and rewarding of individual initiative and enterprise, and so on. The FBI plays foil to the *Post* in much the same way here, as Woodward and Bernstein learn of its inadequate investigation, presumably constrained by institutional loyalties or bureaucratic limitations. The ideological work undertaken by the *Post*/government dyad thus requires a kind of sleight of hand, in which the negative term of readily recognizable oppositions (past/present, old/young, establishment/antiestablishment) is transformed into a kind of defective version of the mastery of information and media undertaken by Woodward and Bernstein. As a result, the position of the father or of the establishment becomes one that does not have to be totally rejected, but rather one that simply falls short of what the son can achieve; the father can remain, provided he gets with the times and acts more like Bradlee and less like Nixon. The generational aspect of the conflict here is similar to that noted by Derek Nystrom in several other New Hollywood films, in which the generational conflict between the older and younger members of the professional-managerial class has to be neutralized or drained of radical antagonism in order to ensure the continuity of capitalism.[32]

Conspiracy and Agency

If Woodward and Bernstein function as agents of a conspiracy, what keeps them from being anything more than stand-ins for a force whose ultimate identity (if we assume it is not simply that of the press) and motivation remain obscure, protagonists stripped of any individuality or personal motivation? Neoliberalism's problem of how to seem to deliver greater freedom and uniqueness to individuals while incorporating them ever more fully into a system that dictates their actions is translated here into terms specific to the Hollywood film: how can one maintain the emotional appeal of the protagonist function when it is clearly no longer self-motivated or encompassed by the single individual? This problem is related to one that Jameson identifies in *Dog Day Afternoon*: "how to imagine authority today, how to conceive imaginatively— that is in non-abstract, non-conceptual form—of a principle of authority that can express the essential impersonality and post-individualistic structure of the power structure of our society while still operating among real people ...?"[33] *Dog Day Afternoon* incarnates this authority/agency in the "cool and technocratic" FBI agent, but does not need to make him seem sympathetic, since the viewer is instead invited to emotionally invest in Al Pacino's antihero character, Sonny. *All the President's Men*, meanwhile, subsumes the alienated method actor (this time Hoffman, not Pacino) into a different paradigm, in which he occupies the position not of tragic antihero but that of the agent of a new, better establishment; we might thus say that the ultimate answer to Jameson's question is that somehow, Sonny and the FBI agent (who stands in for the faceless power of corporate America) must become the same person. *All the President's Men* thus faces at once the problem of how to make a protagonist who is merely a cog in a larger machine appealing and compelling and that of how to make us root for the winner or the establishment once again, to dispel the notion that the only way to be a hero is to die or to fail.

Here the differences between the two lead actors become relevant: Hoffman falls into the category of the late-period method actor, much like Pacino, while Redford is far closer to the classic leading man. Both, however, end up carrying out the same actantial function. While I will return in a moment to the implications of this merging, we might posit that this represents something like the synthesis of the irreducibly individualistic New Hollywood star (Hoffman) with the more neutral leading man figure (Redford), the former embodying a kind of antiestablishment ethos and the latter the kind of effectiveness more typical of the Classical Hollywood hero, thus resolving one aspect of the problem posed above.[34] On a broader level, we might simply say that it is the star status of the two main actors that allows the film to offset the characters' lack of individuality and motivation and to make them seem like charismatic individuals despite being drained of almost all of the characteristics we would expect from a Hollywood protagonist. The movie star as "spectacular" individual, the person as image, serves as imaginary compensation (for the viewer) for what has been lost in terms of actual freedom and self-determination, while at the same time making it seem as though the commodification of the human being (or the turning of the human being into "human capital," if one chooses to put it in more neoliberal terms) is a positive and desirable thing.

As far as making these characters interesting despite their lack of discernable motivation is concerned, what we have here is perhaps a revalencing of the unmotivated protagonists of the earlier New Hollywood films: their emptiness or lack of internal drive now becomes valuable becomes it represents a space to be filled, as though anxiously awaiting the appearance of an external force, or frictionless identification with a corporate or collective entity. What are Woodward and Bernstein if not the more knowing and consenting mirror images of *The Parallax View*'s Joe Frady, who mistakes the desires and goals of the conspiracy for his own, unwittingly carrying them out? These are characters who, unlike those in *Easy Rider* or *Five Easy Pieces*, reclaim the ability to act within the world at the price of giving up their freedom, thus reconnecting the individual to the social whole. Of course narratives that stage the negotiation between the individual and the social in the fashion of the Bildungsroman are hardly unique to this period of Hollywood, but now they are resolved rather differently than before: the Classical Hollywood model, at its very origins, resolved the contradiction between the individual and the social by showing how the former's personal characteristics could in fact be useful to the latter. The Western is of course a key generic site for staging this resolution (how can the antisocial element serve the purposes of the social?), but we also find less allegorical models of how the individual might find a place within a corporate structure in early Hollywood films. In a Fairbanks film like *His Picture in the Papers*, the antisocial misfit ends up, after many failed attempts, figuring out how his seemingly useless skills (here, physical fitness and an antisocial tendency to get into brawls, even with the police) can in fact serve capitalism; this is perhaps not that far from the way that, much later, films like *The Dirty Dozen* show, as Robnik notes, how pathological/antisocial characteristics can be harnessed in the service of the social.[35] But in the case of Woodward and Bernstein, this tension has vanished, simply because no individual qualities or desires are relevant any longer. Wendy Brown notes that in neoliberal theory, in contrast to classical liberalism, "reconciling individual with national or other collective interests is no longer the contemporary problem to be solved by markets."[36] This contrast is detectable in the absence in *All the President's Men* of the individual/social tension, as though expressing the supposed lack of conflict with the social that results when the neoliberal individual simply "accept[s] the market situation as imposed on them as 'reality'—i.e. as the only 'rules of the game.'"[37] This is precisely what Woodward and Bernstein, unlike the earlier Hollywood protagonists, accept: they are already part of a system, and very much at home within it, because it is only under these conditions that they can gain any individual identity at all, thus avoiding the death and failure that resulted when their New Hollywood predecessors attempted to opt out.

This lack of individual interest relates to what Jameson repeatedly refers to as the "providential" character of the film: everything will happen as it needs to, almost automatically, if one pulls the right string. It matters little who pulls the string; the fabric will unravel regardless. This also allows for the abrupt conclusion of the film, a kind of transfiguration of the "non-ending" of New Hollywood films: once Woodward and Bernstein have reached a certain point in their investigation, the film no longer even needs to show its unfolding. Instead, its final minutes are occupied by shots of the newsroom accompanied by the sound of typing, whose numbing repetition evokes an automatic process. In the film's last shots, the human-manned typewriters give way to a machine that literally writes on its own, as a teleprinter automatically types out news stories, informing us of the downfall of Nixon's cronies and, ultimately, of the president himself. We reach a different kind of end of history, in which the subject's absence becomes an assurance that all is running smoothly.

This idea that human beings are both interchangeable and dispensable (obviously related to labor under capitalism in general, but whose acceptance or naturalization is particularly important for neoliberal capitalism, as part of its economic rationale and ideological "reality principle") surely holds the potential to be disturbing, yet here seems intended to reassure us. On one hand the film wants to emphasize the individuality of the two characters, yet on the other it shows the desirability of their interchangeability, once again demonstrating the outmodedness of any need to reconcile the individual with the social. Indeed, the idea of the erasure of the individual in favor of a kind of impersonal process in which agency comes through fulfilling the desires of a corporate enterprise is cast as a way to move forward historically, to overcome the ideological struggles of the 1960s by rendering difference irrelevant. In interviews, Redford constantly emphasizes the differences between the characters that he and Hoffman play ("One was a Jew and one was a WASP, one was a radical liberal and one was a Republican") and how much their success depended on "the alchemy of these two guys, considering their differences."[38] The film's concern with reducing difference and with staging a kind of synthesis between opposing terms allows it to turn the reporter duo (already turned into one being by Ben Bradlee, who referred to them as "Woodstein") into the site of the resolution of a number of contradictions simply by implying that these contradictions are irrelevant. The political affiliations and ethnic backgrounds of the two characters have absolutely no bearing on how well they do their jobs; only the first are mentioned in the film, and then only in passing (as something of a joke, when Bernstein learns rather late in the film that Woodward is a Republican, as though to stress the irrelevance of this fact).

Once again, the solution arrived at here is very different from the one we see in earlier "team narratives" like *The Dirty Dozen*, in which, as Robnik argues, "the goal-orientation of the action image depends not on fusing differences or reducing them to presupposed standards of efficiency, but on mining them for their use-values as potential productive forces."[39] While the film takes pains to contrast Woodward and Bernstein, the contrasts end up being extremely superficial (styles of dress, speech, personal tics), the kinds of expressions of "individual identity" that neoliberalism champions.[40] Specialized labor is likewise liquidated: at its outset the film show us that each character has particular strengths (Bernstein is a better writer, while Woodward works better outside of the office and excels in personal interactions), yet by the end such distinctions are no longer sustained (Bernstein ends up being more important in his face-to-face interactions with sources, while Woodward is often depicted surrounded by piles of books and papers). Difference is subsumed through the unification of both into the same actantial function, as specialization gives way to flexibility and interchangeability.

Seduction and Submission

All the President's Men's focus on the work carried out by Woodward and Bernstein allows it to foreground the importance of mastering media and information, providing a symmetry between the two conspiracies and suggesting the centrality of data and surveillance to "the future of our country," which Ben Bradlee declares to be at stake near the end of the film. What is really at stake here, though, is the future of capitalism, as it shifts to a model in which the collection, sharing, and interpretation of information become increasingly indispensable, and in which a huge amount of resources and labor are dedicated to processes of surveillance and the mastery of data. It is the question of how to give figuration to this sort of labor that lies at the heart of *All the President's Men*. Yet the fact that it needs to be allegorized, to be presented in a form that is far more concrete and visible than the one it takes in reality, ends up revealing its most violent and troubling dimensions, and foreshadowing a process in which all human subjects are reduced to instrumentalizable data. Woodward and Bernstein do not search through databases or run algorithms, as their present-day counterparts would, but instead spend most of their time talking to other human beings face-to-face, and it is these human beings who end up being the film's main antagonists. The film depicts the main obstacle to the new paradigm it heralds not as the Nixonians, but as those who refuse to submit to the reporters' demands for information.

As Jameson notes, "It is also important to raise the issue of gender in these encounters, where the proximate other—secretary or intermediary for those absent others who hold supreme power—is almost always a woman, who must in some way or other be victimized or tormented in order to release her secret, or—in the stunning Miami sequence—to remove her from the crucial door."[41] The encounters in question here, particularly the one featuring Jane Alexander as a bookkeeper, are troubling indeed: Bernstein quite literally forces his way inside of her home, and then spends hours forcing her to speak, despite her fear and reluctance, and it would not be far-fetched to see this as a thinly disguised rape, particularly given the film's characterization of Bernstein as a womanizer and seducer, a capacity that he clearly draws upon in order to manipulate women into talking. In two other instances, the reporters instrumentalize female colleagues who have had sexual relationships with people who have information that they need; one sleeps with an old flame at their request in order to obtain this information, essentially pimped out by Woodward and Bernstein.

The tactics Bernstein uses to extract information from women range from seduction (as when he turns on the charm while speaking to an employee of Howard Hunt) to deception (as with the Miami gatekeeper Jameson mentions) and outright use of force (the Jane Alexander scene). In all three cases, what is at stake is the woman's commitment to another man, from whose sway she must be freed: some who refuse to talk invoke their loyalty to the "president's men," but others, like Alexander's character, are shown to be hesitant to speak due to fear of these same men. In the case of the latter, we are ultimately shown that she wants to bring her former boss (John Mitchell) down, so Bernstein's aggressive tactics are cast as justified, a way to force her to do what she really wants to do. The disturbing scenario here is one in which these women are finally allowed to speak, to break out of the closed and secretive conspiracy and become part of the new, transparent one, in which their "voice" is liberated, but only so that it may be instrumentalized. The new order represented by the reporters gives voice to all, and puts an end to bureaucracies and their secrets, but this apparent liberation functions as a way to disavow continuing subjection and, indeed, class conflict (the women in *All the President's Men* are surely only slightly more middle-class versions of the ones Jameson finds in *Dog Day Afternoon*, "those doubly second-class and underpayable beings" who stand in for all of those marginalized and victimized by late capitalism).[42] Bernstein's interactions with these women stage a perverse talking cure, a liberation whose end point is already determined, providential, and resistance to which can thus be seen only as stubborn antagonism. They reveal not only the continuing actual marginalization of women but more broadly the fact that antagonism and difference remain in this new order and, perhaps most importantly, that the mastery of information is a matter of power and of the instrumentalization of others. To accept this as liberation is to accept oneself as a source of information to be used by power, willingly, in the service of good, to accept the erasure of the private (the woman whom the reporters pimp out to her ex-lover voices the quickly overcome objection, "That's personal!"). Here the film functions, to recall Kael's comments about Redford's films, as a very dark kind of "how-to" guide, depicting a world in which subjects will have to willingly consent to continual violations of privacy and personal boundaries in the name of the greater good.

On another, cruder level, perhaps these scenes assure the male viewer that the male impotence of the New Hollywood period (for example, that of Hoffman himself in *The Graduate*) has been overcome, that patriarchal authority has been regained but is nonetheless somehow different from and preferable to that which it has supplanted, insofar as it is desired by those who will be its subjects, who require it to gain their own freedom. Gone is the castrated Oedipus of *Chinatown*, replaced by the one who vanquishes the Sphinx for the good of Thebes, oblivious to the plague that will inevitably follow. This intersection between the mastery of information and a triumphant machismo was already present in Redford's previous film, *Three Days of the Condor*, but takes on a particularly perverse form here, one whose foundations seem to arrive ready-made in the appellation "Deep Throat," conferred upon Woodward and Bernstein's informant by Howard Simons, managing editor of the *Post*. Deep Throat is a kind of Tiresias figure, whose name signals what Jameson identifies as the "pornographic" character of the reporters' inquires:[43] he is masculine insofar as he is indeed a man and situated as a source of authoritative or even patriarchal knowledge, yet at the same time, occupying a dark and womb-like parking garage, he cannot fail to evoke those feminine bearers of knowledge (the Sibyl, the Sphinx, or at moments even Cassandra) who present a threat to the male hero, giving rise to an anxiety that is perhaps dispelled by imagining a (desired) phallus entering the woman's mouth at the very moment it opens to speak the truth, as suggested by the allusion to the pornographic film in which the main character's clitoris is located at the back of her throat.

It is not, however, only on the level of gender that antagonism and the threat of violence reemerge out of the film's ostensible solution to the ideological deadlocks and form-problems of the New Hollywood film. The lack of distance between the solution and the crime that Jameson notes, the reduction of antagonism to competition between symmetrical agents, brings along with it the threat of reversibility, the menace of occupying the position of the loser instead of the winner. The subject who exercises surveillance and extracts data from others may at any moment be repositioned as the object of that same process. Here, that reversibility is given figuration in terms of an absent gaze, conjured up by images that evoke an unknown subject (or even a surveillance camera) looking at our protagonists from a great distance, and more explicitly, by Deep Throat's warning that Woodward and Bernstein are under surveillance. Ultimately, this warning is never proven to be true: the reporters' lives, contrary to what Deep Throat says, do not appear to have been in danger, nor do we ever find out who, if anyone, was watching them. Yet this lack of resolution leaves us not with relief but with the sense that this condition has simply become ubiquitous; it matters not who or what is watching but simply, as Woodward puts it, that "it's being done." Ultimately, the one who watches remains invisible and unnamed, much like in *The Parallax View*, almost as though Pakula wanted to leave a loose end, a remainder, to undercut Redford's triumphalism. The moment in which the suspense would break, in which the watcher would be revealed and thus neutralized, never comes. The threat that remains unnamed and unseen constitutes something like the dialectical complement, the negative mirror image, of the same new paradigm represented by the *Post*. The new surveillance and information-based capitalism is everywhere, and we cannot choose not to be a part of it; it knits the world together, provides a common ground that serves to provide a shared way of understanding and acting within that world, thus giving the impression of equality among all, but cannot liquidate the antagonisms and contradictions internal to it. In its darker moments, then, the film gives us a terrifying glimpse of a postpolitical, globalized capitalism that cannot fully repress or disavow its inherent violence.

The film's darkness perhaps goes some way to explaining why the solution it offers is not one that was subsequently emulated but was instead replaced by a return to the clear ethical and ontological oppositions characteristic of the cinema of the Reagan period. *All the President's Men* is ultimately all too clear in revealing the inextricability of its triumphalism from the dehumanization and instrumentalization at the heart of an ideology that claims to act in the service of individual freedom and dignity.

Yet in other ways the film announces a process that has proceeded with great success, one that happens not in the cinema but in the merging of journalism and entertainment, the end point of a process in which the visibility or "transparency" of the political is insisted upon in such a way that it is subsumed into culture, into spectacle, all the better to conceal the material realities that lie behind the twenty-four-hour news cycle. Contrary to what the film would lead us to expect, such transparency has hardly led to consensus, as the antagonism fundamental to a paradigm marked above all by the primacy of competition breaks apart the common ground that it purports to offer. The myth of the transparency, impartiality, and democratic function of the free press offered by *All the President's Men*, which recasts these virtues in neoliberal terms, already appears suspect in the film itself, which does not entirely conceal the darkness behind the light; it surely can no longer be taken seriously once the *Post* is owned by Jeff Bezos, who incarnates the use of surveillance and data collection in the service of capitalism, and the reduction of the human being to exploitable information, both on the warehouse floor and in the virtual realm.

Notes

1 Fredric Jameson, *Signatures of the Visible* (New York: Routledge, 1990), 143.
2 Fredric Jameson, *The Geopolitical Aesthetic: Cinema and Space in the World System* (Bloomington: Indiana University Press, 1992), 33.
3 The presence of this kind of dialectical process has been posited by Thomas Elsaesser, J. D. Connor, and others as occurring on an industrial level, as well as by Drehli Robnik in respect to how the dysfunctional protagonists of New Hollywood films are "put to use" through new forms of "purposeful action." See Elsaesser, "American Auteur Cinema: The Last—or First—Great Picture Show," and Robnik, "Allegories of Post-Fordism in 1970s New Hollywood: Countercultural Combat Films and Conspiracy Thrillers as Genre Recycling," both in *The Last Great American Picture Show*, ed. Elsaesser, Alexander Howarth, and Noel King (Amsterdam: Amsterdam University Press, 2004), and J. D. Connor, *The Studios after the Studios: Neoclassical Hollywood (1970–2010)* (Stanford, CA: Stanford University Press, 2015), esp. chaps. 2–3.
4 Jameson, *Geopolitical Aesthetic*, 67–71.
5 On this point, see Peter Krämer, *The New Hollywood* (London: Wallflower, 2005), 32–33.
6 Jameson, *Geopolitical Aesthetic*, 67.
7 Jameson, *Geopolitical Aesthetic*, 67.
8 Interview in the film *All the President's Men Revisited* (Peter Schnall, 2013).
9 For a summary of these crises and subsequent transformations, see David Harvey, *A Brief History of Neoliberalism* (Oxford: Oxford University Press, 2005), esp. 5–63.
10 Jameson, *Geopolitical Aesthetic*, 13. This focus on gathering operable information is at the core of Hayek's conception of the market, hence at the heart of neoliberal theory; the kind of information I have in mind here is more related to the mass surveillance / data gathering characteristic of contemporary capitalism, which is far more centralized and comprehensive than (but perhaps the logical evolution of) Hayek's paradigm in which the "price system" serves as the primary means of gathering information. See Friedrich A. Hayek, "The Use of Knowledge in Society," in *Individualism and Economic Order* (Chicago: University of Chicago Press, 1996), 77–91.
11 On "governance," a term initially introduced by Foucault, see Wendy Brown, *Undoing the Demos: Neoliberalism's Stealth Revolution* (New York: Zone Books, 2015), 125 (and the rest of chap. 4).
12 Pauline Kael quoted in John Boorstin, "Notes on the Making of *All the President's Men*," *Los Angeles Review of Books*, March 25, 2016.
13 Geoff King, *New Hollywood Cinema: An Introduction* (London: I.B. Tauris, 2002), 24–30.
14 Michael Ryan and Douglas Kellner, *Camera Politica: The Politics and Ideology of Contemporary Hollywood Film* (Bloomington: Indiana University Press, 1988), 17.
15 Ryan and Kellner, *Camera Politica*, 19.
16 Thomas Elsaesser, "The Pathos of Failure: American Films in the 1970s: Notes on the Unmotivated Hero" (1975), in Elsaesser, Howarth, and King, *Last Great American Picture Show*, 280.
17 Elsaesser, "Pathos of Failure," 291.
18 Jameson, *Geopolitical Aesthetic*, 9.
19 Jameson, *Geopolitical Aesthetic*, 34.
20 Jameson, *Geopolitical Aesthetic*, 33.

21 Jameson, *Geopolitical Aesthetic*, 67.

22 Interview in *Pressure and the Press: The Making of* All the President's Men (1976, uncredited promotional film).

23 Jameson, *Geopolitical Aesthetic*, 69.

24 Jameson, *Geopolitical Aesthetic*, 67.

25 On this second point, see Pierre Dardot and Christian Laval, *The New Way of the World: On Neoliberal Society*, trans. Gregory Elliott (London: Verso, 2013), 191.

26 Here we might recall Jameson's assertion that what occurs in the postmodern situation is not "the death or disappearance of the subject," but rather "the subsumption of all solitary rebels or isolated monads into new forms of group cohesion and affirmation," a process illustrated through the transformation of the private eye into an agent of a larger enterprise. See *Signatures of the Visible*, 173.

27 Dardot and Laval, *New Way of the World*, 260.

28 Michel Foucault, *The Birth of Biopolitics: Lectures at the Collège de France 1978–1979*, trans. Graham Burchell (New York: Picador, 2008), 118–119.

29 Jameson, *Geopolitical Aesthetic*, 68.

30 Robnik, "Allegories of Post-Fordism," 347.

31 Dardot and Laval, *New Way of the World*, 191. Deng Xiaoping famously voiced this sentiment in a more poetic way, asking, "What does it matter if it is a ginger cat or a black cat as long as it catches mice?" See Harvey, *Brief History of Neoliberalism*, 125.

32 Derek Nystrom, *Hard Hats, Rednecks, and Macho Men: Class in 1970s American Cinema* (New York: Oxford University Press, 2009), 21–58.

33 Jameson, *Signatures of the Visible*, 48.

34 Redford's position here is perhaps more complex than Hoffman's, insofar as he had already played a character who represents a failed attempt at this synthesis in *The Candidate* (1972), but that discussion will have to wait until another day.

35 Robnik, "Allegories of Post-Fordism," 337–340.

36 Brown, *Undoing the Demos*, 84.

37 Dardot and Laval, *New Way of the World*, 170.

38 Interview in *All the President's Men Revisited*.

39 Robnik, "Allegories of Post-Fordism," 343.

40 Harvey, *Brief History of Neoliberalism*, 47.

41 Jameson, *Geopolitical Aesthetic*, 72.

42 Jameson, *Signatures of the Visible*, 46.

43 Jameson, *Geopolitical Aesthetic*, 73.

10

The Conspiracy Film, Hollywood's Cultural Paradigms, and Class Consciousness

MIKE WAYNE

This essay discusses Fredric Jameson's insight that the Hollywood conspiracy film is a degraded form of popular intuition concerning capital's hostile class power. But to understand the problems and possibilities of conspiratorial thinking in popular film requires grounding the genre in a discussion of broader cultural forms. Jameson's broader theoretical model identifies three main cultural forms: realism, modernism, and postmodernism. He argues that each of these is "dominant" in three successive historical stages: nineteenth-century nation-based capitalism (realism), monopoly capitalism and imperialism (modernism), and late capitalism (postmodernism). With the passing of each successive stage, the correlating cultural dominant is also marginalized or becomes historically redundant. This, as we shall see, is problematic, but it is characteristic of Jameson's Marxist analysis that a subgenre like the conspiracy film can be unraveled only by thinking big and thinking long, that is, over historical time. However we will need to add a fourth cultural form to Jameson's trinity, one that can give a place to Hollywood as a mass cultural form. As soon as we do that, some questions and problems arise with Jameson's model. For example, in what sense is modernism "dominant" in the face of the rise of mass culture in the monopoly capitalism and imperialism phase? Further we may ask whether the historical schema is too linear in its vision of the rise and fall of cultural paradigms. Has, for example, realism been eclipsed as thoroughly as Jameson's model suggests?

We will see that the conspiracy film can be located in each of these four cultural forms or paradigms (and that they are all still active). While still being recognizable as a type of film, the conspiracy film gets reconfigured differently according to which of these cultural paradigms a given film is primarily located in. The heterogeneity of the conspiracy film will be explained by these larger macro-cultural forms. The question of form will be shown to be important because form is a way of negotiating (with different strengths and weaknesses) the troubling social content of capitalism itself. Cultural forms are made to be read and decoded; they constitute, as Jameson would say, a kind of cultural programming, and so we will want finally in the conclusion of this essay to be explicit about the hermeneutic (interpretive) skills in cognition each of these cultural forms specialize in and how that interacts with the specific (sub)genre of the conspiracy film. To map the four cultural paradigms in a dialectical fashion, I draw on a Jameson device borrowed from A. J. Greimas called the "semiotic rectangle". A critique and modification of Jameson's theoretical model emerges, one that I think better articulates the essential Marxist principle of contradiction. If at one level Jameson himself is one of the foremost practitioners of theory attuned to cultural contradictions, there are aspects of his modeling, such as the historical sequencing of cultural forms mentioned above and the question of the "cultural dominant," that sometimes cut against what Jameson himself knows to be the case.

Cognitive Mapping and Conspiracy

Conspiracy as a model for thinking about social causation, that is, as a framework for literally understanding real-world events, is clearly problematic. The term indicates secret and unaccountable stratagems by an organized group or groups aimed at amassing power against the public interest typically (but not exclusively) involving at least some illegal means up to and including lethal force. Of course conspiracies do happen, but they happen in the context of the relations of advanced capitalism that provide the *motive and the capacity* to exercise conspiratorial agency of a certain type. But even more importantly the vast mass of social causes that operate in the world on a day-to-day basis are *not* the result of conspiratorial activity but are simply the workings out of economic and social power, in and out of public view and according to the laws that have sprung up around (bourgeois) legal norms of private ownership of the means of production and communication.

The real material causal forces that conspiracy thinking seeks to explain have become more powerful recently as globalization develops transnational institutional forms. The IMF, the World Bank, the WTO, and regional free-trade blocs are designed to sever the connections between states and their (national) publics and cement their alliance with transnational corporate interests.[1] Despite responding to real phenomena, conspiracy thinking is not particularly helpful to us in cognitively mapping capitalism. It presupposes the omnipotence of elite actors, excludes chance and contingency, and disavows a proper analysis of the contradictions of capitalism's political economy. Politically it is deeply ambivalent and can be mobilized by the right. So why should conspiracy movies be of interest? Because, as John S. Nelson pithily states, "conspiracy is a trope for system."[2]

While the conspiracy framework is problematic as a social science concept applied directly to the real world, as a way of telling stories it functions as a trope, extended metaphor, or what Jameson would call an allegory, in which class fantasies and anxieties may become representable. The lesson to take from conspiracy movies is not that the state and corporations routinely bump people off, but rather that the capitalist state and corporate power complexes and their representatives obey malignant logics (the profit motive) that are radically hostile to the interests (and lives) of the majority of the audience. These sentiments and feelings will find no expression or recognition in the discourse of the political class, the news media, and commercial speech generally. The modern conspiracy film is an attempt to make something perceptible that is very difficult for the mind to grasp, for all sorts of reasons (because of inherent complexity or the geographically extensive nature of global capitalism and also because this reality cuts against the forms of appearances of capitalist society). And the possibility of making some embryonic form of class consciousness perceptible is where politics and popular culture can meet. As Jameson notes:

> In order for genuine class consciousness to be possible, we have to begin to sense the abstract truth of class through the tangible medium of daily life in vivid and experiential ways; and to say that class structure is becoming representable means that we have now gone beyond mere abstract understanding and entered that whole area of personal fantasy, collective storytelling, narrative figurability—which is the domain of culture and no longer that of abstract sociology or economic analysis. To become figurable—that is to say, visible in the first place, accessible to our imaginations—the classes have to be able to become in some sense characters in their own right.[3]

Jameson argues that the "failure" of conspiracy stories is their "slippage into sheer theme and content." In other words, what the conspiracy film is diagnosing is fundamentally a question or problem of *form*: how to make something as abstract as capital "vivid and experiential." In his groundbreaking analysis of *Dog Day Afternoon* Jameson argues that it is not the performance of the Hollywood star, Al Pacino, that is of interest, with his classic method acting style being the very emblem of the psychologically complex subject with their individual human goals, but the unknown television contract player James Broderick, who as the FBI agent expresses "the essential impersonality and post-individualistic structure of the power structure of our society while still operating among real people, in the tangible necessities of daily life."[4] This points to the fundamental problem of form and the need to modify storytelling (here to develop character types that can represent the corporate subject) in order to cognitively map late capitalism, to make it *figurable*. I argue though that modifications of character types are *not* sufficient transformations of form in and of themselves to meet the challenge of new social content. We need to scale the analysis up to the macrostructures of *narrative* and to map the different options of form that are available for popular Hollywood films in telling conspiracy stories.

Mapping the Cultural Antinomies

As a Marxist Fredric Jameson insists on the relationship between culture and transformations in the mode of production. As modes of production change, new cultural forms emerge as the privileged sites to articulate certain problems of social content through aesthetic form. Jameson calls these forms "cultural dominants."[5] There are three main stages his historical schema works with: nation-state capitalism, monopoly capitalism and imperialism, and our current period, multinational capitalism. To each of these phases in the capitalist mode of production there is a corresponding cultural dominant, respectively, realism, modernism, and postmodernism. Absent from this trinity of forms is the question of mass culture, which consolidates itself in the era of monopoly capitalism and imperialism. Once we reinsert mass culture into the historical schema though, we need to ask on what basis Jameson can argue that modernism was the cultural dominant for the second phase of capitalist expansion rather than mass culture. Jameson has defined a "dominant cultural logic or hegemonic norm" as "the force field in which very different kinds of cultural impulses . . . must make their way."[6] Surely though it was mass culture that was the hegemonic norm, the "force field" in which modernism had to make its way?

Once we establish mass culture as the "cultural dominant" under monopoly capitalism and imperialism, the passage from modernism to postmodernism as the cultural dominant also looks in doubt. Certainly, mass culture has changed in recent decades, and some of those changes are arguably related to postmodern developments (e.g., cultural diversification or even fragmentation).[7] But it is very questionable whether there has been as clean a triumph for postmodernism as Jameson's historical schema implies. Jameson is well aware that any particular phase in the history of a mode of production is always loaded with prior cultural formations reconfigured within it, as well as anticipations of possible future alternatives or lines of development.[8] Yet his linear historical schema has the unfortunate effect of elevating particular cultural formations to the status of a cultural dominant, when there are significant questions to be asked about his selection. Conversely, the linear historical schema has the effect of pushing Jameson (against his better judgment) in the direction of an overly hasty relegation of previous cultural formations to the rubbish heap of history.

What I would like to do is offer an alternative mapping of cultural forms, one in which postmodernism is more emergent than dominant and one that still finds older cultural forms (realism and modernism) to be active. The conspiracy film illustrates what is at stake in the differences between these cultural forms, and the cultural forms in turn situate the conspiracy film within a wider set of contexts and cultural crosscurrents. An important feature of Jameson's decoding apparatus is his appropriation and refunctioning of the "semiotic rectangle" associated with the work of the structuralist theorist A. J. Greimas. We can make use of the semiotic rectangle to map the cultural options available in a given period. The semiotic rectangle is formed by the interplay between a pair of binary oppositions that the theorist "works up" out of the material being analyzed and then uses to map the four possible positions that can be taken up within the parameters or constraints that the antinomies posit.

As Jameson notes in the influential and indispensable book *The Political Unconscious*, the semiotic rectangle, in his reworked version, "maps the limits of a specific ideological consciousness and marks the conceptual points beyond which that consciousness cannot go, and between which it is condemned to oscillate."[9] The rectangle can be used to analyze individual texts or to map positions within a set of cultural options. I use it to map the four cultural paradigms (or forms). To elaborate the rectangle we have to generate our first antinomy or primary opposition, which will be positions 1 and 2: (P1) society versus (P2) the individual or rather the bourgeois monad, the self-enclosed, self-sufficient causal agent of classical bourgeois economics. An in-depth rationalization of this choice is beyond the scope of this essay, but this is one of the classic antinomies of bourgeois culture. The monadic subject cannot be integrated into a model of society, since the free-floating bourgeois monad is fundamentally antisocial as a model. The desocialized monad represents a form of reification, an absolute or polarized subjectivism separated from and confronted with an equally absolute objectivism in the form of functionalist and deterministic visions of society that are logically incompatible with the monad as "free agent."[10]

Yet the nineteenth-century realist novel was a place where the relations between individual and society could be reimagined and worked through (at least partially). However, this becomes increasingly problematic in the age of imperialism from the late nineteenth century onward. Taking the British Empire and English literature as his example, Jameson argues that under colonial and imperial capitalism, individual lived experience in London, say, is silently shaped by the tentacles of power, trade, and exploitation flung around the world, in India, Jamaica, or Hong Kong. "At this point the phenomenological experience of the individual subject—traditionally, the supreme raw materials of the work of art" no longer coincides with its structural conditions of existence. Jameson

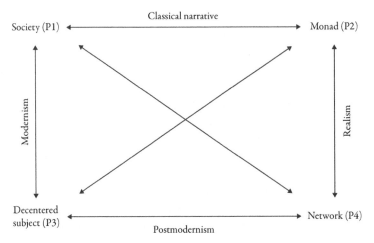

FIGURE 10.1 An adapted version of the Greimas rectangle

associates the nineteenth-century phase of national capitalism broadly with the aesthetic model of realism, although obviously that category will encompass an enormous heterogeneity of approaches. In film however, as opposed to literature, which is Jameson's main case study for his historical schema, it makes more sense to associate this antinomy with what theorists have called the "classical narrative," more of which later. The main point to note here is that attempting to work through the contradiction between society versus the monad (typically the bureaucratic institution versus the outsider/rebel figure in popular cinema) represents the defining characteristic of the classical narrative.

The idea behind the Greimas rectangle is to extend the initial opposition to elaborate the range of options available for trying to resolve cultural and social contradictions. In my adaptation of the rectangle, the initial opposition is extended by alternatives to each term of the first binary. The alternative to "society" will become "network" (P4), and the alternative to the "monad" will be the "decentered subject" (P3). The result is figure 10.1.[11]

The new terms, P3 and P4, provide new options for cultural paradigms to work through the contradictions shaping the initial antinomy (P1 vs. P2). Now P1 can be worked through in relation to P3 and P2 can be worked through in relation to P4, while a new emergent option now exists between P3 and P4. The reader will note that the four positions correspond with our four cultural paradigms or forms: the classical narrative (which stands as the specifically filmic representative of mass culture) now joins modernism (P1 vs. P3), realism (P2 vs. P4) and postmodernism (P3 vs. P4). The latter three terms have been important for Jameson's thinking, and we must now very briefly explain how and why in order for the semiotic rectangle to make sense. I leave the further analysis of the classical narrative, which Jameson has had little to say about, to the next section.

Let us take modernism first. For Jameson, modernism emerges in the twentieth century as one kind of attempt to recognize the new spatial reach of capital far beyond the culture and conventional politics of the nation-state, let alone the individual subject. Modernism has many strands of course, some more orientated to an external world of mass society and industry, such as constructivism and futurism, others more orientated toward an inner world of a subject structured by psychic responses to social forces, such as German expressionism (which as is well documented feeds into American film noir) and surrealism, both of which articulate the paranoid sensibility so important for the conspiracy hermeneutic. But all strands of modernism regard the world and their own means of representation as assemblages that can be constructed and deconstructed, hence the emphasis on self-reflexivity, and the disruption of more "naturalized" conventions associated with nineteenth century realism.[12] A modernist version of society then is quite different from a classical realist version of society in part because it is paired with a different model of the subject. The decentered subject is no longer a self-sufficient causal agent but a construct of the social that is itself conceived as a construct, and therefore potentially both are mutable and open to the aesthetic reconstruction of the artist (and potentially the audience more broadly). Montage, the great unifying principle of so much modernist culture, embodies this principle of assemblage and production and seeks to burst out of the unities of time and space that had shackled storytelling around the individual perspectives of classical realism.[13] These formal strategies are combined in modernism with what Perry Anderson calls "the imaginative proximity of social revolution."[14]

But for Jameson, modernism is an exhausted cultural paradigm and in the contemporary context the dominant cultural paradigm is, for him, postmodernism. Jameson's 1984 essay "Postmodernism; or, The Cultural Logic of Late Capitalism" definitively established the term as something Marxists needed to engage with. For Jameson, postmodernism is not a mere style or set of aesthetic characteristics but is instead integrated into or the logical expression of profound changes in the capitalist mode of production. These changes include the domination of the world economy by multinational corporations (rather than, say, corporations embedded in imperialist nations as in the past), the penetration of previously precapitalist regions of the Third World by capital, the enormous expansion of media and communications technologies through which capital also intensively invades the inner psychic reaches of the individual subject, the new signal importance of knowledge and information to production and product development as it is mediated by computers and scientific research, the connected growth of services, the new technologies of automation, cybernetics and now genetic technologies that allow capital to enter into and reconstruct the inner recesses of nature itself.[15]

What is implied in my Greimas-inspired rectangle of four cultural paradigms is my disagreement with the notion that postmodernism represents a *cultural dominant* (read off from capital's international spatial extension, as with modernism, now coupled with a new technologically assisted commodifying invasion of subjectivity). I see postmodernism as one cultural option, vying with other important cultural habits that just because they are "older" are not necessarily now residual in any permanent sense. In terms of film, the classical narrative, despite modifications, remains I would argue both quantitively and qualitatively (in terms of the appeal of the form) Hollywood's "go-to" formal option. That said, these different cultural options are not sealed off from each other but are dialectically related and so can influence one another.

Just as society is conceived differently between the classical narrative paradigm and the modernist paradigm, so too the decentered subject, which is the joining point between modernism and postmodernism, is conceived somewhat differently in its pairings with P1 and P4 respectively. In the "Postmodernism" essay Jameson argues that the very model of the individual subject has been transformed. The older bourgeois monad (P2) as a site of a unique self, with a unified rational life project, was profoundly problematized by Freudianism, which opened up subjectivity as deeply contradictory and driven by nonrational forces (P3). The great modernist themes of "alienation, anomie, solitude, social fragmentation, and isolation" imply a concern that something is wrong, either with self, with society, or with both.[16] But with postmodernism, "the alienation of the subject is displaced by the latter's fragmentation."[17] The new "schizophrenic" subject of postmodernism can no longer differentiate between reality and mass media simulation (or simulacra) of reality and history.[18] The "constructed" version of the subject that modernism posed has been displaced by a subjectivity trapped in a bubble of commodity relations and psychically penetrated by so many media and communication technological apparatuses as to fragment into an "effect" of unmappable structures with no "center." But under postmodernism, this is a situation without anxiety and even, with the "death" of the autonomous subject, without emotion. Instead there is a "waning of affect," a strange emptying out of feeling and psychological investment.[19] Postmodernism then will fundamentally alter the conspiracy film, since a deep foreboding and sense of anxiety generated by perceived malicious external agents gives way, as we shall see, to a sense of "gaming" and puzzling conundrums.

However, with the vision of a "schizophrenic" subject immersed in a perpetual present and unable to think historically, I think we see both the power and the problems with what we may classify as a certain kind of "science-fiction" theorizing. Certain trends are extrapolated from a context in which there are other competing and contradictory factors at work, and then unfolded and generalized as our imminent future or even current predicament. In the case of some of Jameson's formulations, this acts as a stimulating warning as to the consequences of our situation, an estrangement effect in theory similar to science fiction itself, one that can jolt us into denaturalizing a taken-for-granted world, but at the risk of taking the warning in theory as an already achieved "one-dimensional" reality.

In his earlier work, *The Political Unconscious*, Jameson conceded less ground to the postmodern assault on reality and the impossibility of any coherent sense of self. Addressing himself to poststructuralism, which is the philosophical counterpart to postmodernism and late capitalism, Jameson argues that it has a certain "descriptive value" insofar as it speaks to the experience of the subject in consumer society, one in which "psychic dispersal, fragmentation . . . hallucinogenic sensations, and temporal discontinuities" are part of the cultural landscape.[20] Importantly, and perhaps more robustly in *The Political Unconscious* than in the later "Cultural Logic" essay, Jameson notes that "we may admit the descriptive value of the post-structuralist critique of the 'subject' without necessarily endorsing the schizophrenic ideal it has tended to project."[21]

The decentered subject (P3) in the semiotic rectangle occupies a pivotal position between modernism and postmodernism. The latter emerges in the antinomy between its own version of the decentered but now *schizophrenic* subject and its own alternative to the older model of the social order, namely the network (P4). This fragmented subjectivity still requires at least some sense of "structure" even if it is only a generalized model of power as in Foucault or desire as in Deleuze in order to ground it (one cannot have a "subject" without an "object"). When thinking about how a sociological description of the network society of the kind offered by Manuel Castells may be converted into an aesthetic sensibility or figuration, we get the sense of an older world of discrete and durable centers of power transformed by technologically enabled global networks of connections, with interdependencies that cross boundaries, a sense of structure that shimmers with movement, complexity, risk, and contingency.[22] In these ways the network society appears to be differentiated from the older, more static sociological paradigms of "the social."

However, yet another option is available in our mapping of cultural positions, and this one modifies the older individual subject (P2) as one half of the opposition with the network society instead of the newer schizophrenic subject, which seems the network's more natural compliment. Tethered to this older model of subjectivity, films navigating this binary can be classified as part of a realist paradigm. The monad is modified by exploration of its relationship with the network as opposed to the older model of the social. "Character" becomes part of an ensemble, a *connected self* in what has been called "the network film." This connected self is less determined by its own actions than by chance, by direct interactions with others and/or by *parallel* interactions with others whom characters may never meet. These parallel interactions can in principle extend beyond the nation-state. This cultural paradigm seems in many ways best placed to overcome the central contradiction Jameson has identified between the social and the individual. As he notes in his essay on Third World literature: "We have been trained in a deep cultural conviction that the experience of our private existences is somehow incommensurable with the abstractions of economic science and political dynamics."[23] It is worth reminding ourselves that the appeal of the conspiracy film is precisely its attempt to link the personal with the political, the private with the public. As we shall see, that linking is configured differently according to which cultural form different films are located in. The realist form of P2 and P4 imagines this linkage, develops interpretive strategies to represent it, differently from the other cultural forms. As an aside we may note that in his essay on Third World literature, Jameson got himself into problems, upsetting many because he seemed to be essentializing the category. Jameson argued that compared to the "West," the "we" unable to overcome the dichotomy between individual and society, Third World literature, "*is always an allegory of the embattled situation of the public third-world culture and society.*"[24] Why did Jameson say "*always*," and why was he so sure that such capacities have been completely eliminated from Western regimes of representation? Jameson I think got himself into problems because he overlaid his historical schema (nationalism, imperialism, multinational capitalism) onto the First World, while the Third World was cast as some other zone that had managed to preserve capacities the West had definitively lost. This First World / Third World dichotomy meant each "region" was homogenized internally and absolutized in terms of their mutual difference (one unable to link the private with the political, the other, "*always an allegory*").[25] But this in turn highlights the reservations I have been raising in relation to his modeling of cultural contradictions. In fact, even within an industry as heavily commodified as Hollywood (our particular case study) we must restore *a range of options* (generic and narrative for example) available to it, including strategies that strive to overcome the tension between the personal/psychological and the social/political that Jameson found exclusively in Third World literature.

The Conspiracy Film and the Classical Paradigm

Conspiracy films in the classical mode are in abundant supply, as we would expect since this is in fact *the dominant paradigm*. To mention only some titles from recent years, we have films such as *Enemy of the State* (1998), *The Constant Gardener* (2005), *Michael Clayton* (2007), *The International* (2009), *Captain America: The Winter Soldier* (2014), *The Circle* (2018), and so on. Not every film that has a conspiracy as part of its plot would necessarily be classified as a "conspiracy film." The conspiracy film tends to involve a conspiracy at scale that threatens to engulf the protagonists and society as a whole.

One of the defining features of the classical narrative is that it remains locked into individual cause-effect relations, characters with clearly defined goals (conflicting between main protagonist and antagonist) and usually simple but at any rate easily readable motivations and an omnipresent narrative that, despite leaving a trail of enigmas to sustain viewer curiosity, offers a growing position of knowledge mastery as the narrative unfolds and the key lines of action are resolved. Many conspiracy films still rely on the staples of the classical narrative ideology to resolve problems, such as public exposure (the hero gets the truth out thanks to the media) and/or physical elimination of the chief villain (typically by the hero). This is not to say that the classical narrative remains unchanged by history. Jameson discusses modifications in this structure in relation to the influential trilogy of conspiracy films by Alan Pakula back in the 1970s in his book *The Geopolitical Aesthetic*.[26] These modifications include spatialization of the narrative across many different locations and terrains as attempts to cover all the bases of the conspiracy's sprawling tentacles; socializing the villain (who now embodies the corporate will); the victim (who now becomes the public) and the detective (who now becomes a researcher into a general problem) often accidentally stumbling into the labyrinth.[27] These changes may make it harder for films to come to ideological resolutions. Will the *New York Times* expose the conspiracy at the end of *Three Days of the Condor* (1975)? Or will Turner (Robert Redford) be on the run for the rest of his (presumably short) life?

The film *The International* (2009) is interesting because as with at least some of the 1970s conspiracy films, the problem of responding to the social content of advanced capitalism threatens to overwhelm the limits of the classical narrative form. The villain is collectivized, for example, with the CEO of the bank at the center of the conspiracy surrounded and supported by a management team. The Interpol detective hero Salinger (Clive Owen) is also supported by a team of detectives internationally in all the different locations of the action (Jameson's point about spatializing narratives). At the same time, these modifications of character types are folded back into such classical narrative fundamentals as Salinger's central role as the driving goal-orientated force in the story and the omnipresent narrative, which here gives us early access to the inner sanctum of the conspirators. We may not know exactly what they are doing and why, but the narration identifies whom the antagonists are and offers the viewer a position of evolving narrative mastery by measuring the hero and the collective team's progress in terms of how close they are getting to identifying them. Crucial to that endeavor is another indication of how far this form can typically collectivize the problem. Instead of relying on an anonymous pool of contracted assassins as we might have expected, the International Bank relies on *one* lone assassin who is excessively individualized by having a signature leg brace that in turn leads the detectives to him, which in turn incriminates the bank.

While the causal action that leads to the revelation of the bank relies on this antiquated individualism of the lead assassin, the plot content presents the bank as too powerful, too international, too well supported by governments and other institutions to be either exposed or decapitated. The CEO tells the hero that he knows that if he is killed, another manager will take over, and so on. Thus when the CEO is killed by a revenge mafia hit moments later, a montage sequence of newspaper headlines tells us that a new CEO is appointed, later that the bank is doing well again, that there are problems in the Middle East, which we the viewer (but not the newspaper articles) know are caused by the bank's arms dealing, and finally that a Senate enquiry has been launched looking into dirty money and advised by a district attorney who helped Salinger. But is this narrative ending a note of hope or merely another failed attempt to call the bank to account? Either way, this indeterminate outcome suggests that the social content the film has dealt with is clearly pushing at the individualizing boundaries of the classical form, but as long as the institutional and cultural structures for that form remain in place we can expect its dominance (albeit with contradictions and modifications) to continue.

The Conspiracy Film and the Social Realist Paradigm

In fact there is a specific genre of realism that I want to discuss as a potential solution to the problem of form which the social content of advanced capitalism poses for popular film culture: the "network film." David Bordwell provided an early account of the formal characteristics of what he termed the network film in his 2007 book *Poetics of Cinema*. Formally these are alternatives to "the single-or paired protagonist plot"[28] central to the classical narrative, where a "thrust-counterthrust" dynamic between central characters constitutes the action.[29] Instead, in the network film there are multiple character storylines; it flattens the hierarchy of importance that characters in the classical narrative film have, and there is a corresponding shift of attention to group and potentially institutional dynamics. Although interactions between characters are of course important, the editing architecture of the network film invites us to think about the indirect nature of the relationships *across* the various lines of action (how, for example, characters unknown to each other can still affect each other's lives). Thus the network film constructs a parallelism of "characters, situations and activities,"[30] encouraging comparative evaluations at moral, social, and thematic levels. Compared to the simple linearity of the classical narrative, the network format opens up a space for films to deal with social realities with some degree of complexity.

Bordwell himself, as a leading neoformalist wary of situating films in relation to their social context (let alone the mode of production) and critical of theories that draw on the social sciences, is reluctant to speculate on the wider conditions that might account for the emergence of the form. Yet as Amanda Ciafone notes, Bordwell's filmography of network films between 1920 and 2007 demonstrates, when reorganized historically, a "dramatic upsurge in the number of network narratives in the last two decades."[31] For Ciafone these films are some kind of response to contemporary transformations in global capitalism, although she is skeptical of their cultural politics, describing them, disparagingly, as "melodramas of globalization."[32] Ciafone discusses a number of subgenres of the network format, such as "contingency-narrative films" including *Amores Perros* (2000) and *Babel* (2006), where chance (typically misfortune) is the most powerful determinant in the lives of the characters rather than "structural causes and positive collectivity."[33] The stress on chance would clearly produce an "underdetermined" picture of social causality quite at odds with the structural patterns that social relations and interests tend to produce. If the contingency-narrative film then relies overly much on chance, then this is an unsatisfactory resolution to the antinomy between the individual and the network concept of society.

Then there are what Ciafone classifies as "world system films" that try to map the transnational networks of global power rather than the contingent connections of a large ensemble of characters. Ciafone discusses *Traffic* (2000) and *Syriana* (2005) as examples (but more recently we can identify *The Big Short* [2015] and *The Laundromat* [2019]). She is critical of *Syriana*, bemoaning the absence of positive counterpower and the return to conservative private spheres (homecomings) at the film's conclusion as a consolation to a wider impotence in the public-political sphere. In this reading *Syriana* falls into the trap of imagining a total system of conspiratorial power. Again, this would represent an unsatisfactory resolution to the antinomy that the conspiracy film and the network realist form is in a sense trying to respond to.

However I think this reading of *Syriana* underappreciates the pedagogic opportunities concerning class power that the film offers. *Syriana* has the international spatialization dynamic that we saw in *The International*. The action is spread around the world, including the United States, Switzerland, an unnamed Arab country in the Persian gulf, and many other locales. Unlike *The International*, there is not one single point of origin for an amorphous sprawling conspiracy against which a primary protagonist (albeit with a team of helpers) is pitched. Instead there are loosely related conspiracies on different scales and of different types that emerge as component parts of the dominant interconnected (but sometimes conflicting) interests at play. We can identify three types: type 1 is primarily economic-political, produced in the interface between economic and political power. This is represented by Connex-Killen, two oil companies on the verge of merging but having confirmation by the authorities held up while there is an investigation as to whether Killen broke the U.S. Foreign Corrupt Practices Act in winning a giant new contract in Kazakhstan. Bennett Holiday, an ambitious lawyer, is asked by his law firm whose client is Connex to see if anything untoward has happened and then negotiate with the political-juridical representatives for a solution. Connex, although the larger company, needs the merger to happen because it has just lost a big oil contract in the unnamed Arab country.

The political-juridical domain represents another level of "conspiracy," since Holiday does indeed discover that bribes to a Kazakhstan official facilitated the deal, but the question then is how to finesse that in a way that does not block the merger. Holiday offers up a Killen representative (Dalton) who was involved, but of course Killen will argue that Dalton acted without authority, and Dalton will in turn keep his mouth shut and do a small amount of prison time in exchange for a sizable payoff. Holiday negotiates with the DA, looking for what he calls "the illusion of due diligence." The DA wants another scapegoat, however, to complete the "illusion," and Holiday is given one by Killen boss Jimmy Pope, namely Holiday's own immediate boss who has done something shady in relation to another deal. This amounts to a conspiracy because all the players know that, as Dalton himself puts it, corruption is hardwired into the interface between the economic and the political spheres. Finally there is the vaster conspiracy world of the U.S. intelligence services, which are operating to secure the power of the United States internationally.

Syriana has an omniscient narrative, necessary to cut across all the different story lines. But whereas in the classical narrative this gives the viewer generally easy purchase on the plot action, albeit with enigmas sprinkled along the way, here the viewer has to work extremely hard to make sense of the relationships between the strands of action. We start with migrant workers in an unnamed location trying to get on a bus before cutting to "Bob" (not his real name), a CIA agent who is in Tehran. Bob (George Clooney) sells two rocket launchers to an arms dealer, but only in order to assassinate him. However, one of the rockets is passed to another buyer and ends up near the conclusion of the film being used to blow up an oil tanker in a suicide mission by two Islamic militants, one of whom we see getting onto the bus in the opening shot. But we will get to know this militant, Wassim, *before* he becomes a militant, and see how the life of a migrant worker in an unnamed Arab country is affected by remote economic decisions and police brutality, and eventually ends up getting sucked into the Islamic fundamentalist network. The experience that the film cultivates through its storytelling strategies is of characters not as fixed essences either morally or as functions of a narrative form (helpers, obstacles, sources of wisdom, etc.) but as complex interfaces between the social and the biographical. This network film appropriately diminishes individual causal agency (although it does not eliminate it) and opens up a gap between what characters think they are doing and what they are actually doing or achieving. Thus the liberal ideology of some of the characters that the film could be read as invested in can easily be read as deconstructed by the form itself, something that Ciafone herself notes.[34]

The network film is a kind of cultural training in thinking about consequences (without the easy foreshadowing of the classical narrative) as they are spread around the storylines in complicated patterns. For example, why did Connex lose the contract to the Chinese? We also initially see the impact on Wasim and his father, as they are laid off work at the Connex plant in the unnamed Arab country and their immigration status is thrown into doubt. Later it becomes clear that Connex lost the contract because the Emir's son, Prince Nasir wants to develop geopolitical independence from the United States. Yet that in turn produces a reclassification of Nasir as a threat to U.S. interests by the CIA. In a succession struggle between Nasir and his brother Prince Meshal, the United States backs the latter as he will be easier to control. At the same time, Bob, who has been put on desk duty, is pulled back into the field to assassinate Prince Nasir upon a visit to Beirut, a place that Bob was apparently very active in during the civil war in the 1980s. When that job goes wrong, Bob is scapegoated (as Dalton is, but without the financial compensatory package), and this leads him to reevaluate the interests he has been serving (corporate as much as the U.S. intelligence community). We never see a direct linkage between Connex and the intelligence agencies, but the links are inferred; the strategic connections between the intelligence "community" and the oil industry are the inevitable consequences of the nexus of power. We do hear about and briefly see members of the Committee for the Liberation of Iran, which has nothing to do with the film's plot but tells the alert viewer that the committee, on which Killen men sit and which in turn is active in Washington, is part of a world where the political and the economic merge (if not without tensions that the sort of juridical-political negotiations that Bennett is involved in are designed to clear up).

The comparative dimension of the "crisscrosser" format allows some very nice points about class and power to be subtly registered. Most of the characters are part of the elite networks, but Wasim's storyline (unusual in itself for an American film) is contextualized and contrasted with their powers and decisions. His suicide mission is also interestingly compared with the U.S. drone strike on Prince Nasir's convoy. Wasim's act would typically be framed as "terrorism," but its recontextualization by comparison with the U.S. murder of Nasir (and his wife and kids) calls such easy ideological closures into question. The drone strike scene concludes with an audio bleed-in from the next scene of *applause* as we then cut to Leland Janus, chairman of Connex, giving his acceptance speech after winning "oilman of the year." This montage between image (of the done strike) and audio (of the applause) deftly makes the point about the economic interests that are being served by the U.S. state. Conspiracies, large and small, are, like the actions of the characters in general, contextualized as stratagems that are part of the world of capitalism.

The Conspiracy Film and the Modernist Paradigm

We can see the influence of modernism in the network film insofar as its narrative architecture attempts to break out of the frustratingly narrow causalities and spatiotemporal unities of the classical narrative. We might also see the multiple narrative strands as having roots in the sprawling nineteenth-century realist novel. However, the medium of film imposes its tempo on the spectator in a way the novel cannot, and via the use of editing there is more of a sense of a montage of juxtapositions between the strands, which was a key feature of twentieth-century modernism. We can also see modernist self-reflexivity in such network films as *The Big Short* and *The Laundromat* with their direct-to-camera addresses and autocritique of popular forms (Margot Robbie with a glass of champagne in a bubble bath explaining finance capital!). With the even more extensive Brechtian approach of *The Laundromat* especially, we can see how the network film begins to bend round into the modernist paradigm, which is a warning about constructing mutually exclusive (nondialectical) cultural typologies.

Despite these modernist influences, the network films discussed above have a realist confidence in their capacity to understand a complex world. What distinguishes modernism from realism, I would argue, is that the former is characterized by a more extensive and profound sense of a *crisis* in representation than any of these realist network films want to explore. For Jameson, as we have seen, modernism emerges at a point where an older conception that "society" was coterminous with the nation-state gives way to an international system of imperialism, a new expanded totality that requires a revolution in formal strategies (hence a new self-consciousness in language) to be mapped. Modernism's aggressive assault on narrative coherence and/or reliability means that it is perhaps the least amenable to being absorbed into the Hollywood system, but even here there are examples, such as Darren Aronofsky's recent *Mother!* (2017), that play with a subgenre of the paranoid conspiracy model that explores patriarchal power relations over women.[35] Films like *Flightplan* (2005) and *Unsane* (2018) begin by questioning whether the diegetic reality we took for granted is actually the construction of the traumatized female protagonist. But gradually these films settle into classical narrative plot developments (there really is a conspiracy and the heroine has to bust it wide open). The Buñuel-like *Mother!*, in contrast, insists on exploding any plausible real-world cause-effect relations all the way through, so that the film can "make sense" only if we read it allegorically. In addition to the allegorical, an old hermeneutic that, as Benjamin argued, acquired new meaning and functions within modernism,[36] there is also polysemy. Is the allegory in *Mother!* a theological one, is it about artistic creation, is it about gendered power relations, is it about the tragedy of history?

In an earlier essay on Jameson's postmodern thesis I suggested that the low-budget film *Series 7: The Contenders* (2001) was a more radical modernist critique of the kind of paranoid media-inspired conspiracies found in classical narrative films such as *The Truman Show* (1998) and *AntiTrust* (2001).[37] In *Series 7: The Contenders*, we are locked entirely into the unreliable narration of the series itself, which pitches "contestants" in a fight to the death for mass entertainment. The conspiracy is open and public, and everyone is complicit with it. The crisis of representation is that there is no "outside" this discourse, no *classical narrative* point of omniscience from which we can know the truth of the situation. Yet at the same time the question of truth and the real has not been abandoned (as it is in postmodernism), but in modernist fashion we are invited to decode this televisual discourse, explore its gaps and contradictions, and perform an *immanent* or a *symptomatic* critique of the discourse. Once again immanent/symptomatic critique is central to modernism, along with allegory and polysemy. The immanent critique implies that a normative standard of nonmanipulative representation is being appealed to, that the principle of reality remains necessary, that truths are embodied in the *form* of the critique (rather than the arrival at a singular truth), and that a critical, reflexive subject (the audience of the film performing this immanent critique) is fortunately still possible. For Jameson, the difference between modernism and postmodernism is quite simply that the latter has given up on critique, immanent or allegorical.[38] But as we shall see, postmodernism must be enunciated from a position other than postmodernist in order for it to speak its postmodern concerns at all.

The Conspiracy Film and the Postmodern Paradigm

Postmodernism merges modernist experimentation with popular culture and combines this with a new mood of political acquiescence. This is articulated in a new version of the subject (thoroughly hollowed out by consumer and corporate capitalism) and a new (networked) version of the object world that eludes capture and classification by representation that is merely a simulacrum with no referent. If this is a rhetorical exaggeration for effect (what I have called science fiction theory), it nevertheless speaks to social and historical experiences that must be real enough. The postmodern represents Hollywood's preferred mode of articulating a crisis in representation in a popular entertaining format that suggests that the classical narrative regime can no longer exhaust and contain the new historical experiences that the postmodern speaks to. The stability, the security, the unity inscribed in the dominant form must be supplemented beyond the modifications of character already discussed, with significantly more radical modifications that can speak to the instability of representation (relativism), the insecurity of knowledge and faith in discernible cause-effect relations (epistemology), the disappearance of the real (ontology), and indeed trust (ethics).

Many films that might be classified as examples of what Elsaesser calls the "mind-game film" may in fact be only partial breaks from the classical narrative, not least in that around the forty-five-minute mark the spectator's confusion about what exactly is going on starts to get reassuringly clarified. But this is not always the case by any means, and in any complex and uneven cultural situation one would expect films to incorporate contradictory paradigms. My final case study of the conspiracy film in the postmodern mode reflects this unevenness and perhaps also the fact that it is very difficult for postmodern theory (or culture) to be logically consistent regarding the final eclipse of the real, which always returns in some form since ultimately (from a materialist viewpoint) intelligibility depends on it.

The title of *Cypher* (2002), a science fiction film directed by Vincenzo Natali, is indicative of the new postmodern subject, who is a blank slate, a zero on which any number of constructed personalities or identities can be transposed. In its opening the cypher is a "character" called Morgan Sullivan who is being recruited by Digicorp as a corporate spy to be deployed against commercial competitors. He passes the elaborate lie detector test and is given a new identity, Jack Thursby, and a seemingly pointless set of tasks, to record keynote speeches at various corporate conferences. Sullivan, naïve, unworldly, and dominated by his wife, starts to take on the constructed masculinity that befits the spy. Instead of drinking ginger ale, he starts drinking single malt scotch on the rocks, his voice deepens and becomes more assured, and he acquires a new self-confidence. Sullivan/ Thursby, as played by Jeremy Northam, perfectly captures the postmodern "subjectless subject"[39] and the waning of affect that Jameson famously diagnosed. The postmodern musician or actor is, Fred Pfeil argues, "deadpan, indifferent, depersonalized, effaced." Their performance "effectively cancels the possibility of traditional audience identification" but thereby conveys a postmodern "structure of feeling."[40]

Thursby's identity as a spy seems at odds with his experience, which is to listen to presentations on subjects like "shaving cream distribution outlets in North American markets." The mysterious Rita turns up and seems to know a lot more than Sullivan does. She warns him to take some pills and later injects him with a substance designed to "block the Digicorp narcotic." Later the conference proceedings are revealed to be a simulacrum (as will be his life in general). Undrugged he is awake to experience what really happens when all the other corporate types, budding Digicorp spies like himself in fact, fall asleep listening to the droning keynote address. Enter scientists with brainwashing headsets. The headsets fitted, automated injections go into the back of the neck, miniature steel grips hold open the eyelids (as in the brainwashing scenes in *Clockwork Orange*), and a manufactured narrative of their constructed identity is beamed into the cerebral cortex. Later, boarding a plane home he sees all the other corporates drugged in their chairs, oxygen masks on them, bathed in a sickening green light, before he too is drugged. When he wakes up he is supposed to *be* Jack Thursby (rather than impersonate Jack Thursby). His new life in the suburbs is complete with a new wife, who like his old wife is bossy and domineering.

While Digicorp think that Sullivan now believes he is Thursby, Rita has blocked the brainwashing process so that Sullivan still thinks he is Sullivan (although as we may guess, given the similarity between Sullivan's "real" life situation and the false one set up by Digicorp, the "real" one will turn out to be a simulacrum as well). Although I have conveyed the complex "mind-game" nature of the film, coupled with the postmodern sense that not only identity but the mise-en-scène of real life itself is an elaborate set (up), then it is also true that around the forty-five-minute mark some sense of what is going on emerges. For Digicorp the purpose of the exercise is to create agents who can penetrate the defenses of their competitors by really believing that they are who they say they are. But Sullivan is a double agent sent by Digicorp's competitor, Sunways Systems, to become a Digicorp spy, apparently spying on Sunways and who will then feed Digicorp misleading data via Sullivan. Rita it turns out works for

Sebastian Rooks, who the security chief at Sunways tells us is a ruthless freelance operative who ensured that Sullivan escaped the full brainwashing program in order to work against Digicorp.

At this crucial halfway point then, some spectator knowledge has been accrued, new important variables such as Rooks have been introduced, and outstanding questions and enigmas such as how Sullivan is going to escape the malevolent designs of both Sunways and Digicorp and how his relationship with Rita will develop remain to be resolved. At this point though, while still unorthodox, the film moves back a little closer to the classical narrative form, while the content remains typically postmodern. Toward the end of the film it is revealed that in fact Sullivan is Rooks, who has brainwashed himself into believing that he is Sullivan in order to participate in the spying game for his own purpose. The imagined signifiers of masculinity that Sullivan was adopting to become Thursby actually turn out to be the residual traces of the real person who is Rooks. Rooks's reason for this complex stratagem turns out to be that he wants to retrieve a file in the data banks of Sunways Systems, which has pegged Rita for elimination. The finale of the film sees "Sullivan" converge with his real identity as Rooks in order to be able fly the strange helicopter he himself designed and wipe out the military-style Special Weapons and Tactics Teams sent by both Digicorp and Sunways to unmask his identity and kill him. They discover too late that Sullivan/Thursby is Rooks!

Thus the film finally is revealed to be enunciated from a position heavily invested in a pre-postmodern subjectivity, that of the freelance operative, the individual whose conspiracy outwits the twin conspiracies of the rival corporations and who is motivated by romantic love for Rita. Rooks (as the allusion to the chess piece implies) is not a pawn but the puppet master at the center of this mind game, a very postmodern ludic play ostensibly uncoupled from any real social and historical ground. Yet even the comparatively simple film *The International* did not indulge in such childish archaic petit bourgeois fantasies as the ostensibly more sophisticated *Cypher*! If the final shot of the pair of them sailing in the South Pacific seems as "real" (i.e., fabricated) as anything else in the film, then it remains the case that this ideology of the individual and romantic love (virtually unimaginable in the world of the film) remains operative at some level for the spectator.

Conclusion

The purpose of developing a semiotic rectangle of cultural paradigms for Hollywood films is not to slot films into a particular category but to map the options available within a cultural-political era to address a key contradiction (featured as an antinomy) within the capitalist mode of production. This provides the context for understanding our case study subgenre, the conspiracy film. For we cannot understand conspiracy as a trope without situating it in relation to the contradiction between models of selfhood and models of social order. The semiotic rectangle maps four models of each—four because the two models of social order (society and the network) are each changed by their relationship to the two models of selfhood and vice versa (the monad becomes the connected self in the shift from P1 to P4 and the decentered selfhood becomes the schizophrenic subject in the shift from P1 to P4). I also stressed the dialectical dynamics between the typologies. For example, we saw the modifications to the classical narrative structure that are developed more substantially but also differentially in the other paradigms, the modernist influences at work in the realist network film, and the unexpected return of a classical narrative romantic individualism in the postmodern text of *Cypher*.

Each of the four paradigms operates with different hermeneutic or interpretive models. The classical narrative, despite modifications, still operates in a world of direct cause-effect relations between protagonists and antagonists; the network film as a subgenre of the realist paradigm operates a comparative methodology of decoding ("the crisscrosser"), while modernism deploys allegory, immanent critique, and polysemy. Postmodernism decodes according to the model of the ludic game or puzzle combined with the principle that the real has been displaced by simulacra. The conspiracy framework gets transformed by each of these paradigms. In the classical narrative, the conspiracy has great metaphorical power (a trope of system) but weak social explanatory power. By contrast conspiracy activity can be appropriately contextualized in the network film. Here the conspiracy is less a *metaphor* of capitalism than a component part of capitalism. Realism, as Roman Jakobson argued, leans more toward metonymy than metaphor, in this case piecing together "contiguous relationships" that characterize metonymy through parallelism. I have suggested that this makes for a more complex cognitive mapping than can be achieved by the direct, linear, cause-effect relations of the classical narrative.[41] In modernism the paranoid sensibility is inscribed into various decoding strategies, a heightened sensitivity to malevolence in the environment (more so than with the social realist network film) and with the same kind of metaphorical power of the classical realist narrative, but with a more sophisticated decoding apparatus than the classical narrative paradigm can muster (polysemy, immanent critique, allegory). In the postmodern paradigm conspiracy is inscribed into dizzyingly complex plot patterns in a ludic game that cannot ground why any of this matters, except by reference to principles outside the postmodern.

Finally, the point of the semiotic rectangle is that it shows the cultural scene is a much more contradictory mix of cultural models than Jameson's historical schema with clean transitions to new cultural dominants implies. The present inherits much of its resources from the past and continues to use and reconfigure them, not least because of the inertia of previously accumulated cultural habits and their continuing ability to speak to us. That said, this essay could not have been written without Jameson's sweeping historical vision, his hermeneutic brilliance, such as the use of the semiotic rectangle for analysis of ideological formations and his insights into the culture of capitalism.

Notes

1 Warren Smith, "Conspiracy, Corporate Culture and Criticism," *Sociological Review* 48 (2001): 153.
2 John S. Nelson, "Conspiracy as a Hollywood Trope for System," *Political Communication* 20 (2003): 499.
3 Fredric Jameson, "Class and Allegory in Contemporary Mass Culture," in *Signatures of the Visible* (New York: Routledge, 1992), 38.
4 Jameson, "Class and Allegory," 48.
5 Fredric Jameson, *Postmodernism; or, The Cultural Logic of Late Capitalism* (Durham, NC: Duke University Press, 1991), 30.
6 Jameson, *Postmodernism*, 6.
7 See Carl Boggs, "Postmodernism the Movie," *New Political Science* 23, no. 3 (2001): 351–370.
8 Fredric Jameson, *The Political Unconscious: Narrative as a Socially Symbolic Act* (London: Routledge, 2002), 18.
9 Jameson, *Political Unconscious*, 32.
10 George Lukács, *History and Class Consciousness*, trans. Rodney Livingstone (Cambridge, MA: MIT Press, 1971), 83–84.
11 Fredric Jameson, "Cognitive Mapping," in *Marxism and the Interpretation of Culture*, ed. Cary Nelson and Lawrence Grossberg (Urbana: University of Illinois Press, 1988), 349.
12 See Eugene Lunn, *Marxism and Modernism: An Historical Study of Lukács, Brecht, Benjamin and Adorno* (Berkeley: University of California Press, 1982).
13 See Mike Wayne, *Marxism Goes to the Movies* (London: Routledge, 2020), 31–35 and 172–174 for further discussion of modernism and film culture.
14 Perry Anderson, "Modernity and Revolution," in Nelson and Grossberg, *Marxism and the Interpretation of Culture*, 325.
15 Fredric Jameson, "Fredric Jameson Interviewed by Paik Nak-chung," in *Global/Local, Cultural Production and the Transnational Imaginary*, ed. Rob Wilson and Wimal Dissanayake (Durham, NC: Duke University Press, 1996), 352.
16 Jameson, "The Cultural Logic of Late Capitalism," 6.
17 Jameson, "Cultural Logic of Late Capitalism," 14 and 15.
18 Jameson, "Cultural Logic of Late Capitalism," 25.
19 Jameson, "Cultural Logic of Late Capitalism," 6.
20 Jameson, *Political Unconscious*, 111.
21 Jameson, *Political Unconscious*.
22 See Manuel Castells, *The Rise of the Network Society* (New York: John Wiley, 2009).
23 Fredric Jameson, "Third World Literature in the Era of Multinational Capitalism," *Social Text* 15 (Autumn 1986): 69.
24 Jameson, "Third World Literature," 69.
25 See Aijaz Ahmad, "Jameson's Rhetoric of Otherness and the 'National Allegory,'" *Social Text* 17 (Autumn 1987): 10.
26 The classic trilogy includes *Klute* (1971), *The Parallax View* (1974), and *All the President's Men* (1976).
27 Fredric Jameson, *The Geopolitical Aesthetic: Cinema and Space in the World System* (Bloomington: Indiana University Press, 1992), 33–34.

28 David Bordwell, *Poetics of Cinema* (New York: Routledge, 2007), 191.
29 Bordwell, *Poetics of Cinema*, 192.
30 Bordwell, *Poetics of Cinema*, 211.
31 Amanda Ciafone, "The Magical Neoliberalism of Network Films," *International Journal of Communication* 8 (2014): 2682.
32 Ciafone, "Magical Neoliberalism of Network Films," 2686.
33 Ciafone, "Magical Neoliberalism of Network Films," 2687.
34 Ciafone, "Magical Neoliberalism of Network Films," 2690.
35 Thomas Elsaesser, "The Mind-Game Film," in *Puzzle Films: Complex Storytelling in Contemporary Cinema*, ed. Warren Buckland (New York: Wiley-Blackwell, 2009), 25.
36 Bainard Cowan, "Walter Benjamin's Theory of Allegory," *New German Critique*, no. 22 (1981): 109–122.
37 Mike Wayne, "Jameson, Postmodernism and the Hermeneutics of Paranoia," in *Understanding Film: Marxist Perspectives*, ed. Mike Wayne (New York: Pluto Press, 2005), 105–130.
38 Ian Buchanan, ed., *Jameson on Jameson: Conversations on Cultural Marxism* (Durham, NC: Duke University Press, 2007), 142.
39 See Mike Wayne, *Marxism and Media Studies* (New York: Pluto Press, 2003), 183–219.
40 Fred Pfeil, "Postmodernism as a 'Structure of Feeling,'" in Nelson and Grossberg, *Marxism and the Interpretation of Culture*, 384.
41 Roman Jakobson, "The Metaphoric and Metonymic Poles," in *Metaphor and Metonymy in Comparison and Contrast*, ed. René Dirven and Ralf Pörings (Berlin: Mouton de Gruyter, 2003), 43.

11

A Theory of the Medium Shot

Affective Mapping and the
Logic of the Encounter in
Fredric Jameson's *The
Geopolitical Aesthetic*

PANSY DUNCAN

An extended meditation on the role of filmic representation in mediating late multinational capitalism, 1992's *The Geopolitical Aesthetic* is Fredric Jameson's most sustained engagement with cinema to date. Drawing on a clutch of North American conspiracy thrillers, from *All the President's Men* (Alan Pakula, 1976) to *Videodrome* (David Cronenberg, 1983), the book's lead section famously argues that the filmic "figuration of conspiracy" functions as a vernacular form of "cognitive mapping"—that is, as a popular attempt to represent the world system of late multinational capitalism.[1] But what should we make of the fact that the stills selected to illustrate this section of the book are, with just a few exceptions, medium shots? A still from *Three Days of the Condor* (Sydney Pollack, 1975) shows a denim-shirted, sandy-haired Joe Turner (Robert Redford) from the waist up as he moves through the belly of the New York telephone exchange with a quizzical expression. A still from *Under Fire* (Roger Spottiswoode, 1983) shows the photojournalist Russell Price (Nick Nolte) scrutinizing a photograph he has taken of three Nicaraguan revolutionaries. A still from *Videodrome* shows pirate broadcaster Max Renn (James Woods) staring with rapt fascination at a television screen featuring an extreme close-up of a lipsticked mouth. Certainly, *The Geopolitical Aesthetic* nowhere directly identifies the medium shot as a valuable technique or device for advancing the project of cognitive mapping—and with good reason.[2] Purporting to provide a view of the world that is barely distinguishable from that afforded the naked eye, the medium shot has helped sustain profoundly problematic fantasies of cinematic transparency, fantasies that don't square well with Jameson's own skepticism of the seductions of the visual.[3] Indeed, this unremarkable, undistinguished staple of popular Anglo-American narrative cinema has proven stubbornly resistant to recuperation by almost any radical critical project.[4] Yet across the course of Jameson's discussion of the conspiracy genre, the medium shot—from the common or garden variety, which cuts the actor off at the waist, to the *plan américain*, which ends at the knees or mid-thighs—is a visual mainstay, suggesting that, whatever its existing critical profile, this shot type may, in fact, have a role to play in Marxist critical praxis.

This chapter makes a simple argument about the medium shot in general, and about Jameson's recourse to the medium shot in *The Geopolitical Aesthetic* in particular. It contends that while rarely celebrated for its critical or diagnostic potential, the medium shot provides a visual solution to a crucial impasse within the program of "cognitive mapping" as it is elaborated in that book. As I show, the impasse in question lies in the fact that the practice of cognitive mapping, by Jameson's own lights, is defined primarily by failure, which in turn points to the need for a supplementary account of how we might orient ourselves affectively *toward* this failure. While Jameson's own written texts register this need only symptomatically, Jonathan Flatley's 2009 monograph *Affective Mapping* promises to answer it systematically, through a turn to a series of aesthetic projects that participate in the work of what Flatley dubs "affective mapping."[5] Yet as I finally show, Jameson's engagement with the medium shot in his choice of stills for *The Geopolitical Aesthetic* may be understood as a preexisting reckoning with the need for an ancillary affective geography of late multinational capitalism. Casting the medium shot as the shot of the "encounter," whether between two people or between a person and an object/environment, I argue that Jameson leverages the shot type's affordances to advance not the work of cognitive mapping, but a makeshift form of affective mapping.[6] In this light, then, the medium shot—a shot form as culturally ubiquitous as it is critically neglected—may possess a greater critical and diagnostic purchase on the vicissitudes of capitalism than existing assessments have allowed.

What is cognitive mapping? The model of cognitive mapping that Jameson elaborates across *The Geopolitical Aesthetic* was initially advanced at the 1983 Illinois conference that led to the important 1988 volume *Marxism and the Interpretation of Culture*. In his contribution to that volume, Jameson pointed to the gap between individual lived experience and the complex forces and flows that shape it under what he called "multinational capitalism"—the newly globalized, post-Fordist form of capitalism that emerged across advanced Western societies in the 1970s and that, during the 1980s, resulted in the full privatization and financialization of cultures and economies.[7] According to Jameson, this gap between everyday sensory experience and the abstractions of global capital had led to a collapse or decline of a practice of aesthetic orientation that Jameson— borrowing from the work of urban planner Kevin Lynch—called "cognitive mapping." And for Jameson the failure of cognitive mapping was as debilitating for political action as the failure of spatial mapping might prove for movement through a city. By way of response to this failure, then, Jameson had proposed a return to "one traditional function of the aesthetic that has in our time been peculiarly neglected and marginalized, if not interdicted altogether"—that is, the task of education, or what he later called "the knowledge function."[8] More specifically, he called for a return to "cognitive mapping" as a cultural and representational operation uniquely adequate to the ambitious task of "depicting social space and class relations in our epoch of late or global or finance capitalism."[9]

Despite this call, the 1988 essay had left cognitive mapping's cultural contours unclear. Yet by 1992, with the publication of *The Geopolitical Aesthetic*, the practice had taken vivid cultural shape in the form of the aforementioned series of North American "conspiracy" films. *Three Days of the Condor*, *All the President's Men*, *The Parallax View*, *Under Fire*, and *Videodrome*, while generically diverse and running the gamut from espionage thriller to body horror, are united by their shared commitment to what Jameson dubs "the motif of conspiracy"—a motif organized, according to Bridget Brown, around the conviction that those institutions and social systems commonly thought to enable and protect us are working against us, whether through covert or overt means.[10] The fact that these documents of political or corporate conspiracy were all released within ten years of each other is no accident, nor merely a function of the historical contingencies of *The Geopolitical Aesthetic*'s composition and publication.[11] According to Jameson, the shopworn figure of conspiracy was a means by which these texts sought to provide a "cognitive map" of multinational capitalism's newly complex world system, while also mediating some of the more localized political and economic crises that marked the period, from the economic collapse of the early 1970s to the Watergate scandal that unfolded between 1972 and 1974.[12] The terms in which these texts did so, of course, evolved over time. While the conspiracy narratives played out in *The Parallax View*, *All the President's Men*, and *Three Days of the Condor* had a radical, antiestablishment cast, by the early 1980s this narrative formation had been harnessed by neoconservative forces in the service of a program of social service cutbacks and tax reductions, as films like *Silkwood* (Mike Nichols, 1983), *Videodrome*, and *Under Fire* attest.[13] For Jameson, however, the conspiracy trope is fairly consistent in its status as function of a project of cognitive mapping—"an unconscious, collective effort at trying to figure out where we are and what landscapes and forces confront us in a late twentieth century whose abominations are heightened by their concealment and their bureaucratic impersonality."[14]

Yet while *The Geopolitical Aesthetic* marked the apotheosis of Jameson's account of cognitive mapping, it also underscores some of the limitations of the project—and points to the role of affect in offsetting these limitations. First, even as he advocates for cognitive mapping as a valuable response to the failures of political agency in late multinational capitalism, Jameson repeatedly admits its impossibility—an admission that situates cognitive mapping among the other "impossible imperatives" and "inevitable failures" that sprinkle Jameson's work.[15] Thus Jameson's famous overture to the pioneering 1983 presentation: "I am addressing a subject about which I know nothing whatsoever, except for the fact that it does not exist."[16]

Second, while *The Geopolitical Aesthetic* nowhere broaches affect directly, *The Geopolitical Aesthetic* sees Jameson turning, repeatedly if unsystematically, to the figure of the feeling subject as a kind of rhetorical and theoretical stopgap at points in his account of the cognitive mapping in which its inevitable failure becomes clear.[17] Consider, for example, Jameson's contention, quoted above, that "nothing is gained by having been persuaded of the definitive verisimilitude of this or that conspiratorial hypothesis; but in the intent to hypothesize, in the desire called cognitive mapping—therein lies the beginning of wisdom." Here, the concession that the effort to represent social totality is by definition a failure (the failure of "the definitive verisimilitude of this or that conspiratorial hypothesis") quickly gives way to the valorization of a specific affective orientation toward this failure (in this case, an orientation of stubborn commitment conveyed by the affectively charged terms "desire" or "intent"). In the absence of any actual cognitive map, then, the affects of the mapping subject provide the next best thing: an affective inscription or experiential "analogon" of the desire for and/or failure of this mapping process. And a similar shift in focus—from object to subject, from the failed map itself to the experience of that failure—marks Jameson's famous analysis of John Portman's Westin Bonaventure Hotel, a theoretical set piece that closes the opening chapter of the book *Postmodernism; or, The Cultural Logic of Late Capitalism*. This passage kicks off with the promise that the Bonaventure's "complacent if bewildering leisure time space" might serve as a cognitive map of the late capitalist world system of which it is a function.[18] Yet it ends as a chronicle of the emotional effects of the hotel's failure to deliver on this promise. In place of an account of a building tagged as an *objective* analogon of the late capitalist world system, that is, Jameson delivers a report on his "bewildering immersion" in the hotel ("I am in this hyperspace up to my eyes and my body") that seems intended to serve as a *subjective* analogon of the same.[19]

Given the unexpectedly crucial role of the affected subject in the impossible work of mapping social totality, it should come as no surprise that Jameson's account of the conspiracy films at the heart of *The Geopolitical Aesthetic* devotes as much time to describing the attitude or orientation of the protagonists as he does to describing the maps themselves. These figures, according to Jameson, possess a signature emotional style, displaying what can "variously be characterized as anxiety, concern, Sorge, harassed bewilderment, apprehension, confusion, or disquiet."[20] And they possess a shared social status, as what Jameson's calls the "social detective"[21]—a figure who, while not often an actual policeman or private investigator, has a great deal in common with the policeman or private investigator due to their role as reporter, scholar, researcher, or photographer (even as their investigation distinguishes itself from that of the traditional criminal detective in the sense that they are seeking to solve a crime of a collective rather than of an individual nature).[22] Moreover, this slippage from an account of the map itself to an account of the subjective attitude to its delivery and/or failure is built into the very logic of cognitive mapping itself. Consider the fact that Jameson uses, as the master term for the concept, the gerund "cognitive map*ping*" (a noun formed from the verb "to map") instead of the standard noun phrase "cognitive map." In place of the "cognitive map" as a representational object, that is, Jameson writes of "cognitive mapping" as a human practice or *process*. A similar slippage is at work in his account of what "may be called 'the conspiratorial text'" as "an unconscious, collective effort at trying to figure out what where we are and what landscapes and forces confront us," which see him inscribe the impossibility of cognitive mapping by doubly internalizing, framing the cognitive map not just as something one tries but as something one *tries to* try—again, then, putting the burden on a certain kind of subjective posture (the posture of "trying").[23]

What emerges from Jameson's emphasis on the subjective experience of cognitive mapping's failure, I suggest, is the need for a rigorous account of how the subjects of late multinational capitalism might position themselves *affectively* in relation to this failure. And Jonathan Flatley's attention to the work of "affective mapping" in his 2008 monograph of the same name directly answers this need. Extending and building on Jameson's work, the monograph is animated by a sense that "just as the lack of a cognitive map of one's social space is crippling for effective political agency, so too is the lack of an affective map."[24] To answer this perceived need, Flatley appropriates the term "affective mapping" from environmental psychology, where it is used to designate the affective dimension of the internal maps that guide us through our spatial environment, and demonstrates that certain "aesthetic practice[s] might help with this process of affective mapping" or actually themselves "function as affective maps."[25] Calling on novels by Henry James, W. E. B. Du Bois, and Andrei Platonov as his primary texts, he suggests that the work of affective mapping operates "not primarily through a realist representation of a social space in the world, but through a representation of the affective life of the reader herself or himself" as they seek (and, in Jameson's reading, fail) to navigate that space.[26] His selected texts, that is, at once "provide a nugget of affective experience for the audience, one with direct historical resonance and relevance, and then also tell the reader something about that experience within the narrative itself."[27] In other words, they at once provide an object for the reader to respond to, and a representation of the reader's response, thus, in the process, as Flatley puts it, "narrat[ing] the production of [their] own reader" and serving as spectatorial mise en abymes that dramatize our experience of encounter with these constitutively impossible representations—experiences of desire, frustration and futility.[28] At stake here, then, is an "allegorization of the experience that the aesthetic practice is itself promoting."[29]

Yet while Flatley's work on affective mapping has been celebrated as a necessary codicil to Jameson's analysis of cognitive mapping, this essay's argument rests on the claim that Jameson's reliance on the medium shot in *The Geopolitical Aesthetic* is a preexisting answer to the need ostensibly answered by Flatley's project. But exactly *how* might the medium shot serve as the vehicle for a project of affective mapping, and thus play an unexpected role in radical Marxist film aesthetics?

To answer this question, we must first gain a better handle on the formal architecture of the medium shot itself, and to do this, in turn, it is worth considering Bordwell and Thompson's neoformalist breakdown of the device. Using "the standard measure: the human body" as their guide, Bordwell and Thompson describe the medium shot as a mediation between the properties of the long shot and the properties of the close-up. While framing the human body "from the waist up" so that "gesture and expression . . . become more visible" than they would be in the long shot, it is also able to reveal something of the body of the actor (whether the knees-up or waist-up shot), and of the "ground," whether neighboring people or the external environment.[30] The medium shot, in other words, provides optical access to the upper body of at least one figure (often showing two or more figures in two-shot side-by-side or face-to-face), while retaining the intimate optical access to facial expression that is often lost in the medium-long or long shots. The examples that Bordwell and Thompson select to support this claim are diverse, ranging from shots featuring small groups of figures to shots of pairs of figures and shots of single figures framed from the waist-up against a landscape or beside an object that occupies the same spatial plane. Yet what is important for our purposes is that across Bordwell and Thompson's case studies—and thus both in terms of its formal affordances and in terms of its historical application—the medium shot lends itself to the scene of *encounter*. At stake in the medium shot, that is, is something like what Emmanuel Levinas famously calls the "face-to-face"—a confrontation between two or more entities, a "relation with the other" that Levinas, not accidentally, articulates in the rubric of the "encounter."[31]

Certainly, where the medium shot elaborates the encounter spatially, certain forms of découpage—notably the series of close-ups or medium close-ups

assembled in a typical shot / reverse shot pattern—elaborate the encounter temporally, and in many respects the shot / reverse shot provides an even more
compelling narrativization of the encounter than the medium shot. Yet among
single shots, it is the medium shot that performs this work most efficiently,
capturing the drama of the encounter in a single rich tableau. Indeed, this shot
type's affordances to the logic of the "encounter" are best underscored through
a comparison with alternative framing choices. Take, first, the long shot: while
lending itself even more readily than the medium shot to the imaging of two
entities side-by-side, it isn't quite able to deliver a scene of encounter due to its
failure to yield up "gesture and expression." Take, similarly, the medium long
shot or *plan américain*, popular across classical American narrative genres,
from the Western to the screwball, between 1930s and the 1960s. Generally
organized around two or more players framed from the knees-up, these shots
"favor[ed] the players' bodies" and gestures—and, by extension, put less emphasis on facial expression.[32] Take, in turn, the close-up. Whereas this shot stages
the subject in the act of considering action, recalling action, or absorbing
action, it does not provide any background context, and thus it is the medium
shot that must be understood as staging the moment of the encounter itself, or
what Lauren Berlant calls a "situation": "a state of things in which something
that will perhaps matter is unfolding amid the usual activity of life," and that,
as such, enables the representation of a relationship in emergence rather than a
representation of a relationship's subjective effects on one of the parties.[33]
Take, finally, the medium close-up. Defined, at least by Bordwell, as a shot that
"frames the body from the chest up," the medium close-up is simply not generous enough to credibly accommodate two players or a player and an object in
the frame.[34] It is notable that in his example of the medium and medium-long
shots (lifted, like all the other examples, from *The Third Man*) Bordwell himself includes two figures, underscoring the medium shot's continuing utility as
a two-shot. Every tighter shot, by contrast, including the medium close-up, is a
single.

   Of course, Bordwell's examples of the medium shot are lifted from classical
cinema, and with this in mind it might be objected that the formal transformations associated with various "post-classical" or postmodern styles—in which
"shots tend to be shorter and framed closer to the performers"—have stripped
the medium shot of its credentials as the default vehicle for the encounter.[35] In
fact, the medium shot's status in this respect has been remarkably durable across
the twentieth century and beyond. Indeed, in Bordwell's discussion of the "intensified continuity" of more recent popular cinema, the medium shot marks an
unexpected point of *continuity* between the Classical Hollywood narrative mode
and more recent postclassical modes, with versions of the medium shot featuring centrally in both contexts. As Bordwell puts it, "As plans américains and
ensemble framings became less common, the norms were reweighted . . . the filmmaker began to work along a narrower scale, from medium two-shot to extreme

close-up."[36] Far from expiring with the classical cinema, the medium shot is its residue—evolving, perhaps, from the knees-up of the plan américain or "medium-long" and into the waist-up of the medium shot, but retaining its centrality all the while. And the medium shot's position as the go-to shot for the scene of inter-subjective encounter can be further underscored through an engagement with critical accounts of the close-up. For many theorists, from Béla Balázs to Gilles Deleuze, the access to the face supplied by the close-up cannot be replicated in the medium shot due to the close-up's unique, defamiliarizing capacity to "push us beyond the realm of individuation, of social role, and of the exchange that underlies intersubjectivity."[37] The close-up, that is, produces a peculiarly inhuman face, a face magnified, desubjectivized, and stripped of the possibility of intersubjective exchange. The obverse might be claimed of the medium shot. Where the close-up estranges, the medium shot familiarizes; where the close-up dehumanizes, the medium shot humanizes; where the close-up robs the face of the possibility of intersubjective relation, the medium shot is a vehicle for the drama of encounter.

It is *as* a shot that lends itself to the scene of encounter, I contend, that the medium shot provides an excellent cinematic mechanism for the work of what Flatley calls "affective mapping," a visual means of at once staging and narrating our experience of encounter with these constitutively impossible representations.[38] And the specific medium shots that Jameson chooses to illustrate the opening chapters of *The Geopolitical Aesthetic* bear out this argument. On the one hand, many of these images feature communications technologies, from the television playing "videodrome" in the still from the Cronenberg film of the same name to the telephone exchange in the still from *Three Days of the Condor* and the photograph examined by Nick Nolte in the still from *Under Fire*. And it is worth noting that, for Jameson, communications technologies are understood primarily in terms of their allegorical function as signs of the vast horizon of late multinational capitalism that they serve to facilitate and of which they are prominent products. Certainly, within Jameson's framework, the same could be said of all late capitalist consumer bric-a-brac. Yet it is peculiarly the case for communications technologies. At once mirrors of and functions of quite literal networks, communications technologies are the perfect representational shorthand for "a network of power and control even more difficult for our minds and imaginations to grasp: the whole decentred global network of the third stage of capital itself."[39] It is no accident, then, that Jameson uses communication technologies as a figure for the process of allegorization by which history becomes text and text history—contending that, within the conspiracy film, "the existential furniture of daily life thereby finds itself slowly transformed into communications technology," the bearer of some echo or meaning beyond it.[40]

Yet like any effort to capture or map the sprawlingly complex space of global capital, the image of communications media—particularly electronic communications media—is not, for Jameson, entirely reliable or effective. While in the quotations above Jameson unambivalently identifies these devices' status as figurations of global capital, he is elsewhere less sanguine about their figural or more specifically allegorical power, voicing doubts about "whether representation can draw directly, in some new way, on the distinctive technology of capitalism's third age, whose video and computer-based furniture and object-world are markedly less graphic than the media and transportation technology of the second."[41] Like all commodities, these machines are at once functions of social labor of production and consumption, and serve to dissemble that labor. Yet their status in this respect is amplified by their status as digital technologies. As Alexander Galloway has noted, "The computer consummates the retreat from the realm of the imaginary to the purely symbolic realm of writing."[42] In other words—and as Ian Buchanan has put it—"the older types of machines . . . had an imposing representational power [that] our own feebler looking little plastic boxes and flickering monitors patently lack. We get no sense of what a computer can do, much less how it has been able to have a world-historical impact, simply by looking at it."[43] Rather than figures for the late capitalist world system, digital technologies are ultimately figures for its impenetrable complexity, its refusal to yield its secrets on a phenomenal scale we can comprehend.

It is fortuitous, then, that Jameson's selection of medium shot stills does not simply present a piece of communication technology, proffered as an (inevitably inadequate) allegory for a social totality. Rather, alongside the image of a piece of communications technology, we are provided with the image of a character encountering it, and our engagement with the technology itself will be routed almost entirely through identification with these figures. Joe Turner's gaze is one of intense concentration as he barrels through the underground labyrinth of the telephone exchange in his effort to solve the murder of his colleagues without falling into clutches of corrupt CIA officials. Max Renn, under the influence of Videodrome, is open-mouthed and enthralled as he crouches before a television screen broadcasting a pulsating, hallucinatory image of what appear to be Debbie Harry's lips. Photojournalist Russell Price wears a troubled expression as scrutinizes a photograph portraying the street-level unrest in Nicaragua that will lead to the Sandinista National Liberation Front (FSLN) ousting dictator Anastasio Somoza Debayle. While varying in kind, the emotions these men express all fall into the category of what Adam Morton has dubbed the "epistemic emotions"—emotions that, according to Morton, play an important role in the acquisition of knowledge and that range from curiosity to knowingness, interest, surprise, and concern.[44] What is striking about Jameson's chosen stills, however, is that none of them depicts characters in states of knowingness, realization, or recognition. Rather, they mark knowledge in suspension or in process, in a state of development that may or may not culminate in epiphany. These are images, as Jameson himself has put it, of epistemic "desire" or "intent," which is to say they depict what Ernst Bloch calls "expectant emotion[s]" "aim[ing] less at some specific object as the fetish of their desire than at the configuration of the world in general, or (what amounts to the same thing) at the future dispo-sition of the self."[45]

And it is because they stage both object and figure in a scene of encounter that these medium shots can be understood as a visual example of the work of "affective mapping" that Flatley diagnoses in the novels of James, Du Bois, and Platonov. On the one hand, that is, these shots present to us an object that we cannot understand—in this case, a piece of communications technology that, as Jameson explains at length, functions as a cipher for "the whole unimaginable decentered global network itself."[46] On the other, they map, narrate, or allegorize our affective encounter with the presented object via the presence of human fig-ures in these pictures—an encounter that is, inevitably, one of unsatisfied curios-ity or thwarted aspiration rather than one of triumphal recognition. What these medium shots yield, in other words, is a kind of spectatorial mise en abyme—an image not of the capitalist world system itself but of the affect that arises in our inevitably bruising and futile efforts to grasp the capitalist world system. And, following Flatley, I would contend that the effect of the medium shot's mise en abyme is not merely to reflect our feeling of epistemic frustration back to us. Rather, its effect is to help us position that feeling of epistemic frustration in a broader set of sociohistorical circumstances, revealing it not simply as a personal condition but as a kind of "historical datum."[47] Just as, for Flatley, "mapping" melancholia can turn melancholia itself into "the basis for a potentially politiciz-ing link with others," so mapping our epistemic frustrations can transform these frustrations into the foundation for powerful, transformative political alliances.[48] We are all struggling to map the object world of late capitalism. We are all failing. Yet to paraphrase Jameson himself, in the medium shot's graphic staging of "the intent to hypothesize . . . therein lies the beginning of wisdom."[49]

Notes

1 Fredric Jameson, *The Geopolitical Aesthetic: Cinema and Space in the World System* (Bloomington: Indiana University Press, 1992), 2. Jameson borrows the phrase "world system" from world-systems theory or world-systems analysis, a multidisci-plinary, macro-scale approach to world history and social change that emphasizes the world system as the primary unit of analysis. See, for example, Immanuel Maurice Wallerstein, *World-Systems Analysis: An Introduction* (Durham, NC: Duke University Press, 2004).

2 Even where Jameson does cast his net more broadly to include formal or visual devices—from the host of "geographical motifs" at the heart of *Three Days of the Condor* to the repeated use of the close-up and the fact that the "agents of conspir-acy" all seem to be sweating—the medium shot is not among them (Jameson, *Geopolitical Aesthetic*, 14, 64, 66).

3 David Bordwell and Kristin Thompson, *Film Art: An Introduction* (New York: McGraw-Hill, 2016), 191.

4 Perhaps more to the point: where the close-up, for example, has been variously seen as "the vehicle of the star, the privileged receptacle of affect, of passion, the guarantee of the cinema's status as a universal language," the medium shot has

barely been "seen" at all, except as the foil for its more arresting, up-close cousin (Mary Ann Doane, "The Close-Up: Scale and Detail in the Cinema," *differences* 14, no. 3 [2003]: 90). As Eisenstein puts it, "A cockroach filmed in close-up appears on the screen one hundred times more formidable than a hundred elephants in medium-long shot" (Sergei Eisenstein, *Au-delà des étoiles*, trans. Jacques Aumont et al. [Paris: Union Général d'Éditions, 1974], 112). Here, if the close-up seems to confer force or power (making a cockroach "formidable"), the medium or medium-long shot seems to subtract it, reducing a hundred elephants to nothing more than a cockroach.

5 Flatley, *Affective Mapping.*

6 Flatley, *Affective Mapping*, 83.

7 Fredric Jameson, "Cognitive Mapping," in *Marxism and the Interpretation of Culture*, ed. Cary Nelson and Lawrence Grossberg (Urbana: University of Illinois Press, 1988), 353.

8 Jameson, "Cognitive Mapping," 347; Jameson, *Geopolitical Aesthetic*, 9.

9 Alberto Toscano and Jeffrey Kinkle, *Cartographies of the Absolute: An Aesthetics of the Economy for the Twenty-First Century* (London: Zero Books, 2015), 7.

10 Jameson, "Cognitive Mapping," 356; Bridget Brown, *They Know Us Better Than We Know Ourselves: The History and Politics of Alien Abduction* (New York: New York University Press, 2007), 103. As historian Richard Hofstadter famously put it, conspiracy thinking is animated by anxieties that the visible, knowable surface of life conceals what he dubbed "a vast and sinister conspiracy." Hofstadter, *The Paranoid Style in American Politics* (New York: Knopf Doubleday, 2012), 29.

11 Fredric Jameson, "Periodizing the 60s," *Social Text*, nos. 9–10 (Spring–Summer 1984): 208.

12 Jameson, *Geopolitical Aesthetic*, 3.

13 Gordon B. Arnold, *Conspiracy Theory in Film, Television, and Politics* (Westport, CT: Greenwood, 2008), 114.

14 Jameson, *Geopolitical Aesthetic*, 3.

15 Bill Brown, "The Dark Wood of Postmodernity: Space, Faith, Allegory," *PMLA* 120, no. 3 (2005): 739; Steven Helmling, *The Success and Failure of Fredric Jameson: Writing, the Sublime, and the Dialectic of Critique* (Albany: State University of New York Press, 2014), 111.

16 Jameson, "Cognitive Mapping," 347.

17 Jameson would not fully engage with the question of affect until *Antinomies of Realism* and *The Ancients and the Postmoderns*. See Fredric Jameson, *The Antinomies of Realism* (London: Verso, 2013); Fredric Jameson, *The Ancients and the Postmoderns: On the Historicity of Forms* (London: Verso, 2015). For the claim that Jameson's earlier work does not broach affect directly, see Brian Massumi, *Parables for the Virtual: Movement, Affect, Sensation* (Durham, NC: Duke University Press, 2002); Sianne Ngai, *Ugly Feelings* (Cambridge, MA: Harvard University Press, 2005); Eve Kosofsky Sedgwick and Adam Frank, "Shame in the Cybernetic Fold: Reading Silvan Tomkins," *Critical Inquiry* 21, no. 2 (1995): 496–522. For an argument that Jameson was more fully engaged with questions of affect and emotion in the late 1980s and 1990s than he is often made out to be, see Pansy Duncan, "Once More, with Fredric Jameson," *Cultural Critique* 97 (2017): 1–23.

18 Fredric Jameson, *Postmodernism; or, The Cultural Logic of Late Capitalism* (Durham, NC: Duke University Press, 1991), 44.

19 Jameson, *Postmodernism*, 43.

20 Jameson, *Geopolitical Aesthetic*, 65.

21 Jameson, *Geopolitical Aesthetic*, 37.

22 Jameson, *Geopolitical Aesthetic*, 39.
23 Jameson, *Geopolitical Aesthetic*, 3.
24 Flatley, *Affective Mapping*, 78. As Flatley puts it, "Our spatial environments are inevitably imbued with the feelings we have about the places we are going, the things that happen to us along the way, and the people we meet, and these emotional valences affect how we create itineraries" (Flatley, *Affective Mapping*, 77–78).
25 Flatley, *Affective Mapping*, 80.
26 Flatley, *Affective Mapping*, 7.
27 Flatley, *Affective Mapping*, 7.
28 Flatley, *Affective Mapping*, 7.
29 Flatley, *Affective Mapping*, 83.
30 Bordwell and Thompson, *Film Art*, 191.
31 Emmanuel Levinas, *Totality and Infinity: An Essay on Exteriority*, trans. Alphonso Lingis (The Hague: Martinus Nijhoff, 1979), 22.
32 David Bordwell, "Intensified Continuity: Visual Style in Contemporary American Film," *Film Quarterly* 55, no. 3 (2002): 18–19.
33 Lauren Berlant, *Cruel Optimism* (Durham, NC: Duke University Press, 2011), Kindle ed.
34 Bordwell and Thompson, *Film Art*, 191.
35 Bordwell and Thompson, *Film Art*, 262.
36 Bordwell, "Intensified Continuity," 19.
37 Doane, "Close-Up," 96.
38 Flatley, *Affective Mapping*, 7.
39 Jameson, *Postmodernism*, 46.
40 Jameson, *Geopolitical Aesthetic*, 10.
41 Jameson, *Geopolitical Aesthetic*, 15–16.
42 Alexander Galloway, *The Interface Effect* (London: Polity, 2012), 17.
43 Ian Buchanan, *Fredric Jameson: Live Theory* (London: Continuum, 2006), 99.
44 Adam Morton, "Epistemic Emotions," in *The Oxford Handbook of the Philosophy of Emotions*, ed. Peter Goldie (Oxford: Oxford University Press, 2010), 385–400.
45 Ernst Bloch, *The Principle of Hope* (London: Blackwell, 1986), 74.
46 Jameson, *The Geopolitical Aesthetic*, 13.
47 Flatley, *Affective Mapping*, 92.
48 Flatley, *Affective Mapping*, 92.
49 Jameson, *Geopolitical Aesthetic*, 3.

12

"An American Utopia" and the Politics of Military Science Fiction

DAN HASSLER-FOREST

Mandatory military conscription as the solution to global capitalism's escalating crisis of socioeconomic inequality: one could easily imagine an idea like this to emanate from one of Slavoj Žižek's more outrageous op-ed pieces, or perhaps even from *The Onion* on a slow news day. But this modest proposal is precisely what Fredric Jameson's instantly notorious essay "An American Utopia: Dual Power and the Universal Army" expressed. At a time when "social democracy is ... irretrievably bankrupt, and communism seems dead,"[1] Jameson sought to reignite our utopian imagination by way of a "collectivity one does not choose."[2]

Following an impeccably organized argument, Jameson's ninety-six-page essay—published in book form together with a variety of responses and reflections edited by Slavoj Žižek—makes the case for reintroducing universal military conscription to American society. The army, so he argues, is the only existing institution that provides a means to swiftly transform late capitalism's deeply dysfunctional system of social relations. Not only is the military a truly universalizing institution, where conscripts from all walks of life are brought together, but it also uniquely provides the social benefits of the now-defunct welfare state: access to education, health care, pensions, et cetera. Spinning this counterintuitive logic in an entirely novel direction, his intervention pushes us to think about new ways of socializing and reinvigorating health care, higher education, social security, and collectivity writ large, thereby leveraging America's universal infatuation with the military to miraculously conjure up a close approximation of full communism.

If we do indeed allow ourselves to sidestep the left's decades-old tradition of perceiving the military-industrial complex as nothing but a force of evil that must be rejected on all fronts, it's not hard to see how radical and truly progressive this idea might be.[3] His proposal is one that chooses the truly revolutionary road of dual power, acknowledging in the first place that politics constitutes merely a way of maintaining the existing balance of power with minimal variations. The goal of the left, therefore, should be to enact radical measures that transition us away from these existing mechanisms and force their lingering social, cultural, and institutional remainders to "wither away" as they are replaced by a utopian alternative organized around the collective.[4] Only a true collectivization of our social relations could achieve this necessary revolution, and after dismissing all other existing professional and institutional organizations worth considering,[5] Jameson's essay makes a case for the universal army as an "eminently practical" way of realizing a radical transformation that "necessarily passes over into a utopian projection."[6]

For science fiction fans, this obvious provocation was easier to relate to than it was for our less nerdy leftist comrades. Among sci-fi geeks, even the most pacifist-minded can hardly downplay the genre's persistent association with militarized utopias, or with military hierarchies as one of the most basic structures of interpersonal drama and social relations. And this obsession is hardly limited to those subgenres or texts that are focused primarily on spectacular military conflict—from Robert A. Heinlein's gung-ho space marines to the decades-long cultural phenomenon that is the definitionally belligerent *Star Wars* franchise. Indeed, the genre all too often takes for granted the idea that space exploration, political resistance, or even futurism per se are organized on the basis of military hierarchical structures by default, yielding endless varieties of what has pithily been described as "militainment."[7] In short: American science fiction futures are always-already implicitly or explicitly military.[8]

Star Trek is the best example. The most widely celebrated paradigm for politically liberal science fiction simultaneously conflates its utopian future with ubiquitous military hierarchies. Across its many incarnations over the past half century, the *Star Trek* franchise has consistently reproduced its top-down command structures, its fetishized uniforms and insignia, and its myopic focus on postimperialist "captains" and their motley crews of military-trained specialists. And of course *Star Trek*'s template has been copied by innumerable serialized franchises that reproduce its casual militarism—from *Battlestar Galactica* and *Babylon 5* to *Farscape* and *Stargate SG-1*. As a vivid illustration of science fiction fandom's familiarity with military paraphernalia, one need only visit a sci-fi fan convention, where the cosplaying tradition resembles nothing so much as a more colorful and diverse military parade.

Given the genre's long-standing association with military structures and iconography, I reflect in this chapter on the question whether popular science fiction may also yield some of the revolutionary forms that Jameson attributes to his proposed universal army. Is it shortsighted to criticize a series like *Star Trek* for its military trappings? Does military science fiction articulate a future society where our traditional notions of politics and power have fully withered away, yielding liberatory collective social structures? Or is there a stubborn kernel of antirevolutionary individualism in these texts that undermines the ways in which they articulate a future focused on the collective? Reconsidering some of these works from the perspective of Jameson's intervention, do these entertainments offer us productive glimpses of what this future horizon of transformative dual power could look like, or do they stubbornly reproduce our most unimaginative assumptions about militarism and patriarchal authority?

To examine these issues, I approach some of the most influential military utopias in modern American science fiction from a Jamesonian perspective. Starting with the basic question of hierarchical versus collective social organizations, I first discuss the figure of the ship's captain as the embodiment of the military's traditional patriarchal organization, and therefore as an antiprogressive and certainly antirevolutionary touchstone in the genre. At the same time, I look at ways in which this figure of patriarchal authority can simultaneously be questioned and opposed by its various dialectical counterparts. While *Star Trek* provided a popular template for serialized science fiction—itself continuing a much longer tradition of imperial conquest as a narrative form—other franchises have juxtaposed these traditional forms of command with other (semi) military organizations that offer a much stronger focus on various aspects of collective organization and nonhierarchical social structures.

Starting with *Star Trek* and its idealized militarism, I first contrast Jameson's vision of transformative dual power with the cultural imaginary provided by classic American science fiction. I juxtapose Gene Roddenberry's liberal-humanist neoimperialism with the more ideologically conservative libertarianism of influential sci-fi author Robert A. Heinlein, who presents the military's traditional combination of violence, masculinity, and strict hierarchical organization as a desirable form of social Darwinism. Paul Verhoeven's satirical and subversive film adaptation of Heinlein's 1959 novel *Starship Troopers* (1997) demonstrates how thin is the line separating such visions from outright fascist ones. By the same token, the many space operas that focus primarily on heroic military resistance to evil empires—from Frank Herbert's *Dune* series to the *Star Wars* franchise— too easily conflate the camaraderie of soldiering with the transformative solidarity of antifascist and anti-imperialist struggles. At the same time, the horrific military actions by the U.S. military (the firebombing of Dresden, the atomic bombs dropped on Japan, and the genocidal carpet-bombing of Korea and Vietnam) that ground these narratives historically are conveniently justified as they are transformed into fantasy.

I then turn to popular science fiction narratives in which questions of military conflict and army conscription are employed to engage with forms of social organization that interrogate or even challenge the deeply patriarchal and hierarchical traditions associated with the military. For example, the ongoing book series *The Expanse* by James S. A. Corey imagines a future in which the colonization of the solar system results in a new and deeply unstable division between labor and capital, with each group in this precarious power balance developing its own form of military culture and organization. Similarly, the conflict between organic humans and artificially constructed Cylons in the rebooted television series *Battlestar Galactica* explores military hierarchies and social systems from a more radically posthuman perspective. Both these franchises offer tantalizing glimpses of how a social context of ubiquitous militarism can also explore progressive and even revolutionary ideas in the face of catastrophic and potentially cataclysmic threats to human existence.

Finally, I turn to Chinese science fiction and the global blockbuster *The Wandering Earth* as an example of a new kind of science fiction text that offers familiar genre thrills while also deviating strongly from American narrative fiction and its most basic ideological coordinates. Combining Hollywood blockbuster traditions with China's state-proscribed ideological payload, *The Wandering Earth* constructs its narrative around precisely the kind of collectivity that Jameson seeks to encourage. But at the same time, we must historicize this text and its political unconscious as an ideological expression of a specific form of authoritarian nationalism that clearly runs counter to any truly utopian imaginary. I finish, therefore, by speculating about whether it is even remotely conceivable in our current social, political, and technological constellation to adopt the kind of sweeping radical change that Jameson proposes—and if not, how we might interpret his intervention from the perspective of both political practice (what kind of real-world political groups would be willing to even consider such an idea as an act of policy?) and culture (what narratives would we need in order to help imagine the resulting societal reorganization as a utopian horizon?).

"Captain's Log": Hierarchical Power and Military Command

In his book *Four Futures*, Peter Frase uses science fiction tropes to sketch out four main directions in which social systems could move beyond the current era.[9] The four scenarios he outlines are mapped out through an elegant Greimasian set of semiotic axes: one between scarcity and plenitude, the other between equality and hierarchy. Obviously, the most obviously desirable of the resulting four combinations is the one that combines plenitude with equality—the *Star Trek* future that is sometimes mockingly referred to as Fully Automated Luxury Gay Space Communism.[10] It's a future in which capitalism's existing social hierarchies are eradicated, in part at least by social justice movements, while technological advancements ensure material plenitude. Frase makes it perfectly clear that the material conditions for such a society are already at our disposal. The problem is that this world of equality and abundance requires both the political will and the collective imagination to make it a reality.

While this particular combination is clearly the most traditionally utopian, it is important to note that its details do not convincingly correspond with the narrative organization of *Star Trek*—or at least not to any of its actually existing forms. For while *Star Trek* is set in a future where this ideal of a technologically advanced full communism has supposedly been achieved, the canonical TV series, films, novels, video games, and comics are focused almost exclusively on the military organization of Star Fleet and the specific crews of various starships and space stations. In these countless space adventures, the explicit hierarchies of really existing military forces not only are constantly reproduced but also serve to naturalize this form of social stratification. Therefore, while top-down command structures are not inherent in this future's social structure, it remains—paradoxically—the only kind of social relation we actually witness. As I have argued elsewhere, the key contradiction of *Star Trek*'s politics is therefore that it consistently reproduces the very same patriarchal hierarchies its speculative future society has supposedly moved beyond.[11]

As Jodi Dean points out in her response to "An American Utopia," Jameson does something similar when he "underplays hierarchy and the chain of command" as "key elements of military organization."[12] His basic argument hinges on the assumption that one could bring people from all walks of life together into a military organization in a way that bolsters solidarity, without simultaneously reproducing the brutalizing rituals and violently enforced hierarchies that have been fundamental to modern military organizations and their Foucauldian structures of ritualized discipline and control.[13] Hence, Jameson's provocation is most useful as what Alberto Toscano pointedly describes as "a kind of *reactant* to reveal our deep-seated *fear of the collective*":[14] by proposing universal military conscription as a "solution" to America's out-of-control military-industrial complex, he forces us to reconsider our more general inability to come to terms with a political imagination organized around the collective.

This fear of the collective is more than just the product of capitalism's fundamental individualism, especially in the intensified neoliberal form of the past three decades.[15] Throughout our substantial cultural archive of science fiction films and television series, there are precious few examples in popular narratives that offer positive depictions of the collective as a form of social organization.[16] On the contrary, examples abound of story forms and genre tropes that systematically demonize collectives as incompatible with the values of liberal humanism. This heritage can be traced through genre films from the Cold War paranoia of *Invasion of the Body Snatchers* (1956) and the rise of the zombie movie genre from the 1960s onward, through to malevolent entities like the Borg Collective in *Star Trek: The Next Generation* and the White Walkers in *Game of Thrones*.

All these narrative embodiments of the collective have one basic thing in common: they present collectivity as an ontological threat by reducing human beings to mindless, inhuman, and even monstrous automatons, bereft of emotions, discernible character traits, or complex hierarchical structures.

By contrast, the ways in which hierarchical and even semimilitary forms of social organization have dominated those same narrative traditions can hardly be exaggerated. Leaving aside for now the vast majority of film narratives that focus exclusively on an individual protagonist's specific goals and challenges, popular stories in film and television organized around larger groups of characters have had a very clear hierarchical organization in the power relations they express and embody. Rather than embracing the utopian potential of radically transformed future systems of social relations, the various crews, teams, and fellowships we actually see in science fiction franchises instead have a tendency to double down on institutional stratification, constantly reproducing the very social hierarchies that their postcapitalist storyworlds have supposedly ended. By focusing our attention primarily on commanding officers, *Star Trek* largely contradicts rather than illustrates Jameson's vision of a militarized future and the swift dissolution of capitalism's residual inequalities: even without money, even without scarcity, even without warfare, the only way to imagine military organizations apparently remains by way of naturalized, internalized, and mythologized hierarchical divisions—which more often than not also reproduce the sexist, racist, and homophobic cultural dynamics of capitalism's social organization.

The most recent incarnation of *Star Trek* provides a case in point. *Star Trek: Discovery* (2017–present) is the first series in the franchise not to revolve around the adventures of a particular commanding officer and his or her crew: protagonist Michael Burnham is introduced as an unruly bridge officer whose mutiny sets in motion the new series' chain of events. But after the pilot episode, Burnham spends only a few episodes as a renegade Starfleet officer before establishing herself as a central figure among the main officers on the eponymous space ship's bridge, and the series swiftly returns to the franchise's familiar focus on a starship's main officers and their chain of command. Thus, as so often happens, the producers' initial decision to shift a narrative's focus away from the more traditional top-down structure of power simply leads back to the reproduction of the very same social structures.

A similar dynamic is at play in the *Star Wars* films. The long-running franchise has been devoted to the militarized struggle between the forces of good (embodied by the Rebel Alliance) and the forces of evil (the pseudo-fascist Galactic Empire, later succeeded by its successor, the First Order). As the Rebels constitute a loosely organized group united in its desire to vanquish a military oppressor, one would imagine that the films might explore less hierarchical ways of organizing political and military resistance. But as the saga has progressed, it is striking how the strict hierarchies of American military leadership are unthinkingly reproduced in this galaxy far, far away. And while few of the details of the Rebellion's processes of internal organization are clarified within the films proper, we do see how the main characters are rewarded almost instantly with high-ranking military titles. Thus, the heroic novice Luke Sky-walker and his renegade friend Han Solo, who both join the rebellion in the first film, have been promoted in the first sequel to the ranks of Lieutenant Commander and General, respectively. Similarly, the character of Leia Organa, first introduced as a Princess, returns in the more recent films as a General, commanding the military forces of the Rebels. Eschewing all of the many ways in which characters could be given authority, status, and recognition, the *Star Wars* franchise has tended to equate authority and even narrative significance with high-ranking military titles.

Thus, even though the evil Empire being fought by the Rebels is more overtly hierarchical in its military organization, the rebellion offers no actual alternative apart from their more scruffy-looking uniforms, a command structure that is less obviously dictatorial, and a less explicitly authoritarian sensibility among the commanding officers. Nevertheless, *Star Wars*—like so many other military science fiction properties that resemble it—illustrates how strongly our militainment-driven cultural imaginary is saturated with the automatic assumption of top-down hierarchical command structures, which in turn reflect capitalism's own forms of social stratification. Any utopian project of radical transformation organized around universal military conscription will surely run up against this hurdle. One could even make the argument that there is a virulent strand of fascist thought that pervades our understanding of military organizations in science fiction.

"Service Guarantees Citizenship": Hollywood's Fascist Unconscious

When director Paul Verhoeven's big-budget adaptation of Robert A. Heinlein's science fiction novel *Starship Troopers* was released in 1997 to decidedly mixed reviews, some critics expressed concerns about what they saw as "quasi-fascist militarism" in a mainstream Hollywood blockbuster.[17] But over the years, *Starship Troopers* has cemented its reputation as one of the most slyly subversive political films in Hollywood's science fiction canon. Pushing beyond Heinlein's libertarian depiction of a harshly militarized society in which citizens are afforded rights and privileges on the basis of their physical strength, willpower, and endurance, Ed Neumeier's script gleefully foregrounds the fascist unconscious that informs so much of mainstream Hollywood entertainment.

In the movie—as in the novel—we follow the grueling military career of a young recruit named Johnny Rico. The son of wealthy liberals, he joins the army voluntarily to prove his own worth and impress his girlfriend, and later commits to this calling in order to avenge an attack by an alien species that annihilates his hometown.[18] During his military training, we do indeed observe that

Rico's experience of military life seems utopian in its reorganization of social relations: there appears to be neither racism nor sexism in the army barracks, as men and women share barracks space, shower rooms, and casual sexual encounters with remarkable freedom and camaraderie. In moments like these, we get a sense of what Jameson means when he argues for universal conscription as a tool to break down capitalism's toxic class system by enforcing a nonelective "classless society".[19] Rico's fellow "grunts" are seen sharing memories, ambitions, frustrations, desires, and jokes across lines of class, gender, race, and sexual orientation to form a community that remains meaningfully diverse while feeling united in solidarity and collectivity: a vivid depiction of what Jameson describes as the army's "nonmilitary function which is essentially social in nature and is calculated to serve as a vehicle for the fraternization of classes."[20]

The scenes showing Johnny's life in the barracks thereby offer a helpful approximation of military conscription flattening out distinctions of class-based hierarchies, as the mobile infantry brings together individuals from a wide variety of social, economic, and cultural backgrounds. One scene in particular foregrounds how diverse this group really is, and how their motivations to volunteer for military service also range from a farm boy's desire to flee his surroundings to a prospective writer's will to broaden his horizons. Most, however, indicate specifically that they signed up in order to access facilities that would be more difficult or even impossible to access without the benefits of citizenship bestowed upon all soldiers: these benefits include access to higher education, the ability to develop a political career, and a helpful shortcut to getting a license to reproduce legally.

But as tempting as this fantasy may be, *Starship Troopers'* specific organization of the military also makes it very clear how effortlessly capitalism's system of social organization can adapt to progressive societal values while keeping its fundamental hierarchical nature intact. This is the point where the film's *dramatis personae* is worth discussing in more detail, as the trajectories followed by its three principal characters perfectly map out how resilient capitalism's organized class structures remain, and how conducive this kind of military imaginary is to an "underlying reality" that is suffused with fascist ideology.[21]

Besides the aforementioned Johnny Rico (played by Casper Van Dien), the film focuses on two other protagonists: Carmen Ibanez (Denise Richards) and Carl Jenkins (Neil Patrick Harris) are high school friends of Rico's, and after the film's early scenes sketch out their friendship, the film follows their adventures after the three of them (each for different reasons) decide to enlist in the military. Having already established in no uncertain terms that "service grants citizenship" in the film's future society, the film goes on to clarify that new recruits are assigned to military units on the basis of standardized test scores. The trio of high school friends is therefore immediately broken up, with the high-performing Carmen admitted to flight school, brainy nerd Carl recruited by the secretive and mysterious military intelligence division, and the academically challenged Johnny finding himself shipped off to boot camp as a mere infantry "grunt."

While the film grants us no insight into Carl's environment once he joins the ranks of the intelligence division, the difference between Carmen and Johnny's social environment speaks volumes about the army's reproduction of capitalism's class hierarchies. Carmen's social environment as a pilot-in-training is one of instant comfort, privilege, and authority, while Johnny undergoes the unrelentingly harsh treatment of newly recruited infantry grunts. While Johnny himself comes from an affluent environment, social behavior among the recruited infantry soldiers is emphatically working-class: the recruits treat each other with an easy and convivial familiarity, in visible contrast with the academy's much more formal and clearly upper-class group of officers. His character is therefore the exception that proves the rule: a privileged member of the upper class willfully rejecting his parents' class-based expectations and embracing the colorful richness of working-class life among the grunts.

Many of these details in the screenplay subtly underline the film's main satirical thrust, as it maps out a future American "utopia" that is resolutely fascist in its social and political organization. Therefore, even though the natural solidarity within the mobile infantry offers an attractive depiction of a social organization that appears to transcend boundaries of class, gender, and ethnicity, the fact that it is embedded within this overtly fascist society where violence is glorified and "natural" social stratification becomes fully internalized.[22] So when the trio is finally reunited at the end of the movie, their collective representation of harmonious and mutually beneficial class distinctions naturalizes the fascist notion that a strictly hierarchical division between groups is natural, desirable, and inevitable. It's the kind of worldview that Hannah Arendt famously described as one in which "every man and every thought which does not serve and does not conform to the ultimate purpose of a machine whose only purpose is the generation and accumulation of power is a dangerous nuisance":[23] one where the individual's right to exist is predicated upon their usefulness to the enforcement of authoritarian state power.

Therefore, while *Starship Troopers* is one of the very few Hollywood films that expose and critique military science fiction's latent fascist ideas rather than simply incorporating and reproducing them, it also illustrates the danger of idealizing some aspects of military life while glossing over others. As appealing as Jameson's vision of a socially transformative universal army may be, the concept is just as likely to pave the way for a more deeply rooted authoritarianism as it is to usher in a postcapitalist utopia—if not more so. And given the current state of cultural and political discourse, the rising global tide of neofascism makes it difficult indeed to imagine any such universal army being used to transform the hierarchical organization of global capitalism into a better world.

Kameron Hurley's recent novel *The Light Brigade* (2019) takes the jingoistic "milibertarianism" of Heinlein's novel, multiplies it by Verhoeven's antifascist satire, and fuses both with the time-loop trope so prevalent in contemporary science fiction. Films like *Groundhog Day, Looper, Source Code, Edge of Tomorrow,* and *Happy Death Day*, in which characters experience time loops that cause them to relive the same moment over and over again, give dramatic expression to global capitalism's prevailing sense of futurelessness, in the specific sense that "we know that a time after the present is going to come, but we don't expect that it will fulfill the promises of the present."[24] The shared cultural and political anxiety they articulate is that of neoliberalism's crisis of the imagination, in which the utopian imagination is stifled by the incapacity that Jameson identified in the late 1980s with the oft-repeated statement that it has become easier to imagine the end of the world than an end to capitalism.[25]

Hurley's narrative adopts the first-person limited perspective of Heinlein's genre-defining military science fiction, doubling down on militarism's implicit fascism by shifting *Starship Troopers'* state-centered power to a future society ruled by a small group of competing corporations. In this capitalist dystopia, citizenship is similarly a privilege bestowed upon the wealthy or earned through military service—while those who can't afford to purchase membership to one of the "corps" are referred to as *ghouls*, lower classes that are dehumanized as zombie-like societal detritus. In *The Light Brigade*, first-person narrator and mobile infantry soldier Gina Dietz finds herself bouncing around her time loop as an unwinnable and increasingly horrific interplanetary war plays out on an elaborate temporal loop. As she slowly learns to construct the war's chronology, she also develops a better understanding of the reality behind the war: what the corps' indoctrination had taught her to think of as a conflict triggered by a genocidal attack by Martian terraformers—an obvious reference to a similar attack in *Starship Troopers*—is revealed to be an attempt by fascist rulers to suppress all remaining forms of ideological resistance.

As the book draws to its staunchly optimistic conclusion, Hurley's take on the military science fiction novel emphasizes that utopianism hinges on the existence of political alternatives, which the book dramatizes in two very specific ways. The first is Dietz's discovery that her time loop is not the only one: the eponymous Light Brigade is revealed to be an experimental military project made up of soldiers who—like Dietz—have become "unstuck in time," each of whom has been experiencing a different trajectory of the war. Thus, by incorporating science fiction's long-standing multiverse framework into the novel's narrative framework, the text first reveals that even a chain of events that had previously seemed to be unalterable is in fact just one of many possible futures that have been playing out simultaneously. It is precisely this revelation that enables Dietz to regain a sense of agency in relation to history as an indeterminate process: the existence of alternatives makes her aware that she has options available to her and that they needn't be catastrophic by definition.

Her move therefore from cynical and even nihilistic participation in perpetual warfare to sincere investment in political change results from this most basic acknowledgment of the possibility of alternatives. For while there seem to be no temporal experiences of the conflict with nondisastrous outcomes at first, the discovery of alternative timelines is strengthened by her realization that Earth's Martian adversary isn't so much a military enemy as it is an ideological one: to the still-feeble resistance, opposition to global capitalism's unquestioned hegemony is dependent upon the existence of a Martian community that is organized along socialist lines. Within the historical context of twenty-first-century global capitalism, the mere acknowledgment of a political system that offers an actual alternative—no matter how precarious—is what offers both the novel and its contemporaneous readers a meaningful utopian horizon.

The Light Brigade therefore manages to bring together two contradictory aspects of Jameson's utopian vision, with universal military conscription as the recipe for radically progressive postcapitalism: on the one hand, Hurley's book powerfully dramatizes the transformative solidarity among military conscripts, while maintaining the Heinleinian tradition of regarding the army as an institution that offers access to important state-run facilities, including civil service, health care, and higher education. But at the same time, this novel emphatically underlines how compatible the military's top-down hierarchies are with fascist ideology. The effort, suffering, and sacrifice that are required from Dietz in order to make a better future possible therefore seem to indicate that the slim chance of a noncatastrophic future happens *in spite of* rather than *because of* her military career.

Indeed, the repeated intersections between historical forms of fascism and militarism are uncannily reflected in these science fiction texts—while the explicit combination of a fully developed corporatocracy with authoritarian militarism makes a terrifyingly appropriate dystopian fantasy for our own era of a global capitalist order facilitated by the rising tide of ethnonationalist neofascism. *The Light Brigade* thus stands as a rare example of a science fiction narrative that goes beyond the mere reproduction of the genre's fascist unconscious, pushing it beyond satire into a productive utopian vision. It bears repeating here that Hurley's novel is only one of many such texts within contemporary science fiction literature, while *Starship Troopers* is an outlier in Hollywood's culture industry even with its more implicit ideological critique. While they may share a genre along with certain thematic and political preoccupations, there is clearly a great difference between them as cultural and artistic forms.[26] While Jameson clearly wrote "An American Utopia" as a provocation designed to stimulate new ideas about the radical reorganization of capitalism's existing social hierarchies, the cultural archive of the military science fiction genre otherwise has strikingly few examples that might serve to inspire the actualization of such a vision.[27]

Without a resilient cultural vocabulary of a military that isn't primarily defined by a top-down and strictly hierarchical chain of command, it feels all the more risky to simply trust in the idea that this particular institution will lend itself to the kind of revolutionary change that Jameson proposes. In this sense, military science fiction teaches us not that alternative forms are impossible but that we tend to fall back on already-existing forms and structures even in the imaginative production of wholly speculative futures. In the current political climate, we must even consider the fact that—like the debate surrounding universal basic income and accelerationism—such proposals can easily be hijacked and absorbed by the far right, whose ethnonationalist agenda clearly fits with our existing understanding of the military. But if authoritarianism is indeed the prevailing global political trend, a closer look at Chinese science fiction may help clarify both the potential and the risk involved in fantasizing about a transformative universal army.

Chinese Science Fiction: Authoritarian Collectivism and the Universal Army

Throughout the twentieth century, science fiction has generally been perceived as a cultural form that expressed the core energies of Western modernity.[28] If we limit its cultural history to the past two centuries, with Mary Shelley's *Frankenstein* commonly described as the first science fiction novel, one certainly observes a correspondence between capitalism's intensified processes of imperialism, technological innovation, and primitive accumulation and the genre's most basic elements of cognitive estrangement, the centrality of the Suvinian *novum*, and social processes of alienation, commodification, and reification.[29] As a cultural form, science fiction is therefore generally recognized by scholars as the literature of modernization.

But in the twenty-first century, China is in the process of eclipsing the West both in the speed of its technological transformation and in the sheer scale and impact of its social, economic, and technological modernization. The speed at which China has transformed itself from state socialism to authoritarian capitalism via its creation and exploitation of special economic zones is unparalleled, while the scale at which colossal debt-funded infrastructure projects are in the process of radically transforming the entire Chinese landscape is impossible to exaggerate. Little wonder then that some of the most provocative, dynamic, and innovative science fiction in recent years has emerged from this particular material context of accelerated modernization.

As many scholars and critics have observed, Chinese science fiction has been gaining ground rapidly within the field. And among those Chinese authors whose work has been successful internationally, Liu Cixin has been the most widely read and celebrated. His novel *The Three-Body Problem* (2007)—the first book in a successful trilogy—won the prestigious Hugo Award after its English-language translation was published in 2014, and the Chinese film adaptation of his novella *The Wandering Earth* was a record-breaking blockbuster in early 2019 that established science fiction as a viable commercial genre in mainstream Chinese cinema. Released theatrically in North America and distributed globally via Netflix, the film constitutes a sea change in the international standing and appeal of non-American science fiction cinema.

The Wandering Earth adapts Liu Cixin's generations-spanning novella about a collective global response to a looming catastrophe: faced with the near-future prospect of our sun's cataclysmic destruction, the governments of planet Earth join together to construct thousands of gargantuan rockets across the surface that will propel the globe out into space on a thousand-year odyssey to the nearest star system. Underground cities are built near the rockets, where surviving humanity (chosen by lottery) are to remain for many generations, until the planet's proximity to the Alpha Centauri star system will hopefully make the surface habitable once more. While the novella maps out both the technical challenges and the human conflicts that occur across many decades, the film focuses on a single crisis en route to the Earth's new destination: as it passes Jupiter to slingshot out of the solar system, it comes too close to the gas giant's surface and is pulled out of orbit. To avoid global annihilation, the group of protagonists must find a way to restart the failing Earth Engines and help the planet break free from Jupiter's gravitational pull.

While similar in style and concept to Hollywood blockbusters like *Armageddon* (1998), this Chinese variation on the familiar blockbuster formula introduces key elements that are refreshingly alien to the American storytelling tradition, in ways that resonate strongly with Jameson's attempt to push our cultural and political imaginations from individualism to collectivism. For while American popular narratives of looming planetary disaster—from *Deep Impact* and *2012* to *The Lord of the Rings* and *Avengers: Endgame*—consistently rely on small, elite teams of highly specialized individuals to save the world, *The Wandering Earth* constantly emphasizes the dialectical tension between the particular (individual subjects, relationships, and communities) and the universal (our necessary reliance on the simultaneous existence of many others working toward the same ends). Thus, where Hollywood typically maintains a clear binary distinction between the exceptional (the heroes) and the ordinary (the passive and largely faceless masses), *The Wandering Earth* is organized entirely around concepts of collective action.

This dynamic becomes especially meaningful toward the film's climax. Given the science fiction blockbuster's familiar look and feel, our internalized genre expectations condition us to interpret the on-screen action as a reproduction of the same old formula in which an exceptional team of heroic individuals must save the day. As the motley group of protagonists, organized into an ad hoc semi-military unit, makes its way toward one of the failing thruster engines with a component that will reignite its massive furnace, we automatically perceive them as the sole heroes, tasked with saving the world at the last instant from seemingly inevitable doom. But in one of the film's many great twists, they arrive there only to discover not only that another team had already restarted this engine, but also that their brave efforts and self-sacrifice would have been in vain had thousands of other identical initiatives not been undertaken across the globe at the same time. Rather than demonstrating the exceptional status of the gifted individual, this particular science fiction narrative instead reminds us—unsubtly but effectively—that collective action offers better odds. Indeed, acts of individual heroism become *more* meaningful precisely because they are part of a universalizing collective action. The truly exciting ideological work done by this emergent form of global blockbuster cinema is this investment in the collective, and the casual rejection of Hollywood's reliance on capitalist categories of individualism and exceptionalism.

But at the same time, the geopolitical context in which *The Wandering Earth* was made lies much closer to authoritarian capitalism than Jameson's utopian horizon of dual power. China's nominally communist single-party political system operates as a highly stratified form of authoritarian state capitalism that has easily incorporated the political and ideological powers derived from Western surveillance technology. From this perspective, the heavily militarized collective future articulated by *The Wandering Earth* again veers dangerously close to a particular type of fascist imaginary, where a remarkably homogeneous humankind forms a natural and organic collective that has fully internalized the state's authority alongside the hierarchical military organization of its social system.

Conclusion

Jameson's provocation in "An American Utopia" challenges us to imagine a utopian horizon on the basis of transitional dual power and the universal army. Enforced conscription would provide a shortcut to socialized health care, higher education, a livable pension, and other benefits, while at the same time helping to break down the class distinctions that uphold capitalism's grossly unequal distribution of power and privilege. This kind of leap defies us to imagine a radically different organization of our social relations, moving us toward a utopian horizon where political theory no longer serves any purpose, having "withered on the vine in a society in which money no longer plays a central role."[30]

Science fiction has helpfully provided us with many examples of postcapitalist futures in which the army occupies a similarly central position, and where militarized futures are commonly expressed as desirable, or even utopian. Enduring franchises like *Star Trek* and *Star Wars* are only the most obvious key works in a genre that presents speculative storyworlds defined almost exclusively by military paradigms. But while these futures might seem like helpful illustrations of Jameson's central thesis, they continue to reproduce our own society's ubiquitous reliance upon hierarchical structures, naturalized and mythologized in these narratives by giving the most sympathetic characters military ranks that underwrite their patriarchal positions of leadership and authority. These examples therefore primarily show that our most basic understanding of the military as an institution also includes strict hierarchical stratification and that it is therefore difficult indeed to maintain the notion that it could serve as the primary practical tool to rid ourselves of capitalism's top-down power structures.

Even more alarmingly, military science fiction narratives like *Starship Troopers* and *The Light Brigade* illustrate very clearly how compatible these military systems are with explicitly authoritarian forms of social and political organization. A fascist imaginary lurks in these texts' politics—either below the surface, as in *Star Trek* and other military utopias, or in full display, as in *Starship Troopers* and other more critical texts. They demonstrate how Arendt's observation that the breakdown of traditional class structures into the undifferentiated "masses" has also been a feature of totalitarian systems of control, in which the military has historically operated as a powerful conditioning tool.[31] While Hurley's novel still forges a path beyond its militarized corporatocracy, *The Light Brigade* also still underlines the danger inherent in social and political systems where the military occupies such a central place.

Both sides of this coin are illustrated elegantly by the recent Chinese science fiction blockbuster *The Wandering Earth*, where the realization of a looming global catastrophe forces humanity to embrace collective aims and reorganize society along militarized lines. By moving away from Hollywood's traditional reliance on the individual over the collective, *The Wandering Earth* provides a welcome structural twist to this familiar narrative formula by privileging collective efforts over the inherent individualism of capitalist culture. But as a cultural product of contemporary China's hybrid of state socialism and surveillance capitalism, the film shows at the same time that this kind of utopia remains tainted by an uncomfortably resilient strain of authoritarianism.

These case studies illustrate how difficult it is to imagine the kind of revolutionary transformation that Jameson proposes we must embrace from within the confines of capitalist culture. If the varied thought experiments of military science fiction are anything to go by, it is challenging indeed to conceive of a military institution that isn't always-already overdetermined by the very forms of patriarchal and hierarchical authority that Jameson's military utopia seeks to demolish. And given the military's conceptual *and* historical alignment with totalitarian forms of power, the current dominance of far-right and ethnonationalist politics should at least give us pause before we start working toward an American utopia predicated on the dual power of the universal army.

Notes

1 Fredric Jameson, *An American Utopia: Dual Power and the Universal Army* (London: Verso, 2016), 3.
2 Jodi Dean, "Dual Power Redux," in *An American Utopia*, ed. Slavoj Žižek (London: Verso, 2016), 110.
3 For a more thorough contextualization of the long-standing symbiosis between Hollywood and the military-industrial complex, see Haidee Wasson and Lee

Grieveson, eds., *Cinema's Military Industrial Complex* (Oakland: University of California Press, 2018).

4 Jameson, *American Utopia*, 21.

5 Jameson, *American Utopia*, 14–18.

6 Jameson, *American Utopia*, 20.

7 Tanner Mirrlees, "How to Read *Iron Man*: The Economics, Geopolitics and Ideology of an Imperial Film Commodity," *CineAction* 92, no. 2 (2013): 4–11.

8 See also Patricia Kerslake, *Science Fiction and Empire* (Liverpool: Liverpool University Press, 2007).

9 Peter Frase, *Four Futures: Life After Capitalism* (London: Verso, 2016).

10 Aaron Bastani's book *Fully Automated Luxury Communism* (London: Verso, 2019) flailingly attempts to take the term seriously by advancing familiar form of accelerationism.

11 Dan Hassler-Forest, *Science Fiction, Fantasy, and Politics* (London: Rowman & Littlefield, 2017), 50–57.

12 Dean, "Dual Power Redux," 109.

13 See Michel Foucault, *Discipline and Punish: The Birth of the Prison* (New York: Vintage, 1995).

14 Alberto Toscano, "After October, Before February," in Žižek, *American Utopia*, 234.

15 Jeremy Gilbert, *Common Ground: Democracy and Collectivity in an Age of Individualism* (London: Pluto Press, 2014), 19.

16 For obvious reasons, there is more variety in the far more abundant genre of anglophone science fiction literature.

17 Roger Ebert, *Starship Troopers* review, November 7, 1997, https://www.rogerebert.com/reviews/starship-troopers-1997.

18 Significantly, he does this against his parents' ambition for him to attend Harvard; Verhoeven amusingly paints the Ivy League institution as a privileged finishing school for the children of the elite, with little or no critical or intellectual potential.

19 Jameson, *American Utopia*, 61.

20 Jameson, *American Utopia*, 62.

21 Fredric Jameson, *The Political Unconscious* (London: Routledge, 1983), 24.

22 The fact that the film demands to be read as a propaganda film produced by the fascist world order the film diegetically represents also casts into doubt the credibility of the film's more utopian aspects.

23 Hannah Arendt, *The Origins of Totalitarianism* (Harmondsworth: Penguin, 2017), ebook.

24 Franco "Bifo" Berardi, *After the Future* (Edinburgh: AK Press, 2011), 25.

25 Jameson, *American Utopia*, 3.

26 For the differences between science fiction as a literary genre as opposed to a mass cultural form, see John Rieder, *Science Fiction and the Mass Cultural Genre System* (Middletown, CT: Wesleyan University Press, 2017); for the most elaborate discussion of the ways in which science fiction literature shares certain traits with critical theory, see Carl Freedman, *Critical Theory and Science Fiction* (Middletown, CT: Wesleyan University Press, 2000).

27 Even Kim Stanley Robinson's "Mars Trilogy," about which Jameson has written admiringly and which does to some extent combine hierarchical military-style social organizations with a largely utopian political narrative, struggles constantly to reconcile the imposition of hierarchical ranks with the characters' functions as avatars for divergent political positions and the polyphonic "struggle between a whole range of utopian alternatives" that is ultimately

fundamental to the work's political and ideological power (*Archaeologies of the Future* [London: Verso, 2005], 410).

28 See Andrew Milner, *Locating Science Fiction* (Liverpool: Liverpool University Press, 2012).

29 See Darko Suvin, *Metamorphoses of Science Fiction* (New Haven, CT: Yale University Press, 1979).

30 Jameson, *American Utopia*, 91.

31 Arendt, "The Classless Society," in *Origins of Totalitarianism*.

Afterword

FREDRIC JAMESON

Confronted with this immensely stimulating collection of very different kinds of essays, my first thought is to wonder whether it commits me to theorizing something like some specific and independent form of film criticism which I might characterize as dialectical in a proprietary sense; and without which the varied topics of these essays simply fall apart into matters of personal taste as far as I am concerned. What I can say, at the very least, is that what is exciting about them is that they give you the urge to see all these films again, and that is certainly what good aesthetic criticism is supposed to do (except in polemic situations, it is best for the theorist to ignore bad or mediocre works; although for the good of the public, the critic has to shoulder the job of denouncing them).

I begin with some impressions: Dudley Andrew's unexpectedly rich discussion of *Diva* suddenly makes me wonder whether not all of the films discussed here (or of whom my reactions are discussed here) are not somehow *transitional* as this one is. This leads me to the idea that to insert a film (or another kind of work of art) into a historical narrative—and finally that seems to be the only "method" that interests me personally—will somehow always turn it into something of a transitional object, even when, as with *Diva*, it is a failure and a transition to nothing, to a future that never appears. In this particular case, indeed, I wish he had mentioned the disavowal of the Mitterrand government after only two years of its socialist and utopian ambitions: what better explanation of the expiration of a promise or a potentiality?

Diva is also an occasion to mention another aspect of my critical relationship to film: so I must thank Dudley for omitting to mention the thriller by Delacorta on which *Diva* is "based." Indeed, it has been important to me to insist on the kinship between forms in the arts: and in this case, that between fiction-film and the novel (to which I would also want to add the kinship with the symphony as a form). Not only does Delacorta's novel exemplify a historically important subgenre of the French novel of the time—the political thriller[1]—but the juxtaposition between art forms helps us break out of the specializations of genre in a dedifferentiating postmodernity, and brings into visibility the deeper abstract categories which those forms embody.

This leads me to a second reflection, on the juxtaposition between the studies of Paul Coates and John MacKay, so different in their tone and interests, and yet strangely akin in a specific kind of attention, namely to what I will call the category. For as subjective, impressionistic or even mystical as Coates's meditation on Angelopoulos's mysteries may be—the mists, water, the setting out to sea on an abandoned raft, the suspension of the next step—and no matter how Bachelardian his welcome attention to their elements, these sense impressions also correspond to underlying categories which can be evoked in a more abstract manner without depriving them of precisely that sensuous appearance that makes them what they are. But categories also underpin the multiple *gestus* of Dziga Vertov's extraordinary work: he is no less sensuous, with his geometrical figures and his organized multiplicities, than Angelopoulos, even though he may at first seem "objective" in some commonsense distinction from Angelopoulos's "subjective" perceptualisms. I am most intrigued by these probes, which promise openings to the deeper categorical logic of narrative as such.

With underlying quasi-Hegelian categories also inevitably comes that equally Hegelian phenomenon which is objective appearance, the reality of sheer appearance, and even appearance as opposed to reality: this is then the sensuous itself as category and even ideology, and Szaniawski's subtle and wide-ranging analysis of the modes of appearance which are the ideological message of Pawlikowski's only apparent melancholy and nostalgia is a virtual master-class in such a demonstration. The elegant seductions of black-and-white film offer material for any literary critic daring to ignore the realities of cinema and the suggestiveness of its practices.

No less seductive is fascism, as Dan Hassler-Forest pointedly reminds me, on the occasion of *Starship Troopers* and its seeming dramatization of my *American Utopia*. I come upon the appropriate aphorism of Heraclitus: "Sea is purest and most unclean water: for fish, drinkable and life-saving; for humans, undrinkable and deadly." Collectivity can certainly be a deadly slogan; but it is a mistake to think the function of ideological analysis is immanently to detect the political valence of a text or an idea: only political practice can do that. The function of ideological analysis is structural, to show the inner construction of the text and the multiple ways—for good or ill—it can be used. My purpose, in *An American Utopia*, was not to resolve the internal contradictions of some concept of the collective which remains to be invented. Rather, it was to show how the positive functions of the Constitution could be preserved by way of an organization that cuts across state boundaries in an unexpected way, thereby producing a stereoscopic image of dual power. As for that excellent film called *Starship Troopers* (a sly Dutch glimpse of America), I doubt if anyone, even our local fascists, will be converted by it, save for the countercultural bits duly noted in the essay.

But I am stunned, and grateful, for Pansy Duncan's demonstration of the technical equivalent of the unique interpersonal building blocks of conspiracy film: cinematic technology should always make up to the other face of any phenomenological insight. But I must wonder whether "medium shot" is a technically sufficient working concept: I'm reluctant to abandon my "sweaty faces." I agree, however, that it is as a peculiar and unique mode of "encounter" that these conspiratorial lowest common denominators must be identified. I must still believe that the Sartrean "look" is the more appropriate name for this interpersonality than any Althusserian or Levinasian "encounter"; but the problem is a crucial one, namely the mode in which cinema is able with its visual apparatus somehow to render fitful emergences of the collective. And I think these must be sought in the image rather than in those plot formations of which Mike Wayne gives us a useful inventory, particularly in his discussion of "network films."

At the microscopic level these are certainly affective matters, and the feeling of affect is part of the semantics of the thing (I should add that I would today insist on a sharp distinction between affect and what I call "named emotions," a distinction that has interesting form/content implications for film which I haven't yet developed). But I think that Cramer puts his finger on something fundamental when he reminds us that here conspiracy is a mode of that unrepresentable category called totality, which has its own inimitable affective charge, one I would associate with the sublime, as in that tremendous moment in which the camera rises to encompass the entire reading room as its ultimate universe. I think something similar is happening in that well-nigh symphonic finale he describes so well, in which the tickertape and news bulletins hammer out rising chords of triumphant doom. I agree that the journalists also make up an institutional collective, however positively we may want to judge it in the immediate context. But those final "mechanical" moments show us that there can also be an affective charge to the suprapersonal and depersonalized corporate forces over which we may otherwise think we are triumphing: Is this not itself a kind of jubilation at the annihilation of those bad Nixonian subjects who still believed in their now derisory individual powers? And where is fascist affect in all this?

But I want to return for another moment to Wayne's reservations about the realism-modernism-postmodernism scheme. I had hoped that the structural language of dominant and subordinate would make it clear that these are not boxes into which one drops items in some ultimate classification, but rather systems in which the past persists, layers upon layers, but in now transformed and sedimented forms. Of course there is always a layer of realism underneath whatever veneer of modernism, and a modernist one under some late-coming and hastily assembled postmodern renovation, just as some traditional countries might now house a small elite of hackers and atomic experts. But the medium of film obliges one to see these categories in structural rather than chronological terms, particularly since film also knows its own quite different absolute break or cut with the supersession of the silent medium and later on of black-and-white as its belated sign. Maybe modern was always a code word for transition as I began to suspect above; at any rate I always conceived popular realism and mass culture as a dialectical opposite to modernism in the arts, and not a separate rubric altogether. But is not "classical film"—and I'm afraid this always has to be a euphemism for the more nationalist designation, "classic Hollywood film"— cinema's moment of realism? Which is followed by the great "modernisms" of the postwar period, the great foreigners from Bergman and Rossellini on? (A suggestion which allows us all to play the great game of deciding who, what, and where the postmodern break was. . . .)

But decidedly *Parasite*, however postmodern or not, is one of the signal moments in which the spatiality of the postmodern unavoidably declares itself: all politics today is about real estate, and it was clear enough that the Koreans were not the only public to recognize this strident reality in Bong's wonderful, terrible film. The essays here on non-Western film (Vázquez, Wagner, Wong) now provide a different kind of answer to those questions: for they demonstrate inescapably how that avant-garde function—always an impulse in classic Western modernism—has moved to other parts of the globe. *Parasite* is to be sure only the culmination of a great Korean "new wave"; but Tsai Ming-liang's work (along with Carlos Reygadas, or with Apitchatpong Weerasethakul or Lav Diaz) demonstrates that a stylistic innovation and experimentalism stifled by economic conglomerates and institutional habits in the so-called advanced countries is still fitfully possible elsewhere. (I would be tempted to call it a late modernism rather than that postmodernism better observed over here.)

What I would like to stress, however, is that all these films prove my political point—sometimes with comic literality—namely that all politics today turns on real estate. Space is the dimension in which, after the Deleuzian "time-image" of modernism, reality reappears in its rawest form. What stunned us about Tsai Ming-liang's *Vive l'amour* was its new "third space," the view of the Real from under the bed, so to speak. Thus non-Western film has the ontologically productive advantage of its very marginality in the current world system. On a globe in which translations are still dependent on good luck, it is film which is still our principal vehicle to that world and its otherwise impenetrable languages (making us embarrassed that our own has become a kind of dead lingua franca like Latin, while our commercial images systematically infect the daily life of distant populations).

As for the Japanese philosophers so usefully described in Yamamoto's essay, they have much to tell us both about the construction of postmodern "impersonal" subjectivities and that of totality as well, and they should immediately be translated: but let's also hear about the synchronies or not between Japanese philosophizing and Japanese cinema, and let's greet the institution of the film festival (now in pandemic crisis along with everything else) with some new institution of the film-theory festival, of which this book can stand as an opening salvo!

Note

1 See Kristin Ross, "Parisian Noir," *New Literary History* 41, no. 1 (October 2010): 95–109.

Acknowledgments

We wish to thank all the people who have made *Fredric Jameson and Film Theory: Marxism, Allegory, and Geopolitics in World Cinema* possible: First and foremost, our thanks go to the contributors, for their remarkable and thought-provoking scholarly contributions, and care and patience during revisions.

We also thank Fredric Jameson for his commentary and enthusiasm for the project since its inception, and, most importantly, for having inspired and at times challenged so many scholars and students, and contributed so much to the humanities over the years.

We would also like to express our gratitude to our peer reviewer and endorsement blurb writers, for their kind words, for their positive feedback on the proposal, as well as for raising pointed and helpful questions.

We thank Marie Sempo for the cover artwork, and Sari Fukushima for initial cover artwork proposals—although we ended up not using them, they pointed us in the right direction.

At Rutgers University Press, we salute the work of all involved in making the book a reality, from editors to typesetters to graphic designers.

Our thanks go especially to Nicole Solano, for her trust in the project, guidance, but also patience, as well as to Joseph Dahm for his excellent work copy-editing the manuscript.

Keith B. Wagner would like to thank, in no particular order, the following colleagues for patiently listening to his thoughts about cultural Marxism, Jameson, real estate speculation, and the state of the discipline: Lee Grieveson, Roland-François Lack, Hans Demeyer, Michael Berkowitz, Kimberly Chung, Joseph Jeon, Yingjin Zhang, Tom Zaniello, Yomi Braester, Chris Berry, Seunghoon Jeong, Lawrence Webb, Derek Nystrom, Louis Bayman, JungBong Choi, Doobo Shim, Ying Xiao, Jann Matlock, Jo Evans, Melvin Stokes, Lauren DeCarvalho, Sangmin Lee, and Wonjoon Kang.

Jeremi Szaniawski would like to thank his coeditors for their perceptive and helpful feedback on his chapter and part of the volume's introduction, and all those whose works have inspired him over the years. In particular, to Alexander Nemerov, for his guidance and friendship.

For joining him on screenings of *Cold War*: Mom, Charlotte, Xavier.

As an earlier version of his chapter to this collection constituted his job talk at UMass Amherst, Jeremi also wants to extend his appreciation to his new colleagues, with particular thanks to Moira and Don for their unwavering support.

Most importantly, Jeremi's gratitude goes to all who hosted him over the course of the past four years—particularly Grzegorz Kunicki, but also Božena Welborne, Hatice Aslan, Eset Akçilad, Stephanie and Dudley Andrew, Nathalie and Martin Maynard, and Mary and Lee Faulkner—for their friendship, support, and kind hospitality. Last but not least, a shout-out to Bojana, for cooking delicious Croatian meals during lockdown in Western Massachusetts.

Michael Cramer would like to thank all of those who have contributed to his work on this volume: for his insights on his piece, Dudley Andrew, for his thoughts on neoliberalism and his research suggestions, Jensen Suther, for their invitation for him to join this project and their indefatigable work on this volume, his coeditors, and to all of those whose scholarship on New Hollywood has deepened his own understanding of the period: Thomas Elsaesser, Derek Nystrom, Michael Ryan, Douglas Kellner, and J. D. Connor, to name but a few.

Michael dedicates this book to his brother Elliott.

Jeremi dedicates this book to the memory of friends departed for less dystopian shores: Andrée, Sevgi, Olek, and Michel.

Keith dedicates this book to his darling daughter, Sasha Choi Wagner, "from appa (daddy)" and Jiyung Jung.

Notes on Contributors

MICHAEL CRAMER is professor of cinema studies at Sarah Lawrence College. His areas of interest include world cinema, the relationship between cinema and television, documentary and nonfiction cinema, and the politics of aesthetics. His publications include "Roberto Rossellini's History Lessons" (*New Left Review*) and "Television and the Auteur in the 1950s" in *Opening Bazin* as well as the book *Utopian Television: Roberto Rossellini, Peter Watkins, and Jean-Luc Godard Beyond Cinema*.

JEREMI SZANIAWSKI is assistant professor of film studies and comparative literature, and the Amesbury Professor of Polish language and culture at the University of Massachusetts at Amherst. He is the author of *The Cinema of Alexander Sokurov: Figures of Paradox* and the coeditor, among other volumes, of *The Global Auteur: The Politics of Authorship in 21st Century Cinema* (with Seunghoon Jeong) and *On Women's Films Across Worlds and Generations* (with Ivone Margulies).

KEITH B. WAGNER is assistant professor of global media and culture and director of doctoral research in film and media studies at University College London. He is the coeditor of *Neoliberalism and Global Cinema: Capital, Culture and Marxist Critique, China's iGeneration: Cinema and Moving Image Culture for the Twenty-First Century* and *Korean Art from 1953: Collision, Innovation, and Interaction*. His monographic study entitled *Living with Uncertainty: Precarity in Cinemas from the Global South and North* will be published in 2021.

DUDLEY ANDREW, professor of film and comparative literature at Yale, has authored several books on French cinema and culture, including a forthcoming *Very Short*

Introduction to French Film and, also forthcoming, a collection, *André Bazin on Literature and Adaptation.*

PAUL COATES is an emeritus professor in the Film Studies Programme of Western University, Canada. He has taught also at McGill, Georgia, and Aberdeen. His books include *The Story of the Lost Reflection* (1985), *The Gorgon's Gaze* (1991), *Lucid Dreams: The Cinema of Krzysztof Kieślowski* (ed., 1999), *The Red and the White: The Cinema of People's Poland* (2005), *Cinema and Colour* (2010), and *Screening the Face* (2012). He is currently completing a book entitled *Comparative Cinema: Late and Last Things in Literature and Film.*

PANSY DUNCAN is senior lecturer in the School of English and Media Studies at Massey University, New Zealand. Her articles on film affect and aesthetics have been published in a number of venues, including *Screen*, *PMLA*, *Cinema Journal*, *Cultural Critique*, and *Feminist Media Studies*, and her book, *The Emotional Life of Postmodern Film*, appeared in 2016. Her current book project, *A Natural History of Film Form: Film Aesthetics through Animal, Vegetable and Mineral Matter*, is an eco-materialist counterhistory of early popular Euro-American film aesthetics, told through the lens of the raw materials of early photographic film stock (cellulose, silver, and gelatin).

DAN HASSLER-FOREST teaches media studies at Utrecht University. He has published many books and articles on science fiction, fantasy, and politics. He is the author of several books, including *Capitalist Superheroes* (2012), *The Politics of Adaptation* (2015), and *Science Fiction, Fantasy and Politics* (2016). His current research is focused on racial capitalism and Afrofuturism.

FREDRIC JAMESON is Knut Schmidt-Nielsen Professor of Comparative Literature at Duke University. He is the author of over twenty-five books, including *Marxism and Form* (1971), *The Political Unconscious* (1981), and *Postmodernism, or, the Cultural Logic of Late Capitalism* (1991), as well as two volumes entirely dedicated to the study of film: *Signatures of the Visible* (1990) and *The Geopolitical Aesthetic: Cinema and Space in the World System* (1992). His many awards include the Holberg Prize Award (2008) and the Modern Language Association's Award for Lifetime Scholarly Achievement (2012).

JOHN MACKAY is professor of film and media studies and professor and chair of Slavic Languages and Literatures at Yale University. He is the author of *Inscription and Modernity: From Wordsworth to Mandelstam* (2006), *Four Russian Serf Narratives* (2009), *True Songs of Freedom: Uncle Tom's Cabin in Russian Culture and Society* (2013), the first volume of *Dziga Vertov: Life and Work* (2018), and the forthcoming *Film Theory: A Very Short Introduction.*

MERCEDES VÁZQUEZ is a lecturer and honorary assistant professor at the Faculty of Arts of The University of Hong Kong. Her most important recent publications include a monograph on contemporary cinematic representations of class in the cinemas of Latin America, *The Question of Class in Contemporary Latin American Cinema* (2018), a book chapter comparing diverse figurations of precariousness in Venezuelan cinema, and the *Oxford Bibliography of Latin American Cinema*. At HKU, she teaches Latin American and European cinemas, Spanish language, and Hispanic cultures.

MIKE WAYNE is a Marxist cultural theorist, documentary filmmaker, and professor of media and film studies at Brunel University. He is the author of numerous books including *England's Discontents, Political Cultures and National Identities* (2018), *Considering Class: Theory, Culture and Media in the 21st Century* (2017), *Red Kant: Aesthetics, Marxism and the Third Critique, Television News, Politics and Young People: Generation Disconnected?, Understanding Film: Marxist Perspectives, Marxism and Media Studies: Key Concepts and Contemporary Trends, The Politics of Contemporary European Cinema: Histories, Border, Diasporas* (2002), *Political Film: The Dialectics of Third Cinema*. His most recent book is *Marxism Goes to the Movies*.

ALVIN K. WONG is assistant professor in comparative literature at the University of Hong Kong. His research covers Hong Kong culture, Chinese cultural studies, Sinophone studies, and queer theory. He is writing a book titled *Queer Hong Kong as Method*. He has published in journals such as *Journal of Lesbian Studies, Gender, Place & Culture, Culture, Theory, and Critique, Concentric, Cultural Dynamics, Continuum*, and *Interventions* and in edited volumes such as *Transgender China, Queer Sinophone Cultures*, and *Filming the Everyday*. He also coedited the volume *Keywords in Queer Sinophone Studies*.

NAOKI YAMAMOTO is associate professor in the Department of Film and Media Studies at the University of California, Santa Barbara. His recent publications include *Dialectics without Synthesis: Japanese Film Theory and Realism in a Global Frame* (2020), *Tenkeiki no medioroji: 1950-nendai Nihon no geijutsu to media no saihensei* ["Mediology in a Transformative Period: Reconfigurations of Art and Media in 1950s Japan"] (coedited with Toba Kōji), and "Soviet Montage Theory and Japanese Film Criticism," in *The Japanese Cinema Book*, ed. Hideaki Fujiki and Alastair Phillips.

Index

Printed and bound by CPI Group (UK) Ltd, Croydon, CR0 4YY

09/06/2025